Volume 8 of the American Wildlife Region Series

WILDLIFE AND PLANTS
OF THE CASCADES

Covering most of the Common Wildlife and Plants
of the Pacific Northwest and the area of the
Lava Beds

By Dr. Charles Yocom and Vinson Brown

Edited by Florence Musgrave

Copyright 1971 by Dr. Charles Yocom and Vinson Brown

Paper Edition   ISBN 0-911010-80-7
Cloth Edition   ISBN 0-911010-81-5

DA

Naturegraph Publishers, Inc., Happy Camp, CA 96039

THE CASCADES WILDLIFE REGION
Approximate Extent

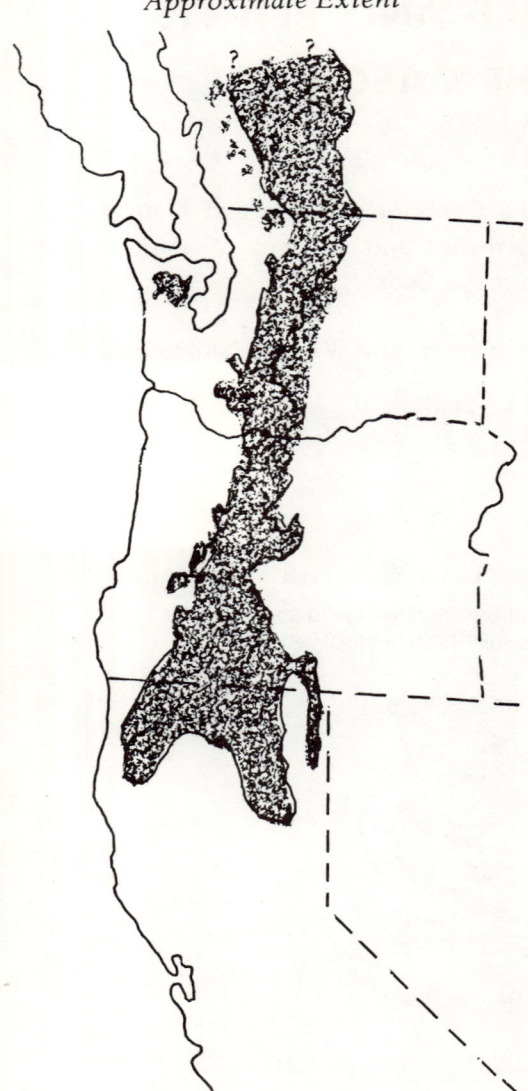

The Cascades Wildlife Region covers the higher mountains of western Oregon and Washington, southwestern British Columbia and far northern California. To the west of it is the Pacific Coastal Wildlife Region, to the east in Washington the Palouse Wildlife Region, to the east in Oregon and California the Great Basin Wildlife Region, and to the south The California Wildlife Region and the Sierra Nevadan Wildlife Region.

The map shows only the general outline of the region, but its extent to the north in British Columbia is not yet clearly defined. There is considerable overlapping with other regions, particularly the Pacific Coastal and the Sierra Nevadan.

For a view of all the wildlife regions of North America, see *Natural Communities* by Lee R. Dice, University of Michigan Press. He calls them Biotic Provinces.

TABLE OF CONTENTS

Vegetation Zones 4
Introduction 6
Mixed Evergreen Forest 9
Streamside Woodland 11
Mixed Coniferous Forest 12
Western Hemlock Forest (West Slope) 14
Sitka Spruce Forest 16
White Fir Forest 18
Pacific Silver Fir 19
Shasta Red Fir Forest 21
Grand Fir Forest 23
Mountain Hemlock Forest 25
Subalpine Fir Forest 27
Juniper Forest 29
Western Yellow Pine Forest 31
Douglas Fir Forest 33
Lodgepole Pine Forest 35
Western Hemlock Forest (East Slope) 37
Whitebark Pine Forest 38
Brushland 39
Sagebrush Plains and Grasslands 41
Mountain Meadows 43
Pumice Flats and Rock Outcroppings 45
Marshes, Lakes and Streams 47
Cultivated Lands 49
Common Plants 50
    Plant leaf and flower types 51
    Fresh Water Plants 52
    Grasses 58
    Coniferous Trees 63
    Broad-leaved Trees 76
    Shrubs and Vines 86
    Herbs 116
Mammals 169
Birds 203
Reptiles 266
Amphibians 272
Fishes 278
Suggested References 285
Acknowledgments 286
Index 287

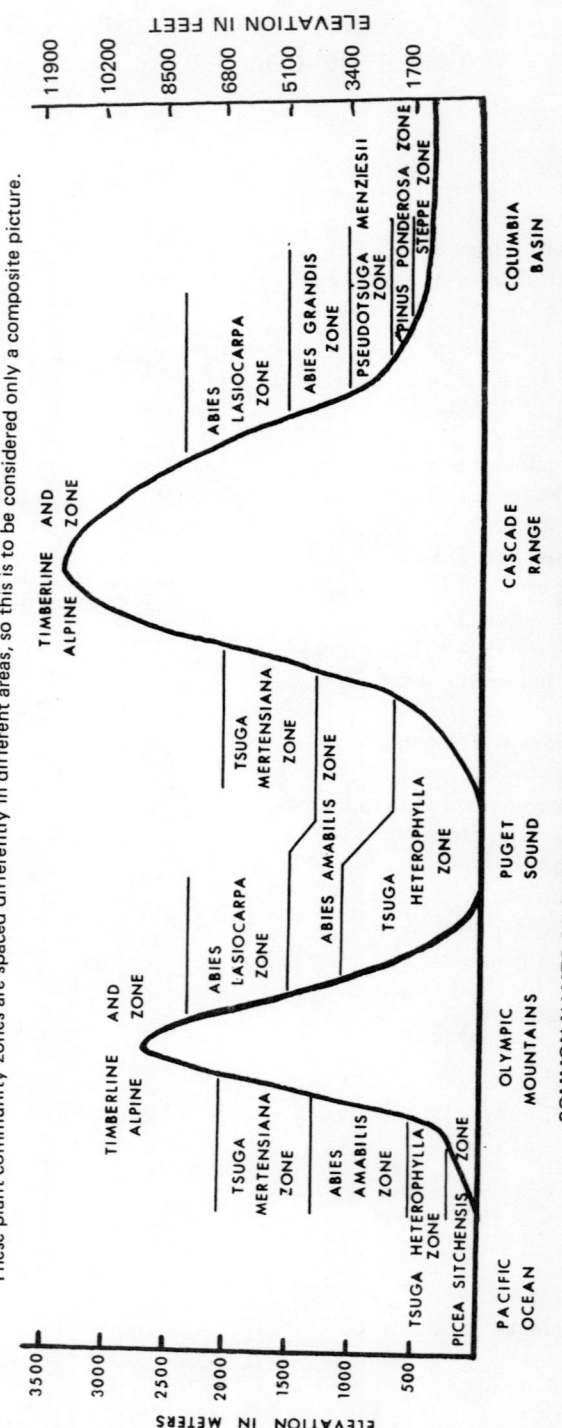

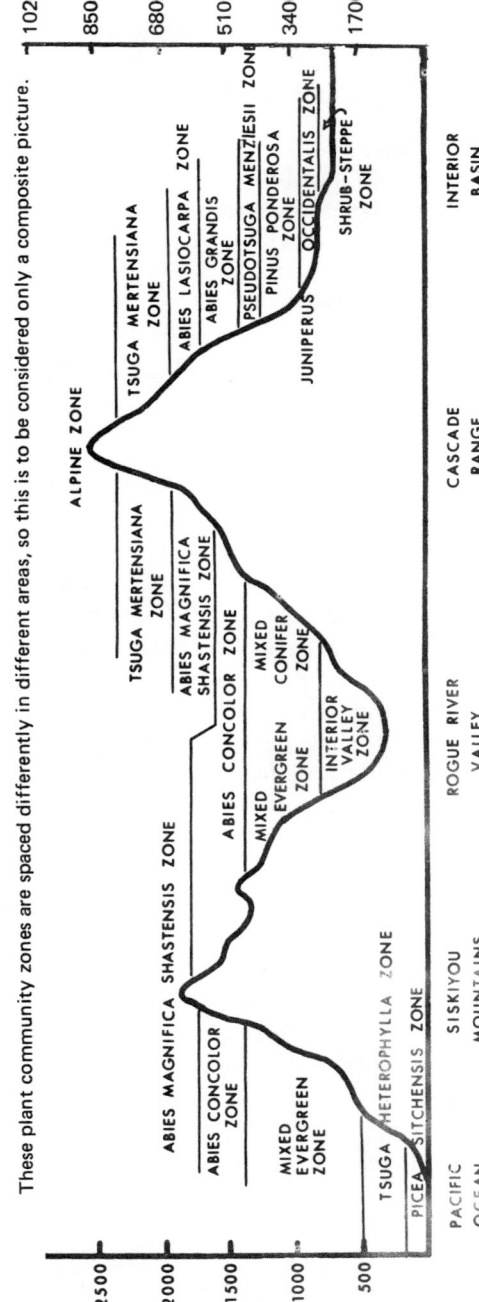

VEGETATION ZONES
Siskiyou Mountains and Cascade Range in Oregon

These plant community zones are spaced differently in different areas, so this is to be considered only a composite picture.

COMMON NAMES OF PLANT COMMUNITY ZONES (Life Zones not given because of complexity of overlapping)

Abies magnifica shastensis = Red Fir Zone
Abies concolor = White Fir Zone
Mixed Evergreen Zone
Mixed Conifer Zone
Tsuga heterophylla = Western Hemlock Zone
Picea sitchensis = Sitka Spruce Zone

Tsuga mertensiana = Mountain Hemlock Zone
Abies lasiocarpa = Subalpine Fir Zone
Abies grandis = Grand Fir Zone
Pseudotsuga menziesii = Douglas Fir Zone
Pinus ponderosa = Yellow Pine Zone
Juniperus occidentalis = Western Juniper Zone

5

INTRODUCTION

This book is the eighth of a series on the wildlife regions of America. Wildlife regions, such as the Cascades Wildlife Region, are distinctive natural geographic areas of similar climate and topography, which tend to have characteristic animals and vegetation within their boundaries. Overlapping between regions makes it impossible to draw a rigid line separating them. Some species of plants and animals appear in several regions, but may be most characteristic of a particular one.

The Cascades Wildlife Region, as defined in this book, covers most of the mountainous areas of northern California from Lassen and Trinity Counties north, and the mountains of western Oregon, Washington and southwestern British Columbia. Because of their proximity to this great wildlife region, we also describe many of the common plants and animals of the nearby lava beds to the east of these mountains. The Pacific Coastal Wildlife Region, which extends from the Cascade Wildlife Region to the Pacific Ocean, intergrades so closely with this region that it is very hard to distinguish any boundary. Consequently many animals and plants are common to both regions. Nevertheless the Cascades Wildlife Region is distinctively different because of its higher elevations, greater cold and generally much greater snowfall. In essence it is an extension of Canada down into the United States and its magnificent volcanic peaks, great canyons, lace-like waterfalls, and beautifully-flowered meadows and wave on wave of mighty forests are without peer in North America. The map on page 2 shows only the general extent of the region, as it is extraordinarily complex.

The purpose of this book is to give you in one volume basic information to help you identify and understand almost all the mammals, birds, reptiles, and amphibians you will find in these mountains, plus also the common plants and fish. The plants will include at least 90% of the individual plants seen, and list particularly those plants that are indicators of particular habitats. For more details the reader should seek the larger and more specialized books listed in the Suggested References at the back of this book.

In the first section of this book the various important plant communities of the region are described, and the common plants that are found in each are listed. Photographs of these plant communities help you identify them, as also does a study of the pictures and descriptions of the common plants found in each community. Notice that each

INTRODUCTION

plant community or habitat is distinctive and different from every other one even though there are many plants found in more than one community. Some communities are particularly distinctive, such as the mountain meadows, while others, such as the ponderosa pine forest and the red fir forest, are superficially alike but can be seen to be different by closer study. Learning to recognize the plant communities, vegetation types or habitats is of great help in later learning to recognize the animals, birds, reptiles and amphibians that live in each of them.

When you are on a hike or visit into any part of the Cascade Wildlife Region, notice what plant community you are in at any time and look at the lists of plants that are shown to live in it. Then study the descriptions and pictures of these plants and creatures and this will give you a good idea of exactly what you can expect to see around you. Each description of a plant, animal, bird, and so forth, has with it a list in small type on the side of the habitats or plant communities with which each is commonly associated. The abbreviations for these habitats are as follows:

Forests from low habitats to high.

Conif. = means found in most coniferous forests of Cascades.

WEST SIDE OF CASCADES

mixed evergreen forest = mix.ev. - see page 9
streamside woodland = str. wd. (found at many elevations) - see page 11
mixed coniferous forest = mix. con. - see page 12
western hemlock forest of the western slope = w. hem. - see page 15
sitka spruce forest = sitk-spr. - see page 17
white fir forest = wh. fir - see page 18
Pacific silver fir forest = sil. fir - see page 19
shasta red fir forest = red fir - see page 21
grand fir forest = gr. fir - see page 23
mountain hemlock forest = mt. hem. - see page 25
subalpine or alpine fir forest = sub.alp. - see page 27

EAST SIDE OF CASCADES

juniper forest of lava beds, etc. = jun. - see page 29
Ponderosa or yellow pine forest = pine - see page 31
Douglas fir forest of east slope = dg. fir - see page 33
lodgepole pine forest = lodg. - see page 36
western hemlock forest of east slope = west. hem. - see page 37
whitebark pine forest = w. b. pine - see page 38

WILDLIFE AND PLANTS OF THE CASCADES

OTHER PLANT COMMUNITIES

brushlands = brush - see page 39
sagebrush plains = sage - see page 41
mountain meadows = mt. mead. - see page 43
subalpine meadows = s.a. mead. - see page 43
alpine fell fields = alp. - see page 44
barren pumice flats = pume. - see page 45
cliffs and large rock outcroppings = rocks - see page 46
marshes and lakes = water - see page 47
streams = streams - see page 47
caves = caves - see page 46
cultivated or urban areas = cult. - see page 49
grasslands = grass - see page 41

In the second part of the book the plants are grouped by type and by systematic arrangements of genera and species. Thus water plants are put in one section, trees in another, shrubs and vines in a third, herbs in a fourth and grasses in a fifth, all for your convenience in finding. But each species is tied in by the abbreviations on the margin to the habitats in which it is found so that you will know where to expect it.

In the third part of the book, all the animals and birds, reptiles, amphibians and fish are described and pictured, again with each species identified by not only its appearance but by habitats or the places where it likes to live.

CLIMATE AND ECOLOGY

The climate of the Cascades varies considerably, from the comparatively dry eastern slopes, especially in southern Oregon, to the lush snow and rain forests of the western slopes, especially in Washington and in the Olympic Mountains. In between are the northern mountains of California and the Klamath Mountains of southwestern Oregon, all of which are fringe areas of the Cascades and grading into the Pacific Coastal and Sierra Nevadan Wildlife Regions. The ecology of the whole region can best be understood by studying the separate plant communities and tying them into the weather and physiographic maps and life zone charts on pages 4 and 5.

MIXED EVERGREEN FOREST

The mixed evergreen forest is composed of conifers and broad-leaved hardwoods. The Douglas Fir and the broad-leaved evergreen, Tanbark Oak, predominate. This zone is noted also for its diversity of soils, providing for a contrast of vegetations. Broad-leaved trees and shrubs and Douglas Fir are found on diorite rocky soil. Gabbro rock soil has more Oregon Myrtle and manzanita species, plus broad-leaved trees and shrubs, Western Yellow and Sugar Pines, and Incense Cedar growing on it. Serpentine soil sites favor Douglas Fir. Among the heavier stands of trees, where soil moisture is inadequate, are cleared patches forming fields of broad-leaved shrubs, such as Wild Blackberry, Oregon Grape and Poison Oak. Where successive burns have occurred the chaparral (or small leathery-leaved brush) is quite dense, and includes manzanita species and wild lilacs *(Ceanothus)* species. Live Oak and Tanbark Oak, Bear Bush, Hoopa Gooseberry, and Pygmy Oregon Grape are plentiful also. However Canyon Live Oak, Greenleaf Manzanita and Mountain Whitethorn predominate in this brush community.

A typical mixed evergreen forest. Photo by David Lehning

TYPICAL PLANTS

TREES
Western Yew 26
Sugar Pine 28
Western Yellow Pine 31
Douglas Fir 40
Incense Cedar 48
Golden Chinquapin 57
Tanbark Oak 58
Sadler's Oak 61
Canyon Oak 62
Huckleberry Oak 63
Oregon Myrtle 64
Vine Maple 71
Madrone 72
Pacific Dogwood 68

SHRUBS
Oregon Grape 74
Pacific Blackberry 101
Wood Rose 104
California Coffeeberry 114
Mountain Whitethorn 118
Fremont's Silk-tassel 125
Salal 136
Greenleaf Manzanita 139
Poison Oak

HERBS
Hooker's Fairy Bells 176a
Rattlesnake Plantain 182
Vanilla Leaf 207
Yerba de Selva 215
Twin Flower 264

STREAMSIDE WOODLAND

The streamside woodland is composed of mostly broad-leaved trees, which are the Black Poplar, Oregon Alder, Willows, Oregon White Oak, and Big-leaf Maple, although Douglas and Grand Firs of the conifers are plentiful. Artificial stands of Black Poplar were planted and some since harvested in the Willamette River area; however, this area was really prairie and oak savannas before it was settled. The dense forests were more in the mountains and delta areas. It is believed that fires have been instrumental (perhaps originally started by Indians) in the maintenance of the savannas and subsequent change over the dense forests with the successive and replacement growths. The dense Oregon White Oak stands have been gradually replaced by Douglas Fir (Oregon Pine), Grand Fir and Big-leaf Maple. Thickets of Mazzard Cherry *(Prunus avium)* and Poison Oak abound, being one of the last replacement growths and good shelter for the Douglas Fir seedlings.

Soleduck River Photo. Courtesy of National Park Service.

TYPICAL PLANTS

TREES
Western Yellow Pine 31
Douglas Fir (Oregon Pine) 40
Grand Fir 42
Oregon Alder 53

Willow species
Black Cottonwood 56
Oregon White Oak 60
Big-leaf Maple 69
Madrone 72

MIXED CONIFEROUS FOREST

This is a scattered individual conifer region that contains stands of Douglas Fir (Oregon Pine), Yellow Pine, Sugar Pine, White Fir and Incense Cedar, occuring in many combinations as well. The elevation is approximately 2,400' to about 4,500' in the southwestern Cascade range and slightly higher elevations in the eastern Siskiyou Mountains. The 36 to 52" of rain fall in winter so subsequently summers are warm and dry. This is more moisture than the Black Oak region or Yellow Pine region receives. Soils are varied and tend to be acidic. Douglas Fir is very abundant but pines are increasing. Protective draws and north slopes have Western Hemlock seedlings and broad-leaved trees as well as Giant Red Cedars and Yews. Incense cedar likes the driest terrain. Brushlands have developed because tracts were burned over or even logged at one time or several times. The *Ceanothus* species (Wild Lilac) dominates these areas. Otherwise for ground cover the White Fir seedlings are getting a good start among the mixed conifers.

Oregon Douglas Fir timber. Credit USDA Forest Service for photo.

MIXED CONIFEROUS FOREST

TYPICAL PLANTS

TREES
Yew 26
Western White Pine 27
Sugar Pine 28
Western Hemlock 38
Douglas Fir 40
White Fir 46
Incense Cedar 48
Giant Red Cedar 49
Chinquapin 57
Tanbark Oak 58
Pacific Dogwood 68
Big-leaf Maple 69
Vine Maple 71
Madrone 72

HERBS
Vanilla Leaf 207
Yerba de Selva 215
White-veined Wintergreen 231
Bog Wintergreen 231c
Twin Flower 264

SHRUBS
Hazelnut 73
Oregon Grape 74
Cream Bush 93
Pacific Blackberry 101
Wood Rose 104
Juneberry 109
Oregon Boxwood 112
Oregon Tea Tree 115
Tobacco Brush 116
Deer Brush 117
Mountain Whitethorn 118
Squaw Carpet 120
California Rose-bay 128
Salal 136
Thinleaf Huckleberry 143
Poison Oak

Western Hemlock Forest. Photo courtesy of Pacific Northwest Forest and Range Experiment Station.

WESTERN HEMLOCK FOREST (WEST SLOPE)

Two different communities belong to this widespread realm that stretches south from British Columbia, containing north slopes and draws of the coast ranges and the Cascades, to the Redwood Belt of California.

One is the Hemlock, plus Oregon Grape and Vine Maple community, and the other is a moist plant rich community of Hemlock, Giant Cedar, Oxalis and ferns. Seasonal rainfall varies from 60-120" with approximately 64" at British Columbia and an average 72-74 degrees yearly temperature. 490-1,800' elevation. Soils are sandy to clay, well-drained and include much rich loam in spots for moisture-needing vegetation. This whole zone (including the east slopes) is important for timber production, and the clear-cut logging and controlled burning of slash, plus replanting of Douglas Fir (Oregon Pine) seedlings, determine the type of growth; but, given much time, the Western Hemlock reinvades even the planted tracts.

TYPICAL PLANTS

TREES
Yew 26
Western White Pine 27
Sugar Pine 28
Western Yellow Pine 31
Sitka Spruce 37 (near coast)
Western Hemlock 38
Douglas Fir (Oregon Pine) 40
Pacific Silver Fir 41
Grand Fir 42
Incense Cedar 48
Giant Red Cedar 49
Port Orford Cedar 50
Oregon Alder 53
Black Cottonwood 56
Giant Chinquapin 57
Tanbark Oak 58
Oregon White Oak 60
Oregon Myrtle 64
Big-leaf Maple 69
Vine Maple 71
Madrone 72

BUSHES
California Hazelnut 73
Oregon Grape 74
Pacific Blackberry 101
California Rose-bay 128
Salal 136
Red Huckleberry 145
Snowberry Bush 149

HERBS
Sword Fern
Large-flowered Fairy Bell 176b
Rattlesnake Plantain 182
Western Wild Ginger 185
Inside-out-flower 208
Yerba de Selva 215
Redwood Sorrel 224
Twin Flower 264

VERY WET AREAS
American Devil's Club 122
False Solomon's Seal 173
Twisted Stalk 177
Columbia Windflower 202
Vanilla Leaf 207
Huckleberry species

Sitka Spruce Forest. Lush growth in the rain forest of the Quinault Natural Area. Credit for photo goes to the "U.S. Forest Service".

SITKA SPRUCE FOREST

This long narrow Oregon and Washington coastal zone is bounded by the Redwood forests of California on the south. The elevation ranges from sea level to about 1800'. The Sitka Spruce predominates, with the long-lived Giant Red Cedar and the Douglas Fir (Oregon Pine) flourishing here also in a climate made moist by heavy winter rains and frequent summer fogs from the ocean. The similar Western Hemlock zone may sometimes take over when these trees are burnt out. The fog adds moisture and the soil is deep and rich and acidic so the undergrowth is luxuriant, with abundant (short-lived) Red Oregon Alder amidst mosses, liverworts and ferns. Logging and fire tracts are common here as in other zones, with the climate being more favorable to the quick growth of berry patches as well as the nitrogen-adding Red Alder. Rotting logs help germinate Sitka Spruce, Oregon Pine, and Cedar seedlings, thus decreasing the more open acreage. The coast has its share of sand dunes and strands where the wind has misshapened the Sitka Spruce and Lodgepole Pine.

TYPICAL PLANTS

TREES
Lodgepole Pine 34
Sitka Spruce 37
Western Hemlock 38
Douglas Fir (Oregon Pine) 40
Pacific Silver Fir 41
Grand Fir 42
Giant Red Cedar 49
Port Orford Cedar 50
Dwarf Juniper 52
Coast Redwood
Oregon Myrtle 64
Big-leaf Maple 69
Red Oregon Alder 76

SHRUBS
Douglas Spiraea 90
Salmon Berry 98
Nootka Rose 102
Western Azalea 127
California Rose-bay 128
Labrador Tea 129
Mock Azalea 130
Salal 136
Evergreen Huckleberry 140
Red Huckleberry 145

HERBS AND FERNS
Sword Fern
Harvest Brodiaea 161
Hooker's Fairy Bells 176a
Douglas' Iris 178
Wild Strawberry 219
Redwood Sorrel 224
Yarrow 277

WET AREAS
American Devil's Club 122

WHITE FIR FOREST

The White Fir zone, elevation 4,500-5,200' in the Cascade range, 4,550-5,850' in the western Siskiyou, to 5,280-5,850' in the eastern Siskiyou Range, is a cold and rather humid area. In extent it is both narrow and scattered, being limited to a gray, acidic soil that is thin to moderately thick over clay. There is good snow accumulation and thus more summer season moisture also. The White Fir predominates, but Incense Cedar favors sheltered draws and its seedlings invade mountain meadows. Douglas Fir (Oregon Pine) favors the drier slopes. One also finds brush in tracts large enough to be called fields in which plentiful Tobacco Brush or Greenleaf Manzanita reign supreme.

"Lake of the Woods", Oregon. Photo by C. F. Yocom.

TYPICAL PLANTS

TREES
Sugar Pine 28
Western Yellow Pine 31
Lodgepole Pine 34
Douglas Fir (Oregon Pine) 40
Shasta Red Fir 45
Incense Cedar 48
Bush Chinquapin 57
Mountain Maple 70

SHRUBS
Hazelnut 73
Oregon Grape 74
Cream Bush 93
Pacific Blackberry 101
Wood Rose 104
Juneberry 109
Tobacco Brush 116
Greenleaf Manzanita 139

PLANTS
Wake Robin 171
Single-flowered Clintonia 172
Sandwort 198b
Columbia Windflower 202
Vanilla Leaf 207
Inside-out-flower 208
Sugar Scoop 212
Wild Strawberry 219
Virgate Phacelia 240b

PACIFIC SILVER FIR FOREST

The Pacific Silver Fir zone is found between the Western Hemlock (even moisture conditions) and the Mountain Hemlock Subalpine zone (colder mountain conditions). The elevation range is 3,250-4,880' in Oregon and 2,450-4,250' in northern Washington. This includes the western slopes and also the eastern slopes where the conditions are similar; that is, wet and frosty, plenty of moisture from snow, cool mountain meadows, wintertime snow packed draws and springs, and near clay soil that produces some poorly drained boggy ground. Well-drained light acidic soil with a thin layer of humus is the rule. Sloping masses of fragmented rocks and out-crops exist in this zone. The Mt. Rainier area has ideal requirements. The Silver Fir, found mostly as seedlings and small trees, wins out in this environment even though it is a late seeder and has tough competition from (but uses for protection) the shade tolerant and fast growing Douglas Fir and some competition from Western Hemlock and Noble Fir. It thrives because it can tolerate the rough treatment from the snow season (cold as well as seasonal wearing down of the top soil). The heavy snow fed moisture determines the lush berry bush communities, with cedar trees, ferns and moss in the very wet sections. Stunted growth of Oregon Grape and Salal and quantities of Bear Grass point out tracts of cut-off seasonal water or drier and non-humus undersoil.

TYPICAL PLANTS

TREES
Western White Pine 27
Lodgepole Pine 34
Western Larch 35
Englemann Spruce 36
Western Hemlock 38
Douglas Fir (Oregon Pine) 40
Pacific Silver Fir 41
Grand Fir 42
Subalpine Fir 43
Noble Fir 47
Giant Red Cedar 49
Cedar species
Alder species

SHRUBS
Oregon Grape 74
Creeping Raspberry 97

American Devil's Club 122
California Rose-bay 128
Mock Azalea 130
Blueberry & Huckleberry
  (species 140-141)
Thinleaf Huckleberry 143

HERBS
Inside-out-flower 208
Bear Grass 158
Single-flowered Clintonia 172
Vanilla Leaf 207
Sugar Scoop 212
Oregon Oxalis 224
Bunchberry 229
Wintergreen (Pyrola
  species) 230-231

20 WILDLIFE AND PLANTS OF THE CASCADES

Pacific Silver Fir Forest. Taken at Sloan Creek National Forest Camp. Credit to "U.S. Forest Service".

SHASTA RED FIR FOREST

The Shasta Red Fir Forest is situated between the subalpine Mountain Hemlock and White Fir zones, a heavily and varied timbered area. Elevations are 5,200-6,500' in the Cascades, 5,850-7,150' in the Siskiyou's. Crater Lake is an ideal community, although this zone shows up also in the dry interior and on eastern slopes. Like other subalpine zones considerable snowfall (7' or more) adds to the yearly moisture, which keeps the ground (western slopes) moist throughout the summer season. Darker color, well-drained, fairly clay free, plus moderate humus soil predominates, though central Oregon's pumice soil must be included. Shrubs and plants are sparse or absent under the dense growth of trees, except for saprophytic types (plants that live on dead organic matter.) Shasta Red Fir is compatible with Red Fir and Western White Pine in the brushy areas, and holds its own while shading considerable Lodgepole Pine. But White Fir, Pacific Silver Fir and Mountain Hemlock give Shasta Red Fir stiff competition, especially closer to their respective zones, though Red Fir may have the final showing. Plateau regions favor Yellow Pine over Shasta Red Fir. Berry bushes, Tobacco

Shasta Red Fir Forest in Coffee Creek Drainage of Siskiyou Mountains. Photo taken by C. F. Yocom.

Brush, Honeysuckle and Mountain Mahogany reign in fire produced fields, pointing out both wet and dry soil communities.

TYPICAL PLANTS

TREES
Western White Pine 27
Whitebark Pine 29
Western Yellow Pine 31
Lodgepole Pine 34
Engelmann Spruce 36
Western Hemlock 38
Mountain Hemlock 39
Douglas Fir 40
Pacific Silver Fir 41
Subalpine Fir 43
Red Fir 44
Shasta Red Fir 45
White Fir 46
Incense Cedar 48
Giant Red Cedar 49
Western Juniper 51
Giant Chinquapin 57

Mountain-Mahogany 65

SHRUBS
Sticky Currant 81
Tobacco Brush 116
Pinemat Manzanita 138
Greenleaf Manzanita 139
Thinleaf Huckleberry 143
Purple Flower Honeysuckle 151
Giant Sage 156

HERBS
Sandwort 198b
Columbia Windflower 202
Vanilla Leaf 207
Valerian 265
Seep-spring Arnica 278
Heart-leaved Arnica 281

GRAND FIR FOREST

The most heavily forested area is the Grand Fir zone with even moderate temperatures and plentiful moisture from winter snowpack. The elevations range from 3,575-4,875' in central Oregon to 4,875-6,500' in the Blue Mountains. Grand Fir is found at elevations 5,360-6,500' in the White Fir zone and in the Western Hemlock zones. The Grand Fir zone is bounded by the Subalpine Fir zone for the upper limits and Douglas Fir or Yellow Pine and Sage plateaus for the lower limits. This Grand Fir joins good growths of Pacific Silver Fir, Western Hemlock, Giant Red Cedar and Mountain Hemlock, and in time to

Tree portrait of Grand Fir 3 miles s. w. of Gotchen Creek Ranger Station. Photo credited to "U. S. Forest Service".

come may be replaced in some spots by these same species, excluding Mountain Hemlock. Lodgepole Pine shares billing with Grand Fir, but is first dominated by the fast growing, shade and drier-soil-loving, Douglas Fir, or very seed productive Englemann Spruce. Western Yellow Pine might be a final occupant over the Grand Fir, save for selective logging practices tending to eliminate this. The soil is gray-brown and fairly acidic with small amounts of clay and a thin layer of humus. Volcanic ash and pumice areas must be included also. Successional stages are important and widespread, usually cleared in the beginning by forest fires. Grand Fir subsequently shares the brushland with pure young stands of Western Larch or Oregon Boxwood, or the predominate Thinleaf Huckleberry, or Grand Fir, and Western Yellow Pine may make with the huckleberry a threesome. Other berry and brush species often crowd in. Mountain Meadows are very lush, but grasslands, where over-grazed, are losing the good Tufted Hairgrass and turning to weed species.

TYPICAL PLANTS

TREES
Western White Pine 27
Sugar Pine 28
Western Yellow Pine 31
Lodgepole Pine 34
Western Larch 35
Engelmann Spruce 36
Western Hemlock 38
Mountain Hemlock 39
Douglas Fir 40
Grand Fir 42
Subalpine Fir 43
Shasta Red Fir 45
White Fir 46
Willow species

SHRUBS
Prickly Currant 78
Shiny Spiraea 89
Creeping Raspberry 97
Wood Rose 104
Juneberry 109
Oregon Boxwood 112
Oregon Tea Tree 115

Tobacco Brush 116
Pinemat Manzanita 138
Greenleaf Manzanita 139
Thinleaf Huckleberry 143
Snowberry species
Wild Strawberry species

HERBS
Tufted Hairgrass 16
Squirrel-tail Grass 23
Wake Robin 171
Single-flowered Clintonia 172
False Solomon's Seal 174
Western Wild Ginger 185
Bistort 191
Sandwort 198b
Wintergreen 230
White-veined Pyrola 231
Bog Wintergreen 231c
Spreading Dogbane 236
Twin Flower 264
Yarrow 277
Heart-leaved Arnica 281

MOUNTAIN HEMLOCK FOREST

This zone is very moist and cool and is the highest timbered one on the western slopes of the Cascade and Olympic Mountains. 110" of rainfall yearly plus 160-560" of snowfall make this possible. The elevation of 4,425-5,525' in northern Washington varies to 5,525-6,500' in the southern Cascades. The Mountain Hemlock is replaced by Subalpine Fir east of the Cascades and in the rain shadowed forest of the Olympic Mountains. However Mountain Hemlock shares the northern Rocky Mountain regions equally with Subalpine Fir and Engelmann Spruce. Moderately well-drained, acidic light colored soil with an under layer rich in iron and some humus grows thick forests of Mountain Hemlock and Pacific Silver Fir. Subalpine Fir and Lodgepole Pine get a start on drier ground and then later Mountain Hemlock invades and reigns. The Mountain Hemlock doesn't easily reseed under its close shady clumps, but seedlings seem to grow slowly in the clearings. The much burned-over slow-to-reforest, upper part of the zone is mostly patches of Mountain Hemlock, Pacific Silver Fir and Thinleaf Huckleberry (a threesome) plus meadows and brushland containing Heath, Rose, and Sunflower species or, on the drier areas, stunted growth of

Mountain Hemlock zone, by C. F. Yocom.

Thinleaf Huckleberry, Bear Grass, Wintergreen (Pyrola spp.) and Creeping Raspberry. Tracts were purposely burned over by the Indians to perpetuate their Huckleberry patches.

TYPICAL PLANTS

TREES
Lodgepole Pine 34
Western Hemlock 38
Mountain Hemlock 39
Douglas Fir 40
Pacific Silver Fir 41
Subalpine Fir 43
Shasta Red Fir 45
Noble Fir 47
Giant Red Fir 49
Cedar species

BRUSH
Spiraea species

Creeping Raspberry 97
Mountain Ash species
White-flowered Rhododendron 126
Mock Azalea 130
Pinemat Manzanita 138
Thinleaf Huckleberry 143
Grouse Huckleberry 144
Bear Grass 158
Wintergreen (Pyrola spp.230)

HERBS
Twayblade 180
Valerian 265

SUBALPINE OR ALPINE FIR FOREST

Coolness and moisture, even glacial spots (valley floors) are representative of this zone. The lower limit elevations are 4,875' in the Cascades and 4,225' or as high as 5,525' in other mountain ranges, where Subalpine Fir blends with Mountain Hemlock close to their respective boundaries. In the majority of the zones, Subalpine Fir forms a twosome with (long-lived) Engelmann Spruce or Whitebark Pine, with the latter combination found more in the open uplands. Subalpine Fir replaces Engelmann Spruce completely on the eastern Cascade range slopes. The very acidic, too well-drained, thinly humus layered,

Subalpine treeline communities, photo by C. F. Yocom.

forest soil, is well-suited for the growth of thick stands of Subalpine Fir alone or combination shrub, trees and meadow communities. This zone has high wind-dried grassy places. Some typical combinations with Subalpine Fir are: Oregon Boxwood (lowest part of shrub area), Bear Grass (stunted growth,dry upper ridges),Mock Azalea (cool ravines or wettest areas,) widespread Grouse Huckleberry areas and the cold-loving Giant Sage communities. The Subalpine zone as a whole has lower winter and higher summer temperatures with less rain and snow accumulation than the Mountain Hemlock Zone.

TYPICAL PLANTS

TREES
Western White Pine 27
Whitebark Pine 29
Western Yellow Pine 31
Lodgepole Pine 34
Western Larch 35
Engelmann Spruce 36
Western Hemlock 38
Mountain Hemlock 39
Douglas Fir 40
Pacific Silver Fir 41
Grand Fir 42
Subalpine Fir 43
Noble Fir 47
Giant Red Cedar 49
Dwarf Juniper 52
Quaking Aspen 55
Mountain Maple 70
Bitter Cherry 105

SHRUBS
Shiny Spiraea 89
Thimbleberry 96
Juneberry 109
Oregon Boxwood 112
White-flowered Rhododendron 126
Mock Azalea 130
Dwarf Huckleberry 142
Thinleaf Huckleberry 143
Grouse Huckleberry 144
Giant Sage 156

HERBS
Blue Bunch Fescue 19
Blue Bunch Wheat-grass 21
Bear Grass 158
Single-flowered Clintonia 172
Sandwort 198b
Alpine Knotweed 192
Aster species
Heart-leaved Arnica 281

JUNIPER FOREST (LAVA BEDS)

The Western Juniper zone is the driest and most widely spaced area between the timbered zones and the high grassland areas. This zone is limited to central and eastern Oregon, northwestern California and a little bit in the Ochoso and Blue Mountains of Washington. Elevations of 2,470-4,560' and many of 3,900-4,560' are the rule with the exception of the High Lava Plains province where it forms a Western Juniper Belt (community of Juniper, Sage and Fescue grass) at elevations of 5,690-6,340' on rocky out-crops and in draws on northern slopes. The Western Juniper zone requires less moisture than Yellow Pine but more moisture than pure grassland or steppe regions. The rainfall has an overall average of 13" seasonal but within the zone 8-10" seasonal is common, so the summers are very dry. Western Yellow Pine is sparsely found on northern slopes or in draws. Otherwise the low-to-high-alkaline soil communities are of the dry shrub variety such as Sage, Sunflower and Gooseberry species and grasses. A community of Juniper and Sage with Blue Bunch Wheat grass may predominate, or Fescue Grass, in the shade of Juniper (most dry areas), or a community of Juniper,

Juniper Forest, photo by Pacific Northwest Forest and Range Experiment Station.

WILDLIFE AND PLANTS OF THE CASCADES

Sage and Antelope Bush. Burning or deer over-browsing kills the Juniper and Antelope Bush and over-grazing kills off the Blue Bunch Wheat Grass and Blue Bunch Fescue, leaving an aftermath of weedy species.

TYPICAL PLANTS

TREES
Western Yellow Pine 31
Western Juniper 51

GRASSES
Blue Bunch Fescue 19
Downy Brome Grass 20
Blue Bunch Wheat Grass 21
Squirrel-tail Grass 23

SHRUBS
Squaw Currant 79
Plateau Gooseberry 85
Antelope Bush 95
Gray Rabbit Brush 155
Giant Sage 156
Spineless Horsebrush 157

HERBS
Buckwheat species
Lupine species 220
Daisy species 275-276
Yarrow 277
False Dandelion 287

WESTERN YELLOW PINE FOREST

The Western Yellow or Ponderosa Pine is an ancient species, openly growing and widely dispersed in the driest sites, second only to the Western Juniper Forest. It is found in a narrow band on the eastern slopes of the Cascade range at elevations of 1,790-3,900', on high pumice plateaus, elevation 4,700-6,700', or the Blue Mountains of Oregon and highlands of northeastern Washington, at elevations of 2,760-4,880'. The Western Yellow Pine blends into the Douglas, Grand, and White Firs at its upper limits and Western Juniper, Giant Sage combinations and grassland or steppe, at the lower dry edges. In a few places

Lassen National Forest. Photo from "U.S. Forest Service".

amongst the Western Yellow Pine regions the Oregon White Oak forms a belt. The rainfall of 14-30" (including the deep accumulation of snowfall) makes for hot, dry, practically rainless, summer days and cold nights. This, plus the moderately dark-colored, lightly acidic, sandy and clayish soils, determine the associations of the Western Yellow Pine. The pine roots go deeper in the sandy soil, but the well-drained, poorly-developed pumice soils allow enough food for the trees to grow young abundant seedlings also. However, in such soils, a stunted associate plant layer may be formed. Western Yellow Pine combines with Western Juniper and Antelope Bush (driest areas); Antelope Bush and Greenleaf Manzanita (best for tree production); Quaking Aspen (water and poorly drained sites); Lodgepole Pine (sheltered draws); Oregon White Oak (east slopes); Douglas and White Firs (pumice regions); and Antelope Bush and Fescue (steppe).

Fires and bad logging practices and livestock over-grazing have changed the environment at times, because weedy species take over the grasses and the lack of moisture makes reforesting very slow; but selective logging can and has strengthened the Western Yellow Pine (by eliminating unhealthy trees and cutting down strength-reducing brush) and fires have even allowed the rodents' caches of seeds to germinate.

TYPICAL PLANTS

TREES
Western White Pine 27
Western Yellow Pine 31
Lodgepole Pine 34
Western Larch 35
Douglas Fir 40
Grand Fir 42
White Fir 46
Incense Cedar 48
Western Juniper 51
Quaking Aspen 55
Oregon White Oak 60
Mountain Mahogany 65

BUSHES
Shiny Spiraea 89
Cream Bush 93
Antelope Bush 95
Nootka Rose 102
Wood Rose 104
Oregon Tea Tree 115

Tobacco Brush 116
Greenleaf Manzanita 139
Snowberry species
Giant Sage 156

GRASSES
Blue Bunch Fescue 19
Downy Brome Grass 20
Rye Grass species
Squirrel-tail Grass 23

HERBS
White-veined Pyrola 231
Spreading Dogbane 236
Virgate Phacelia 240
Scarlet Paintbrush 261
Arrow-leaved Balsam Root 267
Fleabane 276b
Yarrow 277
Heart-leaved Arnica 281
Rosy Everlasting 284

DOUGLAS FIR FOREST (EAST SLOPE)

Douglas Fir Forest (east slope). Pacific Northwest Forest and Range Experiment Station.

DOUGLAS FIR FOREST (EAST SLOPE)

The Douglas Fir Forest is very well developed in the northwest with the exception of south central and eastern Oregon where the trees are scarce or completely absent. This zone is located between the Grand Fir, upper limits, and the Western Yellow Pine or steppes, on the lower edge.

Elevations are 1,790-4,225'. A balanced moisture supply and better soil conditions grow good combination stands of Douglas Fir plus Western Yellow Pine, Lodgepole Pine, and Western Larch. Since the last three species are more fire resistant than the Douglas Fir, pure stands of these conifers have become possible within the Douglas Fir Forest areas. Selective logging practices are eliminating the competition of Western Yellow Pine though. The conifers shelter thick Grand Fir seedlings, so it is a possible future main habitat competitor. Incense Cedar is an occasional conifer in the drier shadier portions of the region. Shrub associations occur with less variety and fewer berry bushes than the higher colder zones. The plant communities are minor.

TYPICAL PLANTS

TREES
Western Yellow Pine 31
Lodgepole Pine 34
Western Larch 35
Douglas Fir (Oregon Pine) 40
Incense Cedar 48
Western Juniper 51
Quaking Aspen 55
Oregon White Oak 60

BUSHES
Shiny Spiraea 89

Ninebark species
Cream Bush 93
Nootka Rose 102
Kinnikinnick 137
Common Snowberry 149

HERBS
Arnica species

LODGEPOLE PINE FOREST

Lodgepole Pine Forest (east slope). Photo from Pacific Northwest Forest and Range Experiment Station.

LODGEPOLE PINE FOREST

The Lodgepole Pine Forest is widely scattered and abundant in pure stands or "Flats" in very specific localities (often sunken terrain) of Pumice plateaus and volcanic cone regions. The elevations are 3,900-4,960' with a rainfall of 14-28", this is including snowfall. The yearly matured, cold resistant Lodgepole Pine seeds and later saplings thrive on poorly developed thick sandy-ash, alkaline-type, soil in wet poorly-drained, or high water tables on well-drained ground. It invades its seeds quickly into burned over tracts, but its chances are high to be replaced by Western Yellow Pine on the more favorable sunny slopes and draws. The Lodgepole Pine was the first conifer believed to have reseeded after the last glacial period finished. Lodgepole Pine combines with Quaking Aspen to form a community in poorly drained localities. Kinnikinnick or Antelope Bush and grass are two other groups that share a community with Lodgepole Pine. Wet meadows interspersed among the "Flats" are not uncommon.

TYPICAL PLANTS

TREES
Western Yellow Pine 31
Lodgepole Pine 34
Grand Fir 42
Quaking Aspen 55

HERBS
Buttercup species
Strawberry species

BUSHES
Squaw Currant 79

Antelope Bush 95
Kinnikinnick 137

GRASS
Tufted Hairgrass 16
Blue Bunch Grass 19
Squirrel-tail Grass 23
Juncus species

WESTERN HEMLOCK FOREST (EAST SLOPE)

This is the third community of the Western Hemlock Forest zone and receives less rainfall. It includes Willamette and other dry valleys and eastern slopes of the coast ranges and Cascades. Elevation is from sea level to 3,700'. The undergrowth of Cream Bush and the evergreen Salal associates with Western Hemlock and Douglas Fir (Oregon Pine). Broad-leaved trees occupy sandy bank localities but are not common. This community is rarer than the other two of this realm. See west slope page 14.

TYPICAL PLANTS

TREES
Yew 26
Sugar Pine 28
Western Hemlock 38
Douglas Fir 40
Incense Cedar 48
Oregon White Oak 60
Big-leaf Maple 69
Madrone 72
Vine Maple 71

SHRUB
Hazelnut 73
Cream Bush 93
Pacific Blackberry 101
Salal 136
Red Huckleberry 145
Snowberry 149

HERBS
Yerba de Selva 215
Twin Flower 264

WHITEBARK PINE FOREST (EAST SIDE)

Whitebark Pine is a timberline forest occupant, sharing equal billing with Mountain Hemlock, Subalpine Fir and, on the driest sites which Whitebark Pine prefers, sharing a community with Lodgepole Pine. It also blends down into the Subalpine Fir dominated territory. The 975-1,625' wide belt of timberline trees has an elevation that starts at approximately 5,000' in the western ranges and varies as much as 1,600' higher up in the eastern portion of the Cascade ranges. Many mountain peaks do not attain the height for the timberline species. Whitebark Pine, Mountain Hemlock and Subalpine Fir all become stunted and form bushy thickets at the summits, Whitebark Pine being the most resistant to this stunting. A Larch species is a colorful (turning orange-yellow in the fall) occupant of this highest of conifer communities. Clark's Nutcracker Jay's forgotten *Pinus albicaulis* (Whitebark Pine) seed hoards help maintain a good reproduction record of this pine.

Photo of the Whitebark Pine zone taken by C. F. Yocom.

TYPICAL PLANTS

TREES

Western White Pine 27
Whitebark Pine 29
Lodgepole Pine 34
Engelmann Spruce 36
Mountain Hemlock 39

Pacific Silver Fir 41
Subalpine Fir 43
Shasta Red Fir 45
Cedar species
Larch species

BRUSHLAND

Brushland has been described as Chaparral in the Mixed Evergreen and Mixed Coniferous Forests, as berry patches in Sitka Spruce, Pacific Silver Fir and Grand Fir Forests, or as brushfields (Tobacco Brush) of the White Fir and Shasta Red Fir Forests. The Heath, Rose and Sunflower and many stunted species comprising brushland are mentioned in the Mountain Hemlock forest region. Mock Azalea and Grouse Huckleberry (brushland) is listed in the Subalpine Fir forest region, and Antelope Bush and Greenleaf Manzanita brushland in the Western Yellow Pine zone. See their respective habitats for additional soil information, etc., and shrub list. Predominately these tracts were cleared by fires and bad logging practices, and, as a rule, in these particular regions, conifers encroach and, with optimum conditions, and time will reconquer these areas from the shrubs, except for the areas bordering the drier grasslands. The talus or rockslides found in the Western Hemlock forests, as they begin to heal with plants after the slides, can be added to the brushland list also.

Brushlands. After forest lands have been logged *Ceanothus velutinus* (Tobacco Brush) grows here and hinders growth of young conifers. Photo by Pacific Northwest Forest and Range Experiment Station.

WILDLIFE AND PLANTS OF THE CASCADES

TYPICAL PLANTS

Mountain Maple 70
Vine Maple 71
California Hazelnut 73
Oregon Grape 74
Sticky Currant 81
Cream Bush 93
Creeping Raspberry 97
Salmon Berry 98
Pacific Blackberry 101
Wood Rose 104
Juneberry 109
Oregon Boxwood 112
Coffeeberry 114
Oregon Tea Tree 115
Tobacco Brush 116
Deer Brush 117
Mountain Whitethorn 118

Squaw Carpet 120
American Devil's Club 122
Fremont's Silk-tassel 125
California Rose-Bay 128
Labrador Tea 129
Pacific Poison Oak
Mock Azalea 130
Salal 136
Kinnikinnick 137
Pinemat Manzanita 138
Greenleaf Manzanita 139
Evergreen Huckleberry 140
Thinleaf Huckleberry 143
Red Huckleberry 145
Snowberry Bush
Purple Flower Honeysuckle 151
Wintergreen (Pyrola species)

SAGEBRUSH PLAINS AND GRASSLANDS

Sagebrush Plains fading to Grasslands are found scattered through the regions bounded by Sitka Spruce and Western Hemlock. They are also encountered as islands within the Western Yellow Pine forests and on old sand dune surfaces. Large grasslands abound in the interior valleys associated with oaks. "Balds" are the grassy areas associated with the Subalpine Fir region. Soil composition varies, influencing the sage and grass growth, but the arid climate conditions (usually more moisture for grassland) and brush fires plus over-grazing and even past cultivation of land tracts have determined the growth to a much greater extent. The roots of brush and grass species are adapted to underground moisture conditions. Deep gravel or sandy soil with very low moisture produces grass and stiff Sage species. Stony shallow soils, with a tendency to be very hot and dry in the summer and cold and frosty in winter, produce a crust of moss and lichens for an early sequential growth and then sage, grass, and buckwheat species. Salty alkaline soils have no moss or lichen ground cover and add greasewood with the scrubby sage species and Gray Rye Grass. Sagebrush thrives in eastern Oregon.

Sagebrush Plains. Photo courtesy of Southern Pacific

WILDLIFE AND PLANTS OF THE CASCADES

Black Hawthorne, with the Giant Sage and other species and grasses, plus a small variety of bushes occupies the moister draws. The Sage species are non-sprouting, so are not adaptable to cattle grazing and along with Antelope Bush must reinvade the ground instead of regrowing after fire damage. Although Blue Bunch Wheat Grass and Blue Bunch Grass can recuperate after fire damage they cannot withstand heavy grazing. This allows Downy Brome Grass and, to a lesser extent, Gray Rye Grass, to take over. In recently disturbed regions, Gray Rabbit Brush is the only shrub found. Thistle, Teasel and Dandelions are the replacement species in abandoned cultivated fields.

TYPICAL PLANTS

SHRUBS
Nootka Rose 102
White Snowberry
Gray Rabbit Brush 155
Giant Sage 156
Spineless Horsebrush 157
Russian Thistle 195
Tumble Mustard 210
Poison Oak

Northern Bedstraw 263
Cinquefoil Species
Phlox species
Fleabane species
Milkvetch species
Paintbrush species 262
Arrow-leaved Balsam Root 267
Yarrow 277

HERBS
Western Blue Flag 179
Sagebrush Buttercup 206
Wild Strawberry species
Vetch 222
Red-stem Filaree 223

GRASSES
Wild Oat Grass 18
Blue Bunch Grass 19
Blue Bunch Wheat Grass 21
Squirrel-tail Grass 23
Blue Grass species
Needlegrass species
Gray Rye Grass 22

MOUNTAIN MEADOWS, SUBALPINE MEADOWS AND ALPINE FELL FIELDS

Burned over tracts have formed mountain meadows in the Pacific Silver Fir and Mountain Hemlock forests. Meadow communities with good moisture conditions enabling bracken ferns and thimbleberries to flourish, and meadowland that reaches up into subalpine meadows associated with the Sitka Alder, are found in the Pacific Silver Fir forest. The Mountain Hemlock territory has rich meadowlands and farther up the harsh alpine environment, between the timberline and shrub line, permits meadow patches. The cooler, moister western slopes permit the growth of Red Mountain Heather and Western Cassiope plus huckleberry species. Grasslands dominate meadows in the eastern areas with high plant coverage. In both the western and eastern Mountain Hemlock region tree species invade and expand and thus are constantly decreasing these mountain meadows. The Sitka Spruce borders sandy-soil coast line meadows, featuring grass and Lupine species. The Grand Fir

Photo of Mountain Meadow by Pacific Northwest Forest and Range Experiment Station.

forest has permanent and important mountain meadows near headwaters of streams. Many perennial grass meadows were over-grazed and allowed to erode and the result was a weedy growth took over with a slow healing process. The wet meadows of the Lodgepole Pine regions on poorly drained pumice ground have already been mentioned. Fescue filled meadows are found on drier subalpine regions. The subalpine meadows reach up into alpine communities and high plateaus showing an association of saxifrage and heather and partridgefoot at elevations of 7,475-8,450'. There is little vegetation above this elevation.

TYPICAL PLANTS

SHRUBS
Willow species
Thimbleberry 96
Huckleberry 144
Huckleberry species
Gray Sage 156

HERBS
Bracken Ferns
Spreading Phlox 147
Bistort 191
Alpine Knotweed 192
Newberry's Knotweed 193
Alpine Saxifrage 211
Indian Pink species
Lupine species
Partridgefoot 216

Cinquefoil 218
Long-stalked Clover
Silverleaf 240a
Valerian 265
Dwarf Hulsea 269
Paintbrush species
Subalpine Daisy 274
Arnica species

GRASSES
Tufted Hairgrass 16
Tall Trisetum 17
Squirrel-tail Grass 23
Needlegrass species
Rush species
Sedge species

BARREN PUMICE FLATS, CLIFFS, CAVES AND LARGE ROCK OUTCROPPINGS

A thin layer of volcanic ash material, sometimes undetected, is a part of the soil of most of Washington and Oregon and down into the Lassen and Shasta mountain areas of northern California, but the thick layers of ash and lava, so evident in sunken areas, volcanic cones and caves, are located mainly in southern central Oregon. Approximately 4,000 year old deposits have formed flats of thick layers of pumice and cinder. The amount of plant growth on these flats is sparse to none on the driest places, but here and there the underdeveloped pumice soils provide adequate soil food for Lodgepole Pine, but little else. The other plants and shrubs are as a rule stunted. Thinner layers of pumice soil were mentioned to support growth in the Yellow Pine forest. Rock outcroppings are found in the timberline forests, subalpine parklands and alpine communities. Mountain Hemlock, Subalpine Fir, Whitebark Pine and Subalpine Larch are dispersed on rocky points or are found in

Barren Pumice Flat, taken by C. F. Yocom.

groups associated with meadows and patches of snow. Plants are compact perennials (cushion plants) with large taproots and found on dry exposed ridges. Partridgefoot is one plant that stabilizes these ridges and rock slides. In Washington the open woodlands and barren slopes that support sparse growth of grasses and close-packed stunted trees are likely to be made of serpentine rock and soil. Western White Pine, Jeffrey Pine, Canyon Oak, Oakleaf Buckwheat, Pinemat Manzanita, California Rosebay, Bear Grass, Spreading Phlox, and Yarrow, thrive on this serpentine soil, and can be classed as indicators of this habitat.

TYPICAL PLANTS

TREES
Western Yellow Pine 31
Lodgepole Pine 34
Douglas Fir 40
Port Orford Cedar 50
Dwarf Juniper 52
Tanbark Oak 58
Huckleberry Oak 63
Oregon Myrtle 64

SHRUBS
Tobacco Brush 116
Red Mountain Heather 132
Kinnikinnick 137
Greenleaf Manzanita 139
Grouse Huckleberry 144
Red Huckleberry 145

HERBS
Bistort 191
Newberry's Knotweed 193
Pumice Sandwort 198a
Western Windflower 202
Alpine Saxifrage 211
Partridgefoot 216
Fan-shaped Cinquefoil 218
Valerian 265
Dwarf Hulsea 269
Cascade Aster 272
Butterweed 283
Arnica species
Lupine species
Paintbrush species
Penstemon species

GRASSES
Squirrel-tail Grass 23
Alpine Rush 25

Rock Cliff. Photo by Pacific Northwest Forest and Range Experiment Station.

MARSHES, LAKES AND STREAMS

Giant Red Cedar and Oregon Alder swamps are found in the Sitka Spruce and Western Hemlock forests, near the coast. Marshes are common on the coastal plains. These swamps and marshes require a high water table and support a large variety of shrubs and plants. Tule and bulrush marshes are located in the Klamath Lake and similar regions to the east.

The lava flows in the eastern areas of our region have created unique water communities in the bogs, marshes and seasonal lakes that are filled with water during the winter and become dry in the summer months. Other high mountain lakes have been formed by glacial action and support much water plant growth during the spring, summer and fall after the ice has melted. The slower-moving streams everywhere afford growing places for water plants in their shallow margins. The commoner of these plants are described and pictured from pages 52 to 59.

Mountain Lake. Photo by Pacific Northwest Forest and Range Experiment Station.

MARSHES, LAKES AND STREAMS

TYPICAL PLANTS

WATER PLANTS
Broad-leaved Cattail 1
Narrow-leaved Bur-reed 2
Small Bur-reed 3
Small Pondweed 4
Slender Najas 5
Water Plantain 6
Broad-leaved Arrowhead 7
Greater Duckweed 8
Water-shield 9
Western Yellow Pond-lily 10
Hornwort 11
Parrot's Feather 12
American Milfoil 13
Whorl-leaved Milfoil 14
Mare's-tail 15

GRASSES
Gray Rye Grass 22
Alpine Rush 25
Sedge species

TREES
Lodgepole Pine 34

Sitka Spruce 37
Western Hemlock 38
Douglas Fir 40
Pacific Silver Fir 41
Subalpine Fir 43
Giant Red Cedar 49
Oregon Alder 53
Quaking Aspen 55
Black Cottonwood 56
Willow species
Oregon White Oak 60
Big-leaf Maple 69
Hawthorn species

SHRUBS
Douglas Spiraea 90
Salmon Berry 98
Kinnikinnick 137
Western Bog Blueberry 141

HERBS
Youth-on-age 213
Lewis' Monkey-flower 245
Willowweed species

CULTIVATED LANDS

The interior valleys are the cultivated lowlands. They are in the Pine, Douglas Fir and Oak forest regions. The climate is warm and dry with a variety of soils from sandy, rocky to clay, and the natural vegetation is grasslands, oak knolls, chaparral hillsides and conifer stands. Logging, grazing and farming are the chief occupations. Land of the dry steppe regions is also cultivated or grazed. Wheat, peas etc., are planted. Overgrazed land has been taken over by weedy species. Mountain meadows are used to graze sheep, and have been badly over-grazed also. See Western Yellow Pine and Whitebark Pine forests.

TYPICAL PLANTS

TREES
Kellogg's Oak 59
Oregon White Oak 60
Big-leaf Maple 69
Madrone 72

GRASSES
Hazelnut 73
Juneberry 109

Snowberry Bush species
Poison Oak
Mazzard Cherry *(Prunus avium)*
Bent Grass species
Wild Oat Grass 18
Plantain species
Vetch 222
Sword Fern

COMMON PLANTS AND HOW TO IDENTIFY THEM

There are certain immensely successful and numerous plants in each wildlife area that help to identify that area or habitat. In the streamside woodland are the willows, alders and cottonwoods; in the chaparral, the manzanita, wild lilac and mountain mahogany; and in the mixed evergreen, the black oak, Douglas fir and madrone. This book helps you get acquainted with these and other common plants, which are the ones you are far most likely to see.

The trouble is, because of the presence of less common plants, you may confuse a rarer kind with one of the commoner kinds described in this book. This is why it is necessary for you to carefully follow the directions given below.

The pictures shown on the next page will help you understand the different kinds of flowers, flower formations, and leaves that are useful in identifying plants. Study these pictures carefully so you understand the meanings of the words used.

Each picture or figure in this section is named. When you see one of these names in a description of a plant turn to the correct figure in this section and you will find a helpful illustration of what the description is talking about.

Besides the general pictures on plants, a number of separate pictures are given with the plant descriptions. Use these also to help you with identification. When you are studying a plant to determine its name, carefully look at every part of it, the leaves, the flowers, the fruit, the seeds, the bark and even the way the branches are formed. When you add all this knowledge together and compare what you have learned with the pictures and descriptions, you are soon likely to come up with the correct name. If you get in too big a hurry, however, and do not carefully double check everything, it is also easy to make a mistake. Unless otherwise noted most plants described are assumed to be found over most of the Cascade Wildlife Region.

(Special Note: An * in front of a plant name means some parts of it are edible. For directions of use see books on edible plants listed in the Suggested References. When the word "leaflet" is used in the pages that follow, it means that the leaf of the plant is compound or made up of many leaflets. Abbreviations: * indicates that some part of the plant is edible, " = inches, and ' = feet.)

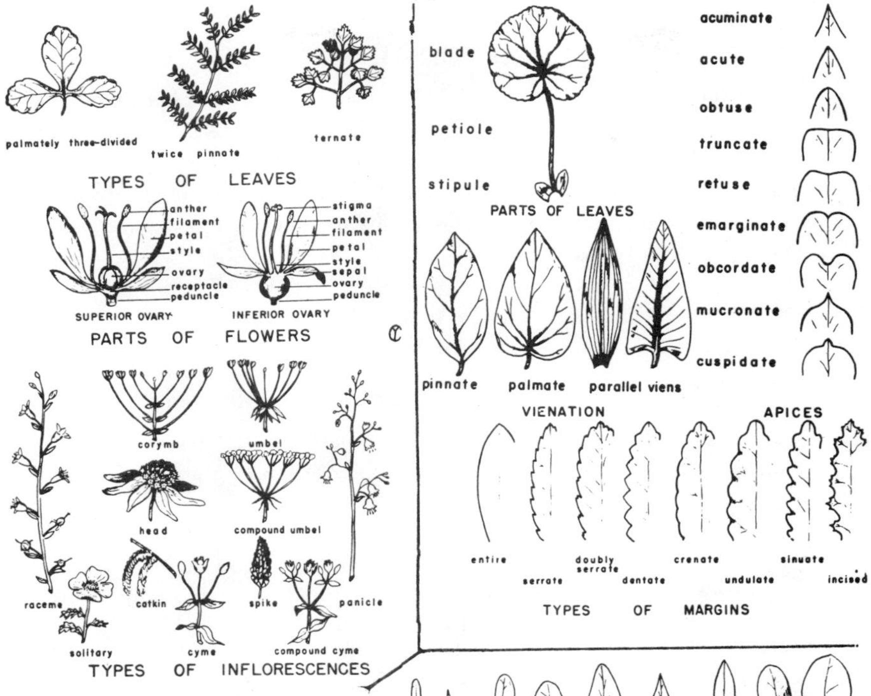

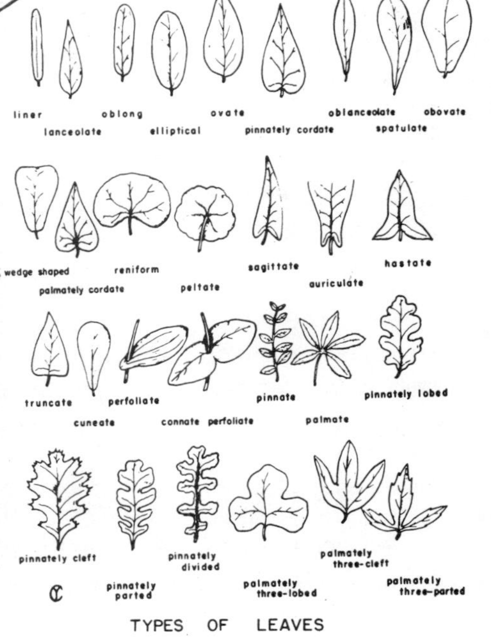

KEY TO PLANT PARTS 51

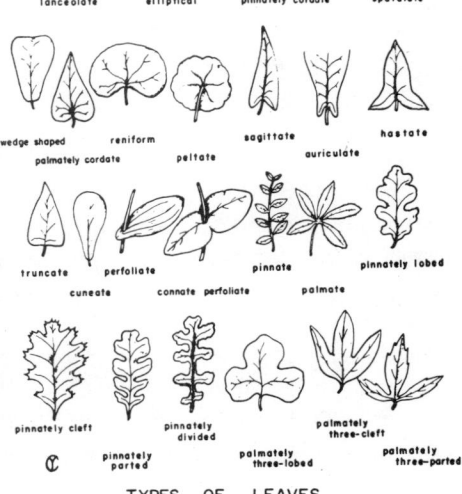

As you study plants in the field or those of your collection, note how their parts compare with those shown on this page. Also turn to this page when you find a plant part named in the descriptions of wild plants that are to be found on the pages that follow.

Practice in this sort of comparison will greatly help you in correctly identifying the common plants you find.

COMMON PLANTS

(NOTE: All trees and bushes are assumed to lose their leaves in winter unless they are called "evergreen" or "coniferous". To help with quick identification, the plants that follow are divided into: A. Fresh Water Plants; B. Grasses; C. Coniferous Trees; D. Broad-leaved Trees; E. Shrubs and Vines; F. Herbs with Parallel-veined Leaves; and G. Herbs with Net-veined Leaves.

A. Fresh Water Plants
(no habitats marked on margins)

CATTAIL Family - solid, jointless and circular stems.

*1. COMMON CATTAIL, *Typha latifolia*. 3-6' tall; leaves very long and flat with sheaths at base; **flowers in dense spike.** Marshes, edges of ponds.

BUR-REED Family

Leaves are sheathed on stem at base, some floating and limp, others stiff and erect; **flowers appear like dense circular burs.**

*2. NARROW-LEAVED BUR-REED, *Sparganium angustifolium*. 12-20" long, floating or high, erect stems; the **brown bur-like fruits about 1/8" wide, and shaped like a spindle;** leaves flat and not keeled; very narrow.

3. SMALL BUR-REED, *Sparganium minimum*. Floating stems reach out to about 32"; some short emergent stems; the **dark green leaves are mostly flat and floating;** the female flower heads 1-3 on upper parts of stems.

PONDWEED Family

The underwater leaves are very thin; and the flowers are very tiny.

4. SMALL PONDWEED, *Potamogeton pusillus*. 12-40" long; **very narrow leaves are submerged, 1-2½" long;** a pair of hollow-formed or tube-like leaf-like stipules at the base of each leaf. Slow streams and ponds.

WATER-NYMPH Family

Submerged annual herbs with slender branches.

5. SLENDER NAJAS, *Najas flexilis*. 3-6½' long stems; **very slender**

WATER PLANTS 53

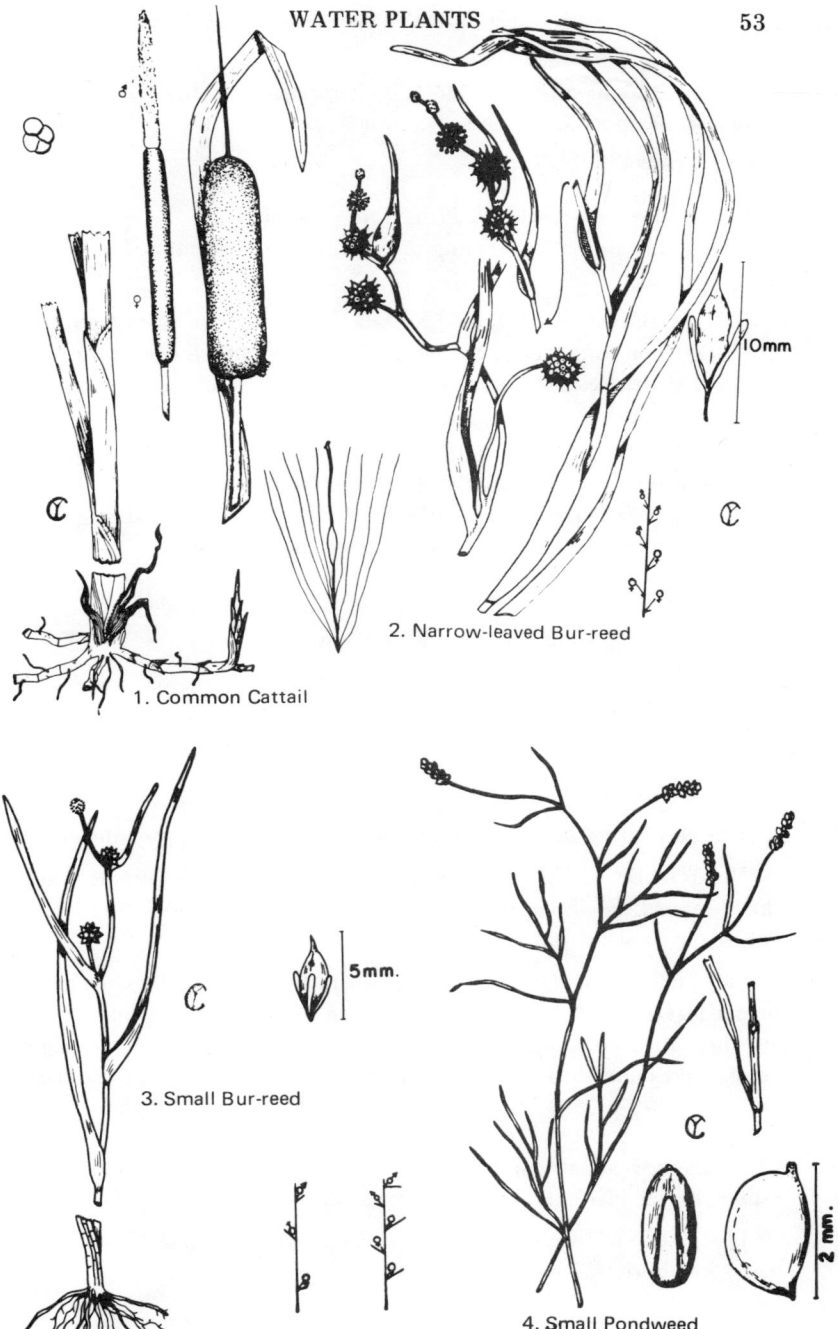

1. Common Cattail
2. Narrow-leaved Bur-reed
3. Small Bur-reed
4. Small Pondweed

leaves with 20-30 tiny teeth along their margins and the leaves usually crowded on upper branchlets. In ponds and slow streams at lower elevations in the mountains.

WATER PLANTAIN Family

The leaves are either floating or erect, and with sheaths; the flowers are in whorls.

*6. COMMON WATER PLANTAIN, *Alisma triviale*. 2-6' high, with 2-9" leaves on long stems; **the white flowers in umbels that form pyramid-like structures on the stems;** fruits ¼-½" in diameter. Margins of ponds and marshes.

*7. COMMON ARROWHEAD, *Sagittaria latifolia*. Mostly underwater plants, with leaves 4-15" long, the flower stems slender; flowers in 3's, **leaves in 3 parts of about equal length;** seed with a strong beak. Quiet water. Indians baked or boiled roots like potatoes.

DUCKWEED Family

Tiny, floating aquatic herbs without leaves.

8. GREATER DUCKWEED, *Spirodela polyrhiza*. **Stems appear frond-like;** the 2 male flowers and 1 female flower appear in a sac-like pouch.

WATER-LILY Family

The very large simple leaves are usually seen floating, or submerged.

*9. WATER-SHIELD, *Brasenia Schreberi*. 1¾-6" long stems; **leaves shield-shaped;** small purple flowers with 3 each similar petals and sepals. Ponds and slow streams.

*10. YELLOW POND-LILY, *Nuphar polysepalum*. The **large heart-shaped leaves, 6-12" broad and 6-14" long are very distinctive;** they are attached to a creeping rootstock by means of a long stem or scape. Ponds, lakes and slow streams. Edible seeds (fried) and tubers(boiled).

HORNWORT Family

Submerged aquatic herbs with the whorled leaves branched into rather stiff slender and tiny-toothed divisions.

11. HORNWORT, *Ceratophyllum demersum*. Stems 2-8' long; 5-12 leaves in whorl. Found in slow streams and ponds.

WATER PLANTS

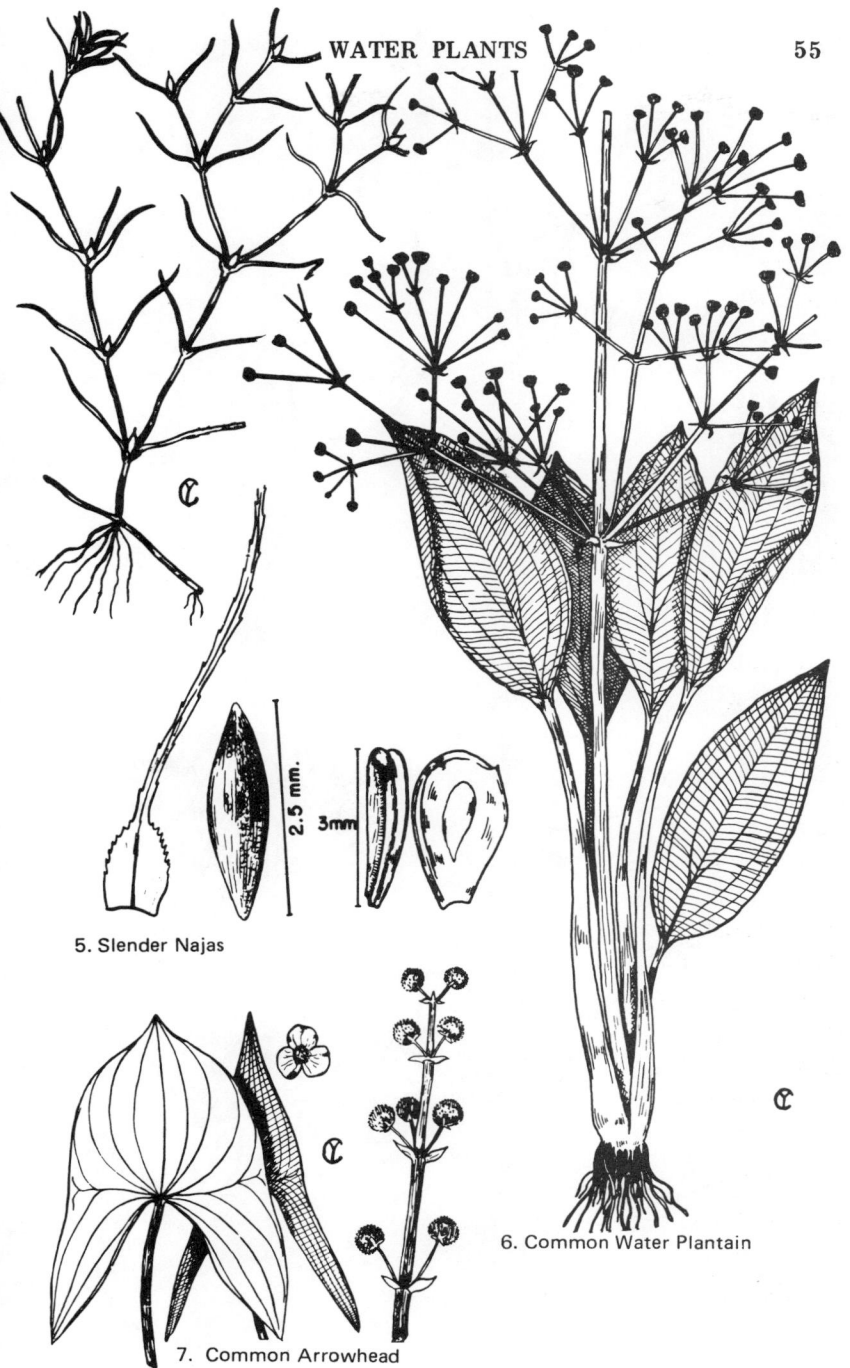

5. Slender Najas
6. Common Water Plantain
7. Common Arrowhead

WILDLIFE AND PLANTS OF THE CASCADES

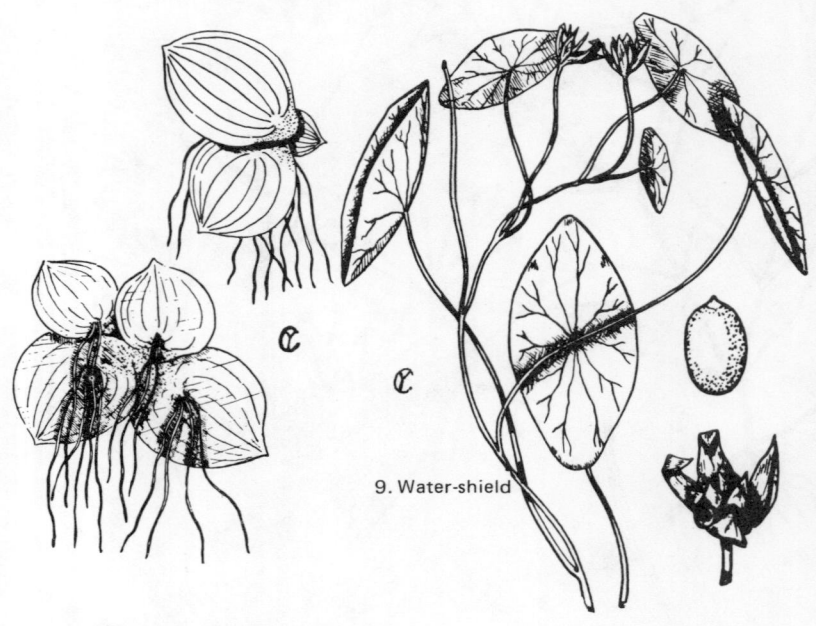

9. Water-shield

8. Greater Duckweed

10. Yellow Pond-lily

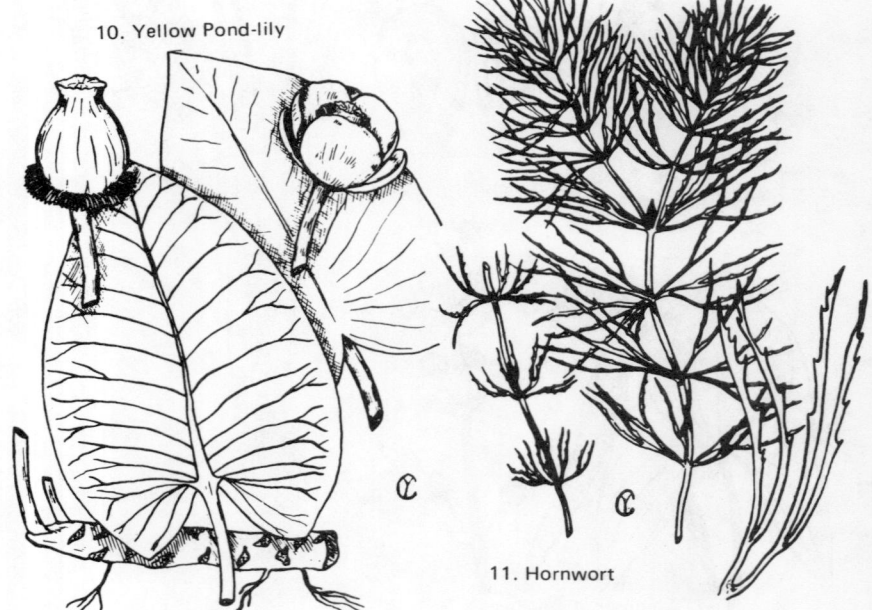

11. Hornwort

WATER PLANTS

12. Parrot's Feather

13. American Milfoil

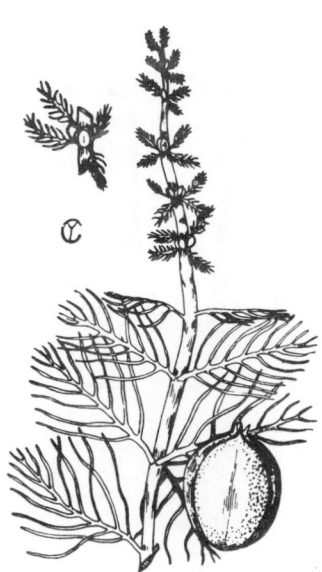

14. Whorl-leaved Milfoil

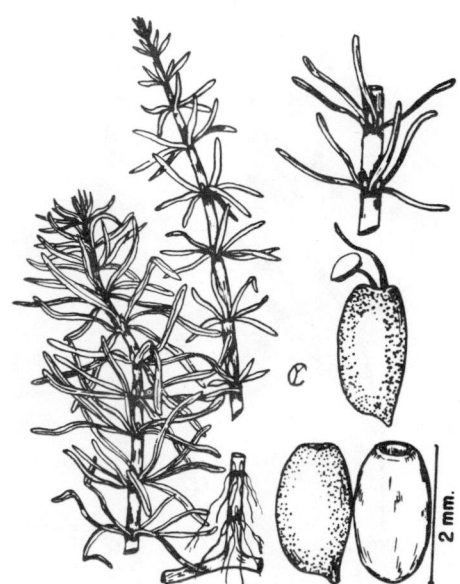

15. Mare's-Tail

WILDLIFE AND PLANTS OF THE CASCADES

WATER-MILFOIL Family

The submerged leaves usually whorled and very finely divided into thread-like parts.

12. PARROT'S FEATHER, *Myriophyllum brasiliense*. An escaped plant from S. America, now found in our lower streams; growing 4-6" out of water, **showing 4-6 feathery whorls of leaves.** Slow streams.

13. AMERICAN MILFOIL, *Myriophyllum spicatum* ssp. *exalbescens*. Stems about 3-3½' long, forked or simple and of a purple color; **leaves in whorls of 3-4; tiny flowers usually underwater on almost naked spikes.** In slow or quiet water.

14. WHORL-LEAVED MILFOIL, *Myriophyllum verticillatum*. Very similar to above, **leaves in whorls of 4-5.** Quiet water in foothills of mountains.

15. MARE'S-TAIL, *Hippuris vulgaris*. **Simple stems are 8-20" high; with many whorls, 7-10 leaves per whorl.** Quiet water below 9,000'.

B. GRASSES

The grasses are commonly found mainly in the mountain meadows, but some are also encountered in open spaces in the woods or along the streams. Just a few of the common kinds are mentioned here. To aid in identification, study the descriptive drawings of grasses and their parts shown at the bottom of this page.

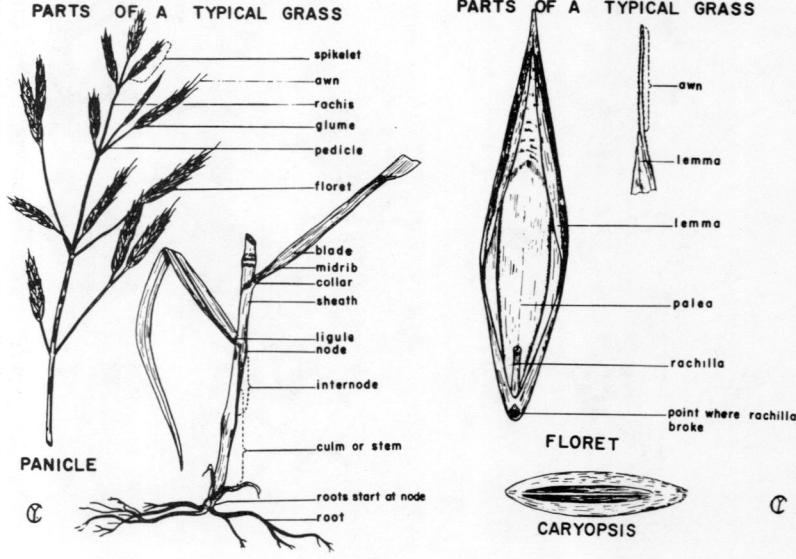

GRASSES

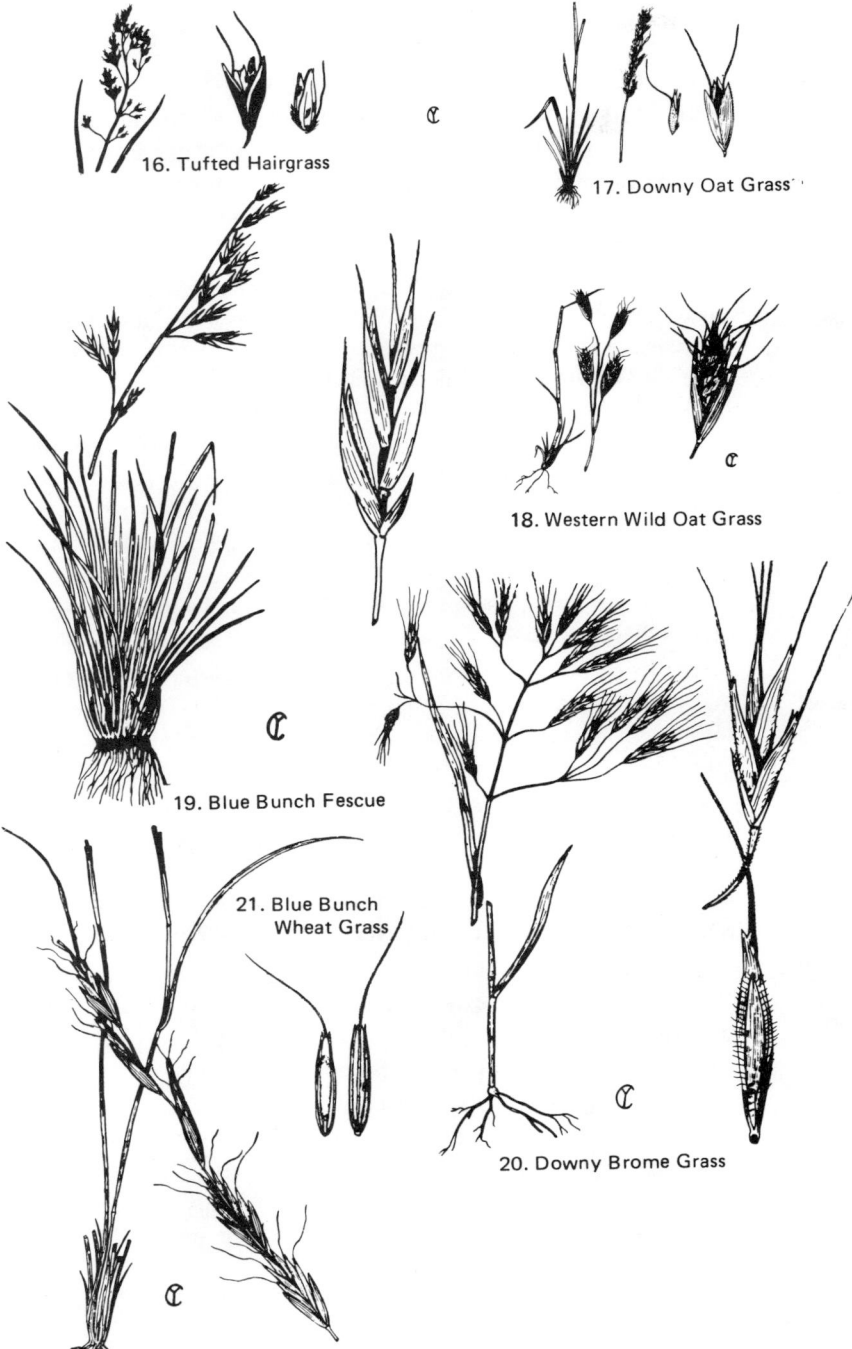

16. Tufted Hairgrass
17. Downy Oat Grass
18. Western Wild Oat Grass
19. Blue Bunch Fescue
21. Blue Bunch Wheat Grass
20. Downy Brome Grass

WILDLIFE AND PLANTS OF THE CASCADES

GRASS Family
Flowers in typical spikelets with long hairs or awns.

mt.mead.
water

16. TUFTED HAIRGRASS, *Deschampsia caespitosa.* 16-48" tall; densely tufted, forming large clusters of spikelets; **grass blades stiff and rough to the touch;** spikelets 1/8-1/4" long, in open panicles 4-16" long; rachis covered with tiny dense hairs. Swampy ground. Transition to Hudsonian Life Zones.

mt.mead.

17. DOWNY OAT GRASS, *Trisetum spicatum.* 6-20" tall; stems rather stout; leaf blades flat; 1/8-1/4" wide, **both blades and sheaths usually covered with tiny hairs, often soft and thick;** panicles 2-6" long, rather dense and spike-like, shining pale greenish to purplish in color; spikelets ¼-2/5" long, usually with two florets. Mainly in Canadian and Hudsonian Life Zones, on both sides of the Cascades.

brush
grass
mix.con.

18. WESTERN WILD OAT GRASS, *Danthonia californica.* 2-3' high, with the flower spikes covered by hairless sheaths; the **grass blades rough to the touch;** a small panicle with 2-5 large spikelets; **the lower sheaths of the spikelets may be much swollen or mis-shapen at times.** Transition zone, west side of Cascades.

conif.
grass

19. BLUE BUNCH FESCUE, *Festuca idahoensis.* 16-40" tall; **leaf blades more than ½ length of stalks;** panicles 4-8" long; forms large leaf tufts; leaves whitish-green and rough. Open woods, arid Transition zone.

grass
conif.

20. DOWNY BROME GRASS, *Bromus tectorum.* 1-2' tall; **the drooping panicles are 2-6" long and reddish;** lemmas usually covered with soft hairs; awns are 1/3-2/3" long; 2nd glume is less than 1/3" long. Introduced from Europe, but common along roads, in waste places, etc. at lower elevations of mountains.

rock
sage

21. BLUE BUNCH WHEAT GRASS, *Agropyron spicatum.* 2-3½' high; **lemmas with sharply-bent awns;** spikes very delicate and slender; leaf blades hairy on upper surface; leaf sheaths smooth. Arid Transition and Upper Sonoran zones of foothills on east side of Cascades, on rocky hills and flats.

grass
mt.mead.

*22. GRAY RYE GRASS, *Elymus cinereus.* 3-9½' high; thickly tufted, coarse and **stiff grass, with blades 3/8-7/8" wide, all rough to the touch and very long;** glumes narrow and awn-like; lemmas awnless. Edible seeds, but hairs must be singed off. Arid Transition zone, mainly east side of Cascades.

GRASSES AND RUSHES

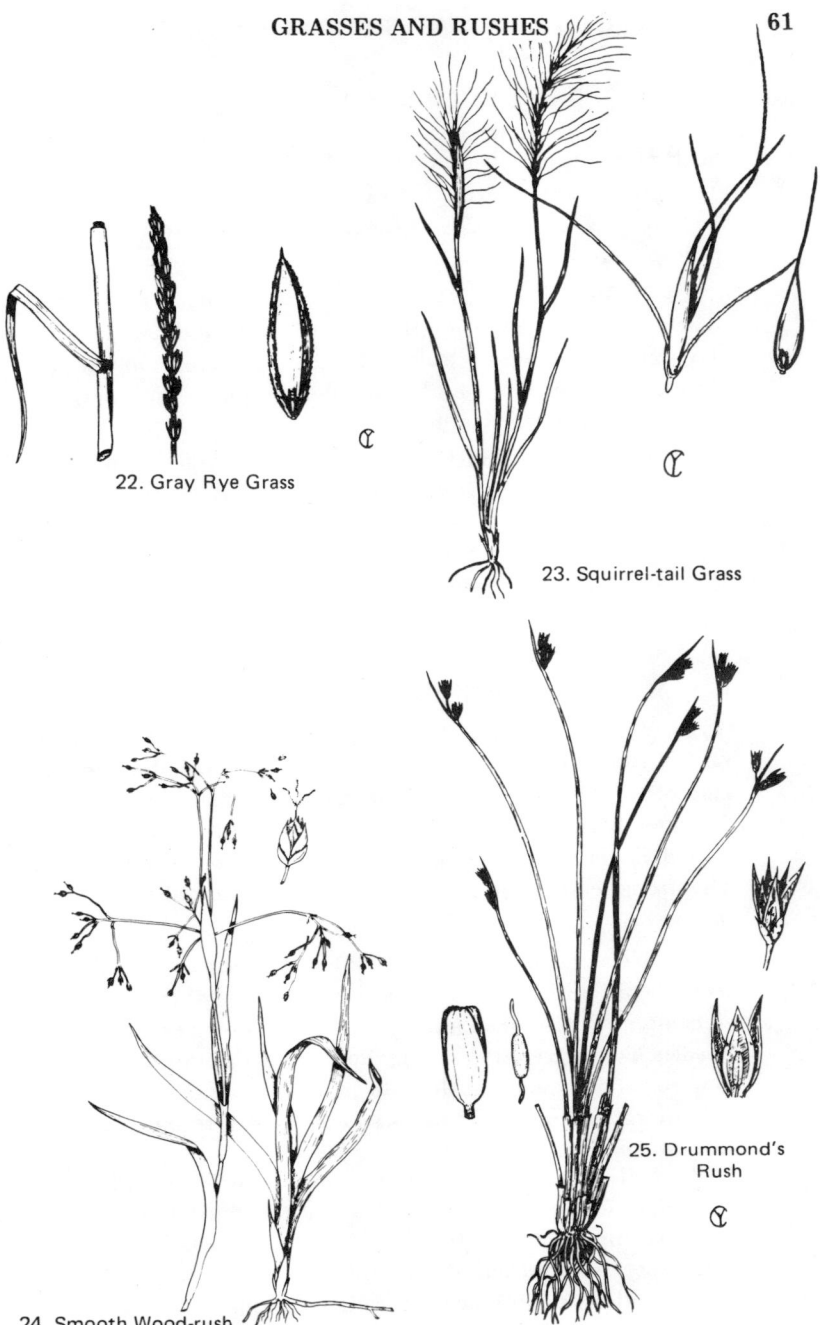

22. Gray Rye Grass

23. Squirrel-tail Grass

24. Smooth Wood-rush

25. Drummond's Rush

WILDLIFE AND PLANTS OF THE CASCADES

conif.
rocks
mt.mead.

23. SQUIRREL-TAIL GRASS, *Sitanion Hystrix*. 4-20" tall; tufted at base; stems erect or spreading; **glumes have 1-2 long, bent awns;** 2 spikelets on each swollen joint of the flower stem. The spikelets often pierce faces of grazing animals, causing inflamation. Mainly east side of Cascades in Transition to Arctic-alpine zones.

mt.mead.
sub.-alp.

24. SMOOTH WOOD-RUSH, *Luzula glabrata*, 8-20" tall; stems rising from basal branches that take root and start growing; 4-5 stem leaves; upper leaf blades 1¾-2½" long, smooth and flat; basal leaves 4-8" long; small flowers appear dark purplish-brown. Hudsonian Life Zone.

mt.mead.
sub.-alp.

25. DRUMMOND'S RUSH, *Juncus Drummondii*. 8-18" high; from well-matted rootstocks; basal leaf-sheaths show no blades or only tiny remnants; flower clusters 1-3, or rarely 4-5 flowered, each flower with a pair of small bracts at the base. Rushes of this kind and similar are very numerous in damp parts of mountain meadows, especially in the Canadian to Arctic-alpine zones.

C. CONIFEROUS TREES

mix.ev.
pine
dg. fir

26. YEW, *Taxus brevifolia*. Evergreen tree or shrub with brown or dark purple scaly bark; spreading horizontal branches; **linear to lanceolate, stiff, entire, spirally arranged leaves that usually appear 2-ranked because of the twisted petioles;** red berry-like fruit. Found in damp canyons in Siskiyou mountains, and Cascades. The strong heavy wood was used by Indians to make bows, spears, paddles, etc.

red fir
gr. fir
west.hem.

27. WESTERN WHITE PINE, *Pinus monticola*. Tall, slender tree, 75-150' high; trunk 2-4' in diameter; bark grayish-purple to cinnamon color, broken into small square to rectangular blocks. **Needles bluish-green, 2-4" long, borne 5 in a group;** cones 6-10" long, sometimes curved at the base. A minor species in the forests of western Washington; found in southwestern Oregon at mid elevations.

mix.con.
gr. fir
mix.ev.

* 28. SUGAR PINE, *Pinus Lambertiana*. Grows to be from 200-220' high, with a trunk from 6' to an occasional 13' diameter; has a flat-topped crown, from 60-70' across, of **slender branches that sweep outward and downward.** Bark on young stems and branches thin, smooth, dark green, becoming 2-3" thick and

YEW AND PINE

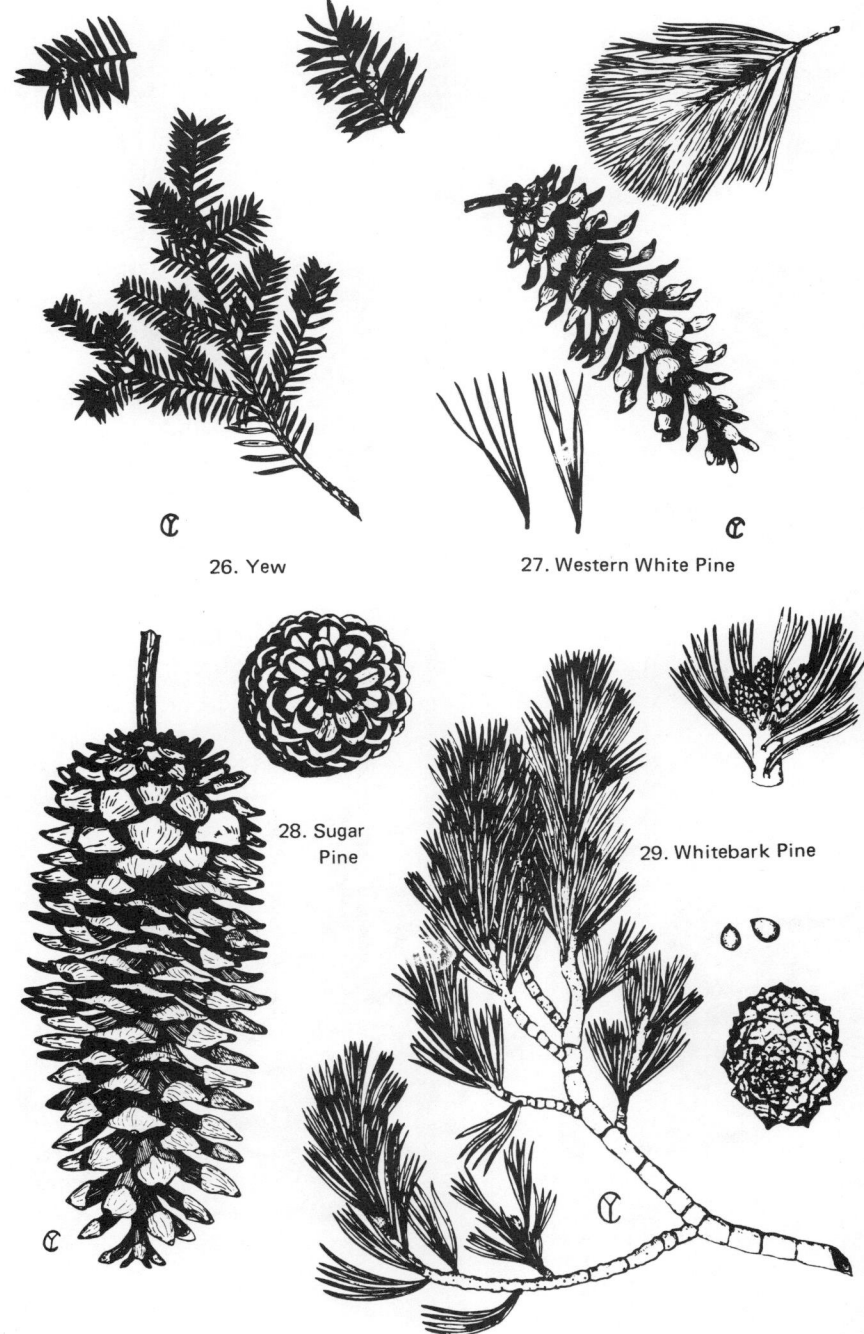

26. Yew
27. Western White Pine
28. Sugar Pine
29. Whitebark Pine

64 WILDLIFE AND PLANTS OF THE CASCADES

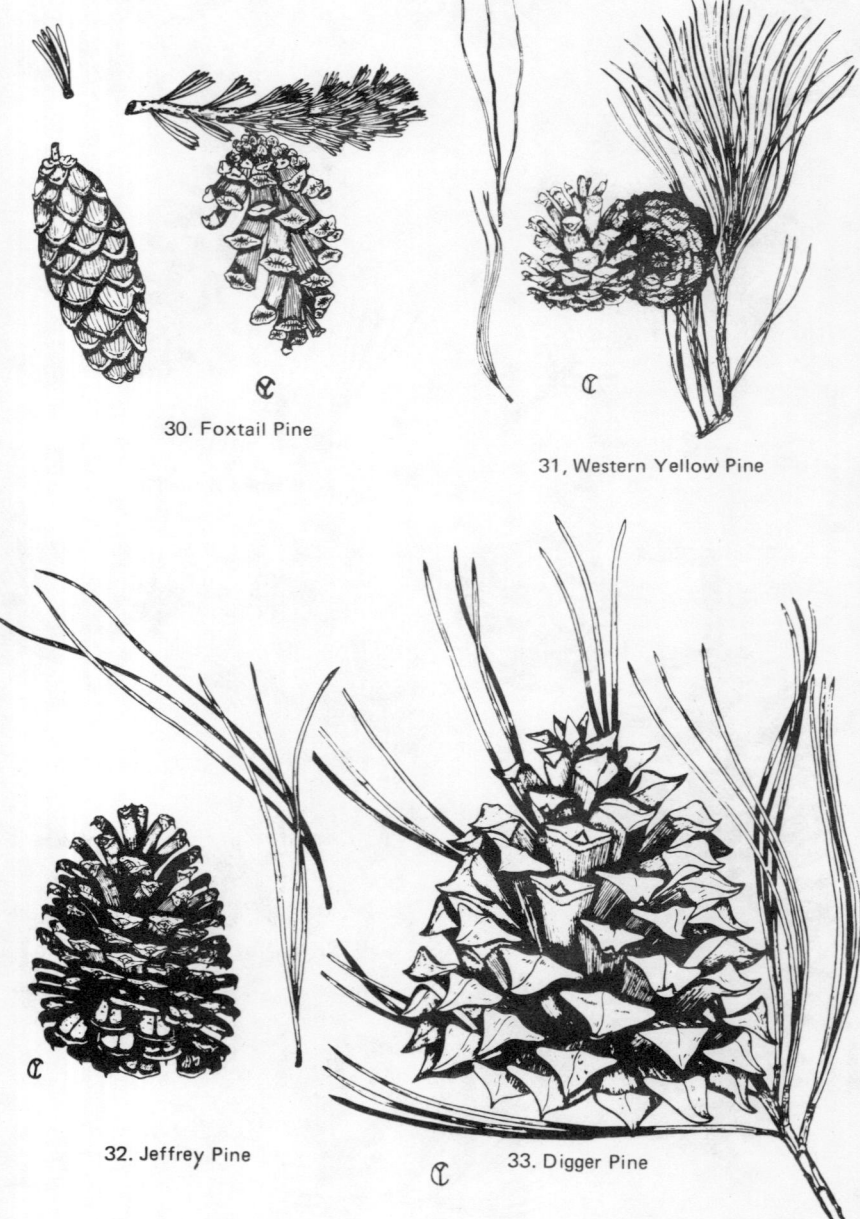

30. Foxtail Pine

31. Western Yellow Pine

32. Jeffrey Pine

33. Digger Pine

deeply and irregularly divided into long thick plate-like ridges covered with large loose purplish-brown or cinnamon colored scales on old trunks. **Cones fully grown in August and open in October; they grow from 11" to as much as 21" long. 5 needles per bundle. Occurs from** Santiam River in Oregon south in Cascades, at 2,100-4,500' elevation, and Coast Range. Sap produces a useful sugar.

29. WHITEBARK PINE, *Pinus albicaulis*. 16-50' tall, **crooked trunked tree with bark split by narrow crevises into white or brown plates;** usually 5 needles per bundle. Needles stout, 1" to over 2" long, dark green. Cones, which ripen in August, are oval or sub-globose, horizontal, sessile, dark purple, 1½-3" long. This is a common tree of the Timberline Regions of the Cascades and Olympic Mountains. It is a major Timberline species in the northeastern Washington and central Oregon Cascade Range. sub.-alp.

30. FOXTAIL PINE, *Pinus Balfouriana*. This interesting tree (rare for this area), usually from 30-40' high, has a trunk from 1' to rarely 5' in diameter, with short stout branches, forming an open irregular pyramidal picturesque head and long rigid dark orange-brown to nearly black branchlets, **clothed only at the extremities with long dense brush-like masses of foliage.** It occurs in Siskiyou County, California, as groves on Scott Mountain at elevations of 5,000-8,000' and in the mountains in the headwaters of the Sacramento River and its tributaries in northern and northwestern California. Needles in clusters of 5, incurved, less than 2" long. Short stalked cones armed with minute incurved prickles. sub.-alp.

31. WESTERN YELLOW PINE, *Pinus ponderosa*. Large conifer, 50-200' tall; the **reddish bark of older trees thick and deeply checked in jig-saw puzzle-like plates; leaves pale green,** in groups of 3 per bundle 3/5-1" long. Cones ovate, reddish-brown, 3-6" long, often several in a cluster; scales relatively narrow, the broad prickles are short and incurved at the tips, often deciduous. Forms open forests on the dryer slopes especially on the east slopes of the Cascades; also found to the west coast in dryer areas, and in Rogue River Valley and the Siskiyous. pine

32. JEFFREY PINE, *Pinus Jeffreyi*. A conifer 90-200' tall; bark on old trees reddish-brown, divided into large plates, irregular in size, but not so jig-saw puzzle-like as in Western Yellow Pine; **leaves 3 per bundle and dull blue-green in color.** This species pine red fir

66   WILDLIFE AND PLANTS OF THE CASCADES

35. Western Larch

37. Sitka Spruce

36. Engelmann Spruce   34. Lodgepole Pine

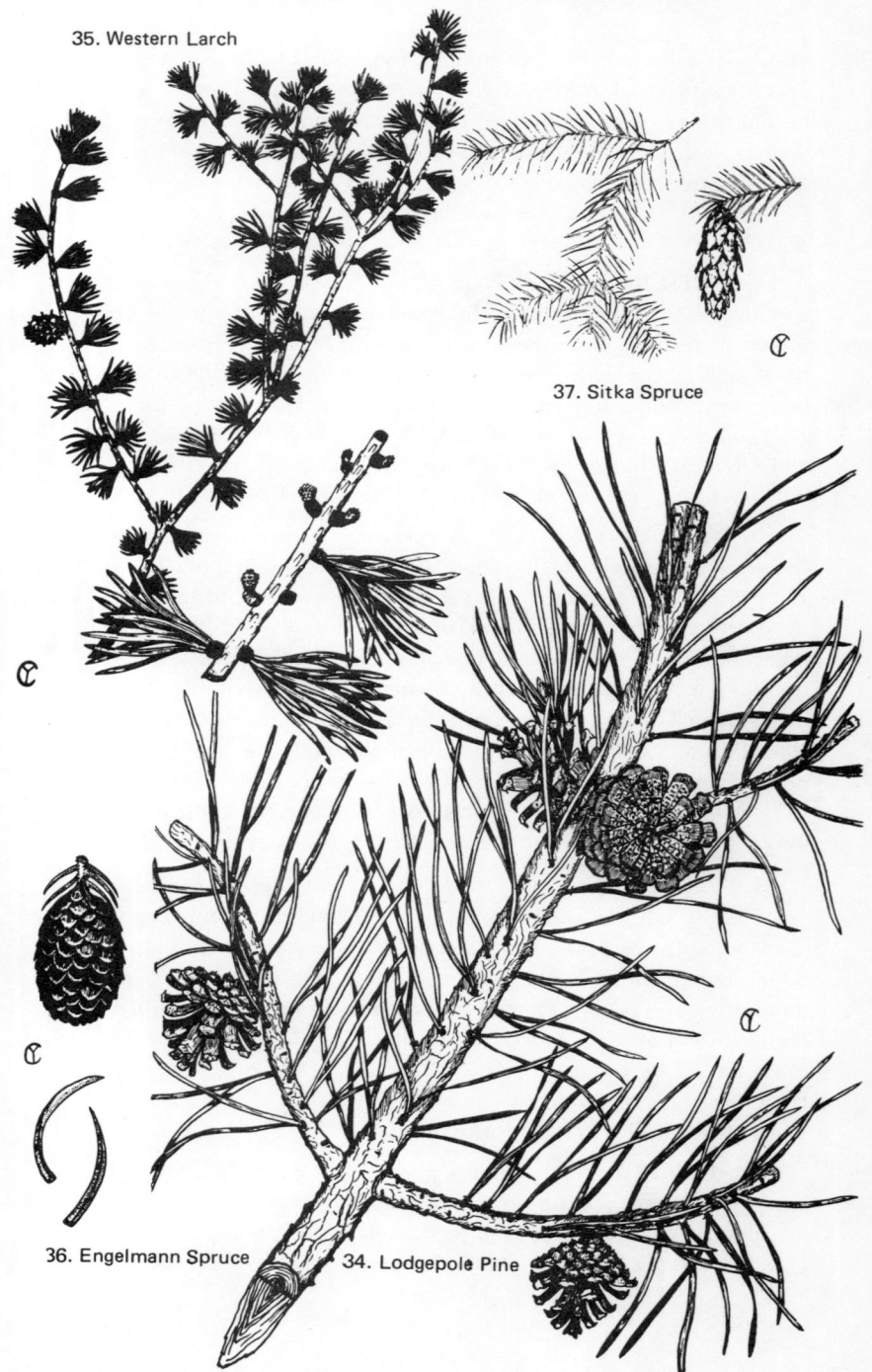

PINE AND SPRUCE

is a dominant conifer in the serpentine soils of the Siskiyou Mountains on the most dry sites from 900-6,000' elevation. Forms great forests from the headwaters of the Pit River in northern California and extends south along the eastern slopes of the Sierra Nevada Range. Cones larger than Western Yellow Pine.

*33. DIGGER PINE, *Pinus Sabiniana.* 30-60', rarely 90' tall; with **several large secondary trunks, making tree seem spread-out;** foliage appear smoky gray-green; **needles in 3's, very long;** cones thick, 6-11" long, chocolate brown. Upper Sonoran and Transition. Edible seeds.   mix.ev.

34. LODGEPOLE PINE,*Pinus Murrayana.*Slender conifer, 60-150' tall, trunk usually 2-3' in diameter; spreading branches relatively short forming a narrow spire-like crown. Bark thin, close, dark brown to light orange-brown, covered with small loose scales; **bright yellow green needles are stout, 1-3" long, two to a bundle.** Small cones 1-2" long, asymmetrical at base; often clustered.   lodg. sub.alp

35. WESTERN LARCH, *Larix occidentalis.* Tall pyramidal trees, 50-90' high, with a narrow open crown; trunk 5-8' in diameter; bark deeply furrowed at base, reddish-brown with large scaley plates; **needles triangular, 1-2" long in tufted clusters of 12-30 on the branches,** after frost, turning yellow in the fall before falling off. Cones 1-1½" long with bracts extending beyond the scales. Found in moist benches and east slopes of the Cascades of Washington and northern Oregon associated with Western Yellow Pine. Subalpine Larch *(Larix lyallii* - not illustrated), which looks much like Western Larch but has leaves that are 4-angled, occurs as a Treeline species of southern British Columbia, southward along the e. slopes of the Cascades to Mt. Stewart at the head of the Yakima River in Washington and in the Okanogan Mountains.   sub.alp.

36. ENGELMANN SPRUCE, *Picea Engelmannii.* **Leaves 4-angled with stomata (tiny holes) on all sides,** cone scales truncate or acute at apex; cones oblong-cylindric or ellipsoidal; branchlets pubescent (covered with fine hairs), needles soft and flexible with sharp pointed tips. Large spire-shaped tree up to 150' tall, shorter at high elevations. Bark light reddish-brown, thin, loose-scaley; branches spreading. Cones pendulous, oblong, 2-3" long; scales usually truncate, toothed or rarely entire at the tip. This is a major seral species and a minor climax species in the Subalpine Fir zone.   sub. alp.

38. Western Hemlock

39. Mountain Hemlock

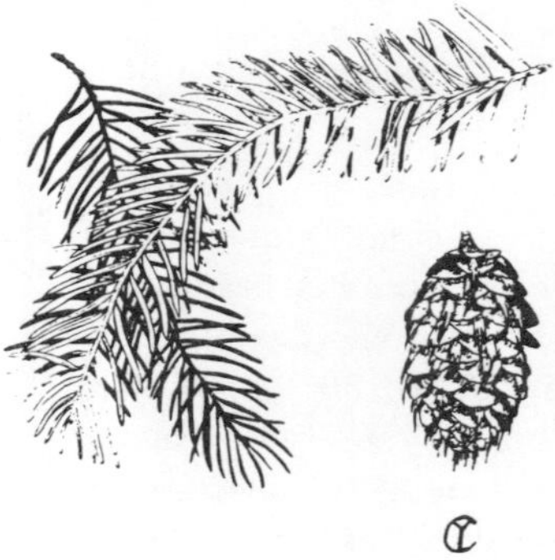

40. Douglas Fir

41. Pacific Silver Fir

SPRUCE , FIR

37. **SITKA SPRUCE**, *Picea sitchensis*. This large tree often grows 200' tall in the moist soils along the coast, but smaller trees found higher. It can be identified by its **very stiff, pungent-smelling leaves which are whitish above and with a ridge in the middle and rounded strongly outward below.** Cones short-stalked, pale yellow or reddish-brown, 2½-4" long.

sitk.-spr.

*38. WESTERN HEMLOCK, *Tsuga heterophylla*. This tall pyrimidal tree is the climax species in the most extensive conifer zone (Western Hemlock zone) of the Cascades, Puget Trough, and Coastal Ranges. **The contracted bark is deeply furrowed and is bright cinnamon-red under the surface.** Cones, (½-¾" long, ovoid), are sessile; cone scales oval, often contracted near the middle, their bracts gradually narrowed to an obtuse point. Leaf flat, stomata (small holes) only on lower surface. **The weeping-willow-like top is distinctive.** Indians steeped leaves for tea.

west.hem.
str.wd.
sitk.-spr.

*39. MOUNTAIN HEMLOCK, *Tsuga Mertensiana*. An important timberline tree species throughout the Cascade Range and Olympic Mountains except for the northeastern Washington Cascade Range. It forms the Mountain Hemlock zone (the highest forested zone) along the western slopes and crest of the Cascades and the Olympic and Siskiyou Mountains. It grows from 70-150' high, has a trunk 4-5' in diameter, gracefully pendant slender branches and a drooping, leaning top similar to the Western Hemlock which is found at lower elevations. **Leaves convex or keeled above, blunt pointed, stomata (small holes) on both sides.** Cones oblong-cylindric, scales longer than broad. The Indians steeped the leaves for tea.

sub.-alp.

*40. DOUGLAS FIR, *Pseudotsuga Menziesii*. Tall tree with compact pyramidal crown; bark brown, thick and furrowed; needles flat and stalked; **small cones hanging, with 3-pointed conspicuous bracts between the scales.** Our most widespread and numerous coniferous forest tree. Indians steeped leaves for a refreshing tea.

dg.fir
sitk.-spr.
mix.ev.
mix.con.
west.hem.

41. **PACIFIC SILVER FIR**, *Abies amabilis*. Leaves are flat and grooved above, with stomata (small holes) on lower surface, rounded and often notched, borne on sterile branches pointing forward, dense and crowded, dark green and shining above, pale below. **Cones deep rich purple,** 3½-6" long, borne erect. This

sil.fir
conif.

WILDLIFE AND PLANTS OF THE CASCADES

43. Subalpine Fir

42. Grand Fir

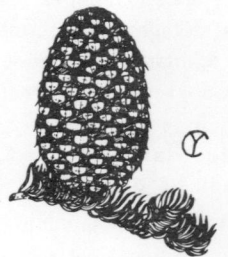

45. Shasta Red Fir

44. Red Fir

46. White Fir

tree forms the Pacific Silver Fir zone that lies between the Western Hemlock of the lowlands and the Mountain Hemlock zone on the western slopes from British Columbia south to Old Bailey Mountain, Oregon. Found at sea level in the north to 3,000-6,000' in its southern range. Attains its largest size on the Olympic Mountains where it is the most abundant fir. It is a minor timberline species in Cascade Range of northwestern Washington and Central Oregon.

42. GRAND FIR, *Abies grandis*. The **leaves of this attractive tree are 2-ranked and form flat sprays. The upper surface of the leaves is dark green but leaves have white bands below.** Cones bright green, 2-4" long. Ranges inland on the slopes of the Siskiyou Mountains and southern flanks of Mt. Shasta, California. Most abundant north of the Rogue River, Oregon, in the Western Hemlock zone. Occurs as a dominant with Douglas Fir in the Mixed Evergreen zone, Siskiyou Mountains.

gr.fir conif.

43. SUBALPINE FIR, *Abies lasiocarpa*. A spire shaped tree that grows at timberline (40-90' tall) and forms climax forests which are best represented on the high ranges extending east from the crest of the Washington Cascade Range and the Okanogan Highlands Province. It occurs as a sub-alpine tree in the Olympic Mountains and south in the Cascades to about Crater Lake, Oregon. **Needles flattened, strongly turned upward, 1-2" long, dark bluish-green, tinged with silver;** cones cylindrical-oblong, dark purple 2½-4" long, born erect on the twigs; **cone scales broadly fan shaped,** falling one at a time.

sub.-alp.

44. RED FIR, *Abies magnifica*. This fir forms well developed forests in the mountains of northern California and extends into the southern Oregon Cascades at 5,000-7,000' in elevation. **Leaves stiff and 4-angled, stomata (small holes) on all surfaces, bluegreen.** Cones dark purplish brown, 6-9' long. Occasionally grows 200' high with 8-10' diameter trunk, and often lacks branches for half the height of the tree.

red fir conif.

45. SHASTA RED FIR, *Abies magnifica* var. *shastensis*. This is a minor timberline species in central Oregon Cascades and forms the Shasta Red Fir zone between the Mountain Hemlock zone and the White Fir zone of southwestern Oregon and the Siskiyou Mountains, extending south on the Sierras. Well developed forests occur near Crater Lake. This tree can be told from the Red Fir by

red fir conif.

WILDLIFE AND PLANTS OF THE CASCADES

bright yellow bracts that cover about half of the scales on the upright cones.

wh. fir
pine
red fir
mix.con.

46. WHITE FIR, *Abies concolor*. This is the major species of the White Fir zone along the southern and southwestern flanks of the Oregon Cascades. It is well developed at Lake of the Wood, and Mt. McLaughlin areas, Oregon. A strip extends eastward into southeastern Oregon. Can be told from Grand Fir by pale blue or glaucous needles that often have stomata on the upper surface.

conif.

47. NOBLE FIR, *Abies procera*. This fir is a minor component of the tree species in the Mountain Hemlock zone of western Washington Cascades. However, it extends south to the Mackenzie River in Oregon and the Siskiyou Mountains. It may hybridize with *Abies magnifica*. Can be told by the **cones which have pale green spatulate bracts full and rounded above and nearly or entirely covering the scales.**

pine
mix.con.

48. INCENSE CEDAR, *Libocedrus decurrens*. These tall (80-150') **resinous, aromatic trees with very scaly bark, and scale-like needles,** have 6 scales per cone and only the middle ones are fertile; seeds unequally 2-winged. Leaves light green; cones about 1" long, hanging.

sitk.-spr.
west.hem.

49. GIANT RED CEDAR, *Thuja plicata*. This attractive tree is associated usually with moist bottom land or occasionally on dry ridges from sea level to 6,000' elevation. It extends from the coast in Mendocino County north to Alaska. It is a dominant tree in the Sitka Spruce and Western Hemlock zones in western Washington and Oregon. It occurs in the northern end of the Willamette Valley and in the more wet habitats of the Mixed Conifer zone in southwestern Oregon. **The minute scale-like leaves cover the branches, which form into flat sprays.** Short cones with 8-12 scales are held on short lateral branchlets. Bark cinnamon-red.

west.hem.
mix.con.

50. PORT ORFORD CEDAR, *Chamaecyparis lawsoniana*. Cones sub-globose, scales peltate (shield-shaped) maturing in one season; seeds 2 under each scale; **branchlets flattened; leaves scale-like.** This tall (often 200' high) resinous tree, with 10" thick bark at base, occurs as small groves from Coos Bay, Oregon to the mouth of the Klamath River in California. It is found in small groves from the southeastern slope of Mt. Hood, Oregon, south in the Cascades. Also occurs in the high mountains of northern Cali-

FIR AND CEDAR

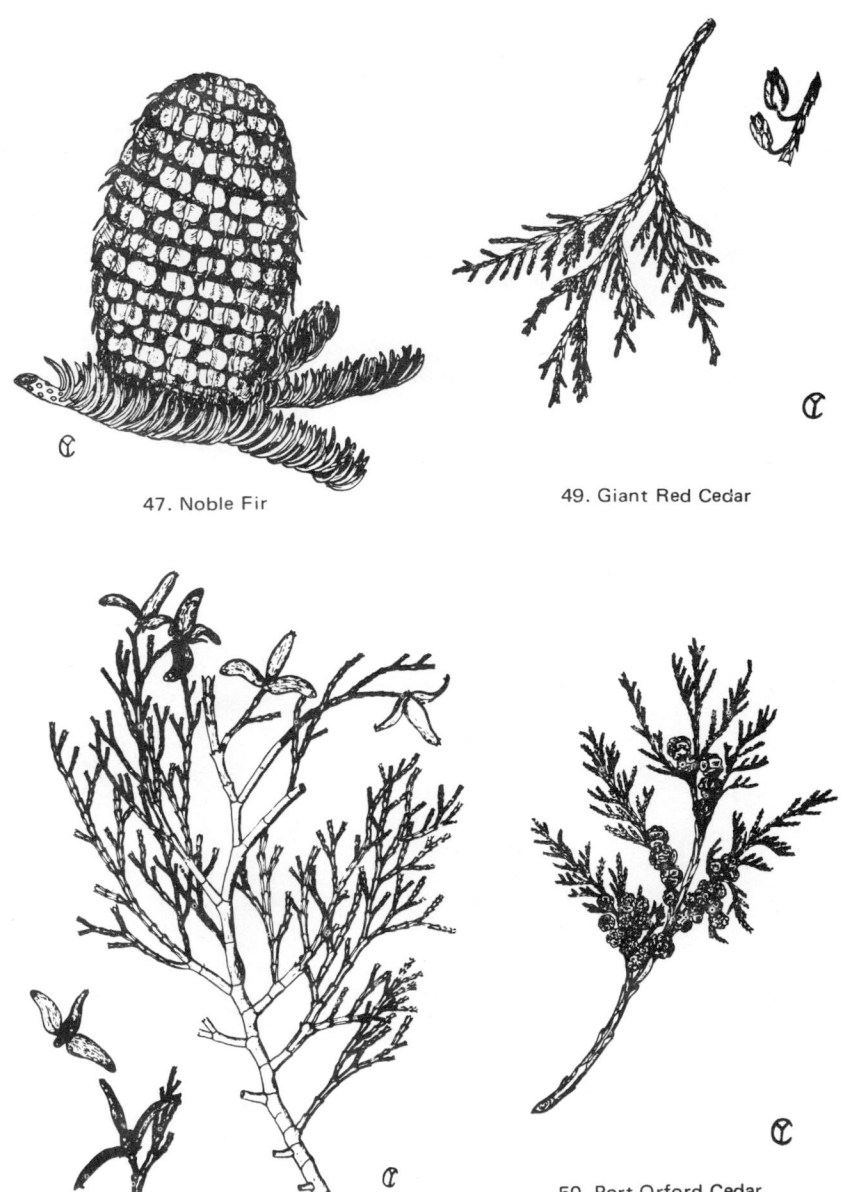

47. Noble Fir

49. Giant Red Cedar

48. Incense Cedar

50. Port Orford Cedar

74 WILDLIFE AND PLANTS OF THE CASCADES

fornia. A close relative, Alaska Cedar *(Chamaecyparis nootkatensis)* occurs as a timberline species from Washington Cascades north and Olympic Mountains.

jun.
pine

*51. WESTERN JUNIPER, *Juniperus occidentalis.* This **pungent aromatic tree or shrub-like tree,** with its **thin shreddy bark,** soft close-grained durable wood, slender branches and **scaley naked buds,** occurs along the foothills of the east flank of the Cascades where it is the dominant tree in the Steppe Region which borders the Yellow Pine forests in Oregon and California. Leaves acute (sharp-pointed), conspicuously glandular; flowers terminal; blue or blue-black fruit, maturing in one season, is oblong and ¼" to ½" in diameter, seeds 2 or 3. Edible berries, best when dried, ground into meal and made into mush or cakes.

sub.alp.
rocks

*52. DWARF JUNIPER, *Juniperus communis.* A low or prostrate shrub with flower at tip of branch. **Flower tips persistent on the bright blue fruit, covered with a white bloom.** Fruit matures in the third year. Found on stony or wooded slopes at 6,400-11,000'. Edible berries as in no. 51.

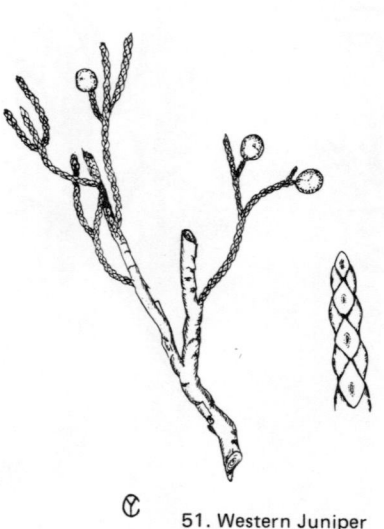

51. Western Juniper

52. Dwarf Juniper

WILLOW, ALDER, ASPEN 75

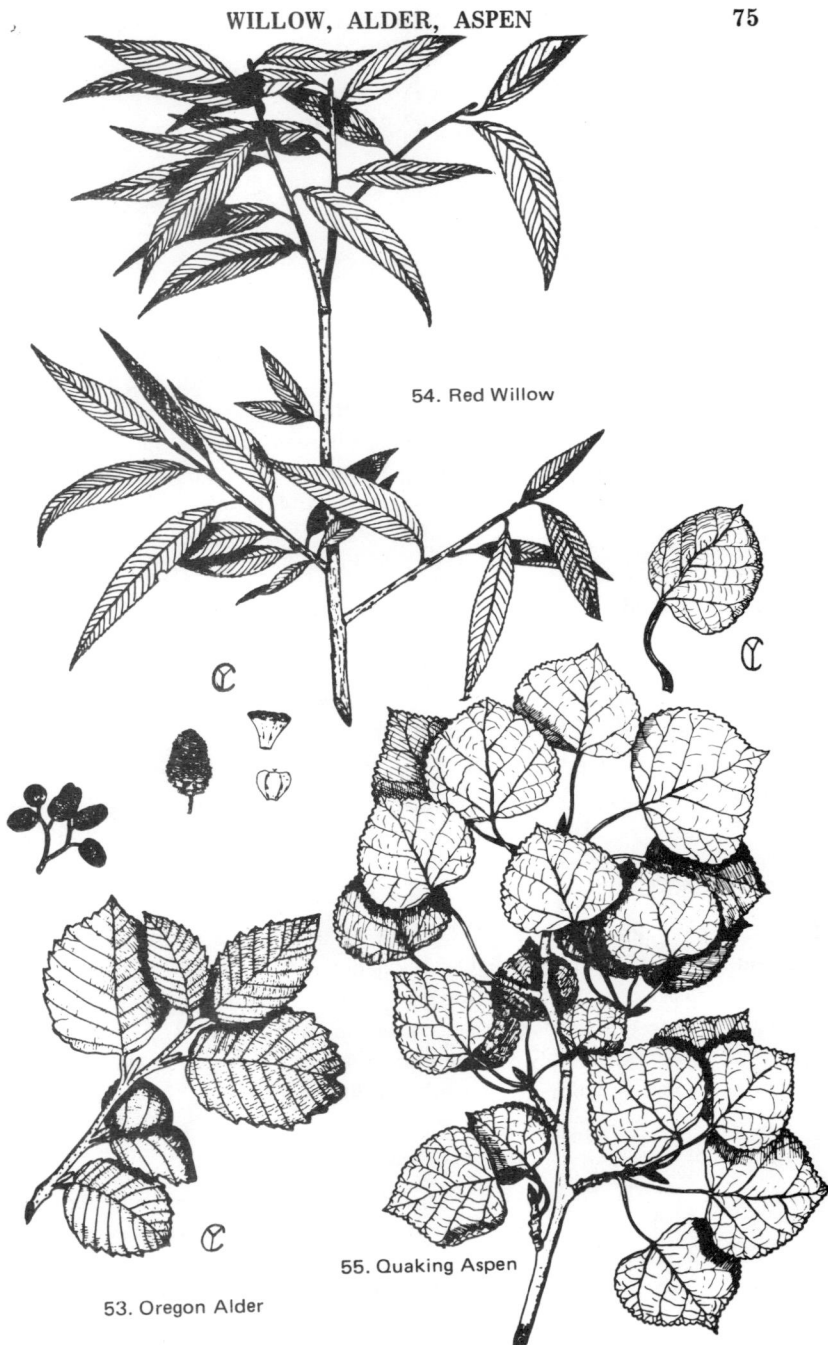

54. Red Willow
53. Oregon Alder
55. Quaking Aspen

D. BROAD-LEAVED TREES AND OAK SHRUBS

Other plants that may grow tree size are numbers 73, 95, 110, 123, 128a, 145, and 148a.

BIRCH Family

str.wd. 53. RED ALDER or OREGON ALDER, *Alnus oregona.* Tree from 30-75' high, flowers develop before the leaves and on last year's twigs. **Leaves are rusty pubescent beneath, and are revolute (rolled back) on the edges.** Nutlets are narrowly winged. Found along stream banks and moist places usually below 1,000' elevation. California to Alaska. Mountain Alder, *Alnus tenuifolia,* is a shrub with similar appearing leaves and nutlets.

WILLOW Family

str.wd. *54. RED WILLOW, *Salix lasiandra.* Up to 48' high tree. Leaves narrow with dark furrowed bark. Slender branches have **red or reddish-shining twigs.** Found along streams or lake sides. Catkins; scales yellow; 4-5 stamens. Bitter inner bark, palatable when dried and ground into flour.

str.wd. 55. QUAKING ASPEN, *Populus tremuloides.* **Leaves green**
mt.mead. **and broad; pale beneath, trembling in slightest breeze.** Catkins; bracts 3-5 lobed; 6-12 stamens. Tree usually small from 8-65' tall with greenish-white bark, (fissured in older trunks) and grows in thickets along stream borders and moist slopes.

str.wd. *56. BLACK COTTONWOOD, *Populus trichocarpa.* Trees 120-175' tall, with broad open crowns, grayish furrowed bark, leaves ovate finely toothed, slightly heart-shaped at the base. Leaves shiny dark green above and paler below. Usually occur below 1,800' elevation, common throughout the lowlands in Cascades and along streamsides. Edible catkins.

BEECH AND OAK Family

str.wd. *57. GIANT CHINQUAPIN, *Castanopsis chrysophylla.* Also
sitk.-spr. Bush Chinquapin *(Castanopsis sempervirens).* *C. chrysophylla* is a tree, 45-150' high, trunk to 3' thick, with **heavily furrowed bark** and stout spreading branches. Leaves oblong to lanceolate,

POPLAR, OAK

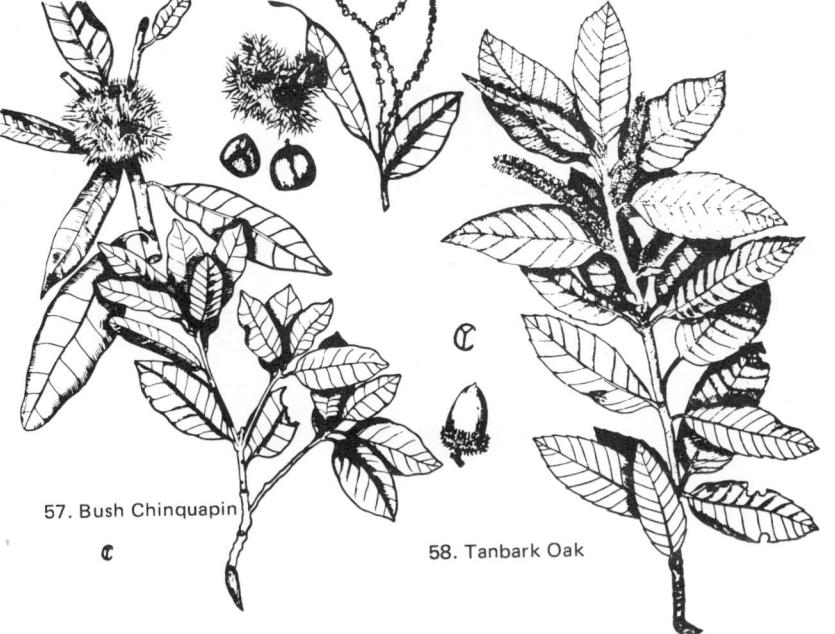

57. Giant Chinquapin

56. Black Cottonwood

57. Bush Chinquapin

58. Tanbark Oak

2-6"long, thick leathery, dark green above, golden-wool-like or olive-yellow below. **Bur, chestnut-like, 4-valved.** Forested slopes usually below 1600' elevation from northwestern California to Washington. *C.sempervirens* is very similar, but is a low spreading bush, and the leaves are blunter; bark smooth. Found in southern Oregon, Cascades, and south. Edible nuts, especially when roasted.

str.wd.
mix.ev.

*58. TANBARK OAK, *Lithocarpus densiflora*. Grows from 50-150' tall; **leaves are oblong and noticeably parallel-veined on the underside.** The slender catkins are from 2-4" long; the acorns mature the second year. The sharp-toothed leaves remain on the tree from 3-4 years. Edible acorns when properly leached, as on all following oaks. From southern Oregon into California.

mix.ev.
pine

*59. CALIFORNIA BLACK OAK, *Quercus Kelloggii*. This broad round-topped tree grows from 30-80' tall. The leaves are 3-lobed on each side and have from 1-4 spine-tipped teeth. **The acorns are deep set in their burs or cups.** This is a common tree in the Siskiyou Mountains of California and southern Oregon.

mix.ev.

*60. OREGON WHITE OAK, *Quercus Garryana*. This typical round topped oak grows from 25-60' tall. The round tipped lobed leaf is from 3" to 6" long. The acorns are smooth and shiny, borne in a shallow cup, and are important as food for many birds and mammals. This oak is common in the foothills of the interior coastal mountains, along the rivers of northern California, Oregon, and in the foothills of Willamette Valley and Puget Sound, and in the Columbia Basin.

pine
red fir
mix.con.

*61. SADLER'S OAK, *Quercus Sadleriana*. 2-8' high shrub, but so distinctly an oak that it is included here with the trees. **Has stiff, very brittle and widely spreading branches, the young twigs shiny or slightly fuzzy; evergreen leaves strongly toothed and grayish-green;** acorns oblong with a thin cup. From southern Oregon south in California Cascades and the Siskiyous and Klamath Mountains at high altitudes on barren slopes and ridges in the Canadian zone.

str.wd.
mix.ev.

*62. CANYON or MAUL OAK, *Quercus chrysolepis*. This oak grows from 30-65' high; young twigs covered with whitish fuzz; has **smooth ashy-gray bark; dark green leaves that are thick and leathery.** Some leaves are toothed margined and others smooth on the same branch. **Acorns are shallow-set in their cups.**

ACORNS AS FOOD

Since oak trees are so widely available, it seems wise here to give a bit of information on using acorns as an emergency food. The choice of acorns to eat is a matter of taste. Indians we know say the Tanbark Oak acorn is best, while others claim the White Oak or Oregon Oak acorn has the finest taste. Black Oak acorns and Live Oak acorns are liked by many, and in fact, almost any acorn has nutritious value.

The acorns are collected when ripe in the fall and allowed to thoroughly dry in the hot sun (or in an oven). They are then finely ground into a meal and this meal must then be leached to get the tannic acid out. The acorn meal can be put into a fine-mesh large sieve or porous basket, and hot water poured over it continually until all the acid taste is gone, or the meal can be put into strong bags and the bags suspended in the water of a stream for several days or until the acid is washed out. Once leached the flour or meal can be boiled as mush or baked into bread. It is good mixed with other grains.

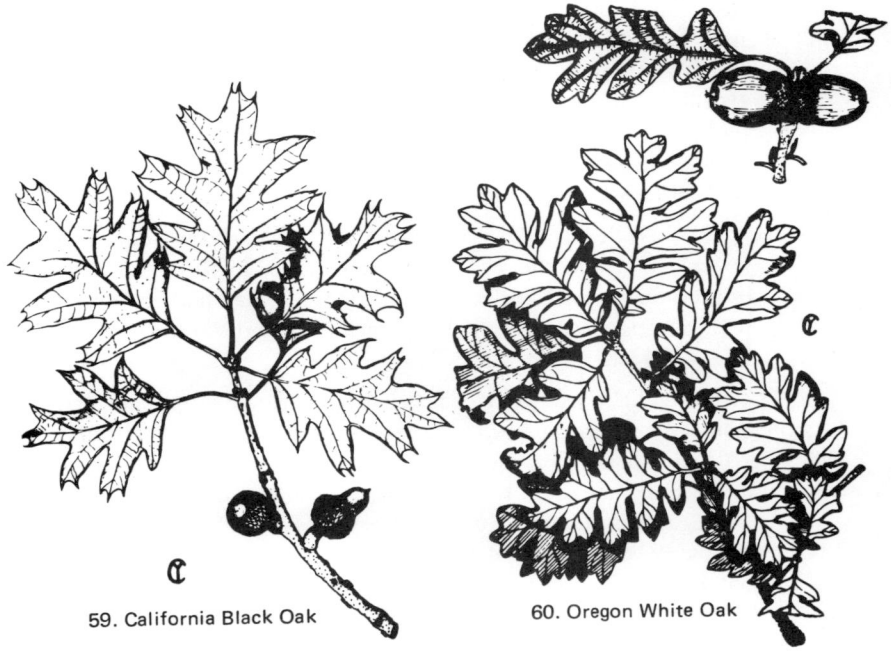

59. California Black Oak
60. Oregon White Oak

Upper Sonoran and Transition zones from southern Oregon southward, in canyons and moist mountainsides.

conif.
brush

*63. HUCKLEBERRY OAK, *Quercus vaccinifolia*. 1-6' high low and spreading shrub, with very flexible and slender branchlets; **evergreen leaves smooth edged and light and shiny green;** acorn with shallow cup and thin walls. Often forms thickets on high mountain ridges in the Subalpine zone and Canadian zones. From southern Oregon into California mountains.

LAUREL Family

brush
str.wd.
mix.ev.
pine

*64. CALIFORNIA LAUREL, OREGON MYRTLE or PEPPERWOOD, *Umbellularia californica*. The **aromatic,** dense-crowned, **evergreen tree** grows from 20-100' tall. It has **long narrow dark green leaves.** Nuts can be parched and eaten or ground into meal.

ROSE Family

brush

65. MOUNTAIN-MAHOGANY, *Cercocarpus betuloides*. Evergreen shrub or low tree 6-25' tall, with smooth gray bark and erect or spreading end branches. Oval shaped leaves entire at lower half and serrate on upper half. 2-3 flowers in a cluster. **Stamens 10-45 in two rows;** pistil 1, style terminal, ovule 1, forming a fusiform (spindle-shaped) akene or fruit with noticeable elongated silky-plumose style. Common in dry areas below 6,000' in northern California, Siskiyou Mountains and southwestern Oregon.

sage
jun.
sub.alp.

66. DESERT MOUNTAIN-MAHOGANY, *Cercecarpus ledifolius*. A tall shrub or scraggy tree (6-30' high) with **narrow leathery leaves with curled-over margins** and **small pinkish flowers** with conspicuously long-tailed carpels. Sagebrush scrub to Subalpine Forest.

brush
pine

*67. WESTERN CHOKE CHERRY, *Prunus virginiana*, var. *demissa* (see also no. 105). An erect shrub or small tree, from 3-18' high. Young twigs are gray-brown; showy white flowers occur in racemes that often terminate in more or less leafy branchlets. **Leaves usually larger than the Bitter Cherry and have one or two glands at base of the blade.** Fruits are red or dark purple, sour but edible when cooked.

OAKS AND MYRTLE

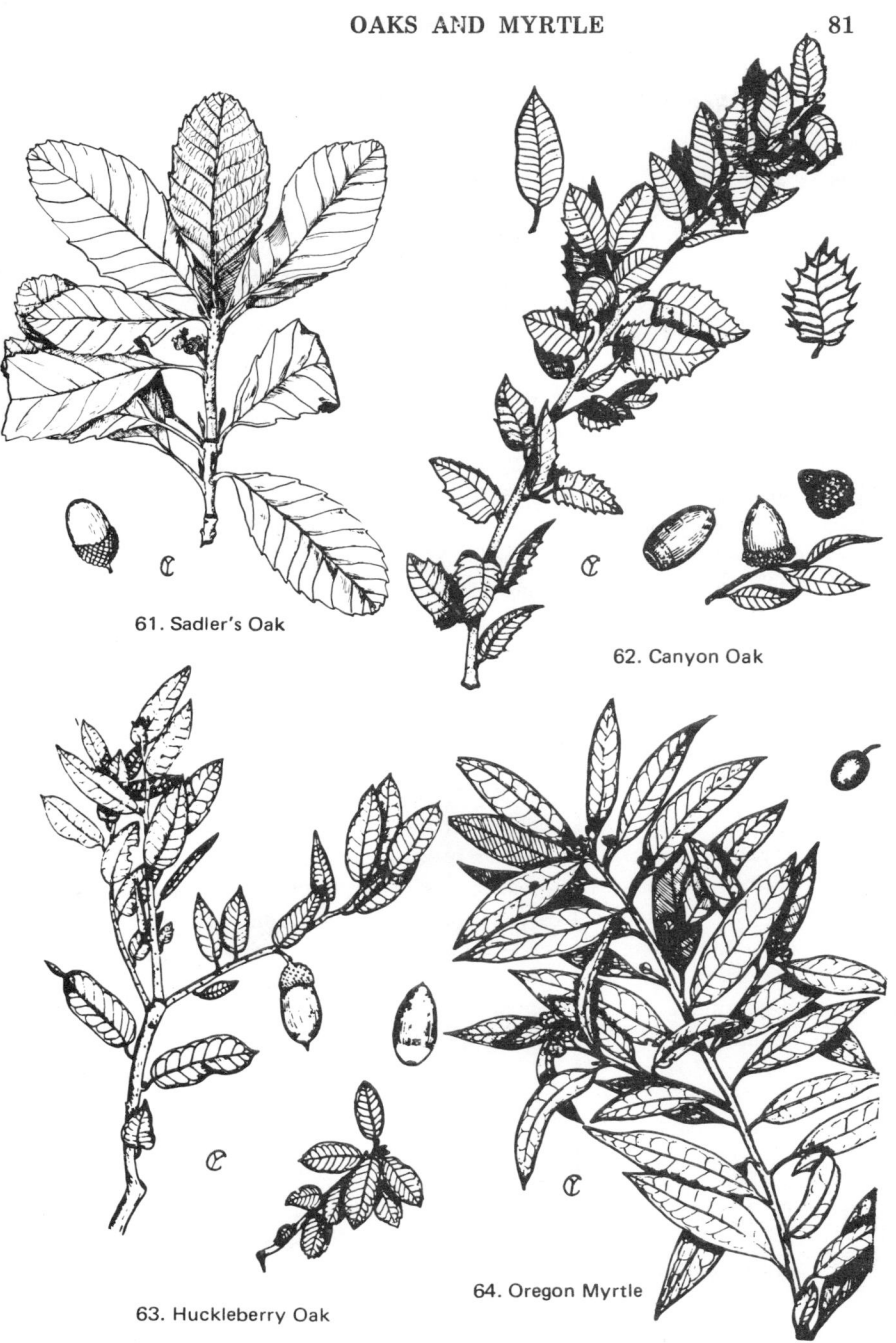

61. Sadler's Oak

62. Canyon Oak

63. Huckleberry Oak

64. Oregon Myrtle

DOGWOOD Family

*68. PACIFIC or MOUNTAIN DOGWOOD, *Cornus Nuttallii.*

str.wd.
conif.
mix.ev.

Tree 18-40' high, bark gray-brown, smooth or on very old trees flaky; **young twigs pubescent (hairy);** wood is white and fine-grained; leaves opposite. Flowers are bracts 4-7 cream colored 1-2½" long and appear before leaves. Seeds are drupes bright shiny orange-red, 25-40 in each cluster. Found from British Columbia to California. Fruits eaten raw or cooked.

MAPLE Family
2-winged fruits

str.wd.
mix.ev.

69. BIG-LEAF MAPLE, *Acer macrophyllum.* This broad-crowned tree grows from 30-100' tall, and has large 5-lobed leaves that are from 4-10" broad; small, greenish-yellow, bell-shaped flowers are produced in corymbs or dense, cylindrical racemes. The typical winged maple fruits are hairy.

str.wd.
conif.
mt.mead.

70. MOUNTAIN MAPLE, *Acer glabrum.* This dwarf maple, 6-20' high, can be told from the Vine Maple by **its 3-5 lobed** leaves. It occurs along the mountain streams and on the east side of the Cascades and on east, in mountains of the Rockies and northward to Alaska. Leaves about 2" in diameter, turning to yellows and reds in the fall.

mix.ev.
pine
str.wd.
west.hem.
sitk.spr.

71. VINE MAPLE, *Acer circinatum.* This maple occurs as a shrub or small tree, 3-20' tall, in the alluvial soil along streams on western slopes of the Cascades and coastal mountains from about 51° N. latitude to Mendocino County, California. The flowers are flat-topped clusters without hairs; fruit and wings widely spreading. **Leaves, from 7-9 lobed, turn purple colored after midsummer and crimson in the fall.** Often dominates the communities on the unforested talus slopes and screes and is a common understory shrub in the foothills of the Willamette Valley.

HEATH Family

dg. fir
mix.ev.
mix.con.

*72. MADRONE, *Arbutus Menziesii.* This **evergreen tree** with glossy, leathery leaves, finely serrate margined, grows from 20-120' tall. **The bark when new is smooth and red to orange-red in color;** with age the bark turns dark and becomes fissured into small plates. Flowers are white, fruit red or orange. Berries edible raw, boiled, or steamed.

MOUNTAIN-MAHOGANY, DOGWOOD

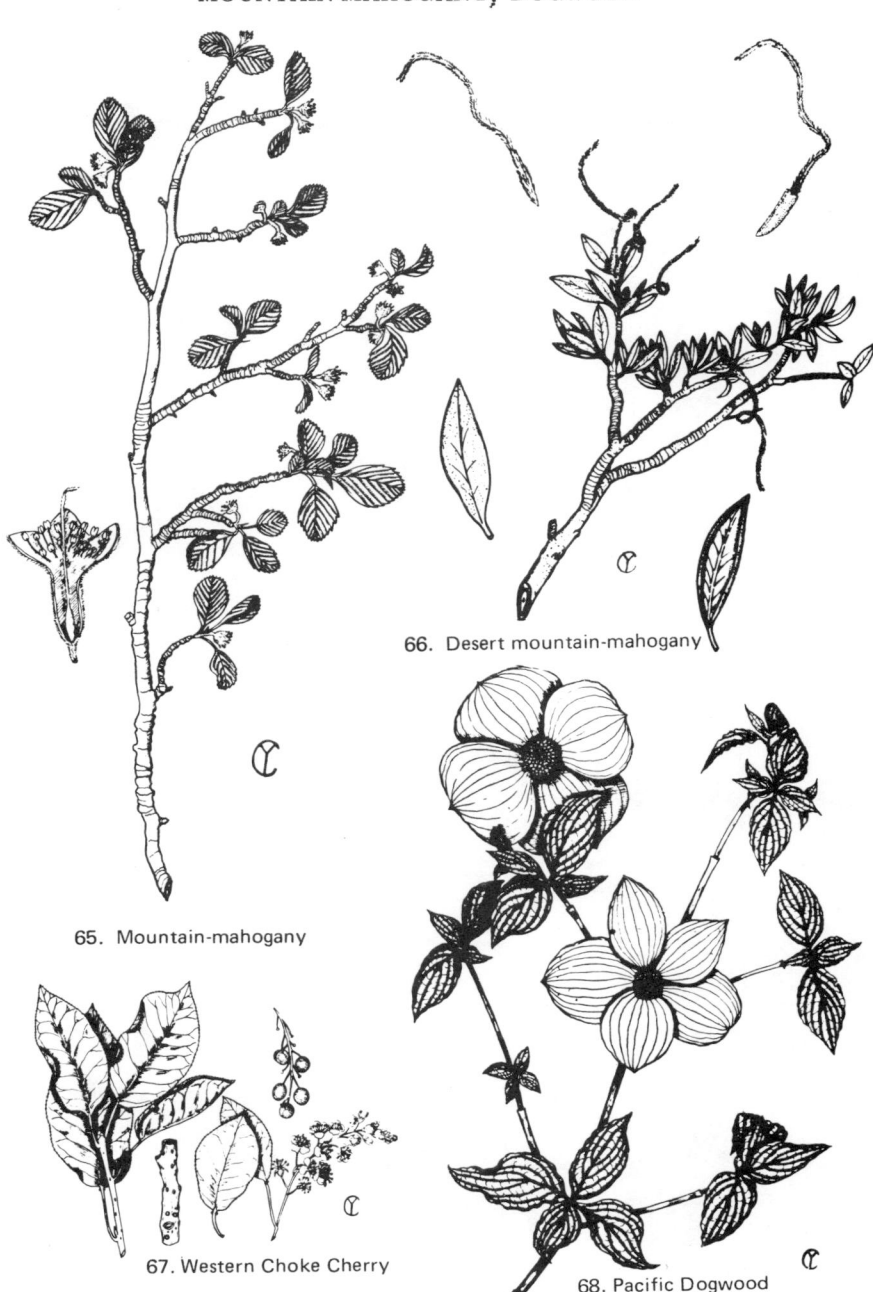

65. Mountain-mahogany
66. Desert mountain-mahogany
67. Western Choke Cherry
68. Pacific Dogwood

84 WILDLIFE AND PLANTS OF THE CASCADES

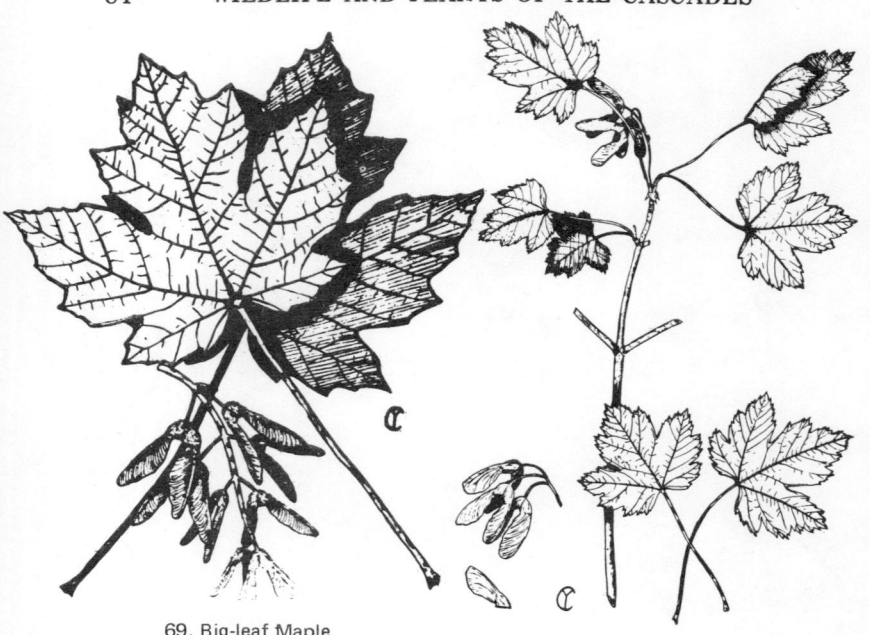

69. Big-leaf Maple

70. Mountain Maple

71. Vine Maple

72. Madrone

SHRUBS

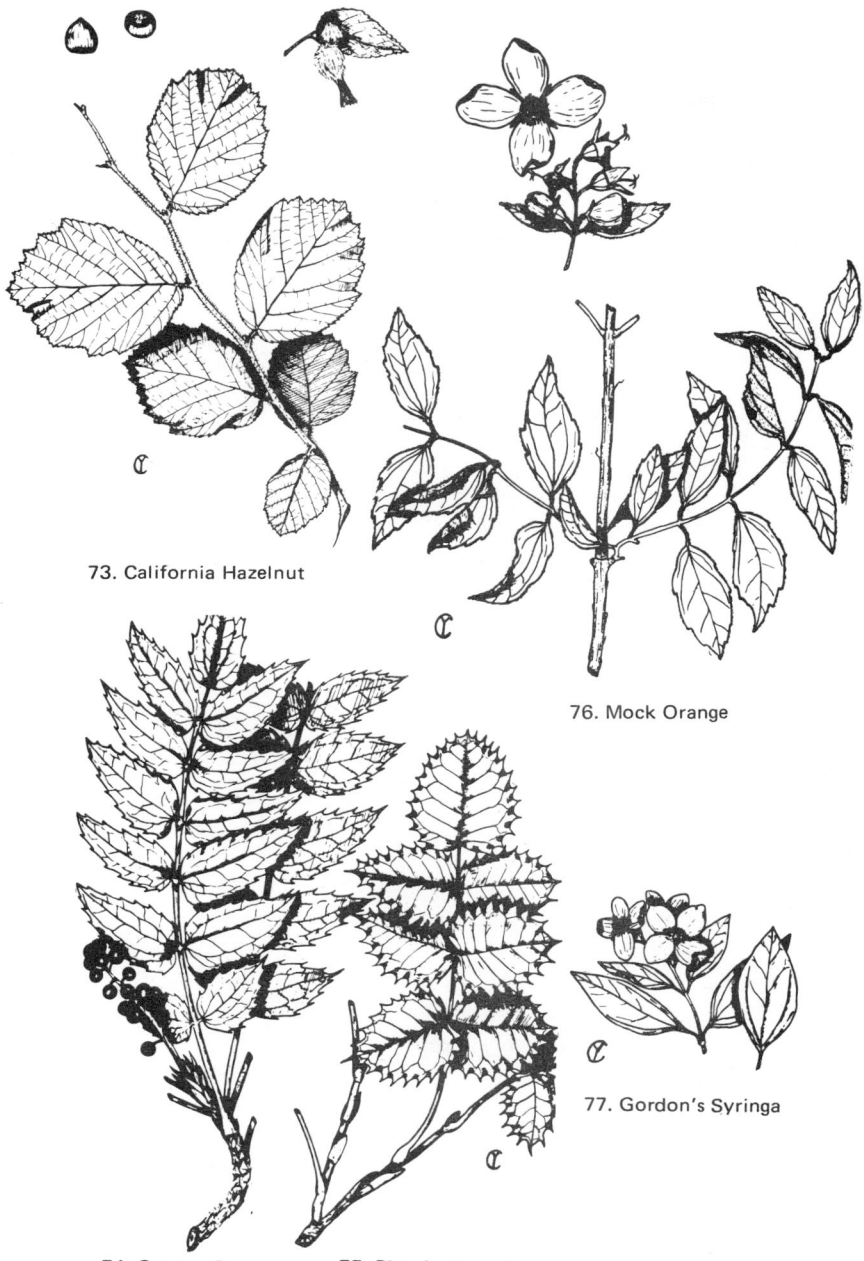

73. California Hazelnut
76. Mock Orange
74. Oregon Grape
75. Piper's Mahonia
77. Gordon's Syringa

E. SHRUBS AND VINES
See also numbers 54, 57, 61, 63, 65, 66, 67, 70 and 71 for other shrubs.

BIRCH Family

str. wd.
mix ev.
west hem.
sitk-spr.

*73. CALIFORNIA HAZELNUT, *Corylus cornuta*. This 6-19' tall shrub has rounded to ovate leaves that are toothed along the margin. **Flowers produced in catkins.** Mature fruit appear as a pair of nuts, base to base, each enclosed by the united bractlets which form a tube, the tube of each pair pointed in opposite directions. Usually at low altitudes. Nuts can be ground into meal to make bread.

BARBERRY Family

str. wd.
conif.

*74. OREGON GRAPE, *Berberis nervosa*. A 1-3' tall shrub with yellow wood and **glossy green leaves with spiny-tipped serrations;** yellow flowers and bluish berries. The unbranched stems terminate in a tuft of compound leaves; leaflets from 7-12. Mainly in western Oregon Cascades and Siskiyou Mountains. Edible grapes.

mix. ev.
dg. fir.
pine

*75. PIPER'S MAHONIA, *Berberis Piperiana*. This 9-24" tall barberry differs from *B. nervosa* in having **branched stems with compound leaves scattered along them.** The leaflets range from 5-9 and have noticeable spine-like teeth along each margin. Edible berries.

SAXIFRAGE Family

pine
str. wd.

76. MOCK ORANGE or WESTERN SYRINGA, *Philadelphus Lewisii*. A tall shrub, 3-9' high, much branched above, with opposite, ovate usually entire leaves and a loose panicle of **large, white, fragrant 4-petaled flowers.** Fruit is a capsule. Common along streamsides at lower elevations. The Syringa is a favorite in cultivation.

str. wd.
mix. ev.

77. GORDON'S SYRINGA, *Philadelphus Gordonianus*. Shrub 6-9' tall; branches curve upwards; leaf margins teeth-like downy on both sides, 1½-3" long. **Flower clusters 5-10; 4-petaled showy white;** ¾" long. Hillsides and streambanks, Siskiyou county to British Columbia.

SHRUBS

*78. PRICKLY or SWAMP CURRANT, *Ribes lacustre*. A prostrate shrub. Prickly currant is so named because of the **many bristles on the internodes and the sharp spines that occur at the nodes of the stems.** Leaves are deeply 5-7 lobed; flowers greenish or purplish, calyx short, saucer-shaped. Berries are black and covered with weak, glandular hairs.

mt. mead.
swamp
red fir
str. wd.

*79. SQUAW CURRANT or WAX CURRANT, *Ribes cereum*. Is a much branched bush with **gummy, shallow-lobed, fragrant leaves.** The white or pinkish flowers are long and tubular, and the berries are usually yellowish-red. Widely distributed in dry open places from the Transition to the Hudsonian Life Zone.

rocks
jun.
alp.

*80. CRATER LAKE CURRANT, *Ribes erythrocarpum*. This is a trailing shrub which roots at the nodes; upright shoots 4-8" tall. Flowers are attractive, variegated copper-colored; bloom in July. The berries turn red at maturity. This plant is of interest in Crater Lake since it was discovered in that area and has been found in only a few areas near there. Canadian zone.

conif.
str.wd.

*81. STICKY CURRANT, *Ribes viscossissimum*. Unarmed, about 3' high shrub; **pubescent throughout and somewhat glandular;** leaves round-heart-shaped to obtusely 5-lobed. Flowers whitish or purplish, about 3/8" long. Berry black. Common on the east slope of the Cascades and at head of Skagit River on the west side. Berries of most species of *Ribes* are edible, some are better cooked.

conif.

*82. RED FLOWERING CURRANT, *Ribes sanguineum*. Unarmed shrub about 3' high, with **a balsamic odor.** The 3-5 lobed leaves are roundish, green above and whitish below. The clustered flowers are red and the **berries are bluish-black with a whitish bloom.** Very showy when in flower; common in moist shaded places.

str.wd.

*83. WHITE-STEM GOOSEBERRY, *Ribes divaricatum*, var. *inerme*. This shrub, 3-10' tall, appears much like the cultivated gooseberry. **Few thorns occur on the branches.** The berries are smooth.

str.wd.

*84. SISKIYOU GOOSEBERRY, *Ribes binominatum*. This shrub occurs as **a trailing plant.** Leaves noticeably pubescent; flowers are villous **(with long soft hairs) and greenish.** The berries

pine
red fir

88   WILDLIFE AND PLANTS OF THE CASCADES

78. Swamp Currant

79. Squaw Currant

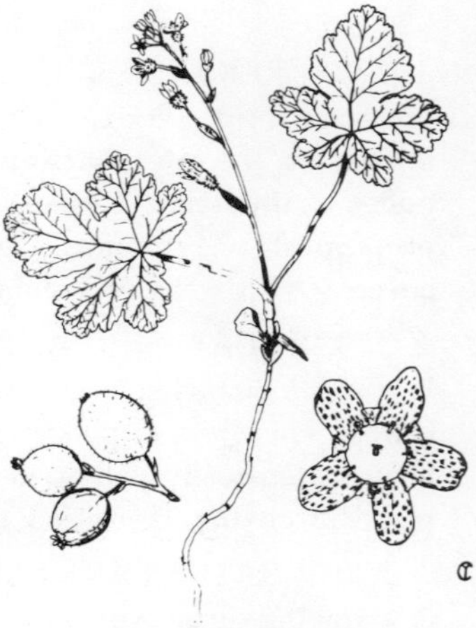

80. Crater Lake Currant

82. Red Flowering Currant 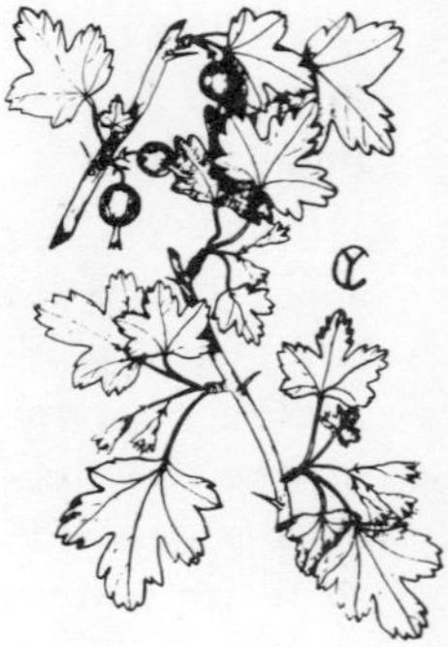   83. White-stem Gooseberry

81. Sticky Currant

84. Siskiyou Gooseberry

85. Plateau Gooseberry

SHRUBS

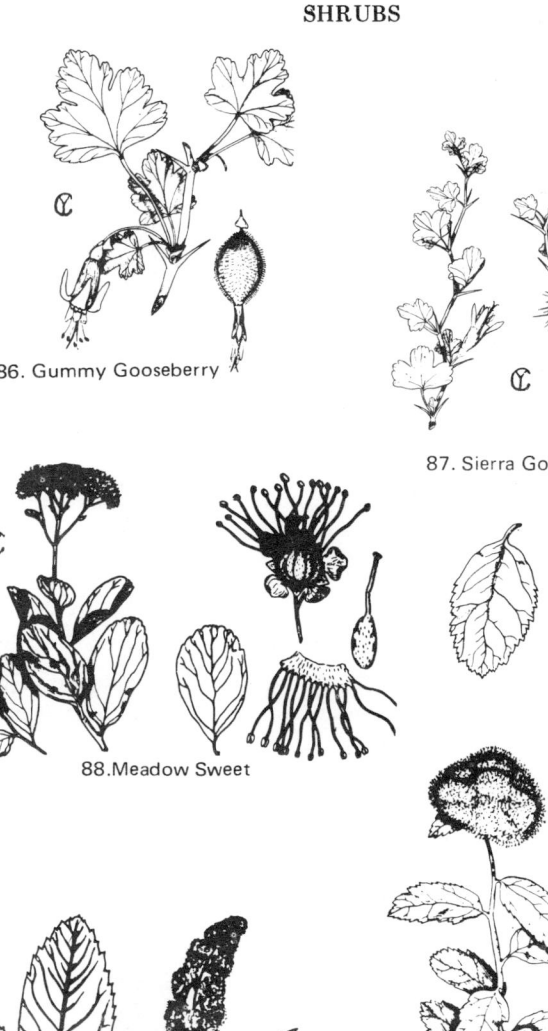

86. Gummy Gooseberry

87. Sierra Gooseberry

88. Meadow Sweet

90. Douglas Spiraea

89. Shiny Spiraea

are often glandular. Common in the area south of Crater Lake in Oregon and northern California.

sage
jun.
pine

*85. PLATEAU GOOSEBERRY, *Ribes velutinum.* A 2-7' tall species with stiff **curved branches beset with mostly solitary stout spines.** From southern Oregon south in dry open ground.

red fir
str.wd.
sitk.-spr.

*86. GUMMY GOOSEBERRY, *Ribes Lobbii.* This bush has **stiff, thorny branches and noticeable pendulous purple-red flowers;** calyx tube bell-shaped. The berries are covered with short, glandular spines. Found from Vancouver Island to northern California.

red fir
pine
brush

*87. SIERRA GOOSEBERRY, *Ribes Roezlii cruentum.* Common shrub, 20-48" tall in pine woods of northern California and southern Oregon. **Fruit with spines;** leaves dark green above paler beneath.

ROSE Family (In part)

rocks
mt.mead.
sub.alp.

88. MEADOW SWEET, *Spiraea densiflora.* The arrangement of the **rose-colored flowers in corymbs or low topped clusters** distinguish this shrub from the Douglas Spiraea. Grows from 1-2' high; leaves ovate or elliptic; serrate near the tip, usually obtuse. Found in Alpine and Subalpine meadows.

str.wd.

89. SHINY SPIRAEA, *Spiraea lucida.* Shrub 2-3' tall, with simple deciduous leaves, serrate without stiples, flowers perfect, white in flat-topped or rounded corymb. Creeping rootstock. Found at timberline in Washington Cascades.

str.wd.
mt.mead
marsh

90. DOUGLAS SPIRAEA, *Spiraea Douglasii.* Grows from 3-6' high. Leaves serrate towards the apex, wool-like beneath; flowers in dense panicles 3-6" long; petals rose-colored. Found at lower elevations around swamps or margins of lakes, mainly west slope of Cascades.

str.wd.
conif.
mix.ev.

91. NINEBARK, *Physocarpus capitatus.* Shrub, 6-15' high, the branches spreading and covered with thin flaky brownish bark; leaves broadly oval to heart-shaped with 3-5 palm-like lobes doubly toothed—without hair above, hairy beneath. 1-3" long; flowers a dense corymb; petals white. Common on stream banks, north slopes below 4,500'.

SHRUBS

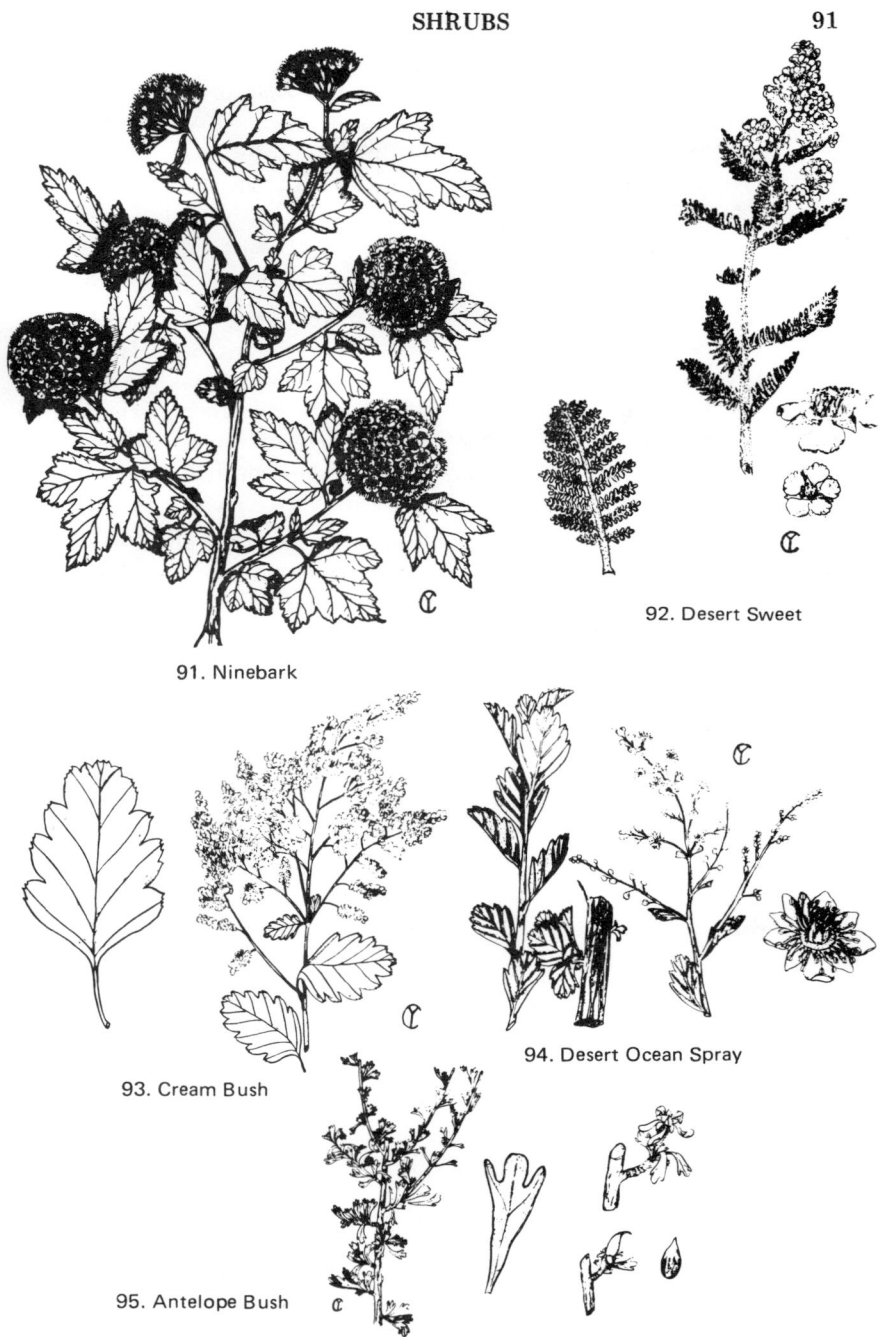

91. Ninebark
92. Desert Sweet
93. Cream Bush
94. Desert Ocean Spray
95. Antelope Bush

92. FERN BUSH or DESERT SWEET, *Chamaebatiaria millefolium*. Widely distributed shrub, 2-6' tall, in the Upper Sonoran zone and Transition zone of northeastern California. Grows in clumps of **cane-like branches, clothed with finely dissected fern-like foliage** and attractive rather large white flowers; leaves and flowers gummy and strong scented. Northeastern California to Oregon.

rocks
sage
jun.

*93. CREAM BUSH or ROCK-SPIRAEA, *Holodiscus discolor*. This large shrub grows from 4-12' in height. It has relatively large **double-toothed leaves** 1-3½" long. The flowers are small white, turning yellowish, borne in a panicle broadly pyramidal, much branched, 4-8" long. These attractive clusters of flowers often bend gracefully downward from the end of the branches. Abundant in open woods. Fruits eaten raw or cooked.

mix.ev.
brush
str.wd.

*94. DESERT OCEAN SPRAY, *Holodiscus discolor glabrescens*. This low spineless shrub with **showy white flowers in clusters** occurs from the Sagebrush Shrub areas to the Hudsonian zone.

sage
rocks
sub.alp

95. ANTELOPE BUSH or BITTER BRUSH, *Purshia tridentata*. A much branched shrub, 6-10' tall, having a dark-colored appearance. The **small three-cleft leaves are covered with whitish-soft, matted hairs on the underside**. Flowers are yellow, fragrant and have a single pistil. This plant of the arid Transition Forest is one of the most important deer foods.

sage
sub.alp.
pine
brush

*96. THIMBLEBERRY, *Rubus parviflorus*. A conspicuous, thornless shrub that reaches a height of 1-6'. **Leaves are large, cordate (heart-shaped) and 5-lobed.** Flowers are white; berries are pale scarlet when mature. Found along streamsides and areas at lower elevations and open woods. All *Rubus* species have edible berries.

str. wd.
str.wd.
conif.
mix.ev.

*97. CREEPING RASPBERRY, *Rubus lasicoccus*. This is a vine of **a creeping type**, and a thornless perennial, often rooting at the nodes; leaves roundish kidney-shaped or heart-shaped. Flowers are white; shoots about 4" tall, fruit greenish or rose colored.

red fir
pine

*98. SALMON BERRY, *Rubus spectabilis*. This is an erect shrub that grows from 6-9' high. The bark is reddish-brown and sparingly thorned except the sterile shoots, which are very well

str.wd.
mix.ev.
sitk.-spr.
west
hem.

SHRUBS

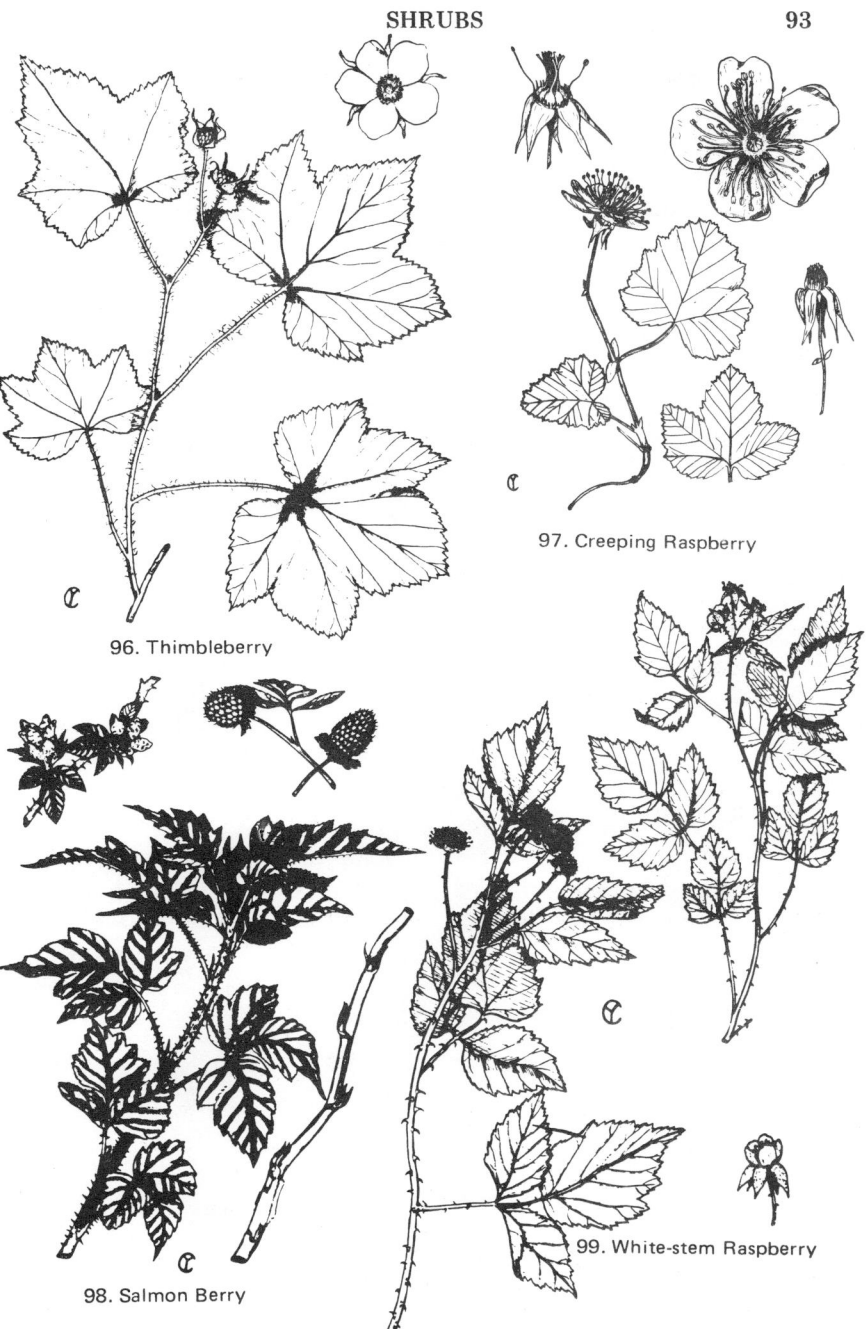

96. Thimbleberry
97. Creeping Raspberry
98. Salmon Berry
99. White-stem Raspberry

thorned. The leaves are formed into 3 leaflets, which have doubly serrated margins. Flowers are from 1-3 in a cluster, petals red-purple; berries scarlet to yellow. Common in the coastal forests in swamps and along streams and in foothills of mountains.

conif.
mix.ev.
str.wd.

*99. WHITE-STEM RASPBERRY, *Rubus leucodermis*. This species has **white, erect, or ascending stems,** to 6' tall. The compound **leaves have white, soft, matted hairs on underside.** Berries when ripe are yellowish-red with a white bloom. Found in open woods.

str.wd.
brush
cult.
mix.ev.

*100. CUT-LEAF BLACKBERRY, *Rubus laciniatus*. A shrub with many branches, up to 9' high; covered with wide-based thorns that are curved and hooked; leaves with **5 leaflets, each about 1-2½" long, and lobed into several sub-leaflets,** so looking much cut up; flowers pink to a rose-red; large black berries. A European import that has spread to many wild areas in foothills of mountains.

str.wd.
mix.ev.
pine

*101. PACIFIC BLACKBERRY, *Rubus vitifolius*. This is an attractive, long, trailing vine-like shrub which is **well-armed with slender prickles.** The leaves are compound and lack the white, soft matted hairs that are so conspicuous on the underside of the leaves of the White Stem Raspberry. White flower clusters to 6" long. Fruits are black and of fine flavor. Common along stream banks at lower elevations.

mix.ev.
dg.fir

*102. NOOTKA ROSE, *Rosa nutkana*. Stout stems of shrub 2-5' tall, **covered with large straight end curved prickles in pairs;** the branches with flowers generally smooth; **leaf with usually 7 leaflets, each ½-2½" long, double-toothed on edges,** and dark green, smooth above; solitary rose-pink flowers. Canadian and Transition zones. Edible fruits and petals.

str.wd.
conif.
mix.ev.

103. SPALDING'S WILD ROSE, *Rosa Spaldingii*. Spalding's Wild Rose is a slender, erect, shrub from 2-6' tall with **broad stiff straight prickles, leaves compound,** leaflets 1/3-2" long, the margins mostly simple toothed. Flowers pink showy, from 2-3" in diameter, often solitary; calyx lobes minutely toothed. Fruit bright red, globose, ½-¾" wide. Found in open woods, British Columbia, Washington and Oregon Mountains.

str.wd.
mt.mead

*104. WOOD ROSE, *Rosa gymnocarpa*. Small shrub about 3' high, armed with many straight prickles, flowers less than 1"

SHRUBS

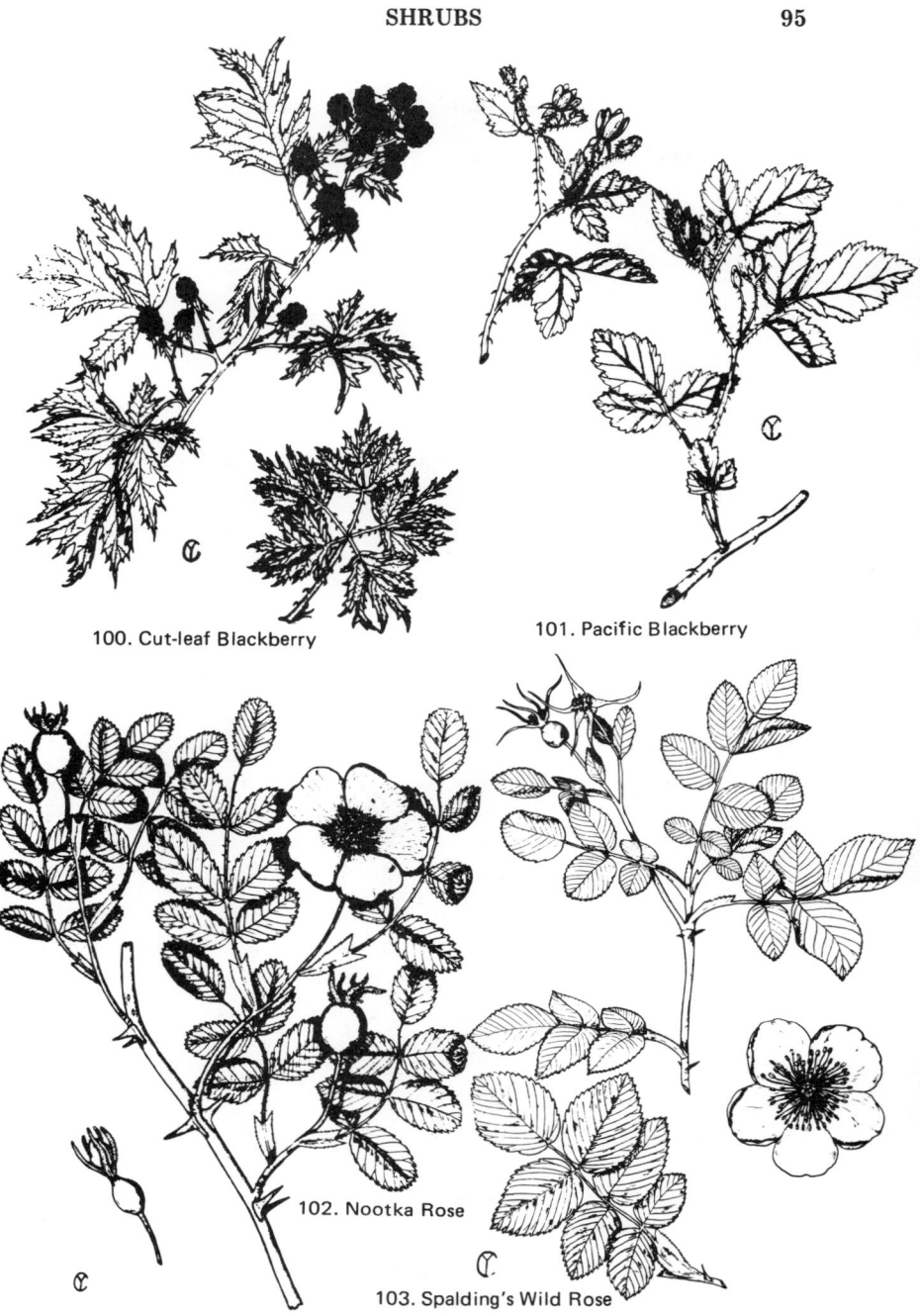

100. Cut-leaf Blackberry
101. Pacific Blackberry
102. Nootka Rose
103. Spalding's Wild Rose

in diameter. **Leaves compound in 5-9 leaflets with serrate margins. Pinkish flowers usually solitary.** Sepals drop from the fruits leaving it "naked." Common in dry woods. Humid Transition zone.

conif.
brush
str.wd.
*105. BITTER CHERRY, *Prunus emarginata*. Shrub with smooth bark. Leaves oblong; acute or acutish at apex; **flowers appear with leaves in small flat-topped clusters; fruit is bright red and very bitter.** Found on mountain slopes and stream banks, Upper Sonoran and Transition zones.

conif.
mix.ev.
*106. SITKA MOUNTAIN ASH, *Sorbus sitchensis*. This attractive shrub has bright green, compound leaves, **small white flowers borne in large flat-topped clusters;** berries coral red when ripe. Berries edible when thoroughly ripe or cooked.

str.wd.
mix.ev.
brush
*107. PACIFIC SERVICE-BERRY, *Amelanchier florida*. Shrub 6-15' high, with reddish-brown branchlets. Leaves broadly oblong to circular; **coarsely toothed above the middle. Rather thin in texture,** bright green above, paler beneath; **fruit dark purple,** glabrous (without hairs) or sparsely hairy. Found in open woods and clearings, mainly Humid Transition zone, western Oregon and Washington. Edible berries.

mix.ev.
conif.
str.wd.
brush
108. PALE-LEAVED SERVICE-BERRY, *Amelanchier pallida*. Tall, much branched bushes with **grayish-red bark,** roundish toothed leaves and **snowy-white flower clusters;** also rigid short branches. Northern California and Oregon, Arid Transition zone.

brush
conif.
*109. JUNEBERRY, *Amelanchier alnifolia*. A 3-10' tall round-topped shrub or small tree of the Interior Valley zone, Willamette Valley, foothills of Cascades, and southwestern Oregon. Flowers with 3/8-1/2" long narrow white petals. Has edible dark berries.

PEA Family

brush
*110. WESTERN RED-BUD or JUDAS TREE, *Cercis occidentalis*. Shrub or small tree, 7-16' tall; simple, pale green kidney-shaped to **heart-shaped leaves** appear on branches usually after the **reddish-purple flowers** in spring. Southwestern Oregon and Siskiyou Mountains and south. Buds, flowers, and young pods may be fried and eaten.

SHRUBS

104. Wood Rose

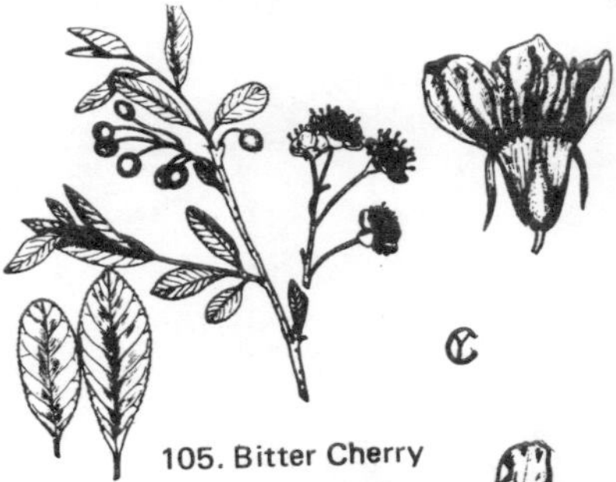

105. Bitter Cherry

106. Sitka Mountain Ash

107. Pacific Service-berry

108. Pale-leaved Service-berry

98 WILDLIFE AND PLANTS OF THE CASCADES

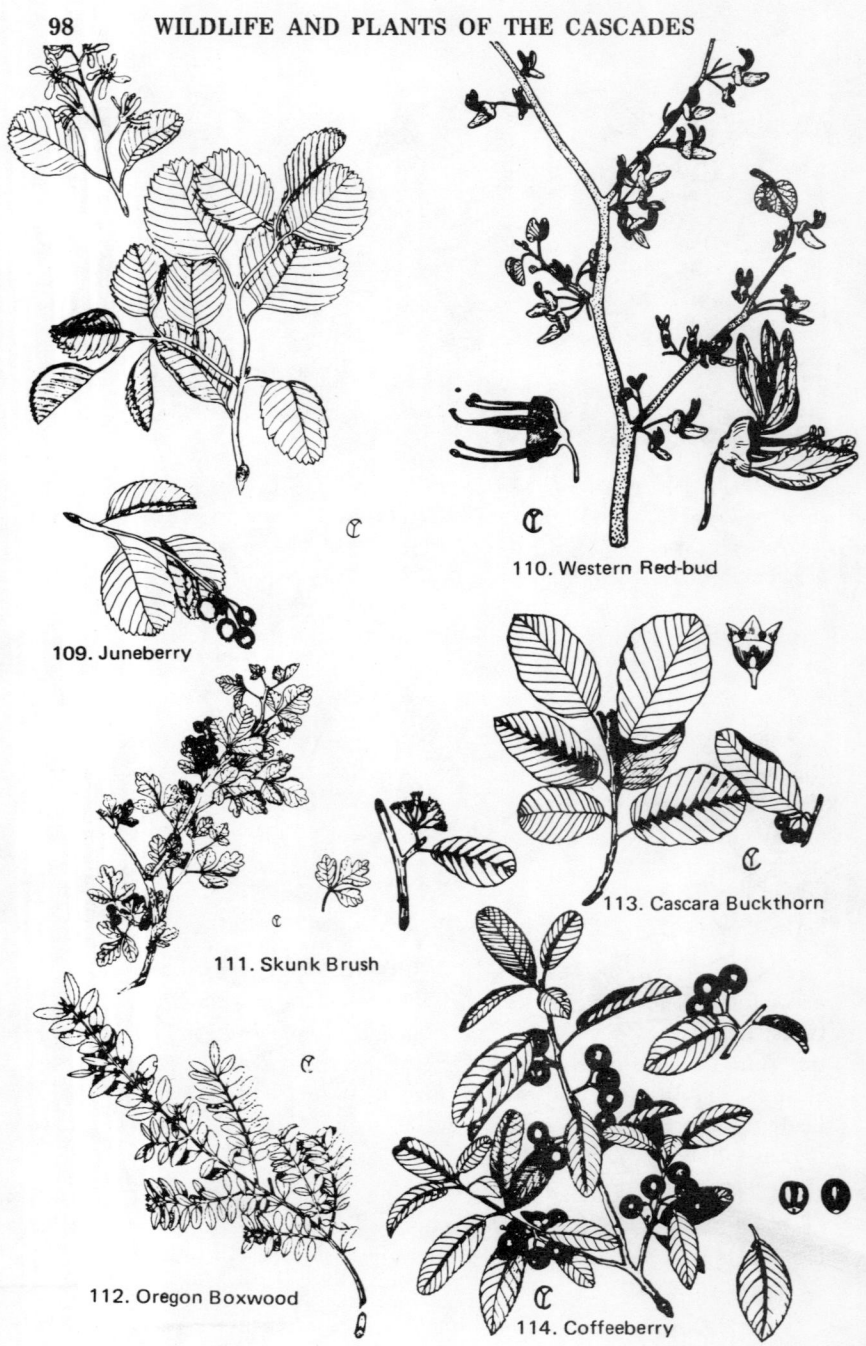

109. Juneberry
110. Western Red-bud
111. Skunk Brush
112. Oregon Boxwood
113. Cascara Buckthorn
114. Coffeeberry

SHRUBS

SUMAC Family

*111. **SKUNK BRUSH**, *Rhus trilobata*. Shrub up to 4' tall, intricately branched; twigs velvety hairy when young. Leaves are alternate, compound with 3-lobed leaflets. Flowers yellowish, appearing before the leaves. Orange-red fruits in a thick cluster. **Plant has an unpleasant odor.** Found in foothills of Willamette Valley and in interior valleys, and foothills down into California. Edible berries.   str.wd. brush

STAFF-TREE Family

112. **MOUNTAIN LOVER or OREGON BOXWOOD**, *Pachistima myrsinites*. **Low evergreen shrub**; 1-3½' very numerous. Leaves opposite, smooth, leathery and serrulate; flowers perfect, very **small, yellowish or purplish**; found solitary in axils of leaves. Found from sea level at Puget Sound to timberline in Cascades, 2,000-6,000', Siskiyou Mountains, Klamath Mountains.   conif.

BUCKTHORN Family

*113. **CASCARA BUCKTHORN or CASCARA SAGRADA**, *Rhamnus Purshiana*. This attractive shrub buckthorn of the Pacific Coast grows to a height of 10' or more tall, being either erect or ascending. **Leaves are about 2-6' long, and minutely notched along their margins.** Flowers are small and greenish. In many places this plant has been nearly exterminated for its medicinal bark, cascara sagrada. Humid Transition zone. Berries edible.   mix.ev pine str.wd. brush

114. **COFFEEBERRY**, *Rhamnus californica*. Upright rounded or low and spreading shrub, 3-12' high; **reddish bark on young twigs**; leaves evergreen, yellowish-green in color, oblong to eliptic; smooth on top and hairless below; small greenish flower clusters; oblong to round; berries turn black or red when ripe. Plant found in southwestern Oregon, south into California. Berries edible.   conif. brush str.wd. mix.ev.

115. **NORTHERN BUCK BRUSH or OREGON TEA TREE**, *Ceanothus sanguineus*. **Deciduous shrub** growing from 3-9' high; branchlets slender, smooth and **usually reddish**. Leaves thin, 2-3" long, elliptical or oval-toothed; flowers white. Mainly Canadian zone.   brush pine dg.fir

brush
conif.

116. TOBACCO BRUSH, *Ceanothus velutinus.* Large upright bush, 6-8' tall, with **large shiny leaves;** flowers in large **white** clusters. Forms dense thickets over extensive areas in pine forests.

conif.
mix.ev.
brush

117. DEER BRUSH CEANOTHUS, *Ceanothus integerrimus.* This tall slender shrub has entire leaves that are much smaller and less glossy than the Snow Bush Ceanothus. The small 5 parted (except for the 3-parted carpel) **usually bluish** or white flowers are produced in elongated clusters. This is one of the most important deer foods where it is found. Common along the Rogue River, Oregon, and Siskiyou Mountains.

conif.
brush

118. MOUNTAIN WHITETHORN, *Ceanothus cordulatus.* 3-6' high, low, spreading shrub, with mainly intricate branches; white bark very smooth; **branchlets rigid and spine-like; leaves rather smooth, light green above, paler green below;** white flowers in simple panicles or racemes. Arid Transition and Canadian zones.

brush
jun.
pine

*119. COMMON BUCK BRUSH, *Ceanothus cuneatus.* Shrub with **erect, rigid, much branched stems;** grows from 3-12' high; twigs gray; leaves opposite, cuneate-obovate or spatulate, denticulate to entire, 2-4" long, somewhat wool-like beneath; flowers white or rarely bluish, in axillary umbels. Found in **dry rocky ground** from Columbia River southward into California. Leaves and flowers boiled for tea.

pine
red fir
brush

120. SQUAW CARPET, *Ceanothus prostratus.* Small prostrate mat-forming shrub with **small coarsely toothed, holly-like leaves.** Purplish blue flowers are produced on short stems in small, compact **clusters.** Transition and Canadian zones. Mainly east of divide, from Klickitat County, Washington, south.

GRAPE Family
Woody vines with climbing tendrils

str.wd.
mix.ev.

*121. CALIFORNIA WILD GRAPE, *Vitis californica.* **Long climbing stems,** 6-45', draping over other plants and clinging by tendrils; **bark shreddy;** leaf-blade generally 3-lobed; fragrant yellowish-green flowers with 5 petals, the purple edible grapes covered with whitish bloom. From southern Oregon south in foothills and mountains to 4,000'.

SHRUBS

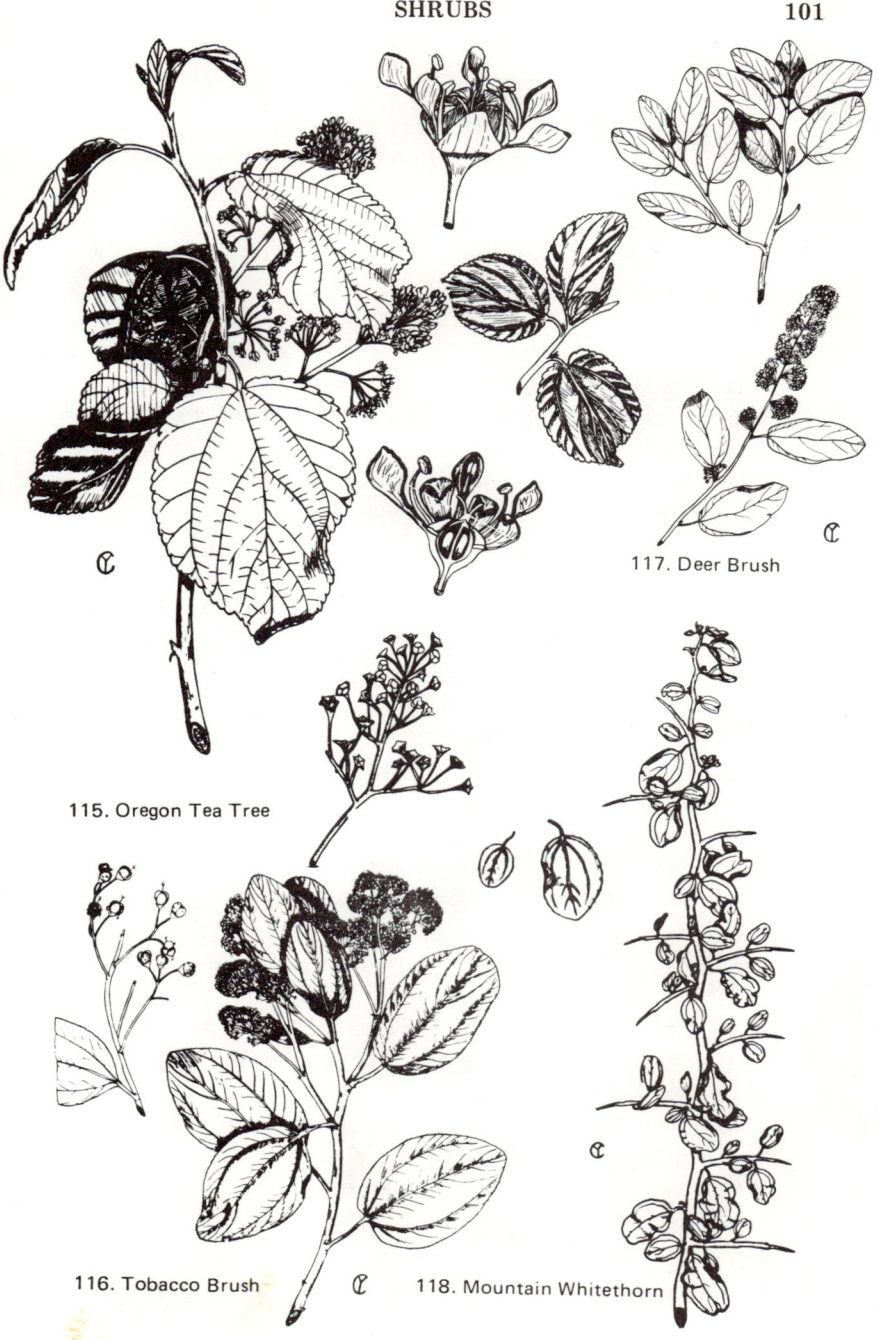

115. Oregon Tea Tree
116. Tobacco Brush
117. Deer Brush
118. Mountain Whitethorn

GINSENG Family

*122. AMERICAN DEVIL'S CLUB. *Oplopanax horridum.*
str.wd.
mix.ev.
w.hem.
sitk.-spr.
Stout shrub, 6-12' high, very prickly; **leaves very large and long stemmed,** roundish, palmately lobed, all at summit of the stem. Lobes acute and finely toothed. Flowers greenish-yellow; fruit scarlet. Abundant in wet places. Plant has a rank odor. Edible young stems.

DOGWOOD Family (In part, see 68, 229)

123. RED OSIER DOGWOOD, *Cornus stolonifera.* Much
str.wd.
conif.
branched shrub, 6-12' high, with **red twigs, these slightly hairy when young;** leaves opposite, oval to narrow, 1½-3" long. Flowers in loose clusters flat-topped. **Fruit is bluish-white.** Common along stream banks and in wet ground.

124. CALIFORNIA DOGWOOD, *Cornus californica.* This
str.wd.
species is much like the Red Osier Dogwood except for the **hairy undersides of the leaves** and the stems; **gray-white fruit.** Common along streams in southern Oregon and northern California.

SILK-TASSEL Family

The apetalous flowers hang down in long tassel-like catkins.

125. FREMONT'S SILK-TASSEL, *Garrya Fremontii.* A tall
brush
mix.ev.
conif.
and erect shrub often 10' high. Leaves elliptical, and leathery; they have a smooth, green upper surface and a lighter, slightly hairy lower surface. **The inconspicuous flowers and their silky bracts are produced on pendulous catkins in early spring.** The round fruits are dark purple to black. Found on dry, exposed areas where it forms dense thickets.

HEATH Family (In part, see 72, 235)

126. WHITE-FLOWERED RHODODENDRON,*Rhododendron*
sub.alp.
albiflorum. A shrub from 3-6' high; not an evergreen; leaves and **white flowers in small side clusters of 1-3, nodding.** Found in the high Washington Cascades at tree line, wetter cooler north slopes. It occurs as a dominant with Nootka Rose (102) in the southern Cascades of Washington, Hudsonian zone.

127. WESTERN AZALEA, *Rhododendron occidentale.* Loose-
str.wd.
mt.mead.
ly branched shrub, 3-12' tall, not an evergreen. The **showy large**

SHRUBS

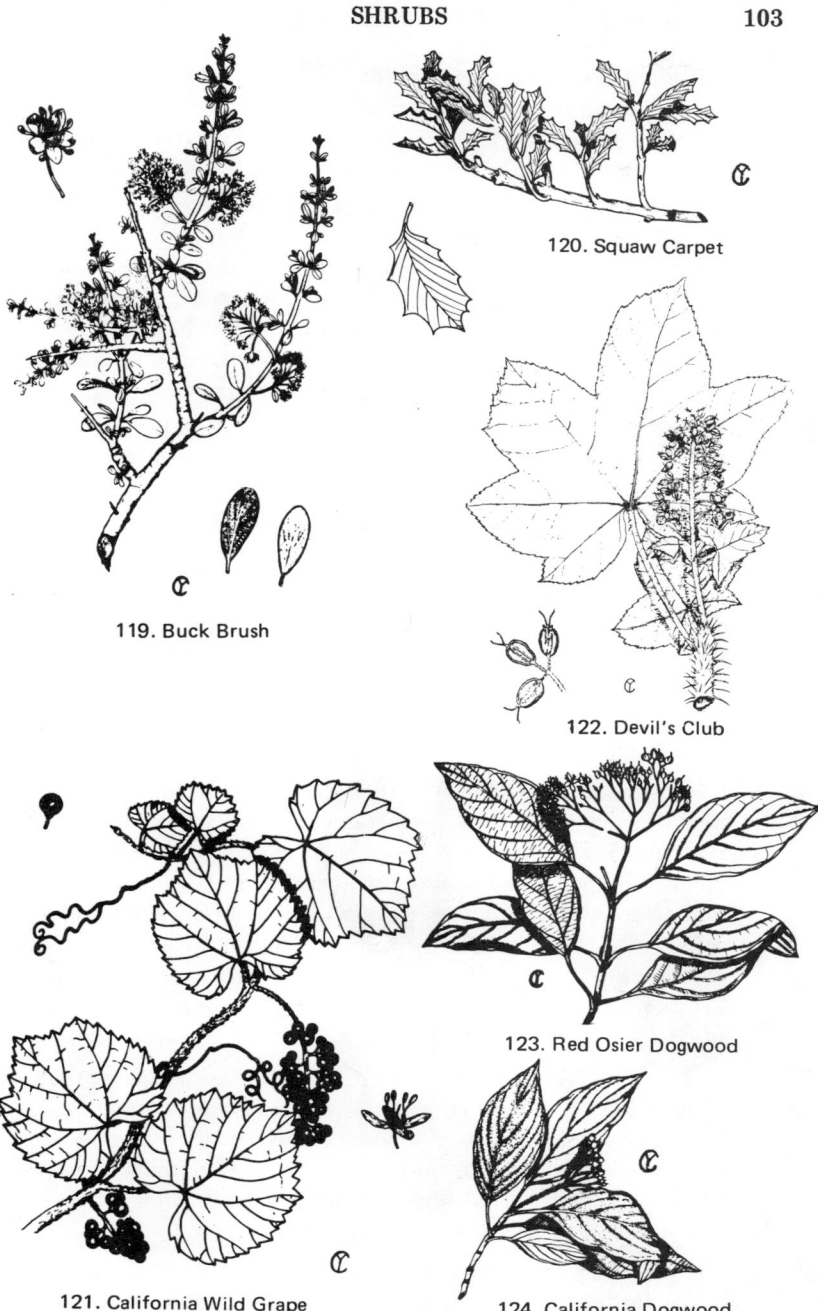

119. Buck Brush
120. Squaw Carpet
121. California Wild Grape
122. Devil's Club
123. Red Osier Dogwood
124. California Dogwood

whitish flowers tinged with yellow and pink make this the most noticed shrub in the coastal areas of California and southwestern Oregon. Found up to about 7,000' elevation in the Klamath Mountains.

str.wd.
mix.ev.
conif.

128a. CALIFORNIA ROSE-BAY, *Rhododendron macrophyllum.* Usually an erect shrub from 4-8' high; but in northern California, it frequently grows 30' high. The large **rose-purple, flowers are borne in clusters at the end of a branch.** The **thick, smooth margined, evergreen leaves** make this an attractive winter plant in the Coastal range, Siskiyou and western Cascades from California to British Columbia, usually below 4,000' elevation.

bogs
water
mt.mead.
sub.alp.

128b. ALPINE BOG KALMIA, *Kalmia polifolia* var. *microphylla.* An evergreen shrub from 1-2" high; leaves oblong, margin curled under, shiny green above, whitish below; flowers in simple flat-topped clusters, **rose purple,** 1/2-2/3" across. Found in **sphagnum bogs,** swamps at high altitude.

water
bogs

129. LABRADOR TEA, *Ledum groenlandicum.* 3-5' tall shrub, with bark coming off in strips; **leathery green leaves usually strongly up-curved edges,** ½-1½" long; flower with white petals, rounded at tip and narrow at base; **foliage resinous and fragrant.** Humid Transition and Canadian zones, south from Alaska to Tillamook County, Oregon.

str.wd.
sitk.spr.
w.hem.
mix.ev.

130. MOCK AZALEA or FOOL'S HUCKLEBERRY, *Menziesia ferruginea.* Tall slender shrub, 1½-6', erect or straggling branches; leaves thin, pale green, obovate to elliptic, round to pointed at apex, margin entire or finely toothed, mostly hairless sometimes with rusty hairs. **Flowers with short stems, copper colored,** ¼" long, urn-shaped, in clusters on end of branches. **Poisonous.** Usually below 1,000' along coastal mountains from California to Alaska, and in southern Washington. Humid Transition and Canadian zone.

rocks
mt.mead.
sub.-alp.

131. CREAM MOUNTAIN HEATHER, *Phyllodoce glanduliflora.* Low alpine heather-like evergreen undershrub, 8-16" high; leaves **numerous, linear, obtuse toothed; petals oval, yellowish and glandular.** Found in Cascades and Olympic Mountains at about 7,500' elevation; rarely found growing with *P. empetriformis.*

sub. alp.
mt.mead.

132. RED MOUNTAIN HEATHER, *Phyllodoce empetriformis.* Much branched evergreen undershrub, 5-20" high; flowers in flat **clusters; rose-red; petal bell-shaped and hairless.** Abundant

SHRUBS

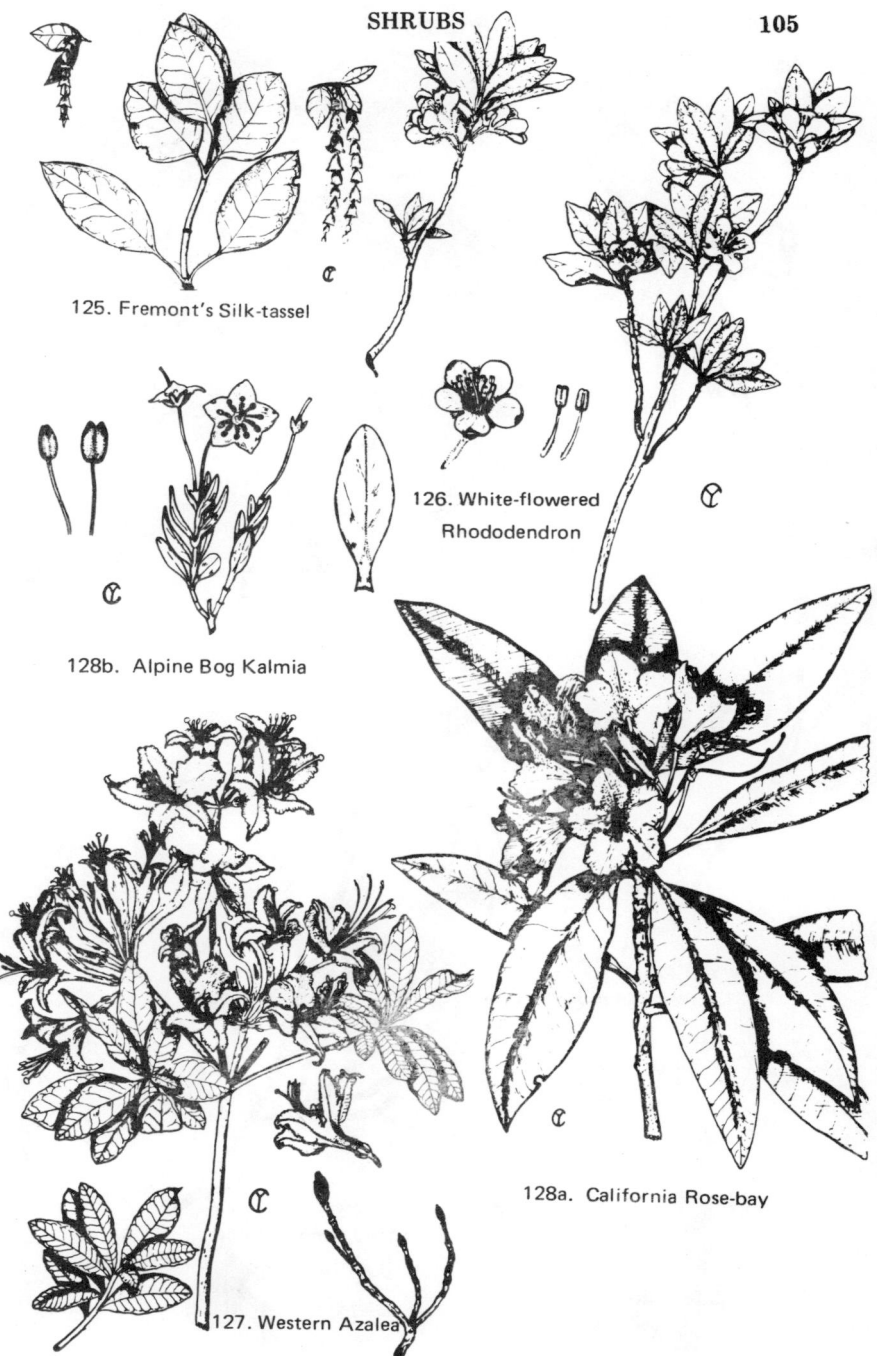

125. Fremont's Silk-tassel
126. White-flowered Rhododendron
128b. Alpine Bog Kalmia
128a. California Rose-bay
127. Western Azalea

106   WILDLIFE AND PLANTS OF THE CASCADES

129. Labrador Tea

130. Mock Azalea

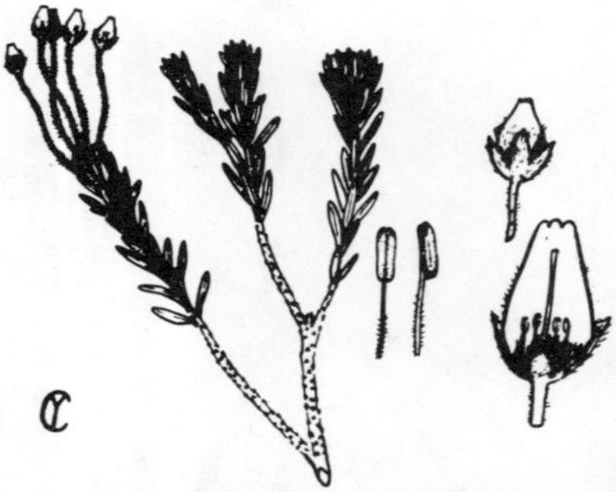

131. Cream Mountain Heather

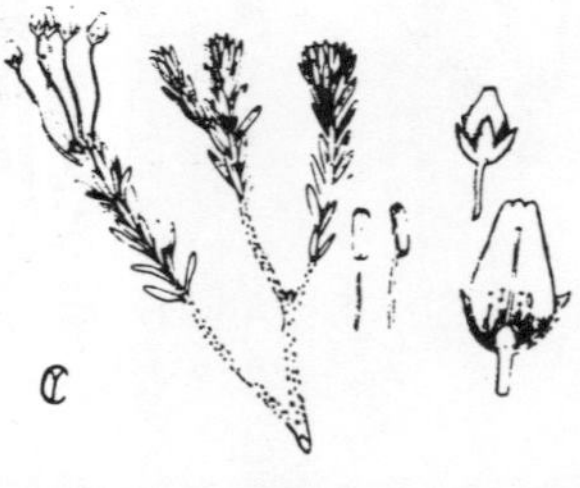

132. Red Mountain Heather

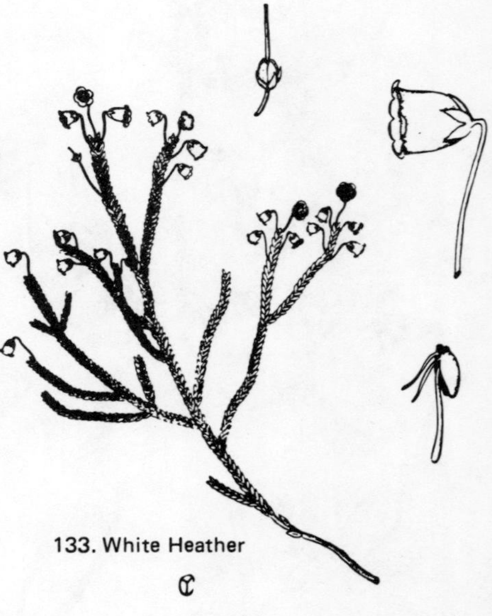

133. White Heather

SHRUBS

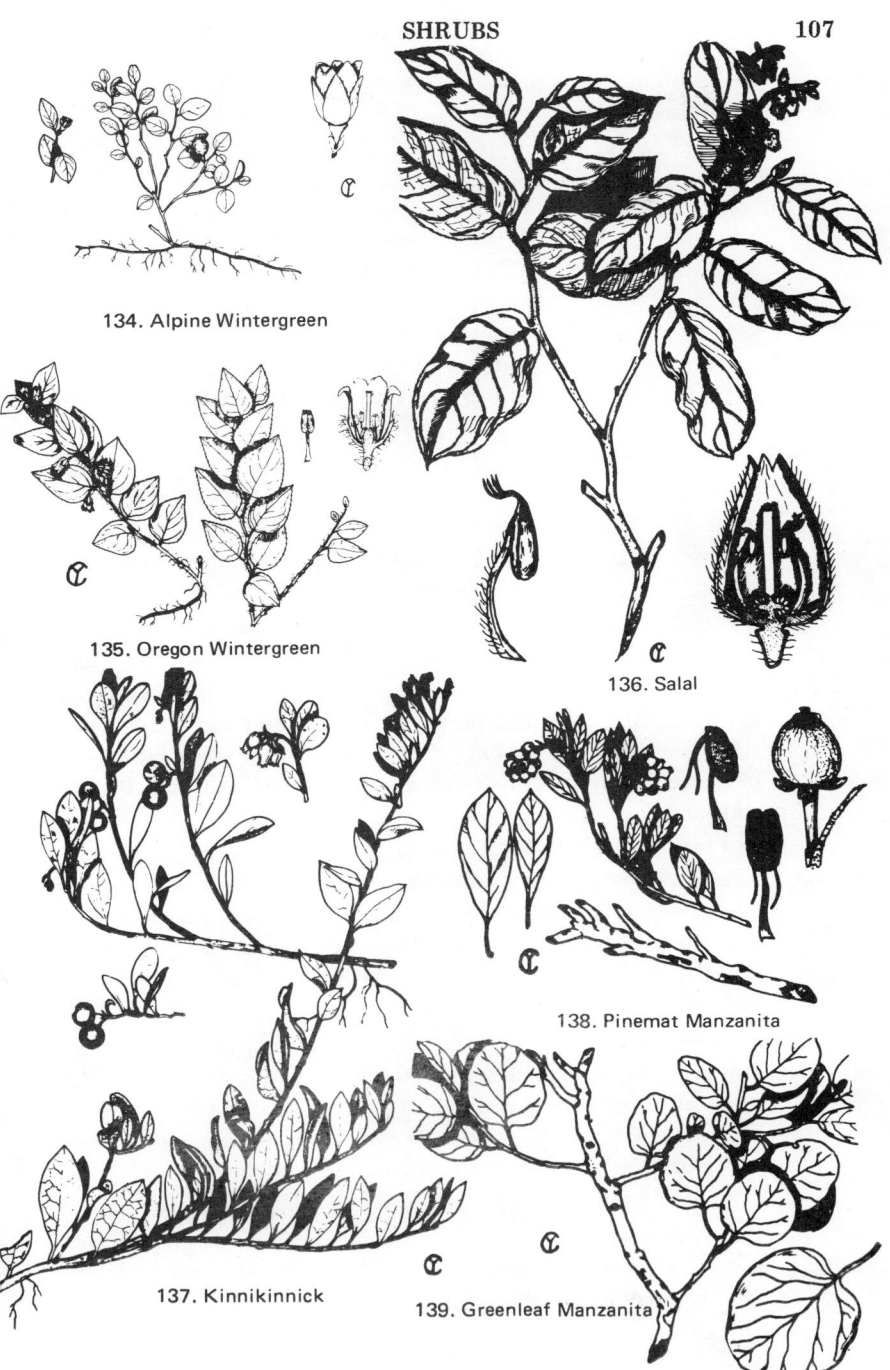

134. Alpine Wintergreen
135. Oregon Wintergreen
136. Salal
137. Kinnikinnick
138. Pinemat Manzanita
139. Greenleaf Manzanita

in the mountains at timberline. Very showy at time of bloom and known as "heather".

rocks
str.wd.
sub.alp.

133. WHITE HEATHER, *Cassiope Mertensiana*. A **creeping alpine shrub**, with some branches reaching 4-12" high; **leaves ridged on back;** flower bell-like with short-lobed petals, white or pinkish.

sub.alp
mt.mead.

*134. ALPINE WINTERGREEN, *Gaultheria humifusa*. This *gaultheria* grows at approximately 6,000' and higher elevation, is **very dwarfed and low growing; often forming close mats.** Leaves are about ½" long and the white bell-shaped flowers occur singly in the axils of the leaves; berries are round, scarlet, edible and spicy flavored.

conif.

*135. OREGON WINTERGREEN, *Gaultheria ovatifolia*. Evergreen shrub from 4-6" high; leaves oval to almost heart-shaped, 2/5-1 1/2" long, **flowers white and bell-shaped.** In open forests in Cascades and Olympic Mountains at approximately 3,600' elevation. Fruit spicy and delicious.

str.wd.
mix.ev.
conif.

*136. SALAL, *Gaultheria Shallon*. Evergreen shrub 1½-6' high, **crooked, often bending down;** leaves oval-oblong, 3-6" long, shiny green above; white to pink flowers are urn-shaped, elongated clusters. Black to dark-purple berries formed from the fleshy calyx enclosing the capsule. Common shrub at lower elevations in the forests from British Columbia south to California. Berries edible raw or cooked.

mt.mead.
brush
sub.alp.
conif.
mix.ev.

*137. KINNIKINNICK or BEARBERRY, *Arctostaphylos uva-ursi*. Evergreen, **trailing, red-barked shrub with thick,** oval-to-long leaves, ½-¾". The **lateral veins inconspicuous;** stems rising 1½-4½" high; bark of **older branches shredded or peeling.** Flowers, pink, urn-shaped, in short elongated clusters. Fruit is bright red. In open woods. Edible berries.

rocks
sub.alp.

*138. PINEMAT MANZANITA, *Artostaphylos nevadensis*. This is a **low, more or less matted species,** with stems rising. The **leaves are bright green, firm and rigid,** ovate to oval. ½-1" long. Flowers few in racemes; petals white, oblong-ovoid; fruit round, red. Found in Cascades at about 7,500' elevation.

pine
brush

*139. GREENLEAF MANZANITA, *Arctostaphylos patula*. This becomes a large 3-6' tall, erect, and robust evergreen shrub with **attractive reddish-colored bark.** The eliptical leaves are leathery. Clusters of urn-shaped pink flowers occur in early summer.

SHRUBS 109

Often forms thickets in the Yellow Pine Forest in northern California and southern Oregon. *Arctostaphylos* berries are edible, but better when cooked.

*140. EVERGREEN HUCKLEBERRY, *Vaccinium ovatum*. Attractive evergreen shrub that grows from 4-8' high. **Leaves very shiny, stiff, toothed and leathery; small, urn-shaped, pinkish flowers borne in elongated clusters.** Blackish fruits furnish much food for birds and mammals, make excellent jams and jellies. Found at low elevations from coastal California to British Columbia.   mix.ev. str.wd.

*141. WESTERN BOG BLUEBERRY, *Vaccinium occidentale*. Also known as Swamp Huckleberry. Grows to a height of about 2' and has **numerous, rather close, erect branches.** The leaves are entire, less than 1" long; flowers solitary, petals oblong-ovate about 1/8" long. Berries black with bloom. Found in wet places, Vancouver Island, British Columbia and south in Cascades mostly on the eastern side to California. All *Vaccinium* species have edible berries, both raw and cooked.   mt.mead. sub.alp. lodg. bogs

*142. DWARF HUCKLEBERRY, *Vaccinium caespitosum*. Low bushy shrub 4-12" high, hairless or minutely hairy; leaves oblong, broad on top to 1" long; flowers solitary in axils, longer than the drooping pedicels, pink petals; berries blue, with a bloom. Found in moist ground; not common in Washington.   mt.mead. rocks sub.alp.

*143. BIG WHORTLEBERRY or THINLEAF HUCKLEBERRY, *Vaccinium membranaceum*. This 3-6' tall, widely branched shrub is locally famous for its annual crop of berries which have been harvested by the Klamath Indians for decades and possibly centuries on "Ewamcan" Mountain near Crater Lake Nattional Park. **Leaves bright green, 1-2" long, and thin.** Berries large and purplish-black when mature.   conif. sub.alp. str.wd.

*144. GROUSE or LITTLELEAF HUCKLEBERRY, *Vaccinium scoparium*. Low bushy hairless shrub, ½-1½' tall, with **numerous erect branches, green and sharply angled; leaves very small, oval to ovate, bright green;** petal urn-shaped, less than 1/8" long; berries light red. In mountains from 4,500-6,000' elevation.   sub.alp. lodg.

*145. RED HUCKLEBERRY, *Vaccinium parvifolium*. This shrub grows from 3' to occasionally 20' high. Leaves thin, oval, not an evergreen. **Branchlets are green and sharply angled.** Flowers are round, greenish or pinkish colored. Berries are bright red   sitk.-spr. red fir mix.ev. str.wd.

and pleasing to eat. Very abundant from California north to Alaska, below 5,000'.

MINT Family

jun.
sage

*146. GRAY BALL SAGE, *Salvia Dorrii* subsp. *carnosa*. A low, 1-3' tall shrub, with numerous branches, making it often as broad as tall; leaves covered with a whitish fuzz and a bran-like scale. Likes gravelly or rocky soil in Upper Sonoran and Transition zones on e. side of Cascades, often in desert. Edible seeds best when parched, ground and baked into bread.

PHLOX Family

conif.
rocks
sub.alp.
alp.

147. SPREADING PHLOX, *Phlox diffusa* var. *Douglassii*. Prostrate shrub, 4-12" with showy numerous flowers ranging from purple to pink or almost white; leaves opposite; petal tube 3/8-5/8". Blooms in spring in pine forests, later at high elevations. Dry slopes and flats.

HONEYSUCKLE Family

conif.
mix.ev.
str.wd.

*148a. BLUE ELDERBERRY, *Sambucus caerulea*. A shrub from 5-18' high. Stems with large pithy centers. **The small white flowers are arranged in flat-topped clusters** (cymes); the blue berries, densely hairless and smooth, mature during July and August. A common shrub at lower elevations. Open places. Edible berries.

str.wd.
mix.ev.
sitk.spr.
w.hem.

*148b. PACIFIC RED ELDERBERRY, *Sambucus callicarpa*. A shrub with pithy centered stems frequently forming thick clumps 3-5' high. **The small white flowers arranged in dome-shaped clusters (cymes).** Bright red berries form in late summer. Mostly w. foothills of Cascades.

str.wd.
mix.ev.
pine

149. COMMON SNOWBERRY, *Symphoricarpos rivularis*. Erect shrub, usually less than 4' high. Leaves opposite, (not toothed) but lobed. **Flowers white or pink, 2-sepaled, small, on very top or between the leaves, clusters.** White berries produced in the fall. A similar species with plants trailing, or low and spreading, and with leaves hairy at least beneath, occurs in southern Oregon and northern California. Sharp-leaf Snowberry *(S. acutus)*.

*150. BLACK TWINBERRY, *Lonicera involucrata*. Upright

SHRUBS

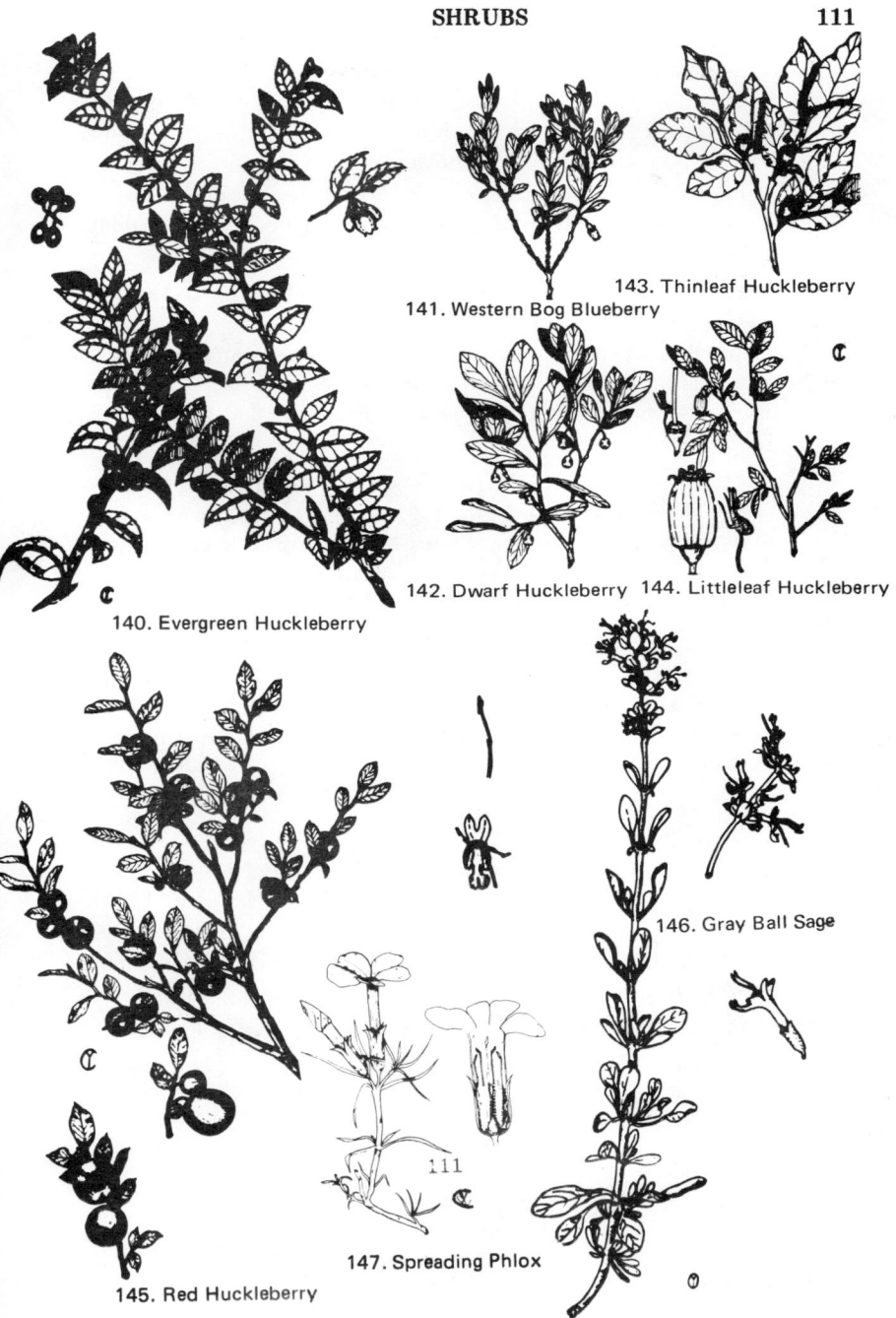

143. Thinleaf Huckleberry
141. Western Bog Blueberry
142. Dwarf Huckleberry
144. Littleleaf Huckleberry
140. Evergreen Huckleberry
146. Gray Ball Sage
147. Spreading Phlox
145. Red Huckleberry

shrub with opposite, not evergreen leaves; **yellow flowers in pairs
on bractlets surrounding the ovaries of the two flowers** forming
a sac-like cup. Each pair of flowers develops a pair of purplish-
black berries above the more or less united, reddish bracts.
Moist places from Coastal Strand to Subalpine Forests. Edible
berries.

151. PURPLE FLOWER HONEYSUCKLE, *Lonicera conjugialis*. Slender-stemmed straggling deciduous shrub with paired
purple flowers that produce two berries that fuse to form a single
fruit as they mature. **The red fused flower petal has a deflexed
lip and a throat filled with white hairs.** Wooded slopes from
4,000-10,000'.

*152. ROCKY MOUNTAIN HONEYSUCKLE, *Lonicera utahensis*. Much branched shrub, 1-3' tall, **not twining**, with paired
white flowers subtended by minute bractlets. **Berries red and not
uniting.** Found in Forest areas in California to treeline in Olympics and common in main Cascades. Edible berries.

*153. ORANGE HONEYSUCKLE, *Lonicera ciliosa*. Climbing or trailing shrub; leaves oval, smooth beneath, obtuse, or small
hairs, short stem. **Yellow, red or orange flowers without stem,**
mostly in 1 whorl. Forest areas in California and open woods in
Washington. Edible berries.

SUNFLOWER Family

154. BLOOMER'S RABBIT BRUSH, *Haplopappus Bloomeri*.
Low spreading shrub, 1-2' high, with abundant heads with bright
yellow rays. **Stems are leafy to the tip.** Blooms in August—especially at higher elevations on the east slopes of the Cascades.
Another form occurs in the Basin Range Country and Forests.

155. GRAY RABBIT BRUSH, *Chrysothamnus nauseosus*.
Shrub without ray flowers; heads with numerous flowers; leaves
gray-green; **stems woolly.** This tall shrub usually occurs in the lower areas along the east side of the Cascades often in more or less
alkaline soil. Also found at higher elevations.

*156. GIANT SAGE, *Artemisia tridentata*. Erect, much-
branched shrub; 3-4' high; appears silvery throughout; leaves 3-
toothed at end. Very common on the east side of the Cascades.
Seeds may be dried into meal after pounding.

SHRUBS

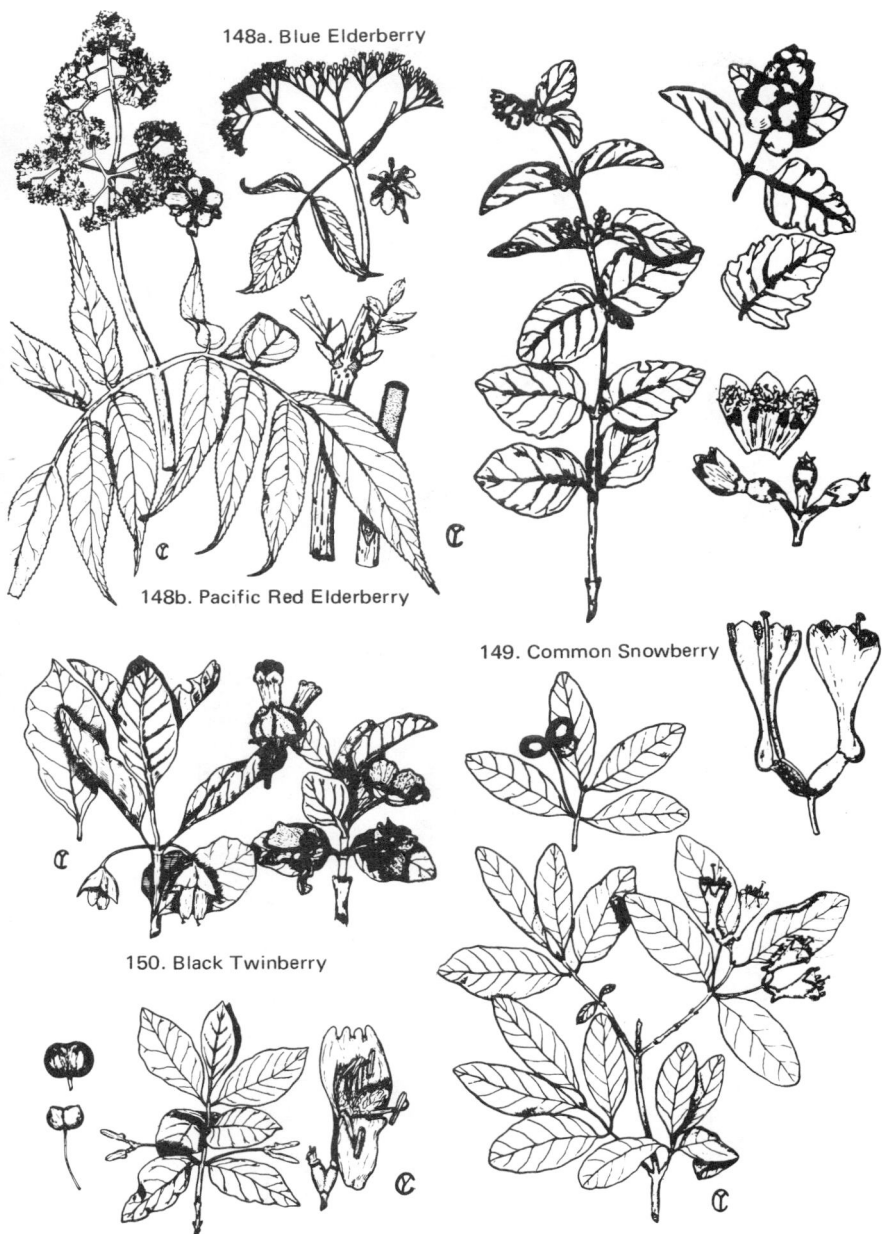

148a. Blue Elderberry

148b. Pacific Red Elderberry

149. Common Snowberry

150. Black Twinberry

151. Purple Flower Honeysuckle

152. Rocky Mountain Honeysuckle

114 WILDLIFE AND PLANTS OF THE CASCADES

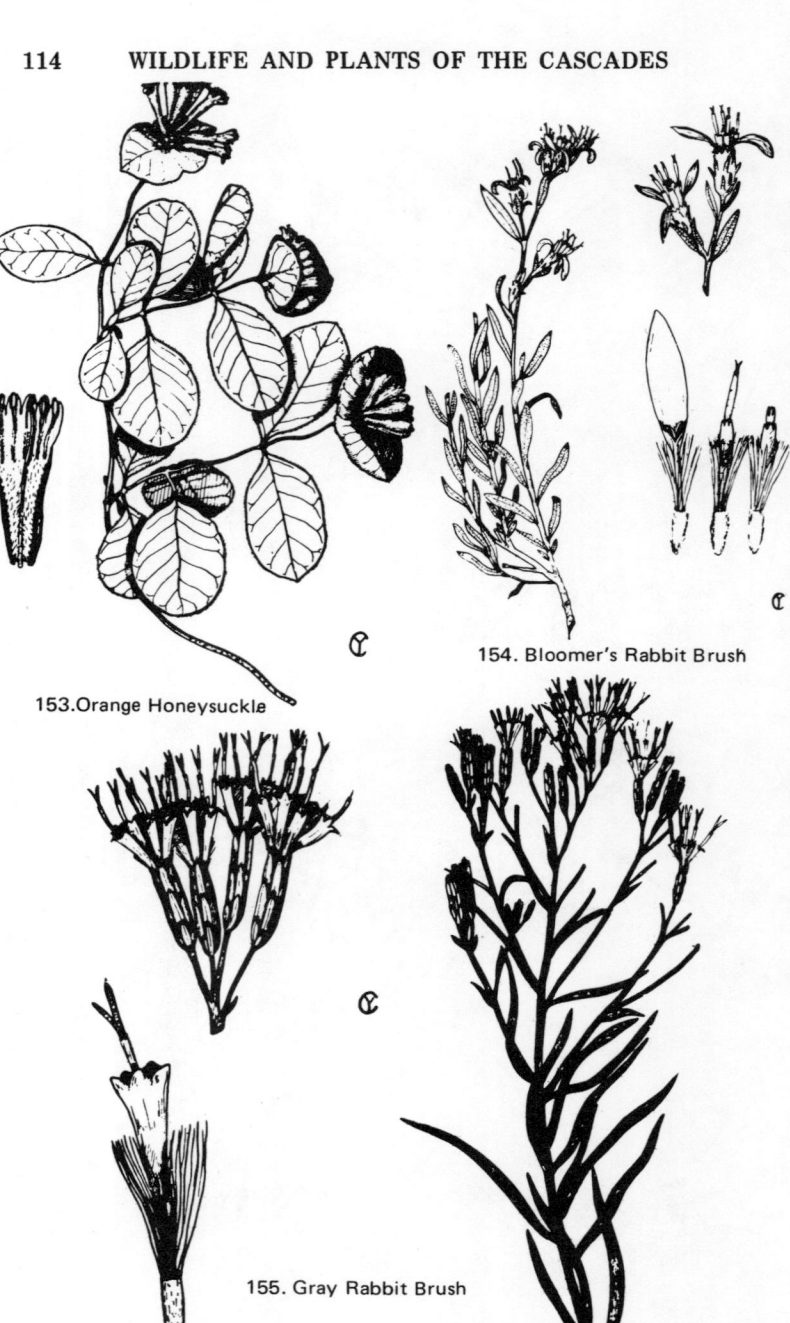

153. Orange Honeysuckle

154. Bloomer's Rabbit Brush

155. Gray Rabbit Brush

SHRUBS, HERBS

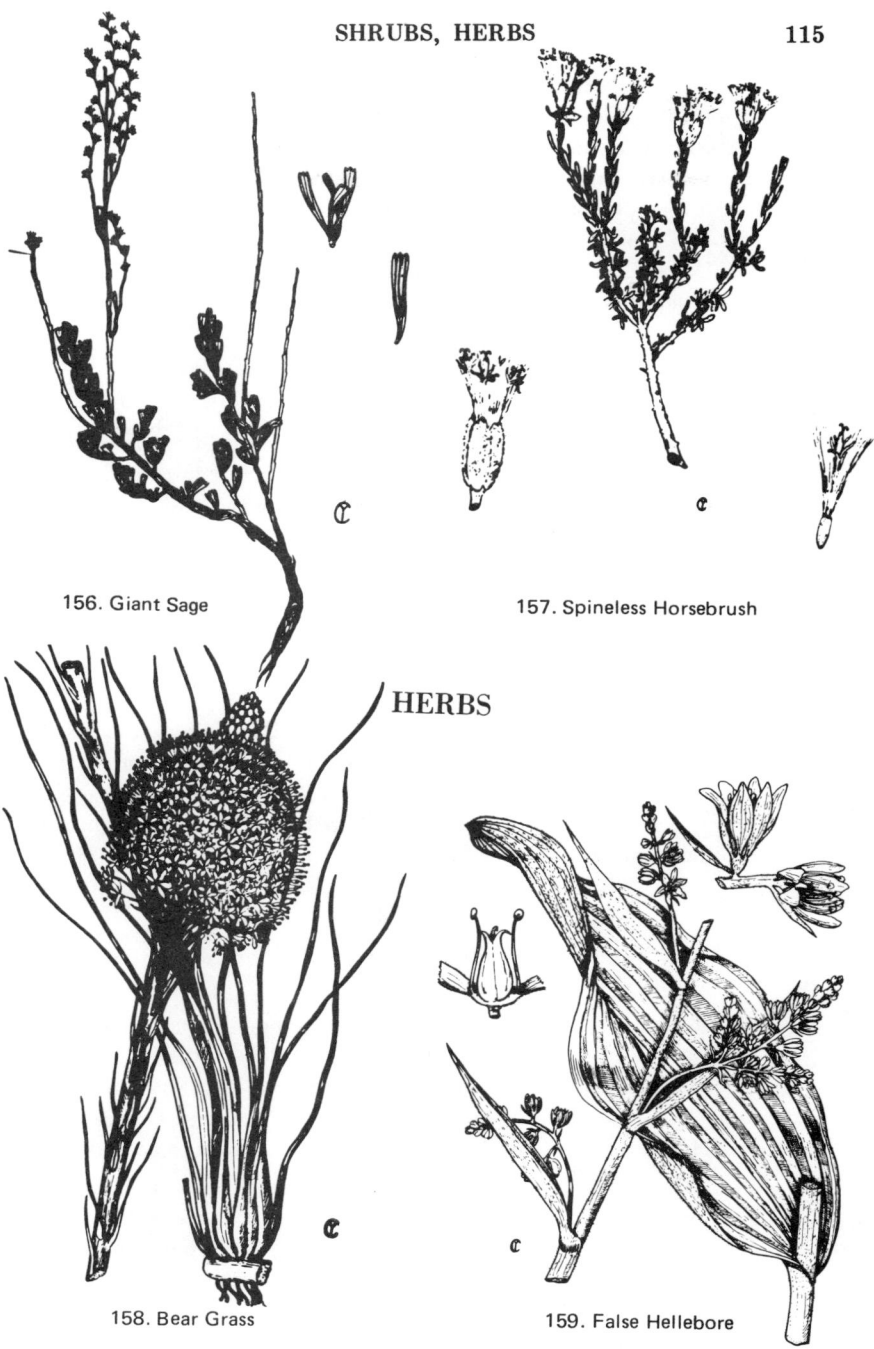

156. Giant Sage

157. Spineless Horsebrush

HERBS

158. Bear Grass

159. False Hellebore

WILDLIFE AND PLANTS OF THE CASCADES

sage
jun.
pume.
pine

157. SPINELESS HORSEBRUSH, *Tetradymia canescens*. A low white, woolly shrub or bush 4-20" tall with **narrow crowded flat-topped clusters of few-flowered heads**. A common plant at Lava Beds National Monument scattered among the Sagebrush and other plants. Found north to British Columbia along east slope of Cascades.

F. HERBS
WITH PARALLEL-VEINED LEAVES

LILY Family

Herbs from bulbs, corns or rootstock; stems parallel-veined.

mt.mead.
mix.ev.
mix.con.

*158. PINE LILY or BEAR GRASS, *Xerophyllum tenax*. Perennial with short thick woody rootstock and very numerous, harsh and stiff, keeled basal leaves. **Flowers white in large dense raceme**. When first blooms appear the raceme is pyramidal, then elongates. Stems from 3-6' high, stiff and erect, common in dry open woods, but not known to occur in western British Columbia. Open dry slopes and ridges usually less than 6,000'; Cascades, north to British Columbia. Forms a climax type community with *Abies lasiocarpa* (43.) in lava flows near Mt. Adams at 3,400'. Fibrous root, roasted or boiled.

mt.mead.
bogs
sub.alp.

159. FALSE HELLEBORE or CORN LILY, *Veratrum viride*. A tall (3-5') corn-like, leafy-stemmed perennial herb from short thick **poisonous** rootstocks; stems woolly-haired; broad leaves clasping and strongly veined, and plaited; flowers greenish in a drooping compound elongated cluster. Found in swampy areas.

AMARYLLIS Family

Flowers if flat-topped or round-topped clusters or single have bracts just below flower cluster.

rocks
mix.con.

*160. WATSON'S ONION, *Allium siskiyouensis*. Flowers 10-20 in round-topped cluster. Main stem about 1-3" high; 2 leaves much longer than the stem. **Flowers rose colored with purple midveins**. Found in Siskiyou Mountains to southern Oregon at high elevations on rocky slopes. All *allium* are known to be edible.

pine
mix.ev.

*161. HARVEST BRODIAEA, *Brodiaea elegans*. This erect leaflets stem herb, 4-15" high, grows from a membranous-coated corm as do all *Brodiaea*. **The flowers in loose flat-topped clusters long individual stemmed, are violet-purple with long droopy-petals**. Found from Vancouver Island to California in dry prairies, grassy hillsides and wooded slopes below 5,000'. Bulbs are edible.

HERBS

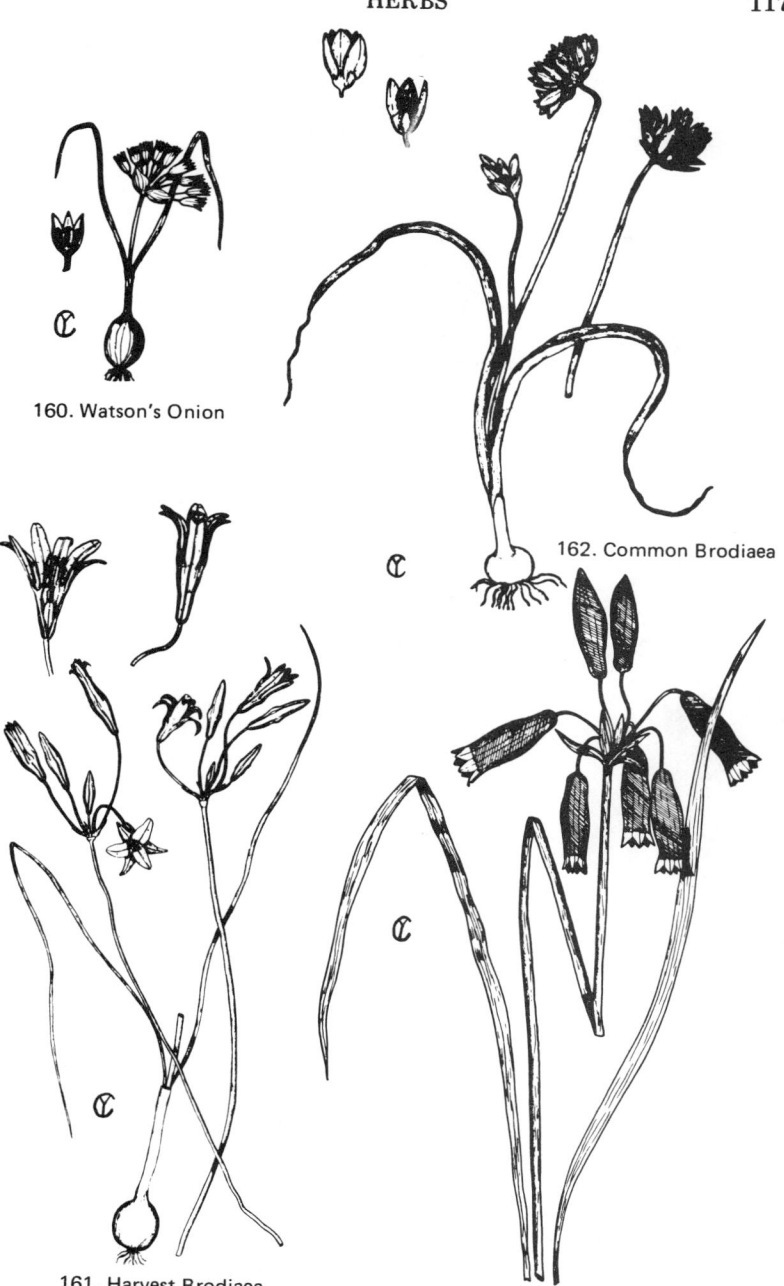

160. Watson's Onion
161. Harvest Brodiaea
162. Common Brodiaea
163. Fire-cracker Flower

118   WILDLIFE AND PLANTS OF THE CASCADES

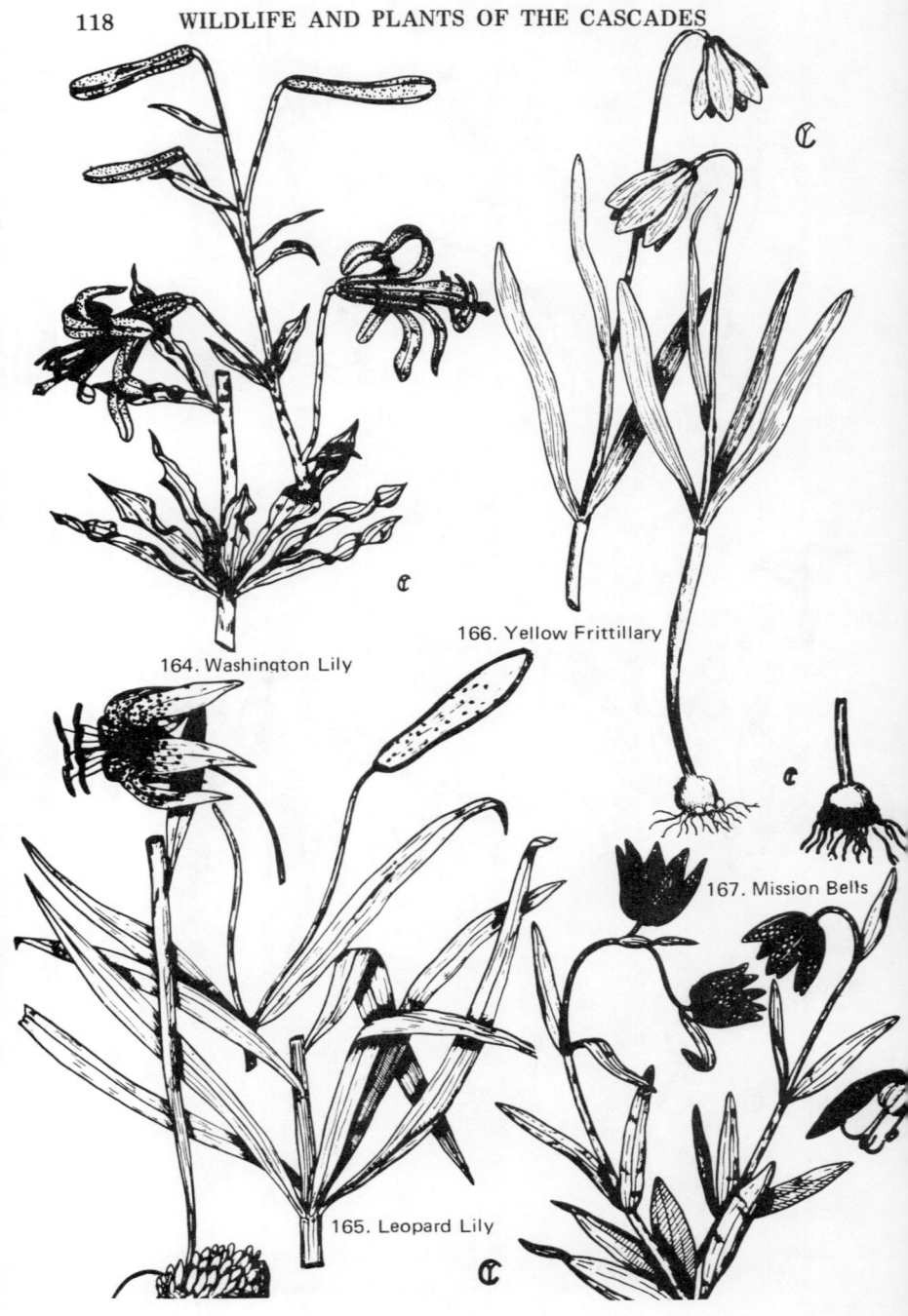

164. Washington Lily
165. Leopard Lily
166. Yellow Frittillary
167. Mission Bells

HERBS

*162. COMMON BRODIAEA or BLUE DICKS, *Brodiaea pulchella* var *capitata*. **Leaves usually shorter than main flower stem.** Flowers 2-20 in a round-topped cluster. Each individual flower stem is 1/8-5/8" long. Petals deep violet-purple broadly funnel-form, 6 stamens. Common on plains and dry open ridges and hillsides below Yellow Pine Forest. Southern Ore. to N. lower California. The bulbs are edible.

grass
pine
mix.ev

163. FIRE-CRACKER FLOWER, *Brodiaea Ida-Maia*. **The red flowers tipped with yellow are borne** on a stalk that grows from 1-3' high. This plant is common near Oregon Caves, Klamath Mountains, Siskiyou Mountains to near the coast in northwestern California.

grass
mt.mead.
pine
mix.ev.

LILY Family (In part, see 158, 159)

164. WASHINGTON or SHASTA LILY, *Lillium Washingtonianum*. Bulbs are 6-8" long; stems 2-5' tall, leaves in whorls, longer than broad. Flowers 2-20 on a single stem, trumpet-shaped. **Pure white becoming purplish as aged.** (Very fragrant) 3-4" long. Among bushes, dry granite-filled slopes. 4,000-7,000'.

brush
conif.

165. LEOPARD LILY, *Lillium pardalinum*. Forms mat like masses of roundish bulbs. Stem stout; 3-7' tall. Shiny leaves in 3-4 whorls and 9-15 in each whorl. Flowers nodding; 2-3" long; **Yellow with red to maroon spots.** Forms large colonies; moist springy places.

bogs
str.wd.
conif.
mix.ev.

*166. GOLD-BELL or YELLOW FRITILLARY, *Fritillaria pudica*. One or more **bell-shaped yellow to orange flower** with flower parts alike, blooming early in the spring, on a single stem about 6" high, bearing several narrow leaves above the middle of the stem. Bulbs eaten raw or boiled; but don't---too rare!

grass
sage
brush

*167. MISSION BELLS, *Fritillaria lanceolata*. Bulbs, with many "rice grain" bulblets. Stem 1-2'. 6-9 leaves in 2-3 whorls. Flowers bowl shaped; **dark purple with mottled greenish yellow.** Shaded slopes and along streams. Bulbs edible. Too pretty to eat!

mix.ev.
str.wd.
pine
brush

*168. YELLOW FAWN LILY, *Erythronium grandiflorum*. Stem erect, 6-16" tall, from a narrow deep-seated corm; leaves 2, bright green, appearing basal; flowers large bright **yellow with purple anthers;** fruit a 3-angled capsule. Moist mountain slopes and the bulbs are edible boiled or dried.

grass
conif.

120 WILDLIFE AND PLANTS OF THE CASCADES

sage
jun.
pine

169. DESERT LILY, *Calochortus macrocarpus.* Large **purplish flower on a single stem from 12-18 inches high.** This showy lily is common in the sagebrush along the dry foothills on the east side of the Cascades. Perianth segments (flower parts) are unlike, the inner large and showy; bell to bowl-shaped, yellow base, with green band down middle.

brush
mix.ev.
sitk.-spr.

170. TRILLIUM, *Trillium chloropetalum.* Stems stout; one or more arising from very stout rootstock, 12-18". 3 large leaves roundish to oval, conspicuously mottled with dark splotches **enclosing long white flower petals** (vary to deep maroon.) Wooded slopes.

mix.ev.
sitk.-spr.
str.wd.

*171. WAKE-ROBIN, *Trillium ovatum.* Usually one stem 10-15" high from horizontal rootstock; 3 leaves in a whorl with a 3 petaled white (turning to purple) flower. Very common in moist woods from California to British Columbia; Coast Range, Siskiyou Mountains and Cascades. Plant boiled as greens.

conif.
str.wd.

172. SINGLE-FLOWERED CLINTONIA, *Clintonia uniflora.* Somewhat hairy herb with slender rootstocks, simple, erect leaves from base. **Flowers white solitary** (rarely 2) on a slender stem (no leaves). Common in shady woods, 3,500-6,000' elevation, montane coniferous forests, Siskiyou Mountains and Cascades to British Columbia.

conif.
mix.con.
str.wd.

173. WESTERN FALSE SOLOMON'S-SEAL, *Smilacina racemosa.* Has white flowers borne in a **compound elongated flower stalk.** Berry is **bright red sprinkled with reddish-purple dots.** Occur at high elevations in the Cascades from California to British Columbia and in the Coastal Range and Siskiyou Mountains.

str.wd.
brush

174. NUTTALL'S FALSE SOLOMON'S-SEAL, *Smilacina stellata.* Has white flowers borne in an **elongated flower stalk.** The berry is **dark purple.** Occurs at high elevations (like above).

mix.ev.
str.wd.
sitk.-spr.

175. FALSE LILY-OF-THE-VALLEY, *Maianthemum dilatatum.* **Like a two-leaved Solomon's Seal, with a much broader leaf.** Blade 2-8" long, 2-4" wide. Elongated flower stalk ¾-2" long. Flowers white; berry round, red. Moist shaded banks near coast.

mix.ev.

176a. HOOKER'S FAIRY BELLS, *Disporum Hookeri.* Perennial mostly woolly-haired herbs with slender rootstocks; stems branched and leafy above. Leaves alternate, clasping. Flowers

HERBS

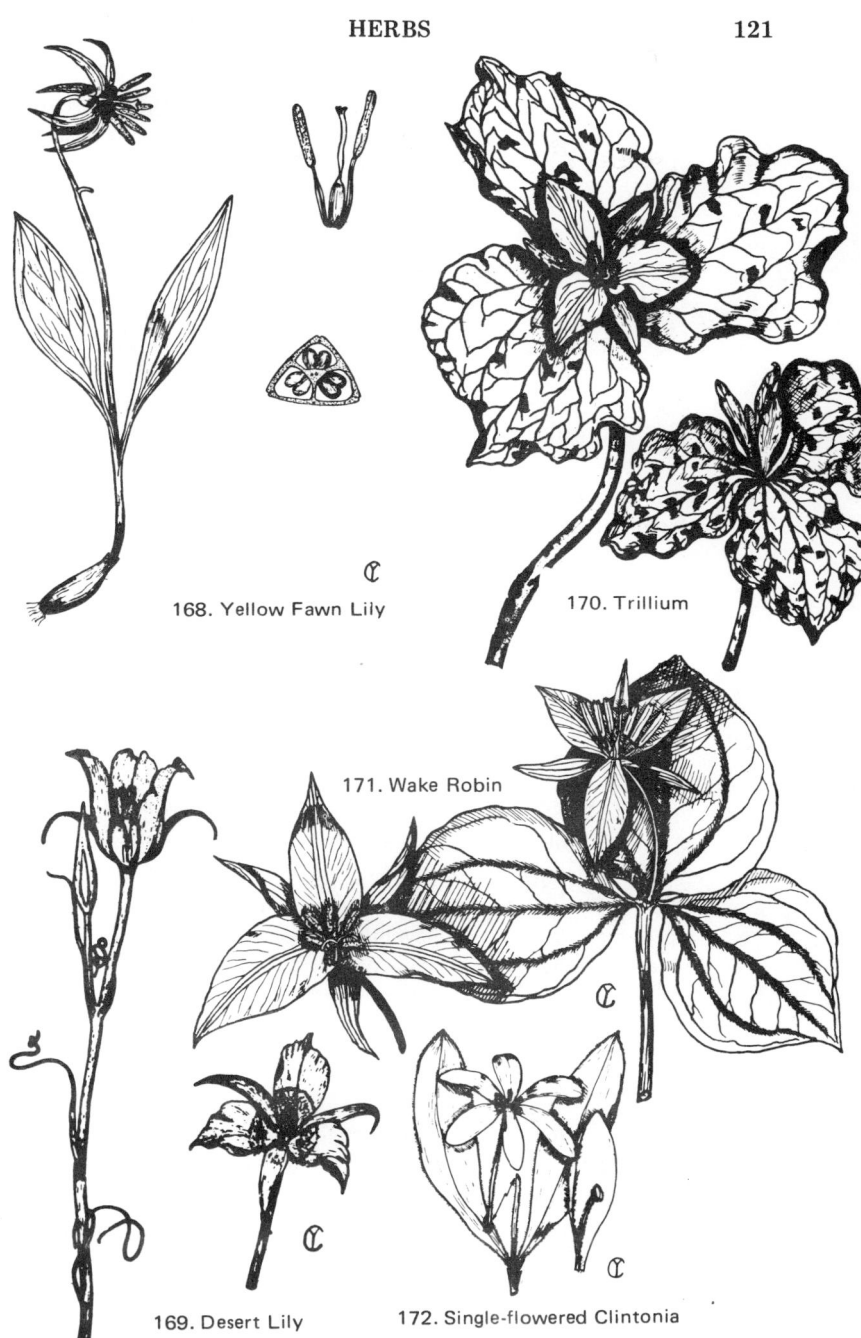

168. Yellow Fawn Lily
170. Trillium
171. Wake Robin
169. Desert Lily
172. Single-flowered Clintonia

greenish yellow, terminal, drooping, few in an umbel (cluster). Has a narrow bell-like flower. Found in shaded woods away from the coast in coastal mountains from California to southwestern Oregon. Moist wooded banks. Not illustrated.

str.wd.
mix.ev.

176b. LARGE-FLOWERED FAIRY BELL, *Disporum Smithii.* It is a larger plant with flowers broad at the base. It occurs along the coast from Nootka Sound, Alaska to northern California.

str.wd.
mix.ev.
dg. fir

*177. TWISTED STALK, *Streptopus amplexifolius.* Perennial herb with stout, horizontal rootstock; stem leafy; clasping, sessile, (close to stalk) alternate leaves on slender bent or twisted stalks. Flowers greenish to yellowish, 1 or 2 together about ½" long bell-like. Oval berry. Found in moist woods usually below 5,000' from California to Alaska. Berries are edible.

IRIS Family

str.wd.
mix.ev.
grass

178. DOUGLAS' IRIS, *Iris Douglasiana.* Leaves ¾" wide to 3' long, prominently ribbed yellow-green to deep green with pinkish or reddish bases. Flower color varies from pale cream through light lavender and dark lavender to deep red purple. Grassy slopes and open places especially in Redwood belt. Forms tufts or small colonies.

mt.mead.
s.a.mead.
slp.

179. WESTERN BLUE FLAG, *Iris missouriensis.* Medium sized, **pale blue-flowered wild iris** similar to our domestic forms, with slender pale green leaves; sometimes purple below. Flowers with spreading sepals; petals shorter than sepals. Common in moist open areas from sagebrush scrub to high elevations on east side of Cascades.

ORCHID Family

Perennial herb from fibrous to fleshy roots. Flowers have pollinia (special pollen masses).

mix.con.
sil.fir
w.hem
gr.fir

180. TWAYBLADE, *Listera caurina.* Stems slender, 6-12" tall, 2 leaves (blunt or rounded at end) clasp stem. **Flowers small 5-40 in number. Greenish on single stalk;** 2 pollina. Found in moist woods 4,000-5,000' elevation from northwestern California to British Columbia and in southern Washington.

181. HEART-LEAVED TWAYBLADE, *Listera cordata.* Small herbs, 4-8" high, with two, opposite, green cordate **(heart-shaped)**

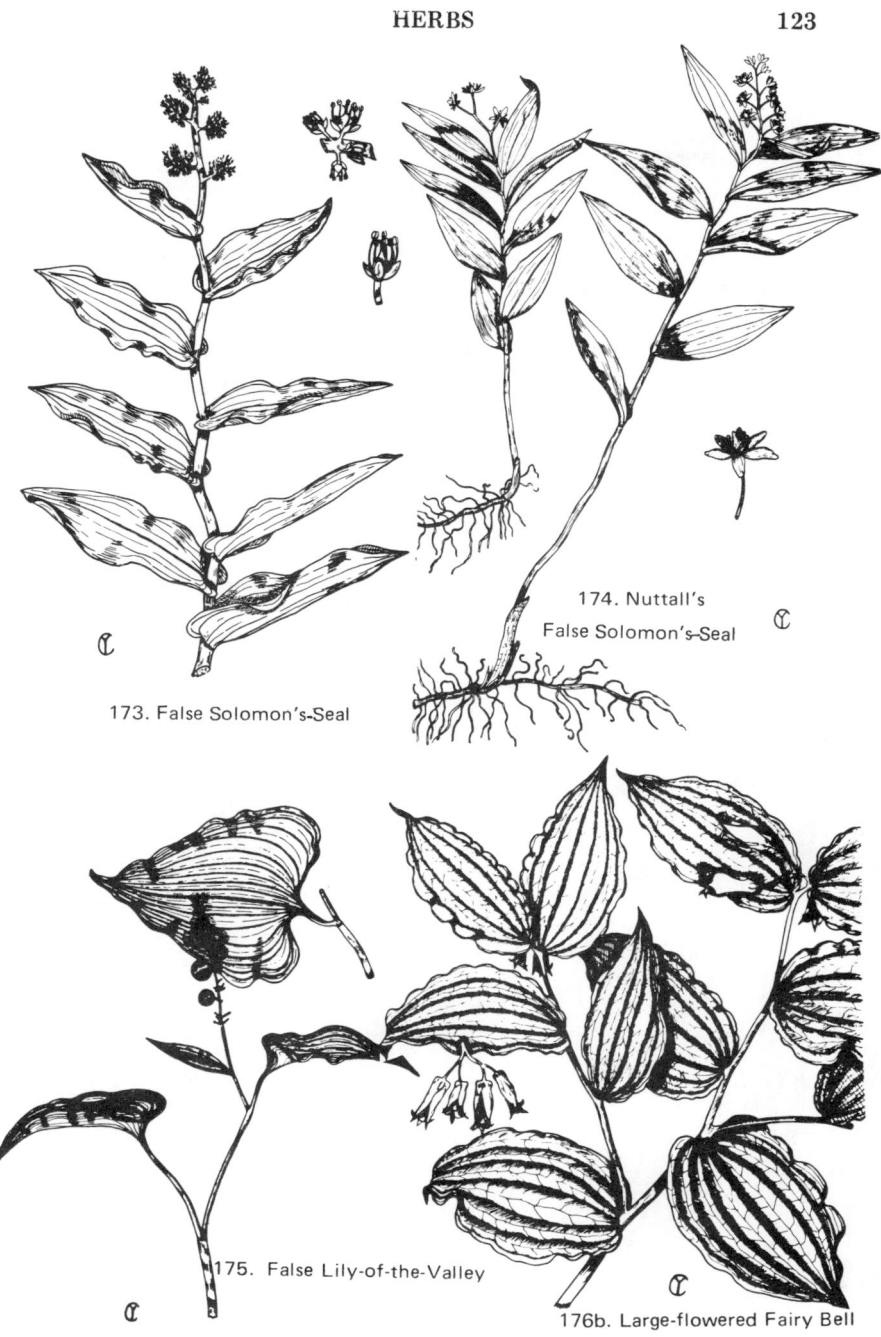

173. False Solomon's-Seal

174. Nuttall's False Solomon's-Seal

175. False Lily-of-the-Valley

176b. Large-flowered Fairy Bell

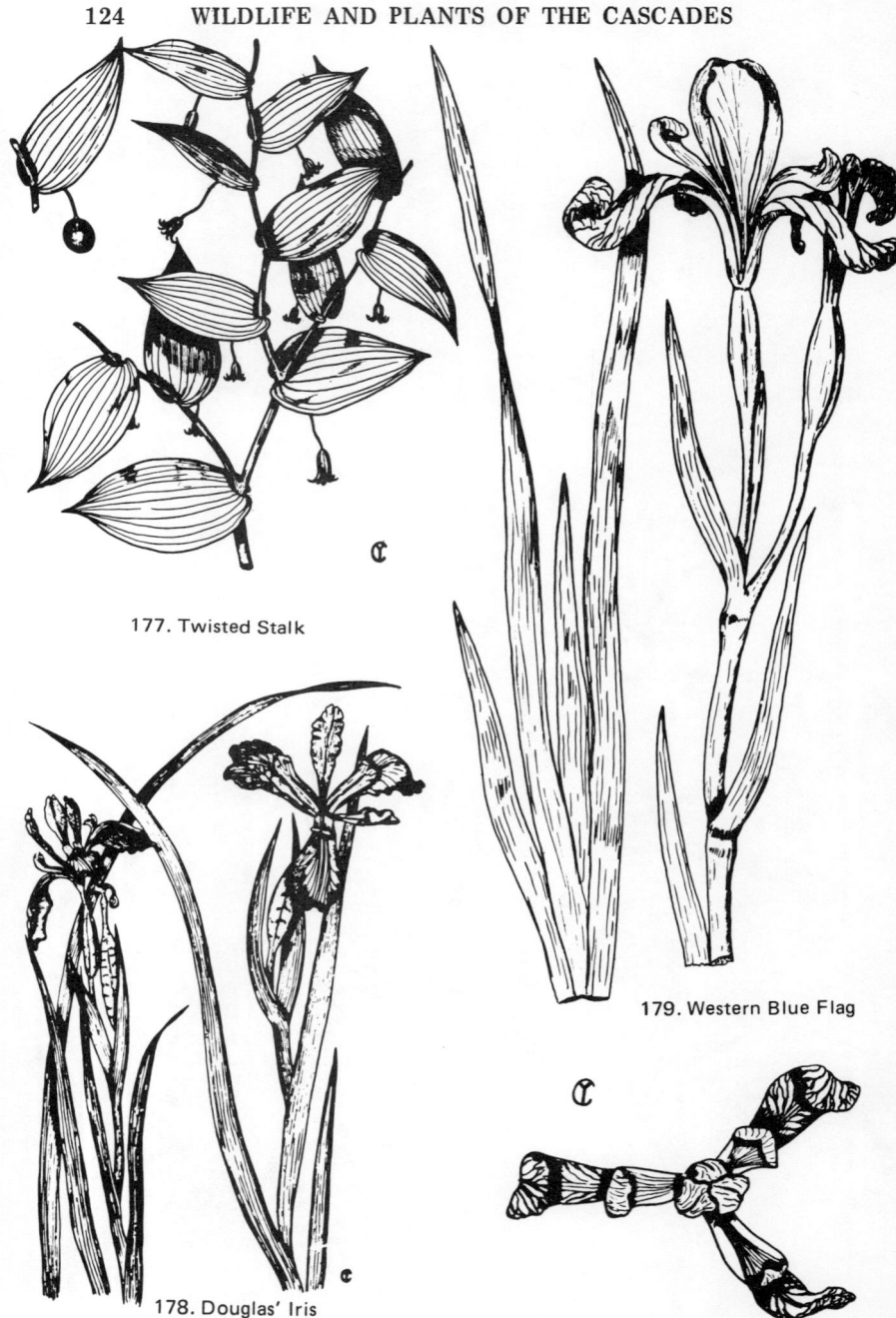

177. Twisted Stalk

178. Douglas' Iris

179. Western Blue Flag

HERBS

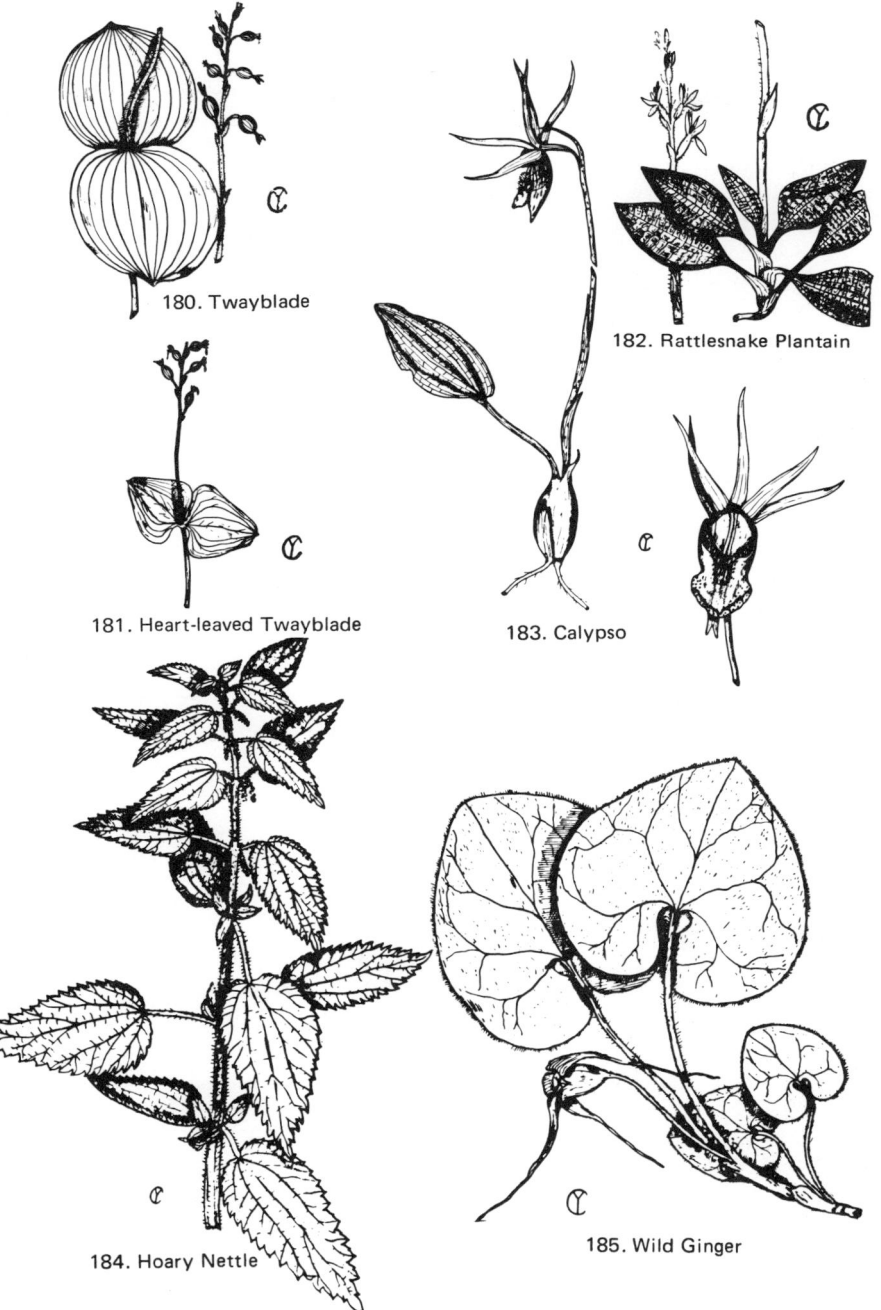

180. Twayblade

181. Heart-leaved Twayblade

182. Rattlesnake Plantain

183. Calypso

184. Hoary Nettle

185. Wild Ginger

str.wd.
mix.ev.
dg.fir

leaves near the middle of the stem; flowers very small, greenish or brownish, 4-20 to the end of the stalk, spurless. Sepals and petals, nearly alike. 2 pollinia. Common in moist mossy woods, California to Alaska.

pine
red fir
dg. fir

182. RATTLESNAKE PLANTAIN, *Goodyera oblongifolia*. Herb, 6-15" high, with bracted erect leafless stem and thick fleshy-fibrous roots; **leaves base situated, often blotched** with white; flowers in bracted spikes. (2 pollinia each). Common on dry forest floors. Found usually below 5,500' in Washington, northern California and southwestern Oregon.

mix.ev.
pine
sil.fir
gr.fir
w.hem.

*183. CALYPSO, *Calypso bulbosa*. Herb with solid bulbs, coral-like roots; **leaf at base of stem solitary**, with leaf stem 1-2"; one-flowered; short leafless stem, 4-10" high. **Flowers, lines and spots of purple.** In bogs and rich woods. Bulb edible.(2 polinnia)

G. HERBS
WITH NET-VEINED LEAVES

NETTLE Family

Annual or perennial herbs. Flowers small greenish in close bundle.

streams
mix.con.

184. HOARY NETTLE, *Urtica holosericea*. Perennial; **male and female flowers in separate clusters;** woolly. Stems whitish-rough-haired; leaves velvety; woolly-haired on underside. **Stinging hairs.** Low damp places below 9,000'.

BIRTHWORT Family

Low leafy stems or non-leafy vines with bitter tonic or stimulating properties.

str.wd.
dg.fir
pine
sitk.-spr.

*185. WESTERN WILD GINGER, *Asarum caudatum*. Stemless perennial herb often clustered from a slender aromatic branched rootstock. Roots thick, fibrous-fleshy; leaves long stemmed, **heart-shaped with smooth margin.** Flowers solitary, large and **brownish purple in color,** and borne near the ground. Common in woods below 5,000'. Rootstock dried and used as ginger.

BUCKWHEAT Family

brush
sage
sub.alp.
pine

*186. SULPHUR FLOWER, *Eriogonum umbellatum*. Perennial herb with spreading woody base. **The naked stems,** from 6-12" tall, bear umbels of numerous deep **sulphur yellow flowers** and leaf-like whorl of bracts. Leaves spatula-like ½-1" long,

HERBS

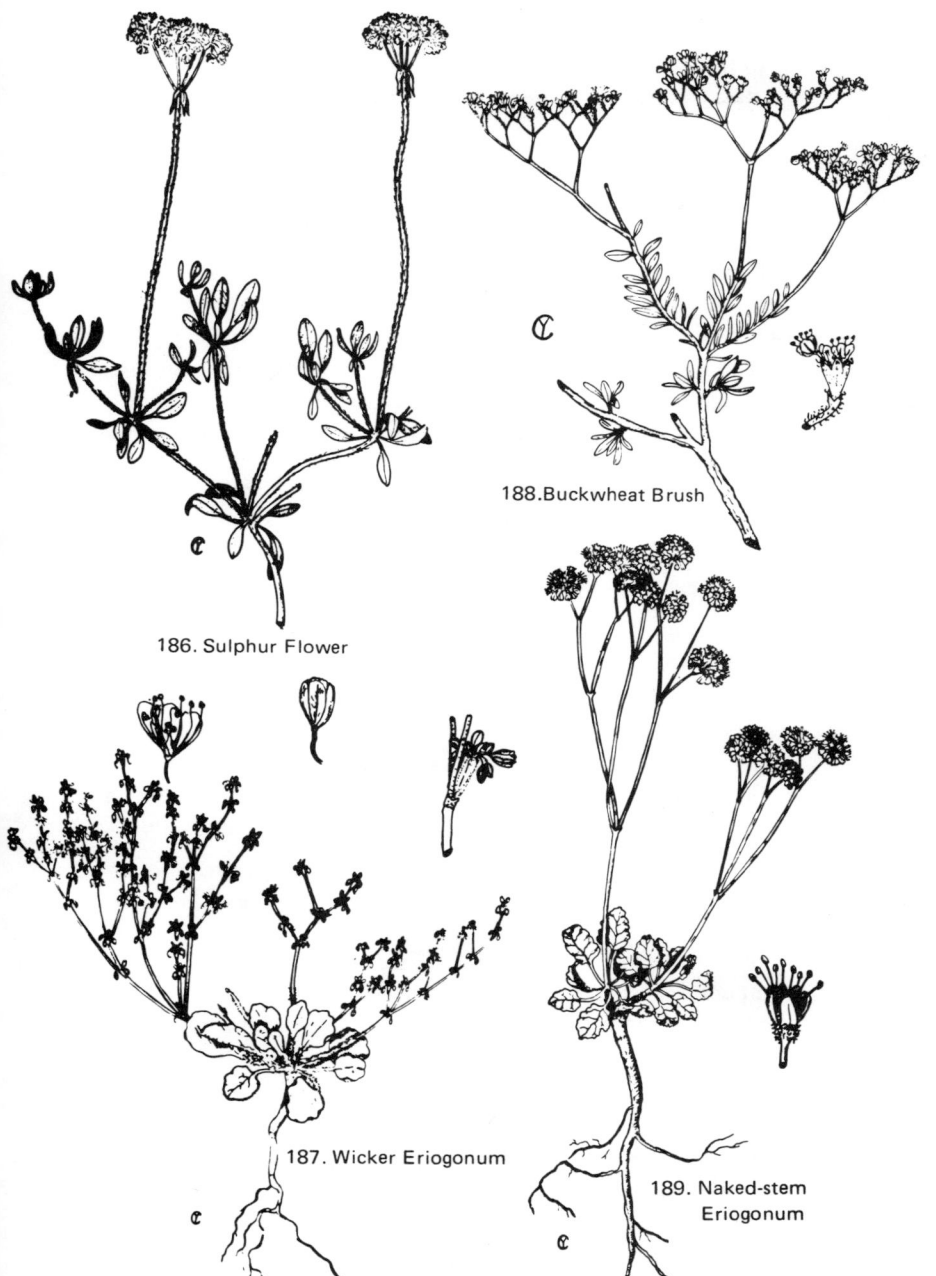

186. Sulphur Flower
187. Wicker Eriogonum
188. Buckwheat Brush
189. Naked-stem Eriogonum

densely white-woolly beneath, green above. *Eriogonum* species may be eaten raw or cooked before they have flowered.

*187. WICKER ERIOGONUM, *Eriogonum vimineum*. Annual plant with **leaves in a basal rosette**. Usually rather low, much branched from near the base, with rose-colored flowers. Dry hillsides and plains below 6,000'.

*188. BUCKWHEAT BRUSH, *Eriogonum microthecum*. Usually grows in large well-rounded bushes with umbels of **whitish flowers** which are above a **whorl of bracts**. **Bark is shreddy.** Dry sandy or rocky soil.

*189. NAKED-STEM ERIOGONUM, *Eriogonum latifolium nudum*. Perennial plant with tall usually hollow stems and spreading **broad basal leaves**. Flowers white some pink (or yellow above a whorl of bracts). Dry-rocky to 8,000'. Coast ranges. Many plant communities.

*190. VEINY DOCK, *Rumex venosus*. A showy sturdy plant 1-2' tall, often growing on sandy banks. **Leaves are smooth blue green** from 3-5" long. The inconspicuous deep rose-colored flowers develop **enormous greenish seeds that later turn to yellow, pink, red and brown.** Edible leaf and leaf stems.

*191. WESTERN BISTORT, *Polygonum bistortoides*. Herb with broadish base leaves and a few stem leaves. Stems to 3' high. Leaves dark green above and smooth beneath. Flowers white or pinkish in an oblong spike. **Stamens slightly protruding beyond petals.** Wet places – 5,000-10,000'. Starchy roots are edible.

192. ALPINE KNOTWEED, *Polygonum phytolaccaefolium*. A bushy, smooth stout perennial 3-6' high, rather fleshy lance-like to oval leaves. 1-6" long and about 1½" wide, all on the stem. **Flowers white to greenish-white.** Flowers in nearly leafless compound cluster. Found in moist and rocky places from 5,000-9,000' elevation in Cascades and Klamath Mountains.

193. NEWBERRY'S KNOTWEED, *Polygonum Newberryi*. Herbage dull green, fleshy and covered with bran-like scales; stems in clumps, more or less spreading; leaves about 2" long and about as broad. Flowers few in leafless joint clusters. A characteristic plant of the pumice fields in southern Oregon Cascades. **In the fall this plant turns a bright red.**

194. SWAMP KNOTWEED, *Polygonum coccineum*. Plant

HERBS

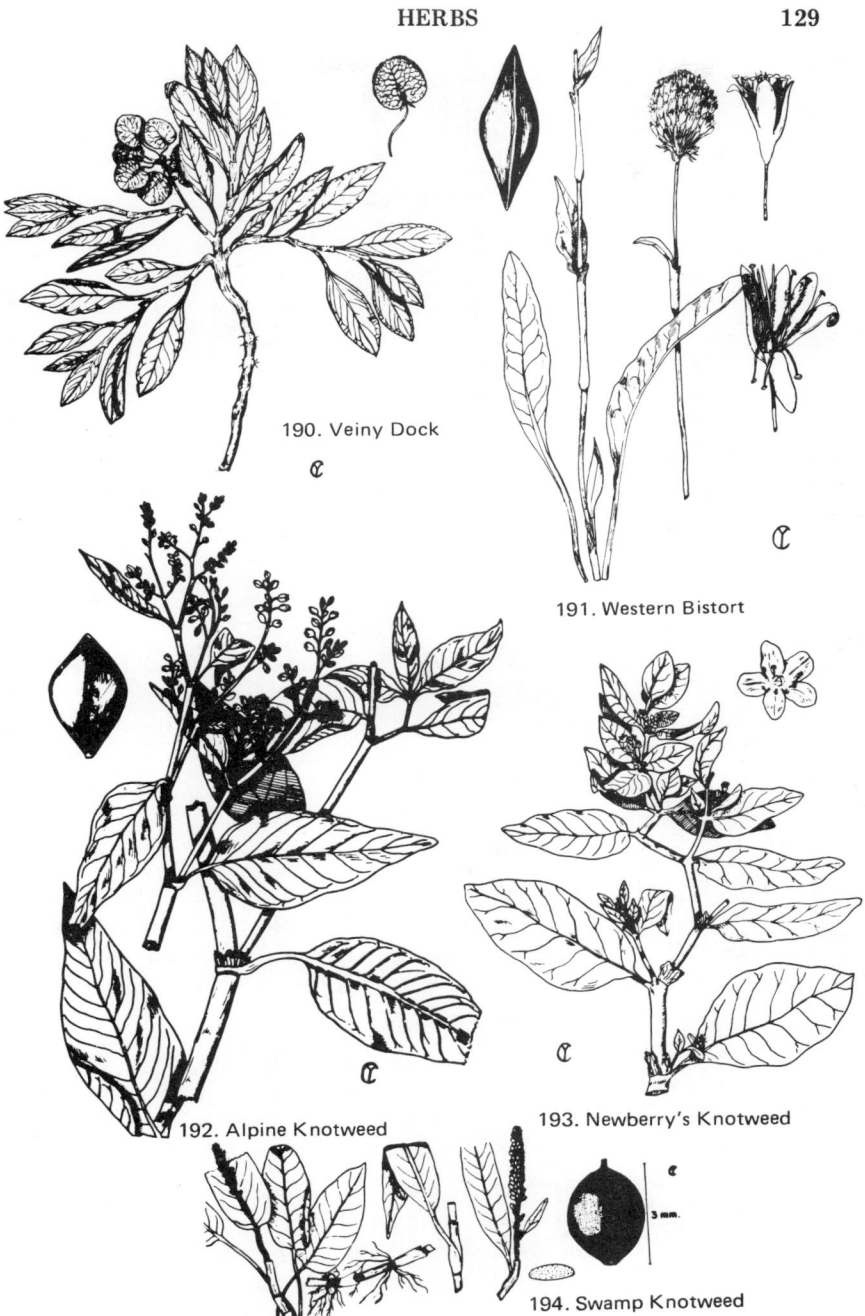

190. Veiny Dock
191. Western Bistort
192. Alpine Knotweed
193. Newberry's Knotweed
194. Swamp Knotweed

WILDLIFE AND PLANTS OF THE CASCADES

water   with tall stems, large pointed leaves and a spike **of red flowers**. Terrestial but in and about ponds to B. C.

GOOSEFOOT Family
Scurfy (covered with bran-like scales) or fleshy plants.

195. PIGWEED or WHITE GOOSEFOOT, *Chenopodium*

cult.   *album*. Naturalized weed of roadsides. 1-4' tall bush with erect grooved stem. Smooth below but often granular above; foliage pale to bright green, leaves toothed or almost smooth on edge, ¾-2½" long. **Small round greenish flowers** usually in small dense spikes. Seeds black shining.

196. RUSSIAN THISTLE, *Salsola Kali* var. *tenuifolia*.

cult.
sage
conif.   Troublesome introduced **tumble-weed type of** plant with bracts broad-based with **stiff flaring reddish, spine-tips**. 1-3' high. Abundant in fallow fields. Seeds black and shining.

PURSLANE Family
Herbs more or less fleshy.

197. HEART-LEAVED MONTIA. *Montia Cordifolia*. Leaves

str.wd.
dg.fir
pine
red fir   fleshy round or heart-shaped, flower stem arising from two opposite leaves. Plant 4-12" high. Flowers white; 4-9 on a stem. Along streams and wet places; 3,500-7,000'.

PINK Family
Nodes on stems and opposite leaves.

198a. PUMICE SANDWORT, *Arenaria pumicola*. Grows in

pume.
lodg.   little tufts or dense clumps, herb about 6" high with **basal leaves thread-like** and **stem leaves paired**. Flowers single, white. Abundant in open pumice areas at Crater Lake.

198b. SANDWORT, *Arenaria macrophylla*. (Not illustrated.)

pine
red fir
mix.ev.   Perennial herb; stems lying down with tips turned up, leaves lance-like to thinner bright green. Flowers small and white, in a cluster at the end of stem, sometimes solitary. 1,500-6,500'. Coast Range, Cascades, California to British Columbia.

199. CALIFORNIA INDIAN PINK, *Silene Californica*. Peren-

pine
brush
mix.ev.   nial herb with stems hairy; from one stout taproot, erect or lying down; 5-15" high. **Leaves oval to elliptical in pairs** and 3½" long. Flowers solitary or few-flowered clusters; **petals crimson** 4-clefted or lobed, the middle lobe broader. Open woods below 5,000'.

HERBS

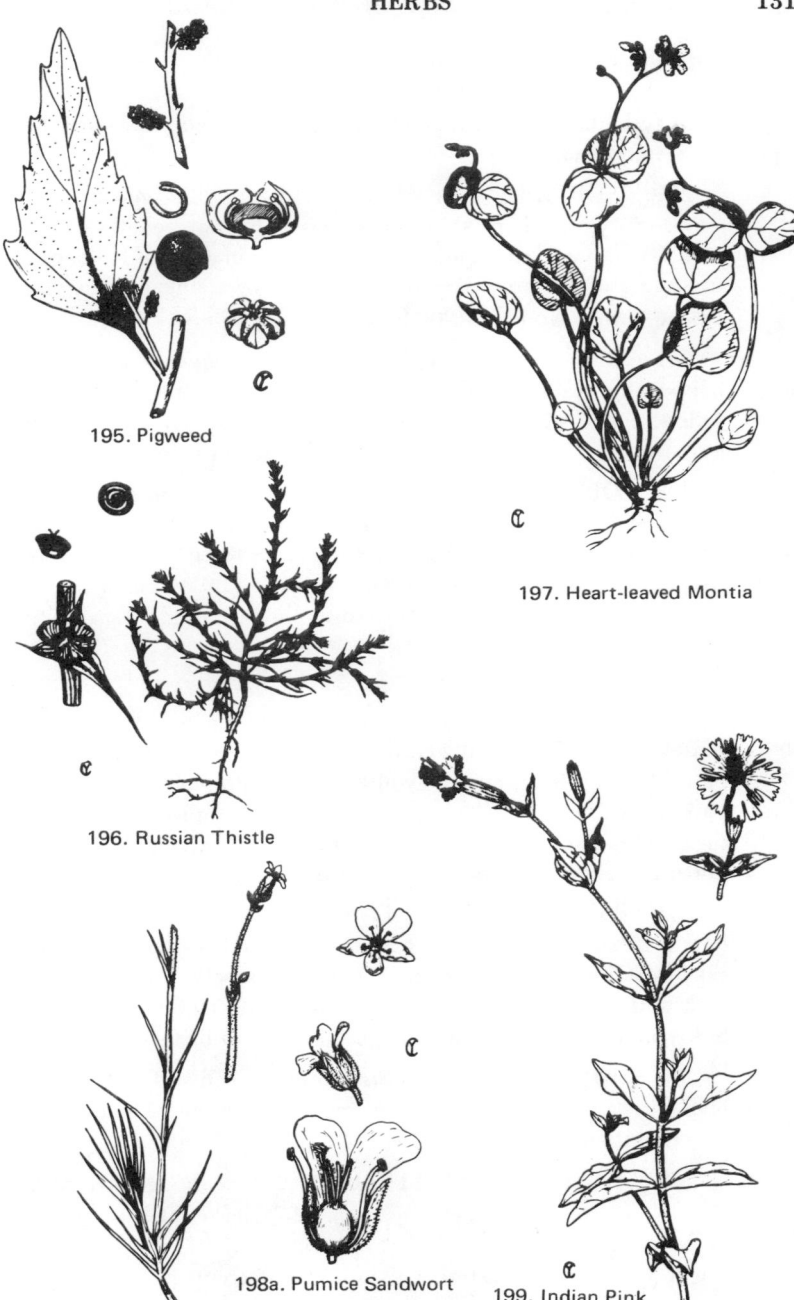

195. Pigweed

197. Heart-leaved Montia

196. Russian Thistle

198a. Pumice Sandwort

199. Indian Pink

CROWFOOT Family

Petals may be lacking and sepals petal-like; sepal and petals may be spurred. Stamens many.

conif.
jun.

200. NORTHWEST CRIMSON COLUMBINE, *Aquilegia formosa.* Stems 1-3' high, shiny smooth, openly branched. Leaves at base few, above, all variously lobed with rounded teeth. **Sepals and spurs of flowers red—other part yellow—stamens and styles extend.** Moist woods. 4,000-9,000'.

brush
mix.ev.
pine

201. RED LARKSPUR, *Delphinium nudicaule.* Plant 8-30" tall with typical irregular larkspur type flowers. **Sepals red; petals yellow tipped with red.** Occurs in the Transition Life Zone down into the sage communities of southern Oregon and South Calif.

pine
mix.ev.

202. COLUMBIA WINDFLOWER, *Anemone deltoidea.* Erect perennial herb, 6-12" tall, from slender running roots, **flowers single** and sepals 5/8-1" long. **Arising from three leaflets (toothed).** Found in dry forests usually below 6,000'. Inland southwestern California to Siskiyou County north through Cascades to British Columbia.

mix.ev.
sitk.-spr.

203. WOOD ANEMONE, *Anemone quinquefolia* var *Grayi.* This anemone differs from; *A. deltoidea* in having a **whorl of 3 leaflets just below the flower,** but the stem is ½-1½" long. The sepals 3/8-5/8" long, may be **white, tinged with purple, or blue or pink in var. oregana.** This species is found in moist woods, near the coast in California, and var. *oregana* in the Siskiyou Mountains, north to Washington mainly east of Cascade crest.

conif.
rocks

204. PASQUE FLOWER, *Anemone occidentalis.* Stem with long soft hairs, leaves at base consisting of three leaflets, also with silky soft hairs, **flowers solitary; petal-like sepals, white-purplish with soft hairs.** Dry rocky slopes from 5,500-10,000' elevation, Siskiyou Mountains north through Cascades to British Columbia.

brush
jun.
mix.con.

205. MOUSE-TAIL, *Myosurus aristatus.* A dwarf plant, 2-4" high, with a tuft of slender leaves and **a narrow spike-like head of very minute white flowers.** Moist places; 4,500-7,000'.

sage

206. SAGEBRUSH BUTTERCUP, *Ranunculus glaberrimus.* Numerous roots, large reclining stems; 2-7" leaves at base, round to oval, thick leaves on stem. Sepals lavender tinged, petals 5— bright yellow. This attractive smooth buttercup is one of the earliest spring flowers on the open hillsides in the lower foothills.

HERBS 133

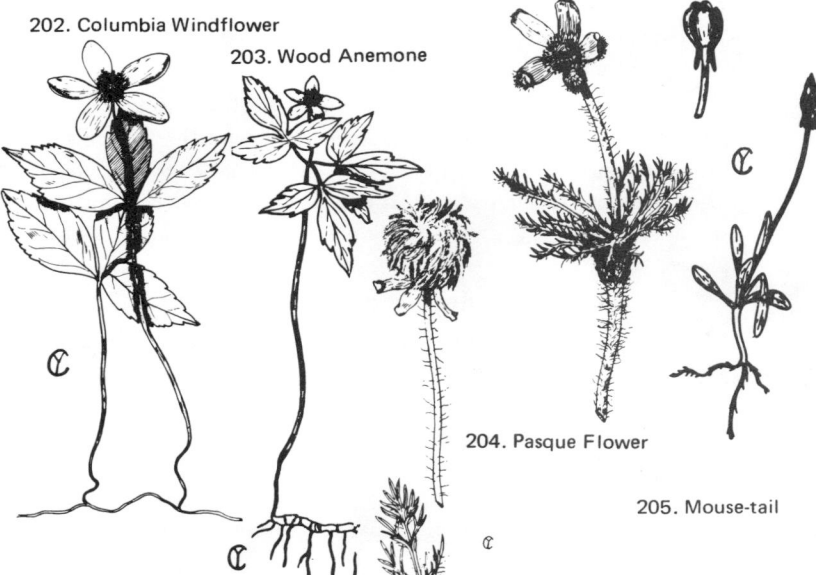

200. Northwest Crimson Columbine
201. Red Larkspur 
202. Columbia Windflower
203. Wood Anemone
204. Pasque Flower
205. Mouse-tail

BARBERRY Family (In part, see 74, 75)

207. **DEER-FOOT or VANILLA LEAF,** *Achlys triphylla.*
Perennial herb with branching scaly creeping rootstock. Leaf solitary; large, 3-parted and long stemmed. **The bractless, flowers are borne on a 1-2" spike.** Fruit reddish tinge but does not split open; becomes dry, broadly moon shaped at maturity. Confined to moist areas in upland forests, north to British Columbia, usually below 5,000'.

dg. fir
pine
mix.ev.
sitk.-spr.

208. **INSIDE-OUT-FLOWER,** *Vancouveria hexandra.* **Perennial delicate stemmed herb** from creeping rootstalk; leaves near base 2 or 3 leaves together of **a 3-lobed leaf;** broadly oval; heart-shaped at base. **White flowers in a loose cluster.** Petal 6, bent downward. Found in shaded areas below 5,000' elevation from northwestern California to Washington.

str.wd.
dg. fir
mix.ev.

POPPY Family

209. **CALIFORNIA POPPY,** *Eschscholtzia californica.* A thick, branching taproot. Stems 8-20". This **showy poppy** which may be **yellow or orange** occurs in the southern Cascades in the Transition and Upper Sonoran zones. Grassy and open places up to 6,500'.

many hab.
grass.

MUSTARD Family

Sepals 4, petals 4, stamens mostly 6.

210. **TUMBLE MUSTARD,** *Sisymbrium altissimum.* This is a common tall tumble weed of disturbed areas in the foothills on the east side of the Cascades. **Petals yellowish white. Stems of flowers stout,** to almost ½" thick, nearly as thick as the fruit; silique (seed cases) widely spreading, rigid, 2-4" long. Waste places.

sage
cult.

SAXIFRAGE Family (In part, see bushes 76, etc.)

211. **ALPINE SAXIFRAGE,** *Saxifraga Tolmiei.* Perennial herb, densely tufted, leafy stems short and branched, nearly prostrate; **spatulate leaves leathery, evergreen,** and smooth margined. Flower stems erect, leafless, 2-4" high, glandular, 1-6 flowered. Petals white and twice as long as the sepals. Abundant along streams and wet areas at 6,000' elevations in Cascades. Moist, rocky places, 8,500-11,000', Siskiyou Mountains and Cascades to Alaska.

lodg.
rocks
alp.

HERBS

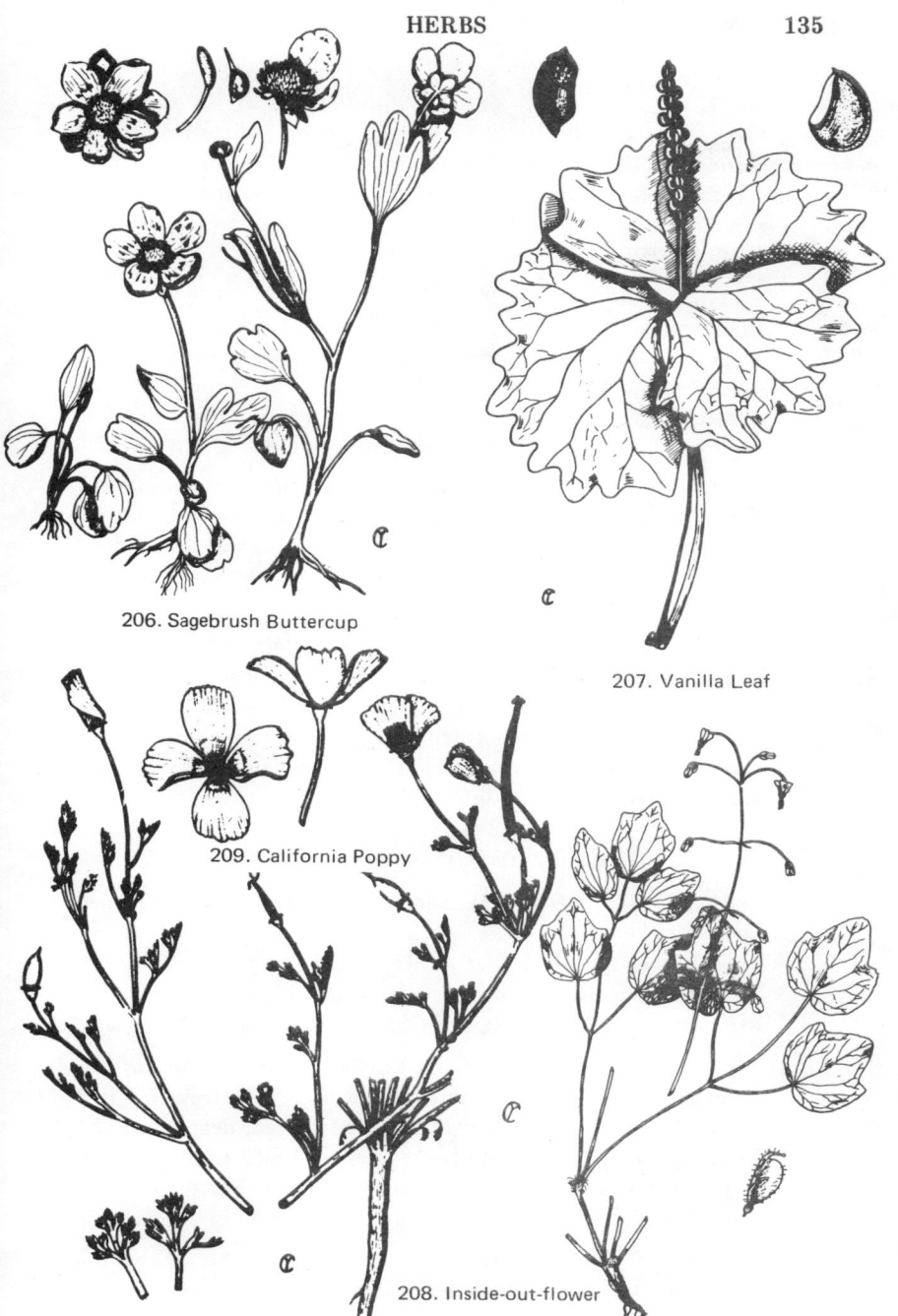

206. Sagebrush Buttercup

207. Vanilla Leaf

209. California Poppy

208. Inside-out-flower

212. COOLWORT or SUGAR-SCOOP, *Tiarella unifoliata.*
Stem 1 to several, 10-20" tall; **basal leaves 3-5 lobed, heart-shaped,** toothed, sparsely hairy, long petioled; stem leaves few, short petioled; flowers small, white, **borne in narrow, elongated panicle;** fruit a capsule with unequal parts. Moist shady woods, north to British Columbia.

str.wd.
mix.con.
lodg.

213. YOUTH-ON-AGE, *Tolmiea Menziesii.* Stems clustered from **woody** base. Stems of basal leaves hairy, blades heart-shaped, 3-lobed and toothed. Leaves on flowering branches, similar but smaller. Calyx of flower long, cup shaped, **greenish veined, tinged with dark red-purple with petals of brown.** Stamens extend slightly. Moist places below 6,000'.

mix.ev.
red fir
dg. fir
str.wd.

214. OVAL-LEAVED ALUM ROOT, *Heuchera ovalifolia.*
This herb has small 5-stamened, **bell-like, yellowish-white flowers** in a spike-like cluster on rather tall, leafless stems, surrounded at the base by **roundish leaves.** Grows in tufts or dense clumps. Common in pine woods.

jun.
red fir
rocks

215. YERBA DE SELVA, *Whipplea modesta.* **Trailing, partly woody** herb with weak, slender branches; leaves deciduous, opposite, ovate, and slightly toothed; **small white flowers** in small crowded clusters located terminally. Found in Klamath Mountains, Oregon, on shaded slopes below 5,000', and on south in coast ranges of California.

mix.ev.
dg.fir
str.wd.
pine

ROSE Family (In part, see bushes 88, etc.)

216. PARTRIDGEFOOT, *Luetkea pectinata.* Luetkea, named for a Russian Commander of an arctic exploration expedition, is a low, woody plant that grows in **turf-like tufts or patches.** The finely cut leaves and the short stems which terminate in an attractive raceme of small, white flowers distinguish this plant.

red fir
sub.alp.

217. MT. RAINIER CINQUEFOIL, *Potentilla flabellifolia.*
Stems slender, 6-12" high, minutely hairy. Base leaves, 3 in a group, with very thin stems. **Leaves fan shaped, deeply cut and toothed.** Few flower clusters, **petals yellow,** to 3/8" long. Found in moist conditions, Siskiyou Mountains north to British Columbia.

red fir
alp.

*218. STICKY CINQUEFOIL or GLANDULAR FIVE-FINGER, *Potentilla glandulosa.* 1-2' tall spreading herb covered with

HERBS

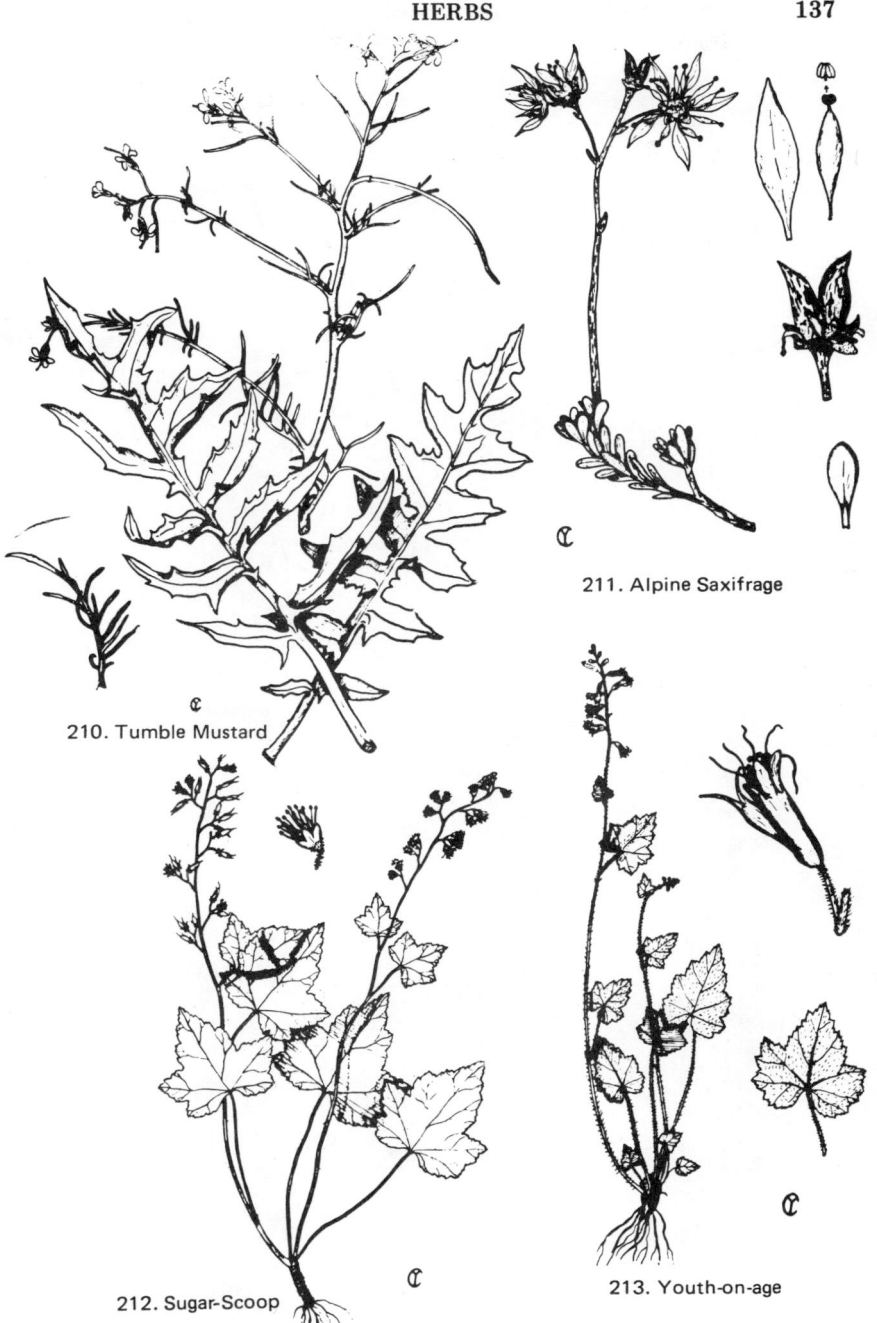

210. Tumble Mustard
211. Alpine Saxifrage
212. Sugar-Scoop
213. Youth-on-age

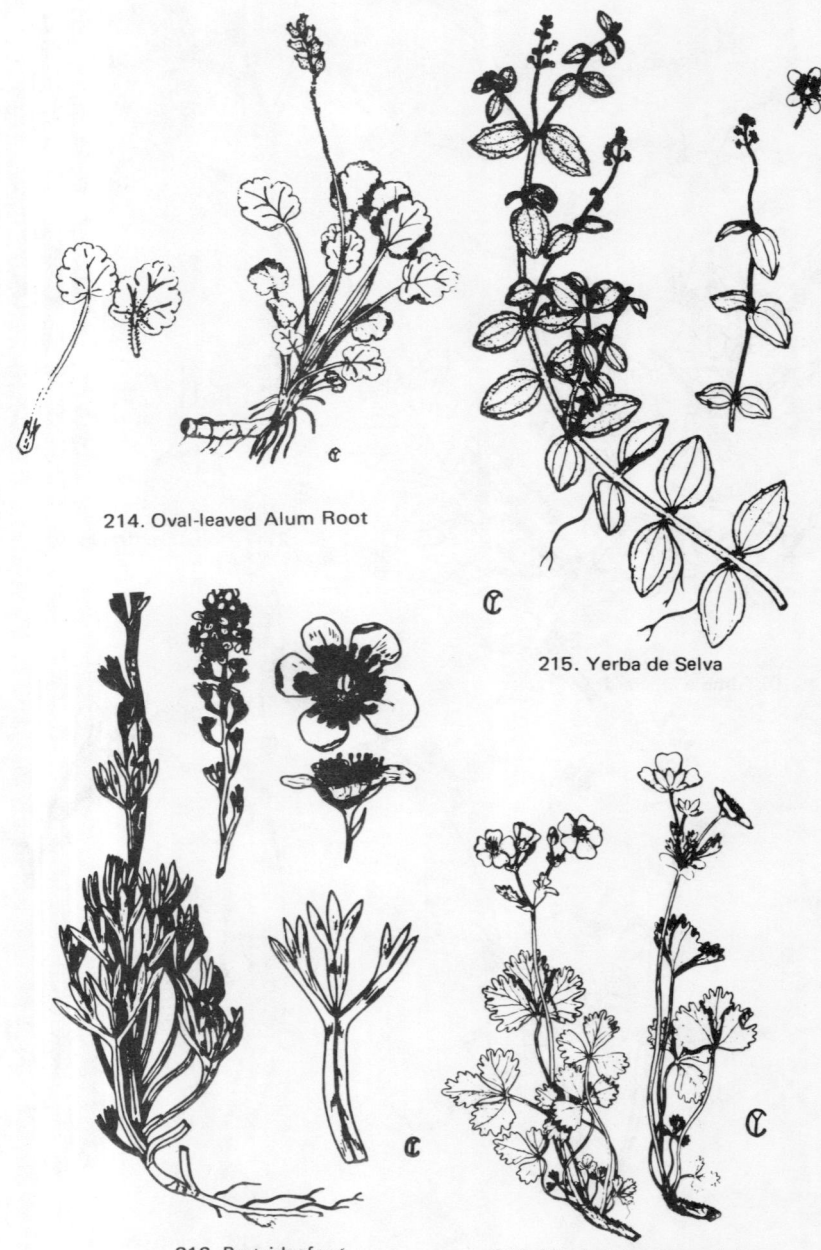

214. Oval-leaved Alum Root

215. Yerba de Selva

216. Partridgefoot

217. Mt. Rainier Cinquefoil

HERBS

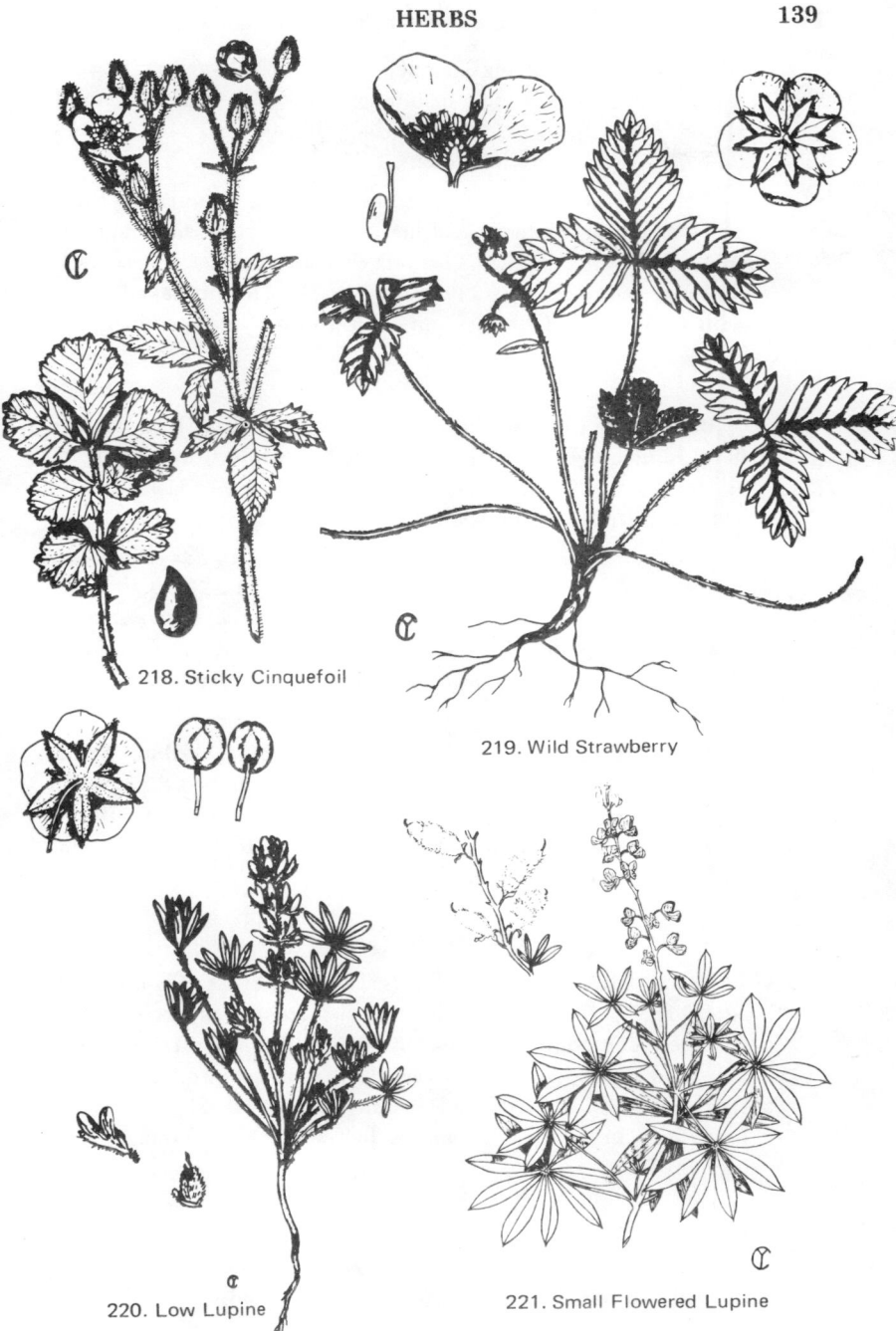

218. Sticky Cinquefoil

219. Wild Strawberry

220. Low Lupine

221. Small Flowered Lupine

140 WILDLIFE AND PLANTS OF THE CASCADES

many hab.
sticky hairs and bearing an open cluster of **pale-yellow flowers.** Lower leaves 4-12" long including stems; 5-9 leaflets, smooth above, hairy beneath, 25 stamens. Roots boiled or roasted. Cascades to British Columbia.

mix.ev.
dg. fir
str.wd.
*219. STRAWBERRY, *Fragaria vesca* var. *bracteata*. Rootstock thick on this perennial herb, propagates by runners; leaves thin, **silky when young**, 3-leaflets that are obovate and coarsely toothed. Flowers white, borne in loose cluster on naked stems, with single bract. Clearings and open woods. Berries edible.

PEA Family

grass
220. LOW LUPINE, *Lupinus subvexus*. Annual, low-growing, hairy lupine, 6-16". Flowers **dark violet purple to rose pink,** ½-¾" long. Seeds rough, dark brown. Northeastern California to southern Oregon below 2,500'.

sage
brush
jun.
pine
221. SMALL FLOWERED LUPINE, *Lupinus argenteus*. Stems erect, branched, hairless to nearly silky; 12-20" tall; leaves compound palmate, leaflets 6-10; calyx 2-lipped; **flowers small, 1/4-3/8" long,** purplish-blue, borne in racemes 3½-7" long. Fruit a densely hairy pod (legume). Hillsides, banks, and open slopes.

conif.
*222. VETCH, *Vicia americana*. **Climbing, trailing,** herbaceous vine; leaves pinnate, tendril-bearing; leaflets 4-8 pairs; 4-8 flowered. **Flowers purple-violet.** In open places from California north to British Columbia usually below 5,000'. Young stems and tender seeds good boiled or baked.

GERANIUM Family

many hab.
cult.
*223. CRANE-BILL or RED-STEM FILAREE, *Erodium circutarium*. Weedy introduced biennial from a tap root; **leaves pinnately compound and divided deeply;** flowering stems sprawling, bent at the nodes; flowers deep pink to purple, petals 5, stamens 10, 5 united seed bearing cases with styles forming **long beak in fruit.** Dry places below 6,000'. Young plants used in salads.

WOOD SORREL Family

*224. REDWOOD SORREL, *Oxalis oregana*. Stems, bearing one white or pinkish flower, purple veined, 5/8-7/8" long.

HERBS

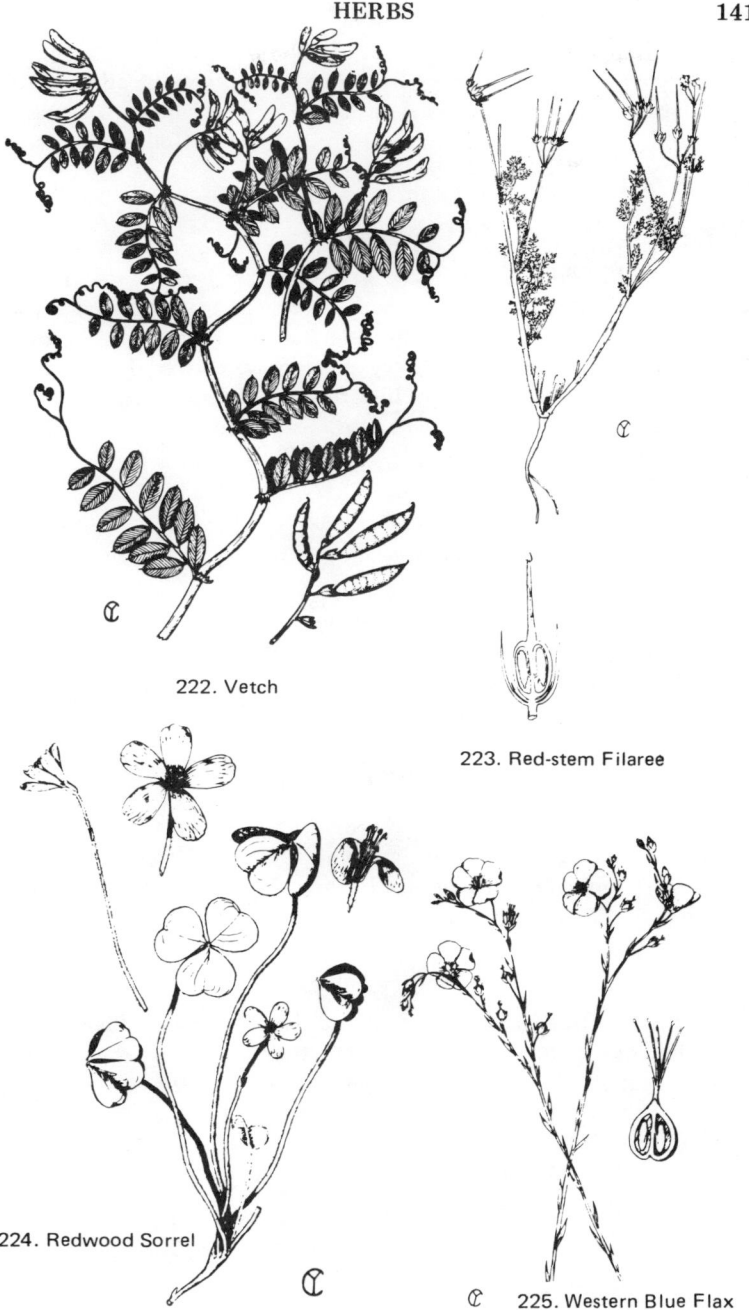

222. Vetch

223. Red-stem Filaree

224. Redwood Sorrel

225. Western Blue Flax

mix.ev.
str.wd.
dg. fir

Leaves many, the stems rusty, long haired, basal; leaflets mostly heart-shaped. Found in deep shade on west side of Washington and Oregon and on south into California Redwood Forests. Leaves and stems edible.

FLAX Family

mix.con.
jun.
mt.mead.

*225. WESTERN BLUE FLAX, *Linum perenne* ssp. *Lewisii.* Stems 8-24" tall with a woody base, simple below and usually branched above; leaves alternate, narrow ½-1" long. Flowers blue, ¾-1" wide, **very showy in a coarse cluster;** fruit a round capsule. **Flowers blossom in early morning and drop petals soon after.** Foothills and middle altitudes. Seeds roasted, dried, and ground.

VIOLET Family

pine
dg. fir
mix.con.

226. YELLOW WOOD VIOLET, *Viola lobata.* Plants arising from shallow rootstocks, 3-8" high. Basal leaves have slender stems, the leaf blades are heart-shaped at base and deeply parted into 3 to several divisions 1-3¼" long. **Flowers yellow, the upper-part brown on the outer surface.** Petals ½-¾" long. Dry slopes and open woods 1,000-6,500'.

EVENING-PRIMROSE Family

brush
sage
lodg.

227. PINNATIFIED SUN-CUP, *Oenothera tanacetifolia.* Grows lying flat on the ground, whorl-like from a tap root. Leaves pinnately divided, to 4" long; **flower petals yellow, aging red,** 3/8-6/8" long. Moist open places.

LOOSA Family

rocks
many hab.

228. BLAZING STAR, *Mentzelia laevicaulis.* Plant coarse **and rough; stem 1-3½" tall,** very stout, branching above; leaves lance-shaped to ovate lance-shaped, wavy toothed to pinnatified, rough-hairy; flowers showy, **bright yellow, large up to 3"** across; stamens yellow, many, conspicuously longer at outer edge. In dry disturbed gravelly and stony places, below 8,500'. Many plant communities.

DOGWOOD Family (In part, see 68, 123, 124)

*229. BUNCHBERRY, *Cornus canadensis.* Perennial herb

HERBS

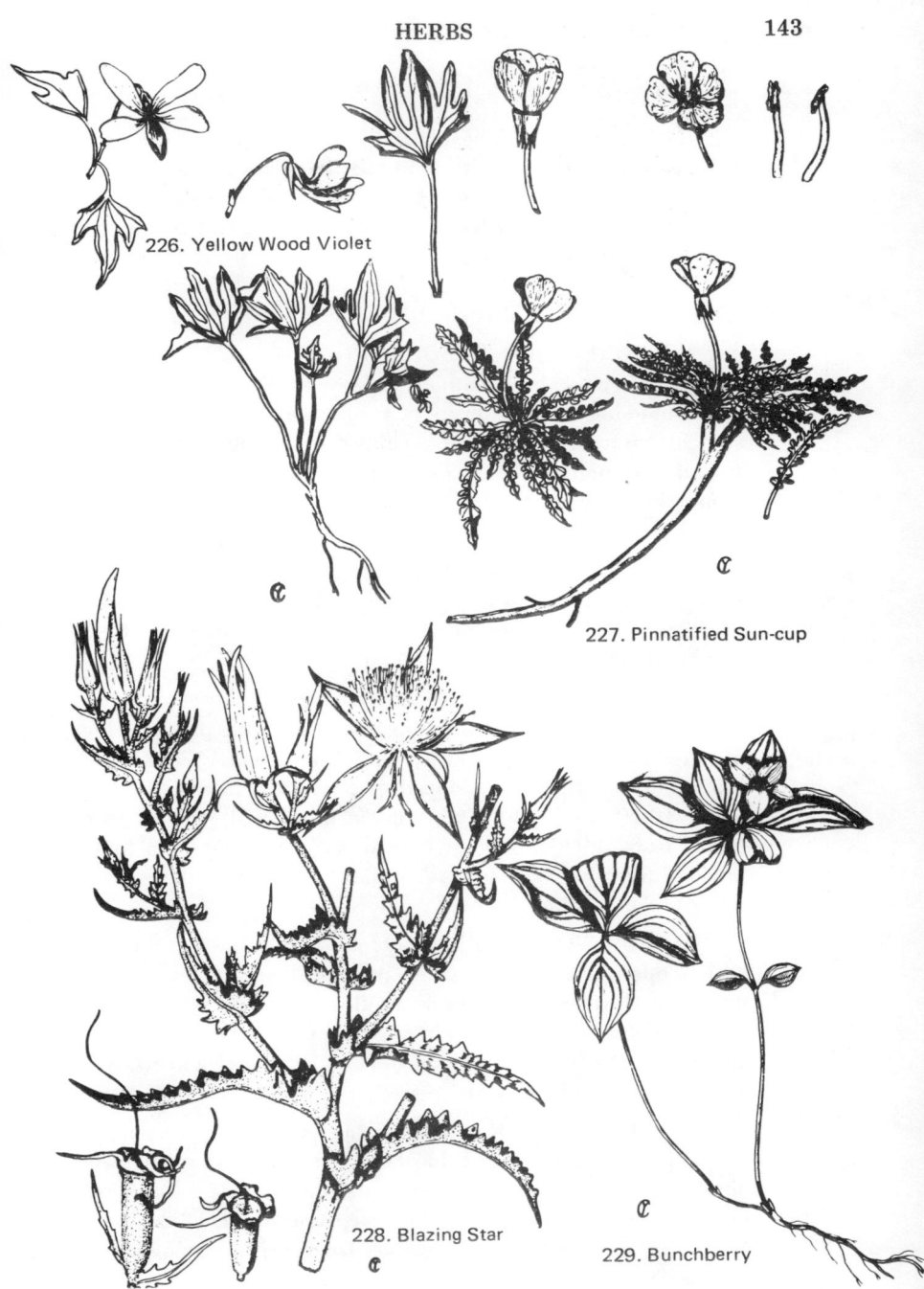

226. Yellow Wood Violet
227. Pinnatified Sun-cup
228. Blazing Star
229. Bunchberry

3-8" high; **flowers are 4 ovate bracts, white,** about ¾" long above
a 4-6 whorl of leaves; **fruit bright red.** Rootstocks woody; stems
scaly below; leaves ovate or oblong. Moist places usually below
3,500', coastal areas in Redwood Forest; north to Cascades and
British Columbia. Fruit edible.

dg. fir
str.wd.
mix.ev.

WINTERGREEN Family

230. ONE-SIDED PYROLA, *Pyrola secunda.* Low and
smooth perennial herb with basal, woody, evergreen, roundish
leaves; nodding white flowers in a simple raceme. The style is
straight. **Racemes one-sided.** Timberline in southern Washington and common in the Siskiyou Mountains in the Klamath
Mountain Province. Shaded woods.

dg. fir
red fir
sub.alp.

231a. WHITE-VEINED WINTERGREEN, *Pyrola picta.* In
P. picta the style is **curved downward** and the **veins of the leaves
have a white border** and often purple beneath. 10-20 flowers
on racemes, petals green to cream. Common plant in the Siskiyou Mountains and Klamath Mountain Province.

pine
lodg.

231b. LEAFLESS PYROLA, *Pyrola picta, Forma aphylla.*
(Not illustrated.) Stems 8-16" tall, erect, the **entire plant** (including flowers) **red** or occasionally with 1 or 2 small green leaves.
Rootstocks stout; **leaves reduced to small, thin bracts.** Raceme
loose, 10-30 flowered. Style curved downward. *Pyrola picta*
found from 3,000-9,500' in Cascades; *Forma aphylla* is found
below 7,500' in Northern California, Southwestern Oregon on
to British Columbia.

pine
red fir
dg. fir.

232. BOG WINTERGREEN, *Pyrola asarifolia.* (Not illustrated.) In this species, the flowers are **dull red,** the ovate leaves basal,
green and leathery; **racemes many flowered.** The style is also
curved downward. Common in southern Washington and Oregon
and also in the southwestern Oregon Cascade Range and Siskiyou
Mountains. In moist, swampy places.

pine
dg. fir
mix.con.

233. SUGAR STICK, *Allotropa virgata.* A plant of remarkable appearance. **Reddish chlorophyll-less herb** with **many scale-like leaves;** flowers without petals in a spike; sepals 5, roundish,
persistent; ovary 5-celled. Stem simple, stout, erect, 12-20" high.
Found in open rather dark woods from British Columbia to
California; from 2,000-10,000'.

dg. fir
pine
sub.alp.

HERBS

230. One-sided Pyrola

231. White-veined Wintergreen

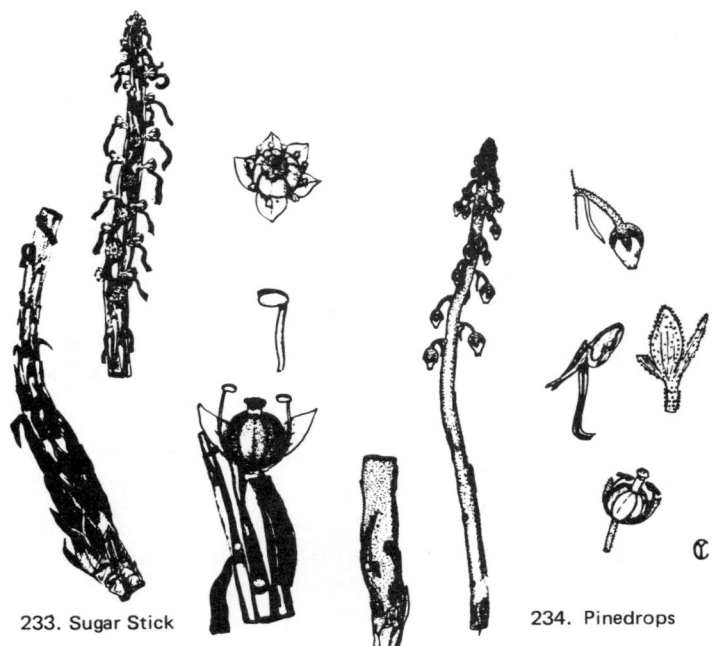

233. Sugar Stick

234. Pinedrops

146   WILDLIFE AND PLANTS OF THE CASCADES

pine
red fir
mix.con.

234. PINEDROPS, *Pterospora andromedea*. Stout, simple, **purplish-brown,** clammy-downy, root-parasitic herb without chlorophyll; **stem wand-like,** with scattered long, thin scales toward the base in place of leaves. Flowers many, nodding, white, in a long bracted raceme, urn-shaped. Found in humus of forests, 2,600-8,500', north through Cascades to British Columbia.

pine
lodg.
dg. fir

235. SNOW PLANT, *Sarcodes sanguinea*. Red **fleshy, downy saprophyte;** stem simple, single or in clusters. Leaves scale-like, long and narrow. Flowers numerous in a stout spike-like raceme, **red above red bracts.** Flower bell-shaped and 5-lobed. Found in rich humus soil 4,000-8,000' in northern California and southwestern Oregon.

DOGBANE Family

pine
red fr
dg. fir

236. SPREADING DOGBANE, *Apocynum androsaemifolium*. Small **shrub-like herb** with milky juice 8-18" high; leaves paired, drooping, ovalish 1-3½" long; flowers small, **pinkish, bell-like.** Common in dry flats and woods and exposed areas at timberline.

rocks
pine
red fir
dg. fir

237. CYCLADENIA, *Cycladenia humilis*. Has short stems flat on the ground, the large roundish leaves are smooth and leathery; **flowers funnel-formed, deep rose colored** nearly an inch long; the large fleshy root penetrates deeply into cinders and pumice. The conspicuous and interesting plant is found on the exposed slopes of cinder cones in Lava Beds National Monument.

PHLOX Family (In part, see 147)

mix.con.
rocks

238. SCARLET GILIA, *Gilia aggregata*. 1-2" high biennial; stems erect, branched from base; leaves pinnated, very thin; flowers tubular, **funnel-formed, bright red** with yellow mottling, ¾-1½" long. Open places, rocky ridges, 3,500-10,000'.

WATERLEAF Family

rocks
red fir

239. PURPLE FRINGE, *Phacelia sericea*. **Perennial herb,** stem ½-1' high; leafy; leaves silky-downy, pinnate, with many narrow lobes; flowers **in a dense spike-like cyme, violet.** Found at timberline, 7,000-8,500', from northern California to British Columbia; in Cascades and Olympic Mountains. A very attractive species.

HERBS

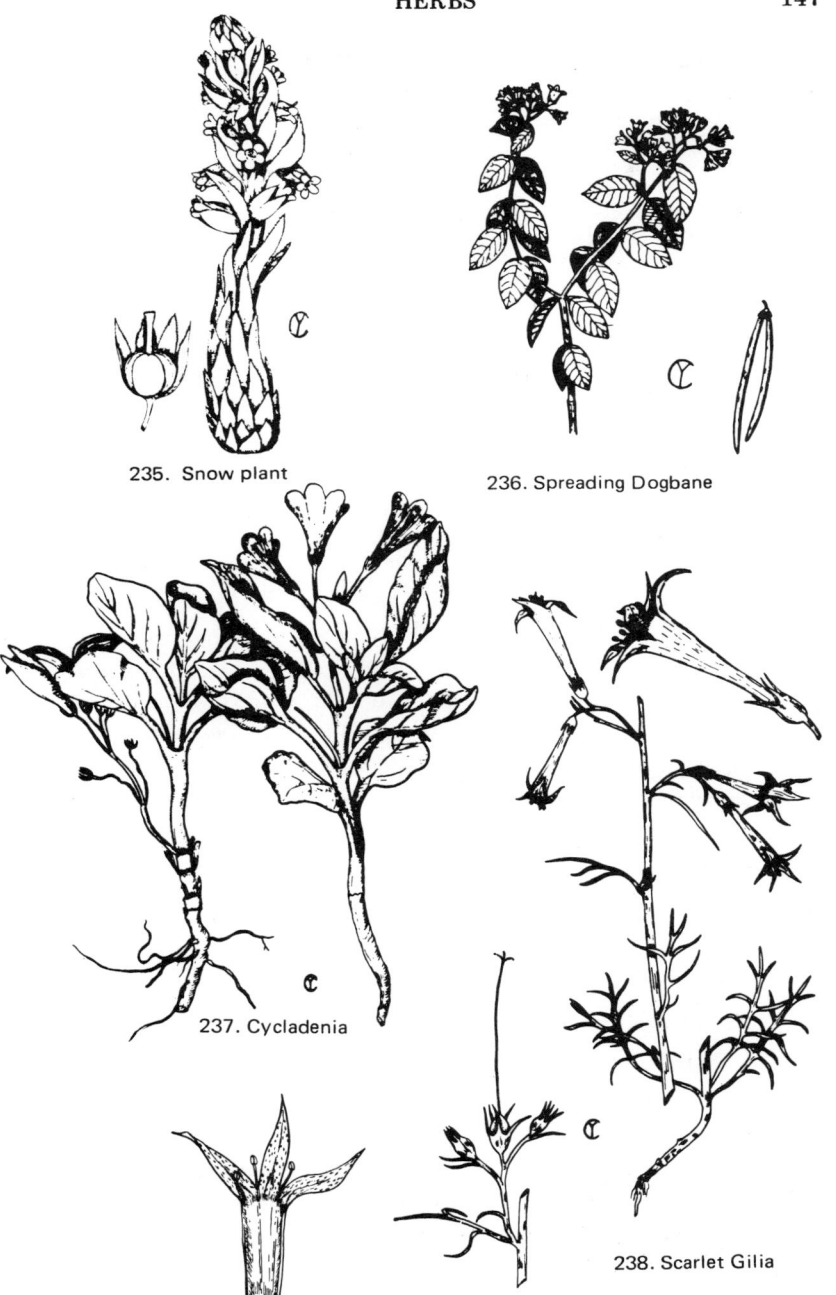

235. Snow plant

236. Spreading Dogbane

237. Cycladenia

238. Scarlet Gilia

148   WILDLIFE AND PLANTS OF THE CASCADES

sage
jun.
pine
red fir

240a. SILVERLEAF PHACELIA, *Phacelia hastata*. Perennial with pinnate leaves; has a small pair of leaflets at the base of the leaf, silvery; **flowers large, bell-like, in spike-like coils,** white to lavender covered with fine white hairs. Found in California north to British Columbia.

red fir
pine
jun.
rocks

240b. VIRGATE PHACELIA, *Phacelia heterophylla*. (Not illustrated.) Biennial or possibly perennial herb; **grayish-green foliage,** stems mostly solitary, simple, coarse, erect, 1-4' high, covered with hairs; **flowers yellow** to greenish white in dense elongated cyme-like spike; leaves with parallel side veins, lower leaflets paired. Found below 7,000'.

MINT Family (In part, see 146)

cult.

*241. COMMON HOREHOUND, *Marrubium vulgare*. Herb 8-24" tall, leaves roundish, margin teeth roundish, white woolly above, hairy beneath; flowers white in dense leaf base cluster, whorl-form around stem. Roadside and waste places. Native of Europe. Dried plant a nutritious tonic.

many hab.
mix.con.

*242. NETTLE-LEAVED HORSE-MINT, *Agastache urticifolia*. Stems several from base, 1-6' tall. Blade ovate, 1-3" long, coarsely toothed. Flowers compact, tapering clusters, petal tube greenish, lobes rose colored. Moist places below 9,000'. California plants usually more downy. Seeds eaten raw or cooked.

sage
mix.con.
sub.alp.
pine
jun.

243. MOUNTAIN MONARDELLA, *Monardella odoratissima*. Plant ½-1' high, woody at base, **paired leaves oblong to thinner,** ½ to just over 1" long, green, short downy hairs by base; flowers pale purple, head 5/8" long, calyx wool-downy. Transition and Canadian Zones. Dry slopes.

NIGHTSHADE Family

mix.con.
brush
grass

244. COYOTE TOBACCO, *Nicotiana attenuata*. Erect simple or branching annual 1-3' high, glandular downy. Leaves with leaf stem oval to narrower; flowers a raceme with a white, long **bell-like star-shaped** top 1-1¼" long. Disturbed places below 8,500', many places and communities.

FIGWORT Family

245. LEWIS' MONKEY-FLOWER, *Mimulus Lewisii*. Herb

HERBS

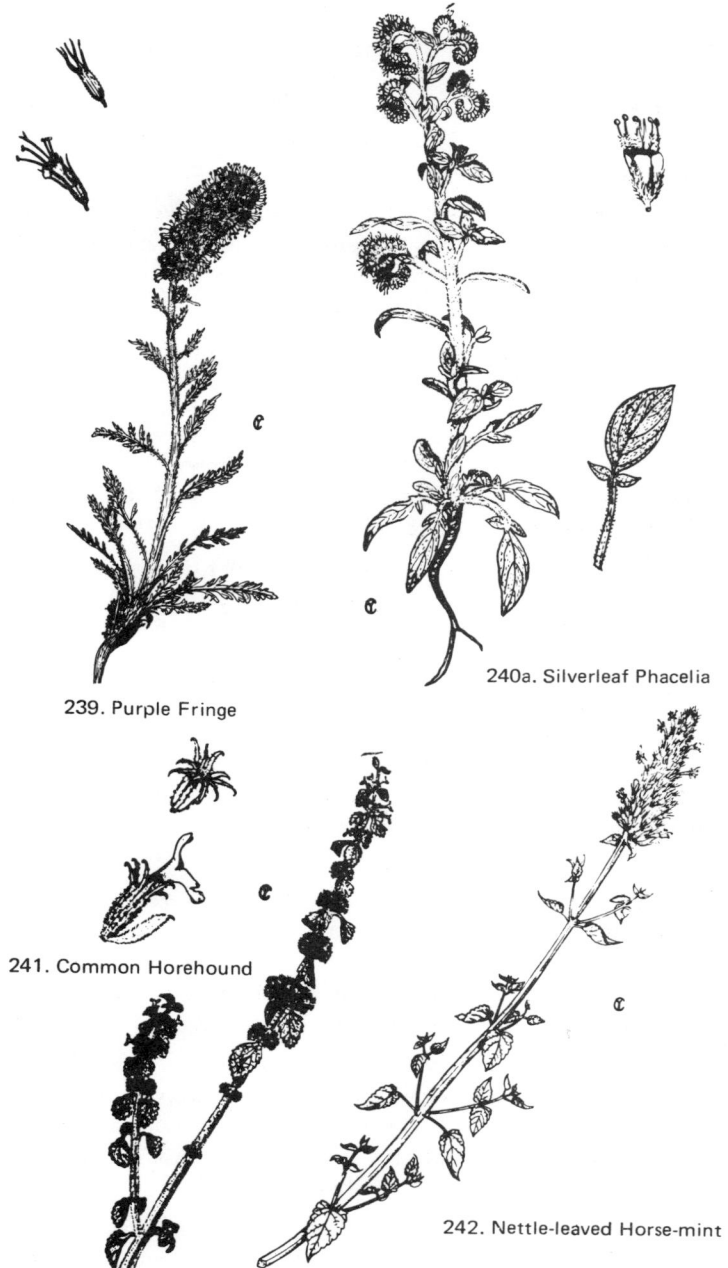

239. Purple Fringe

240a. Silverleaf Phacelia

241. Common Horehound

242. Nettle-leaved Horse-mint

150 WILDLIFE AND PLANTS OF THE CASCADES

str.wd
conif.
with sticky-hairy stems 1-2' tall; leaves close to the stem 1-3" long, sharply toothed on the margins; flowers usually **rose-red** (rarely yellow or white), large, showy, tubular, about 1" wide and 2" long, darker lines down throat, often **blotched with maroon**. Common in wet meadows, 4,000-10,000'.

pine
lodg.
246. PRIMROSE MONKEY-FLOWER, *Mimulus primuloides*. Short stem perennial from running rootstock. Leaves pinnately divided, ½-1½" long, **form a rosette**. Flowers about 1" long, **yellow**, funnel-form to bell-like, the **throat has red-brown spots**. Wet grassy banks.

many hab.
*247. YELLOW or COMMON MONKEY-FLOWER, *Mimulus guttatus*. Annual or sometimes biennial herb. Stems erect or lying down, loosely branched, 1-3' tall. Leaf blades oval to round, toothed, paired. Flowers **yellow, showy**, 1-2½", throat hairy brown spotted ridges. Common on foothills, in **shade along streams**. Plant eaten raw in salads.

brush
jun.
pie
red fir
248. DWARF PURPLE MONKEY-FLOWER, *Mimulus nanus*. Annual 1-6" tall, leaf blades oval to narrow 1 1/8" long. Flowers showy, purple **with white or yellow patches** on floor of throat, 1¼" long. Common in sandy places, often in colonies, California to Washington.

mix.ev.
str.wd.
sitk.-spr.
249. PURPLE FOXGLOVE, *Digitalis purpurea*. Stout plant 4-6' tall, the base leaves are large, oblong to narrow with toothed edges, the flower stem has smaller leaves, the raceme is showy, **purple to white (spotted on the lower paler side)**. Found in shaded places. Native of Europe.

sage
jun.
pume.
250. ASHY PENSTEMON, *Penstemon cinereus*. A plant with many stems which **form clumps** 1' high. Leaves about 2" long, mostly basal **(a rosette)**, ashy-gray color, rough but not hairy, with long slender petioles. **Flowers blue or purple** about ½" long. Volcanic gravels of California and Oregon, 3,500-6,000'.

rocks
pine
red fir
251. ROCK PENSTEMON, *Penstemon deustus*. Stems woody and much branched. Leaves bright green, coarsely toothed, narrow, ¾" long. Flowers **tubular, yellowish-white** marked with **purple** 5/8" long. Abundant in dry rocky areas on ledges in foothills, California north to Washington.

252. SHOWY PENSTEMON, *Penstemon speciosus*. Herb with tall, erect stems 8-30" high, anthers not woolly; flowers

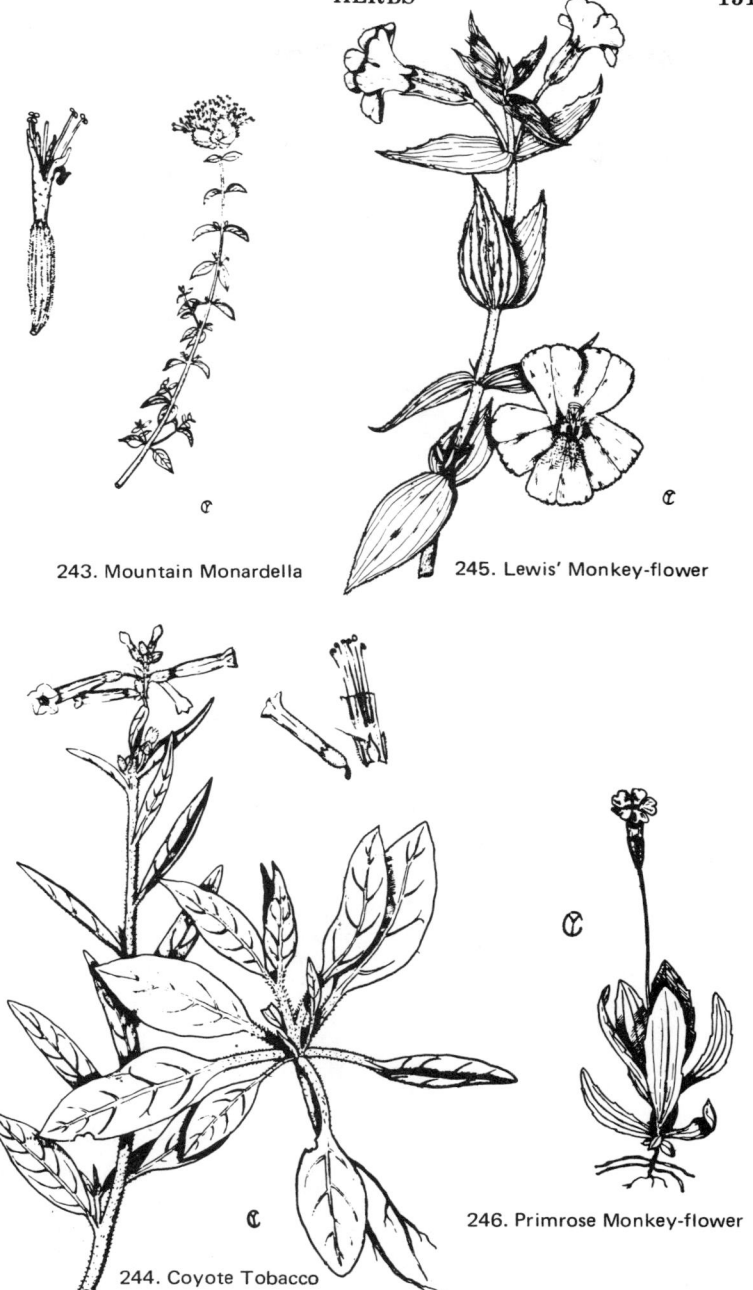

243. Mountain Monardella
245. Lewis' Monkey-flower
244. Coyote Tobacco
246. Primrose Monkey-flower

152 WILDLIFE AND PLANTS OF THE CASCADES

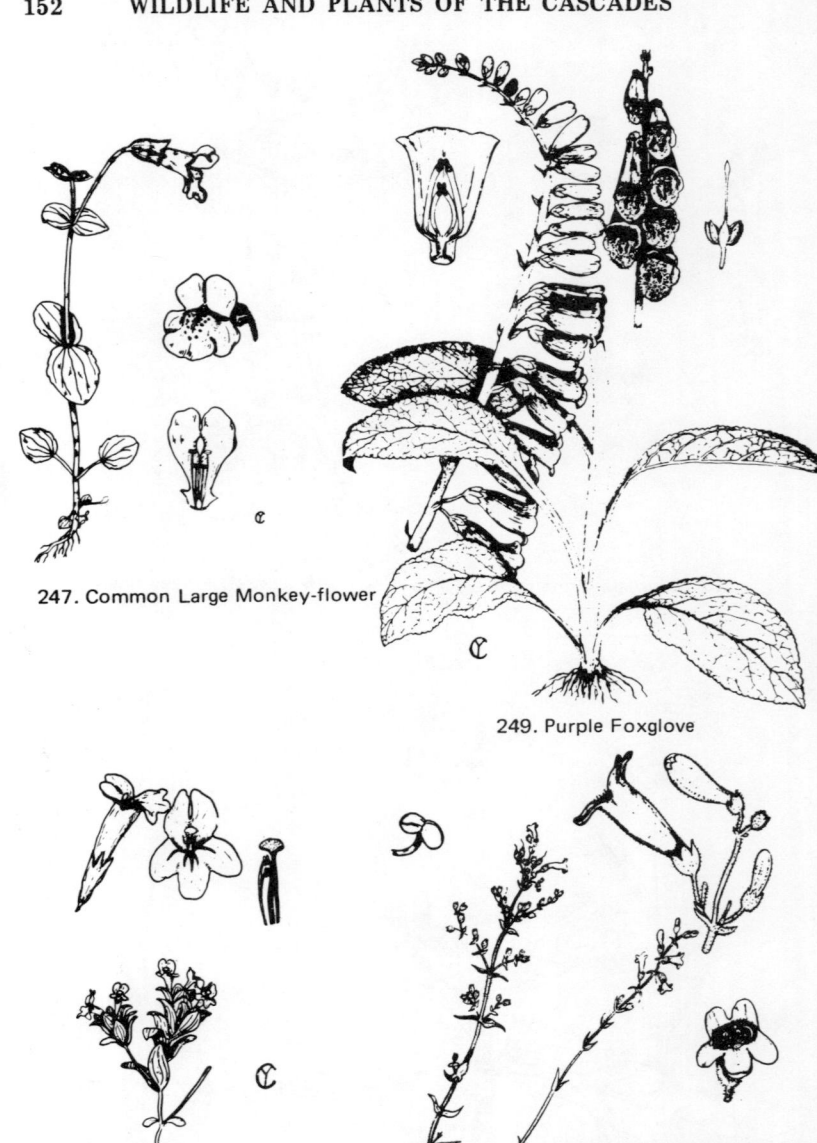

247. Common Large Monkey-flower

249. Purple Foxglove

248. Dwarf Purple Monkey-flower

250. Ashy Penstemon

HERBS

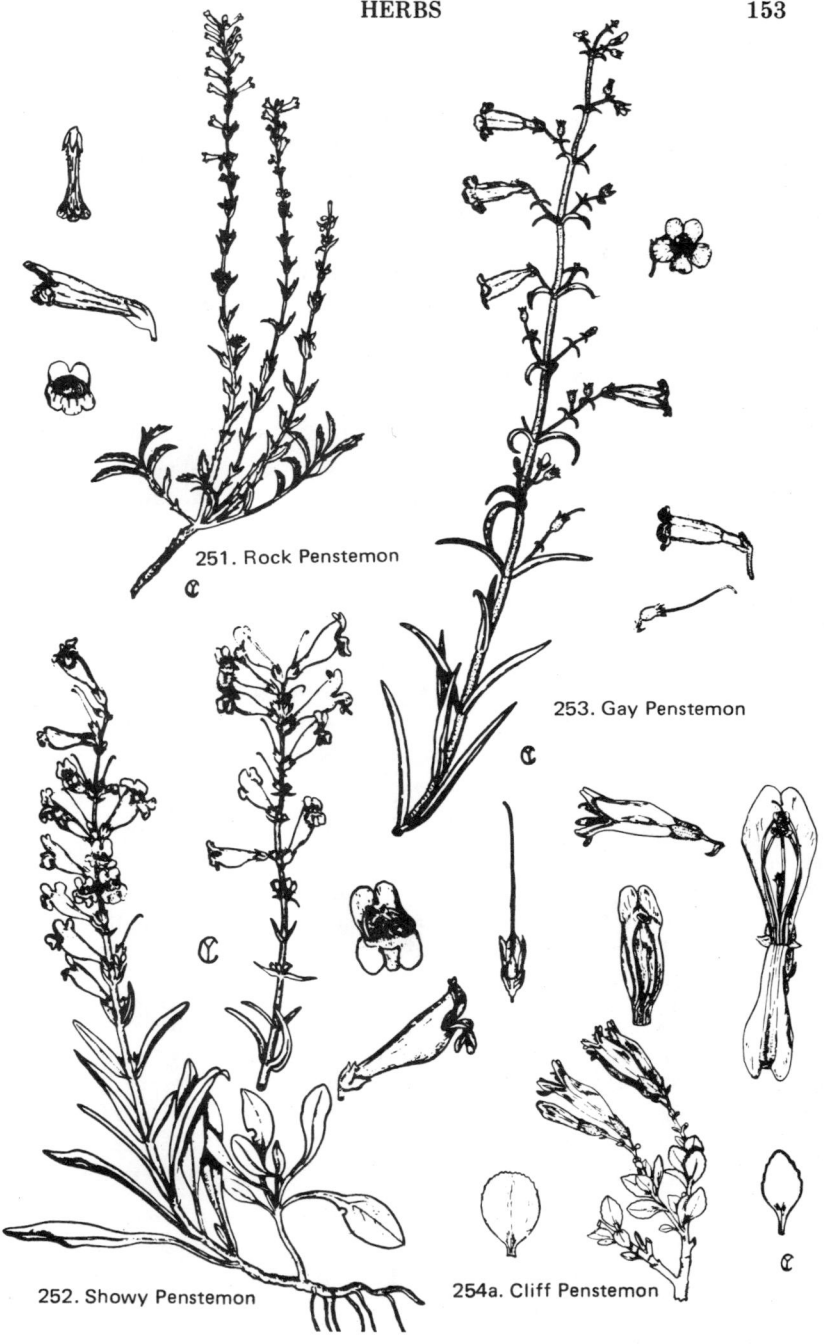

251. Rock Penstemon
253. Gay Penstemon
252. Showy Penstemon
254a. Cliff Penstemon

154 WILDLIFE AND PLANTS OF THE CASCADES

sage
red fir

bright blue-purple, broad, 1-1½" high, in clumps. Leaves thick and smooth, oblanceolated, 1/3-6/8" long. Found in sandy places, California to Washington.

brush
red fir

253. GAY PENSTEMON, *Penstemon laetus*. Plant woody at base, gray or yellow green, **stems often purplish**, much like *P. cinereus* but with larger flowers and absence of basal leaves. Flowers blue lavender to blue violet, tubular, bell-like. Subspecies *roezlii* found from northern California into Oregon. Dry, rocky places, 1,200-8,500'.

rocks
dg. fir
red fir

254a. CLIFF PENSTEMON, *Penstemon rupicola*. This **prostrate, matted**, woody at base penstemon can be distinguished by finely toothed leaves covered with whitish bloom, ¾" long. **Flowers rose colored** 1-1 1/8" long with a noticeable hump in flower tube. Probably hybridizes with *P. davidsoni*. Rocky places, 6,000-7,700'.

rocks
sub.alp.
alp.

254b. DAVIDSON or CREEPING PENSTEMON, *Penstemon Davidsonii*. (Not illustrated.) Prostrate woody-based plant often forms **dense mats several feet across.** Leaves somewhat **circular, smooth margined, leathery,** and green. **Flowers purple-violet,** 1-1 3/8" long, corolla tube straight on top. Stamens 5, four of these anther-bearing, fifth sterile stamen is an elongate, bearded filament. Occurs on rocky upper slopes and ledges. Mt. Rainier south through the Cascades.

dg. fir
red fir

255. WOODLAND PENSTEMON, *Penstemon nemorosus*. Erect plant 1-3' high, **few stems,** woody at base. Leaves thin, evenly spaced on stem, 2-4" long. Few flowers, terminal, glandular on outside, markedly 2-ridged on floor of throat and keeled on top, **color rose-purple to maroon,** about 5/8" long, anthers densely hairy. Moist rocky shaded slopes, 4,500-5,000', Siskiyou Mountains north to British Columbia.

brush
lodg.
mix.ev.

256. COAST FIGWORT, *Scrophularia californica*. Tall, erect, **coarse-stemmed plant**, 3-5' tall, triangular oval toothed leaf 1-4" long. **Dull red or brown irregular flowers ¾" long. Stamens 5,** four anther-bearing and the fifth sterile. Common in moist places, sandy soil, rocky limestone, in the southern Cascades.

brush
pine

257. INDIAN WARRIOR, *Pedicularis densiflora*. Perennial plant 4-20" tall, many basal leaves, pinnately divided (fern-like). **Flower spike deep purple-red,** dense, **terminal end maturing last.** Dry slopes below 6,000'.

HERBS

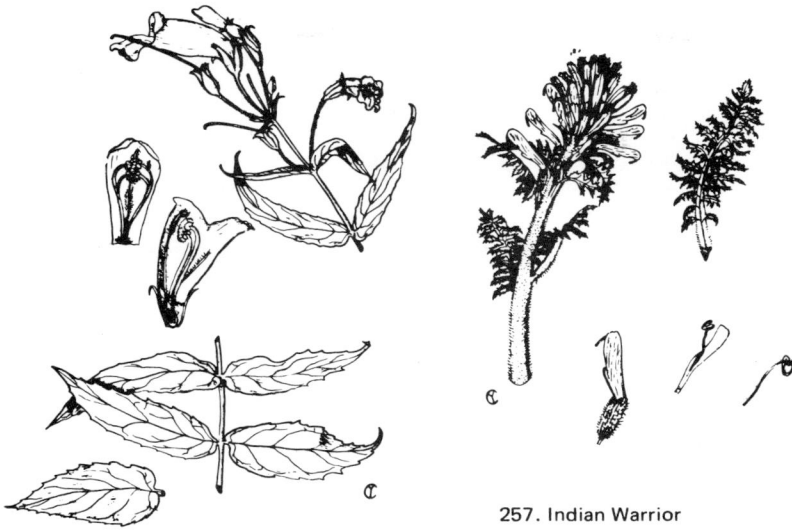

255. Woodland Penstemon

257. Indian Warrior

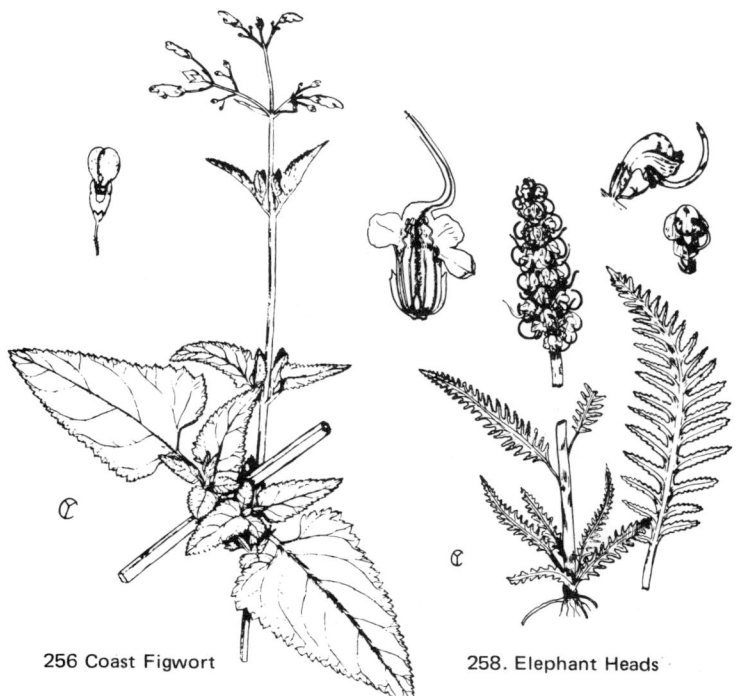

256 Coast Figwort

258. Elephant Heads

156 WILDLIFE AND PLANTS OF THE CASCADES

mt. mead.
mix.con.

258. PINK ELEPHANT HEADS or ELEPHANTELLA, *Pedicularis groenlandica*. Herb with stems erect, 6-16" tall, without hairs. Leaves basal and on low stems 1-3½" long, pinnately divided, narrow, and toothed. **Pink flowers resembling an elephant's head** borne on a white, woody, elongated spike. Dry slopes below 6,000'.

pume.
red fir
alp.

259. PUMICE INDIAN PAINTBRUSH, *Castilleja payneae*. Stems with soft, slender, entangled hairs at base. Leaves cut into narrow segments. Flowers **pale greenish-red to dull orange-red**, clustered on stem 4-20" tall. Gravelly pumice or granitic soil, 7,000-9,000'. Northern California to Cascades in Oregon.

sage
sub.alp.

260. PINE PAINTBRUSH, *Castilleja Applegatei* var. *pinetorum*. Leaves broad, wavy margined, slender lobes; **flowers and foliage mixed with red**; flower cluster varies from scarlet or orange and occasionally yellowish; stems lower than *C. linariaefolia*, 8-24". Dry places 2,000-11,000'.

mix.con.
mt.mead.

261. SCARLET PAINTBRUSH, *Castilleja miniata*. Plant 1-3' tall, a very beautiful and common species. Leaves are narrow lanceolate. Cluster of flowers **scarlet red or vermillion**. Bracts usually 3-divided with lanceolate lobes. Streams and wet places below 11,000'.

jun.
sage

*262. DESERT PAINTBRUSH, *Castilleja linariaefolia*. Perennial plant 2-3' tall with highly colored bracts of **scarlet, crimson or rose**; upper flower lip very much longer than the small, 3-toothed or 3-keeled lower lip. Stems tall, **leaves very narrow** and smooth margined ½-8" long. Northern California and Oregon. Flowers edible.

MADDER Family

pine
red fir

263. NORTHERN BEDSTRAW, *Galium boreale*. A robust plant with **rough, square stems, 4-whorled leaves** long and narrow, ½-2½". Flowers small, white, many, in showy terminal, cymose panicle; petals 4, united below; fruits in twos. Dry slopes below 7,000'.

HONEYSUCKLE Family (In part, see 148, etc.)

mix.ev.
mix.con.

264. TWIN FLOWER, *Linnaea borealis* ssp. *longiflora*. Slender-stemmed small, creeping evergreen herb to 3' long, that forms

HERBS

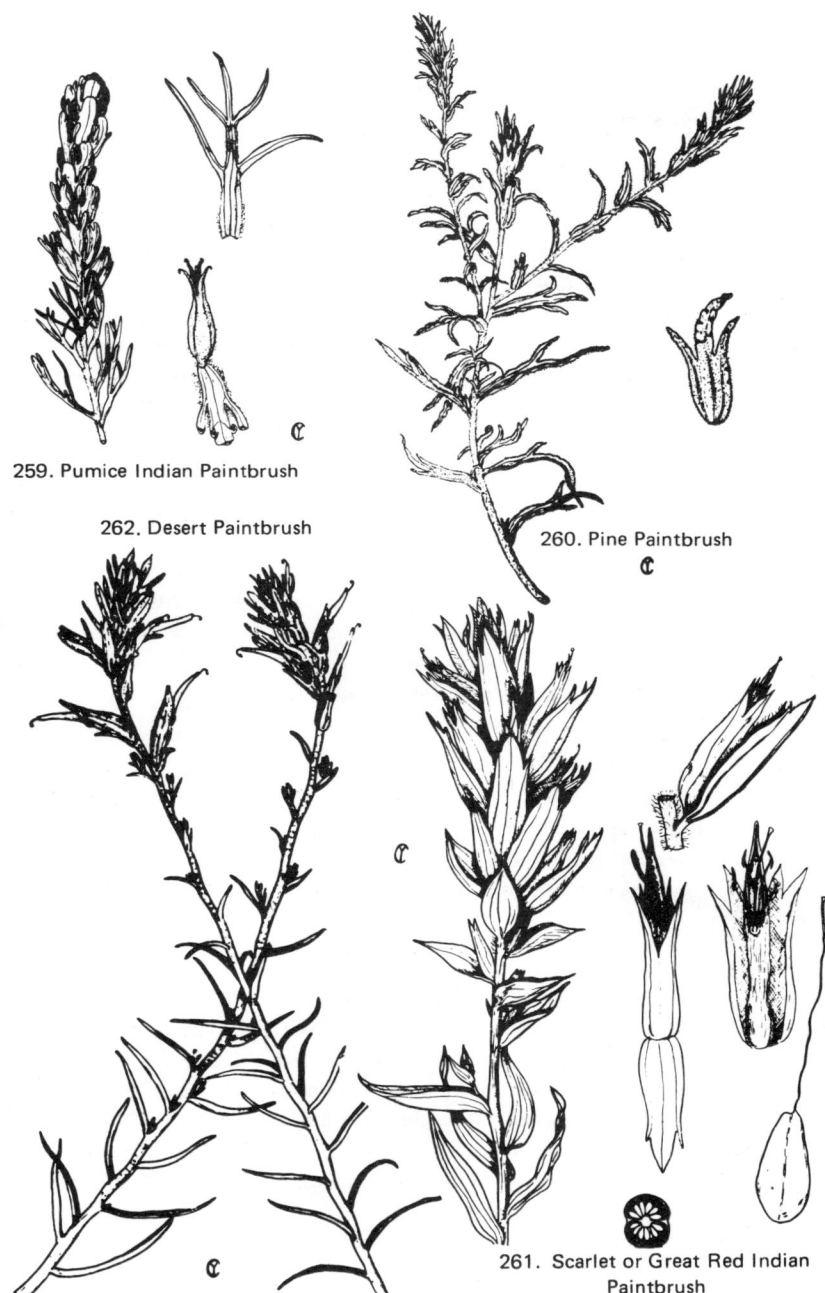

259. Pumice Indian Paintbrush

262. Desert Paintbrush

260. Pine Paintbrush

261. Scarlet or Great Red Indian Paintbrush

networks of mats on the forest floor. Each stem is topped by a single **pair of small, trumpet-like, pinkish flowers,** 1/2-5/8" long. Dense woods.

VALERIAN Family

265. VALERIAN or MOUNTAIN HELIOTROPE, *Valeriana sitchensis.* Tall perennial herbs with **strong-scented, thickened roots;** basal leaves often absent, stem leaves pinnately toothed, leaflets close to main stem. Stems 2-3' high with a flat terminal cluster (11-12 flowers), **white to pinkish, funnel-formed** about 3/8" long, stamens 3. Abundant along streams and bogs in woods and meadows, 4,000-6,000'.

mt. mead.
red fir

BELLFLOWER Family

266a. HAREBELL or SCOTCH BLUEBELL, *Campanula rotundifolia.* Perennial plant from slender rootstocks. Stems erect. Some of **basal leaves ovate to roundish,** ¼-1" long, toothed or smooth margined, often dried and missing by the time of bloom; narrow stem leaves alternate; **bell-shaped flowers bright bluish purple,** ½-1" long, one to several nodding flowers in a raceme. Often along streamsides, moist slopes, 4,500-8,000'.

pine
lodg.

266b. CALIFORNIA HAREBELL, *Campanula prenanthoides.* (Not illustrated.) Perennial herb, **stem angled,** slender, 1-2½' high, with leaves close to stem. Flowers **bright blue, narrow bell-shaped and long lobed,** 3/8-5/8" long. Style longer than and well extended from the flower. Northern California to southern Oregon in dryish wooded areas, below 6,000'.

mix.ev.
dg. fir
red fir

SUNFLOWER Family

*267. ARROW-LEAVED BALSAM ROOT, *Balsamorhiza sagittata.* Broad-leaved herb covered with grayish-white fine hair, leaves pinnately heart-shaped, 6-12" long. **Large yellow flowers.** Disk flowers mixed with conspicuous scales or bracts. Stems 1-2' high, bearing usually a **single large head,** the yellow rays 2" long. Widely distributed on the east side of the Cascades from southeastern California to British Columbia. Large root edible raw or cooked. A similar species, *B. deltoidea,* with herbage sparsely hairy and leaves green on underside occurs on west slopes of Cascades to British Columbia.

brush
sage
jun.
pine

HERBS

263. Northern Bedstraw
264. Twin Flower
265. Valerian
266a. Scotch Bluebell
267. Arrow-leaved Balsam Root

268. CALIFORNIA CONE-FLOWER, *Rudbeckia californica* var. *glauca*. Stems 2-5' high; rays 1-2" long, yellow. Disk flowers, **cone as long as ray flowers, dark brown; leaves narrow 6-12"** long, basal and lower leaves long stemmed. Found in damp places, Grants Pass, in Siskiyou Mountains to Crater Lake and northwestern California, 5,500-7,800'.

mt. mead.
red fir

269. DWARF HULSEA, *Hulsea nana*. Less than 6" high; leaves from woody base, pinnately lobed, 1-3" long. Yellow ray flowers; disk flowers without intervening scales or bracts (naked); **plant a low sticky form** with rather **large flowering heads,** grows in little tufts or dense clumps. Common on cinder slopes on east side of Cascades. 8,000-10,000'.

pume.
lodg.
alp;

270. HOARY CHAENACTIS, *Chaenactis douglasii*. **A woolly herb** about 1' high, leaves cut into small lobes; **heads white.** **Usually several,** forming a loose flat-topped cluster. Found in Lava Beds National Monument. A dwarf form occurs in Crater Lake National Park at high elevations. Found on both sides of Cascades north to British Columbia.

jun.
brush
pine
red fir

271. COMMON ASTER, *Aster chilensis*. A common **fall-blooming, white, bluish-red or bluish aster** of the Coastal Mountains of northern California, growing 1-3' high. Flower heads numerous ½-1" wide. Sea level to 4,500'. A variety occurs in the Klamath Mountains to Siskiyou County in northern California.

grass
many hab.

*272. CASCADE ASTER, *Aster ledophyllus*. Perennial herb, stout woody base, 1-2' tall, with **showy ray flowers, blue to purple. Ray flowers not more than 8.** Stems erect, leafy, forming large clumps; leaves oblong-lanceolate, woolly-haired, 1-2". Common in dry open pumice. Open woods and grassy places from 5,000-7,000', rare in Siskiyou but common in Oregon and Washington Cascades. Leaves boiled as greens.

grass
pume.

273. SHASTA ASTER, *Machaeranthera shastensis*. An herb from a woody taproot with several to many stiff stems that grow about 1' high, forming rather **dense clumps.** Basal leaves spatulate, ½-2½" long. Flowering heads with ray and disk flowers, ray flowers **blue or purple,** ¼" **long;** bracts below ray and disk flowers in several overlapping series (covered with grayish-white fine hairs). Found in sandy places. Mt. Shasta north in Cascades to central Oregon.

brush
pine
red fir

HERBS

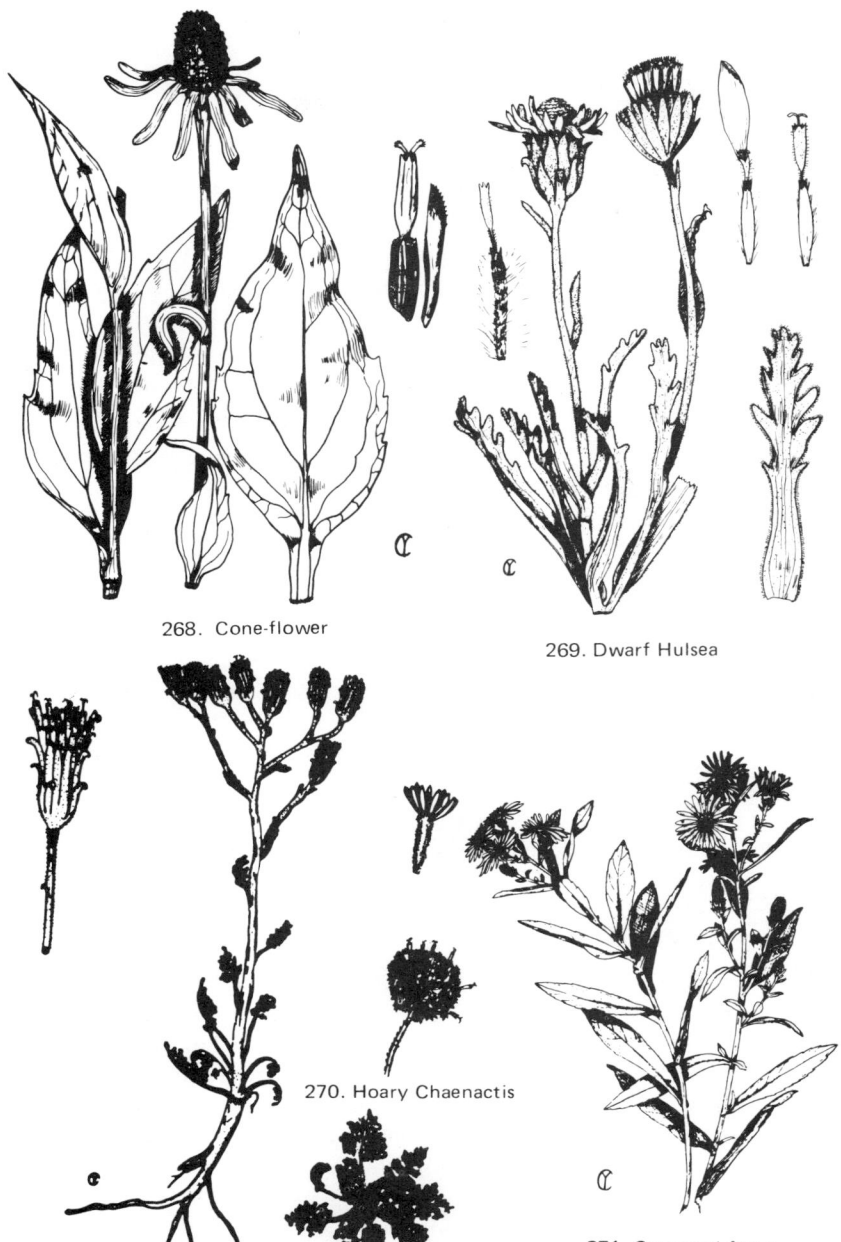

268. Cone-flower
269. Dwarf Hulsea
270. Hoary Chaenactis
271. Common Aster

162   WILDLIFE AND PLANTS OF THE CASCADES

mt, mead.
red fir
sub. alp.

274. WANDERING or SUBALPINE DAISY, *Erigeron peregrinus.* Herb from stout, woody base up to 21" tall. **Basal leaves well developed,** oblanceolate, 2-4" long. Sunflower-like heads that have both ray and disk flowers; rays (30-80) **rose-purple,** 3/8-1" long. Common from Oregon and Washington Cascades to Alaska. Bracts of area below ray and disk flowers in one or 2 series in all *Erigeron.* Moist meadow, streamsides.

mt. mead.
dg. fir

275. SHOWY DAISY, *Erigeron speciosus.* Perennial from woody base, 1-2½' tall and leafy to top, erect leaves lanceolate, ciliated margin, lower leaves stemmed, upper leaves close to stem by a broad base. **Ray flowers narrow,** 100-150, heads few, in a loose corymb. Found in gravelly soil. Open woods.

sage
jun.
pine

276a. HAIRY DAISY, *Erigeron pumilus.* Perennial, sometimes short-lived, woody base, 8-20" tall, stems many and erect, branched from the base. Leaves long, narrow, up to 3" long, hairy. Heads with **many narrow blue, pink, or white rays.** Common in the Basin Range Province, north to British Columbia. Open places in foothills and valley.

rocks
lodg.
alp.
str.wd.

276b. FLEABANE, *Erigeron compositus.* (Not illustrated.) Perennial, tufted from woody crown, 4-10" high, basal leaves stemmed, 3-divided, the side lobes again divided. **Ray flowers pink or white, bracts purplish at tips.** Sandy river banks, 8,000-13,000'.

mt. mead.
pine
lodg.
str.wd.

*277. YARROW, *Achillea Millefolium.* An **aromatic herb** plant 3' high with erect stems, **narrowly and finely cut leaves** and flat-topped heads. Ray and disk flowers, rays white, heads clustered. Found at lower elevations, 2,500-8,000', Cascades and Siskiyou Mountains. Entire plant cooked as broth.

mix.con.
rocks

278. SEEP-SPRING ARNICA, *Arnica longifolia.* This Arnica can be told from the others by its long leaves tapering at both ends. Stem leaves 5-6 pairs, elongated-lanceolate, 2-4¾" long; heads often 2-4 in a corymb. **Rays yellow or orange, 8-13,** about ½-¾" long. One of the most common Arnicas in the upper areas at Crater Lake and on south into California, in well-drained soil, above wet plains. 5,000-11,000'.

red fir
mt. mead.

279. CORDILLERAN, *Arnica mollis.* Perennial herb, stem leaves 2-4 pairs, oblanceolate. Lower leaves generally largest. **Flowering heads erect, broad and rounded,** yellow, with rays

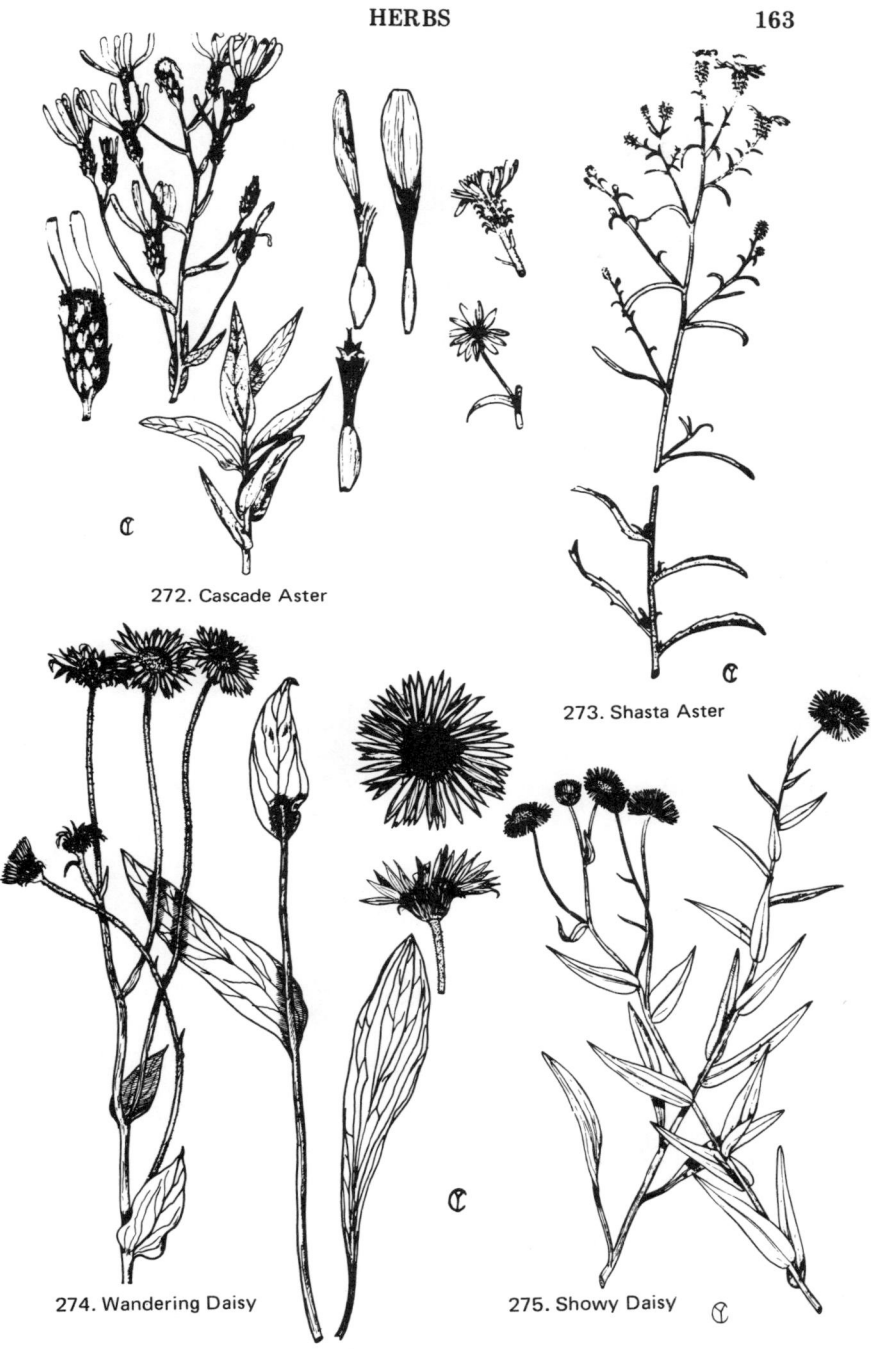

272. Cascade Aster
273. Shasta Aster
274. Wandering Daisy
275. Showy Daisy

164   WILDLIFE AND PLANTS OF THE CASCADES

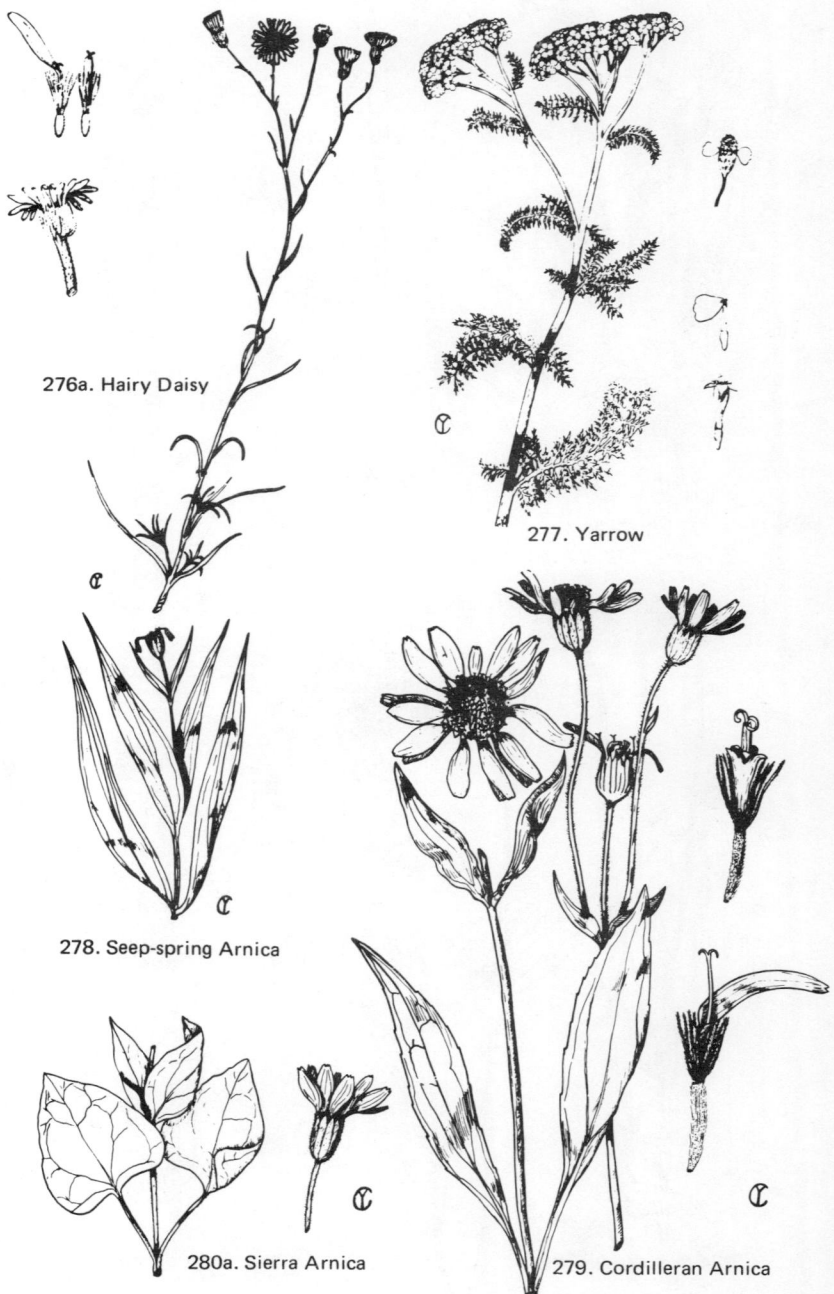

276a. Hairy Daisy
277. Yarrow
278. Seep-spring Arnica
280a. Sierra Arnica
279. Cordilleran Arnica

HERBS

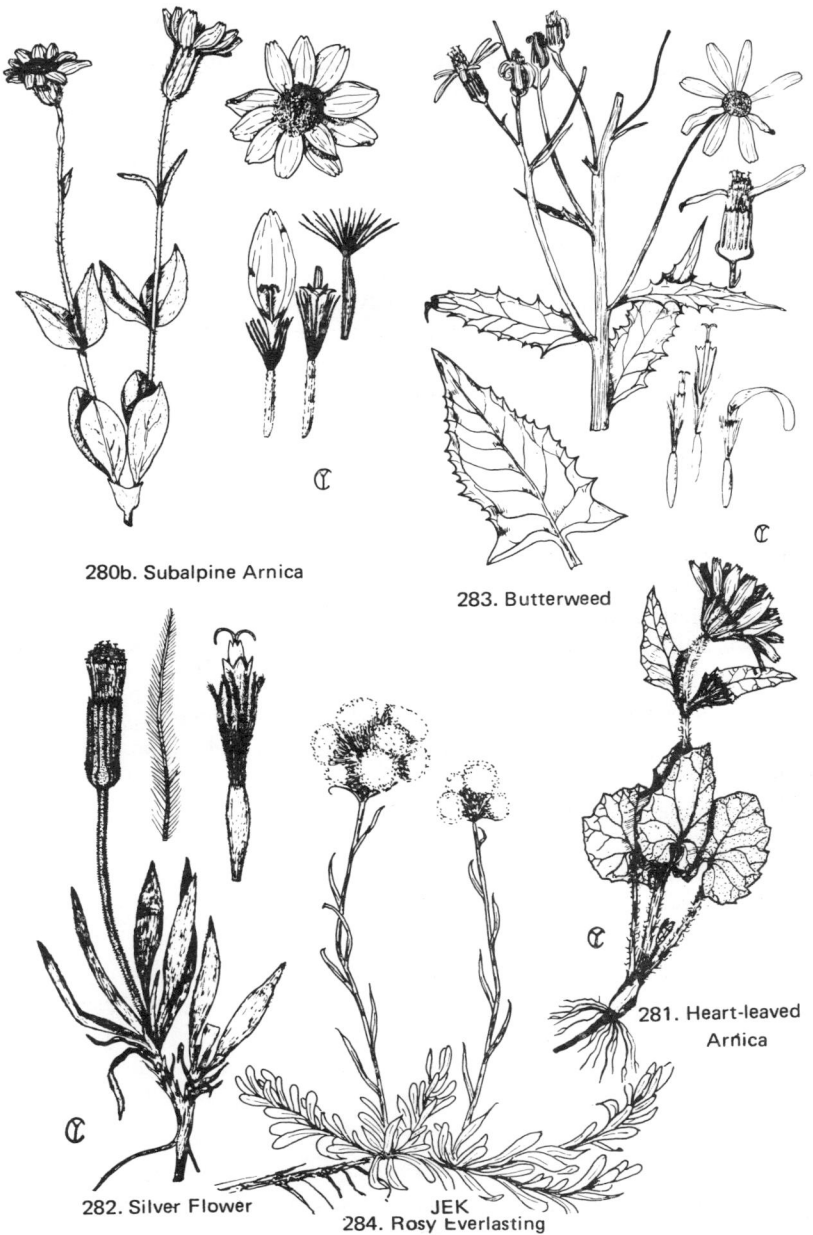

280b. Subalpine Arnica
283. Butterweed
281. Heart-leaved Arnica
282. Silver Flower
284. Rosy Everlasting

(12-18) ½-1" long, crown of bristles tawny. Moist places from 7,500-11,500', California Cascades north to British Columbia.

rocks
red fir
alp.

280a. SIERRA ARNICA, *Arnica nevadensis.* Stem leaves 2-3 pairs, 1-3¼" long; the lower large, stemmed, broadly ovate, smooth edged and rounded or **heart-shape-like at base. Head broadly turbinate to bell-like,** rays 12-20, 1" long, joins white to straw color bristle crown. Open rocky areas near streams, 6,600-11,900' in Cascades from California to Washington.

alp.

280b. SUBALPINE ARNICA, *Arnica rydbergii.* In this *Arnica* the lower stem leaves, **3-4 pairs, are close to the stem.** Heads solitary or few, 8, ray flowers 3/8-7/8" long, form crown of whitish bristles. Forest from Scott Mountains, Siskiyou County, California, north to British Columbia, dry meadows and open slopes.

mix.con.
dg. fir

281a. HEART-LEAVED ARNICA, *Arnica cordifolia.* This Arnica, 8-24" tall, can be told from all the others by the **basal heart-shaped leaves that are toothed.** Stem leaves 2-3 pairs, 1¾-5¾" long. Bracts below rays and disk flowers, with long white hairs. 10-15 rays, yellow ¾-1¼". Found from 3,500-10,000'. Common east of Cascades; upper Nisqually Valley, Washington; northern California, and Coast Range.

lodg.
sub.alp.
str.wd.

281b. STREAMBANK ARNICA, *Arnica amplexicaulis.* (Not illustrated.) Nearly without hairs and somewhat gummy; stems 12-30" tall, tufted; leaves ovate, acute, prominently toothed, hairless and **gummy above,** 1¾-4¾" long; basal leaves stemmed, upper ones close to stem, leaves on stem 4-7 pairs; heads more than one, **8-14 rays, pale yellow,** 3/8-3/4" long. Moist places, 7,000-10,000', in Cascades.

rocks
sub.alp.
alp.

282. SILVER FLOWER, *Raillardella argentea.* An herb without ray flowers; heads yellow; leafless stems 1-5" high; **basal leaves narrowly oblanceolate covered with a silvery felt.** Forms crown of flattened bristles. Dry open rocky places, 9,000-12,000', on the higher points at Crater Lake National Park and elsewhere in the Cascades and northern California.

str.wd
mix.con.;

283. ARROWHEAD BUTTERWEED, *Senecio triangularis.* This perennial herb has noticeable **narrowly triangular, alternate leaves** all along the slender stems that grow 2-6' high. Leaves toothed. Few yellow flowers borne in a flat-topped cluster with

HERBS

5-8 rays about ½". Abundant along stream borders, meadows, and bogs from 4,000-10,000' in Cascades, coastal mountains, on south in Sierras, but occurs near sea level near mouth of Columbia.

*284. ROSY EVERLASTING or PUSSYTOES, *Antennaria rosea*. Low matted, woody base, more or less woolly herb with basal leaves. Slender leaves on stems 3-13" tall. Has flower heads with papery pink bracts below white flower heads, grows a crown of slender bristles. Found in dry sandy or gravelly soil in the Cascades from 4,500-12,000' elevation. Gum of stalk chewed.   mix.con. alp.

285. PEARLY EVERLASTING FLOWER, *Anaphalis margaritacea*. White woolly perennial herb, 1-3' tall, with erect leafy stems and smooth-edged lanceolate, 2-8" leaves; heads numerous, small, disk-like, about 3/8"; **bracts pearly white, bell-shaped, thin, and dry.** Found below 8,500' elevation in many plant communities.   rocks many hab.

286. WESTERN EUPATORIUM, *Eupatorium occidentale*. This is a smooth large, many-stemmed perennial herb, somewhat woody, 1-3' high; leaves ovate, toothed; flowers **crimson, pale purple, pink, or white. Heads compactly clustered at tips of stem.** Found from the east slope of the Oregon Cascades north to Washington and in the Siskiyous east to Lava Beds National Monument, about rocks, 6,500-11,000'.   rocks mix.con. dg. fir red fir

287. MOUNTAIN or FALSE DANDELION, *Agoseris glauca*. Slender perennial plant 8-18" tall, numerous basal leaves long and narrow 2-8". Stems are leafless, each bearing a single head. Flowers are yellow, disk-like, base bell-like. Forms crown of simple bristles or hairs; seeds not toothed. Found on dry, rocky slopes, 5,000-10,500', from Siskiyou and Lava Beds National Monument north to Washington.   sage mix.con. brush

*288. COMMON DANDELION, *Taraxacum officinale*. **Leafless stem 2-12" high;** leaves lanceolate, **deeply toothed 6-12" long;** bracts under orange-yellow flower head narrow, bent back. Seeds toothed. Introduced species found almost any place in meadows, pastures, roadsides. Leaves edible raw or cooked.   conif. cult. mt.mead.

168   WILDLIFE AND PLANTS OF THE CASCADES

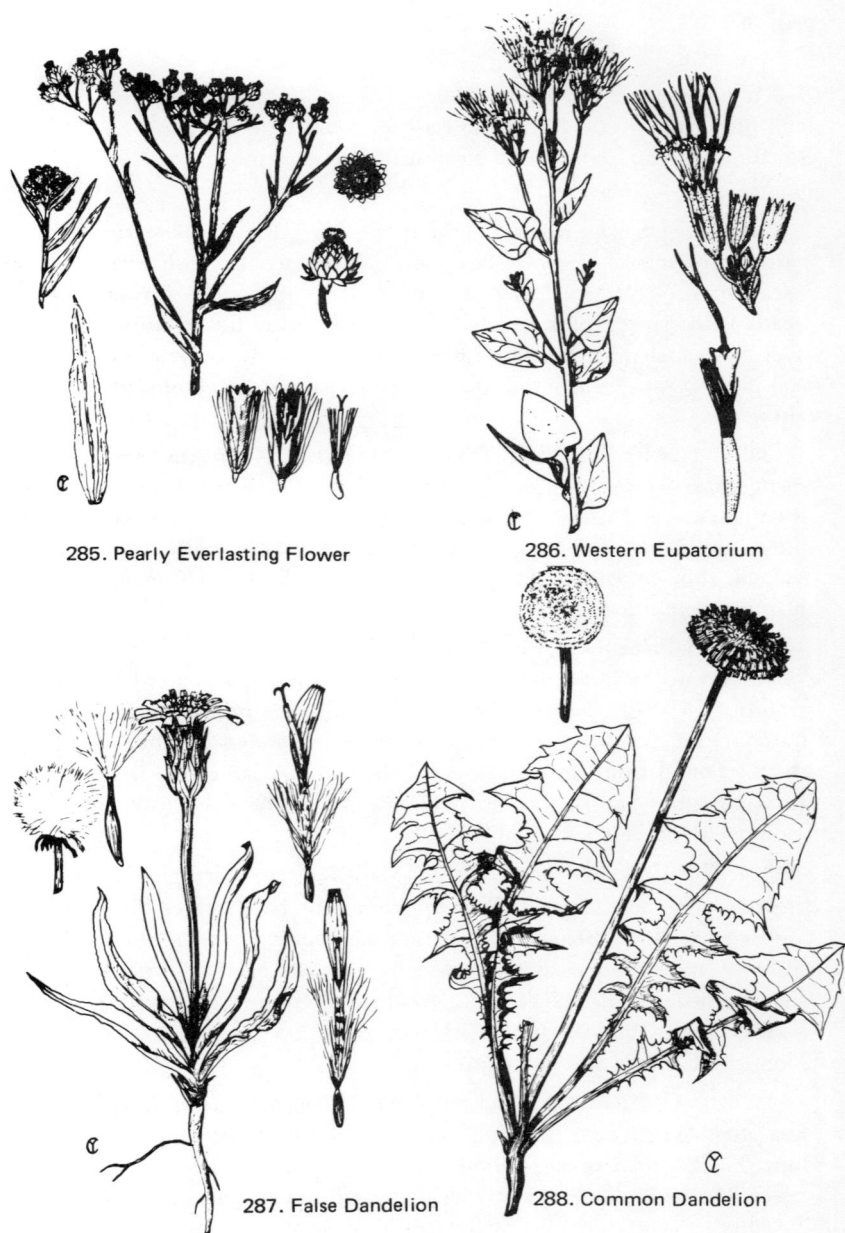

285. Pearly Everlasting Flower

286. Western Eupatorium

287. False Dandelion

288. Common Dandelion

MAMMALS

Mammals is a name applied to animals who have fur or hair on their bodies and give milk to their young. A few mammals, such as the chipmunks, squirrels and rabbits or hares are seen about in daylight, but most mammals are likely to be seen by humans in the very early morning or in the evening. Taking out a flashlight covered with red plastic at night is a useful idea, as many animals are not aware of or not bothered by the red light who are by the white. It is best to sit very still to watch them, or to move very quietly with no abrupt movements. Since most are well-camouflaged with their surroundings, you are likely to catch only glimpses of them and it is wise to look sharply and catch every detail you can. Size is often useful, so try to compare what you see in size to the four common mammals pictured below as similar comparisons are given in the descriptions. Watch also for the many signs of mammals, such as tracks, dens, claw marks on trees, dung (containing parts of what they feed on), and so on.

Most large mammals are easily recognized by distinguishing features described or pictured in this book, but many small mammals, particularly bats, shrews and mice, are hard to tell apart in species form except by experts, but the pictures and descriptions will help. Particularly note the habitats in which each species lives, as this helps with identification.

The chart shown here illustrates the comparative sizes of four well-known species of mammals described in the text. Unless otherwise indicated, the figures following the scientific names in the species account are those of body length followed by the tail length.

Never try to feed bear, deer or other potentially dangerous animals on roads, in the woods, etc., as they can inflict serious injuries if aroused. Conserve our beautiful and interesting wildlife by deed and by word.

Abbreviations: + = larger than; - = smaller than; = for same size as; * = color plate illustration; † = not illustrated; ♂ = male; ♀ = female.

WILDLIFE AND PLANTS OF THE CASCADES

I. Order Marsupialia (Marsupials)

cult.
str.wd.
mix.ev.
brush

1. COMMON OPOSSUM, *Didelphis marsupialis*. Cat size, 15-22". Color grayish, with whitish face; **ears naked,** nose long, **a scaly and prehensile (used for hanging) tail,** and a thumb-like hind toe without a nail. An omnivorous, slow-moving night scavenger, introduced from east. The possum may play dead when attacked; teeth all similar in size.

II. Order Insectivora (Shrews, Moles)

conif.
str.wd.
mix.ev.

2. DUSKY SHREW, *Sorex obscurus*. Mouse-;2½-3", tail 1¾-2". **Reddish to reddish-brown above;** brownish-gray below; tail generally one color; forehead unusually high for a shrew. Like most shrews, it is a ferocious hunter of worms, mice and large insects, eating its own weight in a few hours. Most of region.

sitka-spr.
str.wd.

†3. PACIFIC SHREW, *Sorex pacificus*. Mouse size; 3-3¾", tail 2¼-2¾".[1] A pale or cinnamon brown above, a lighter brown below; more flat-headed than above shrew. Found in Klamath Mts. and central Oregon Cascades.

str.wd.
conif.
mix.ev.

†4. VAGRANT SHREW, *Sorex vagrans*. Mouse-; about 2½", tail 1½-1¾". Brownish above, grayish below; tail usually one color, but sometimes dark above and light below; forehead flat. Found in Transition and Canadian Life Zones, over most of region.

water
streams
str.wd.

5. WATER SHREW, *Sorex palustris*. Mouse size; 3 -3¼"; tail 2½-3¼". Black marked with gray hairs above, whitish to brownish below; **tail distinctly dark above and light below; hind foot with stiff and dense lining of hairs for use in swimming.** Found in most of region, except Klamath Mts. in Canadian and Hudsonian zones.

water
str.wd.
mix.con.
sitk.-spr.
w.hem.

†6. MARSH SHREW, *Sorex bendirii*. Mouse size 3¼-3¾"; tail 2½-3¼". Black above but with silvery-hairs, only slightly lighter below; **tail all dark-colored; hind foot with fringe of stiff hairs that help in swimming.** Found in most of region in Transition and Canadian Life Zones, usually near water.

marsh
water,
str.wd.
mix.con.

†7. MASKED SHREW, *Sorex cinereus*. Mouse -;1¾-2½"; tail 1¼-1¾". Grayish-brown, brown, grayish or tan above and light tan below; tail one color. A rare shrew of Washington.

SHREWS, BATS

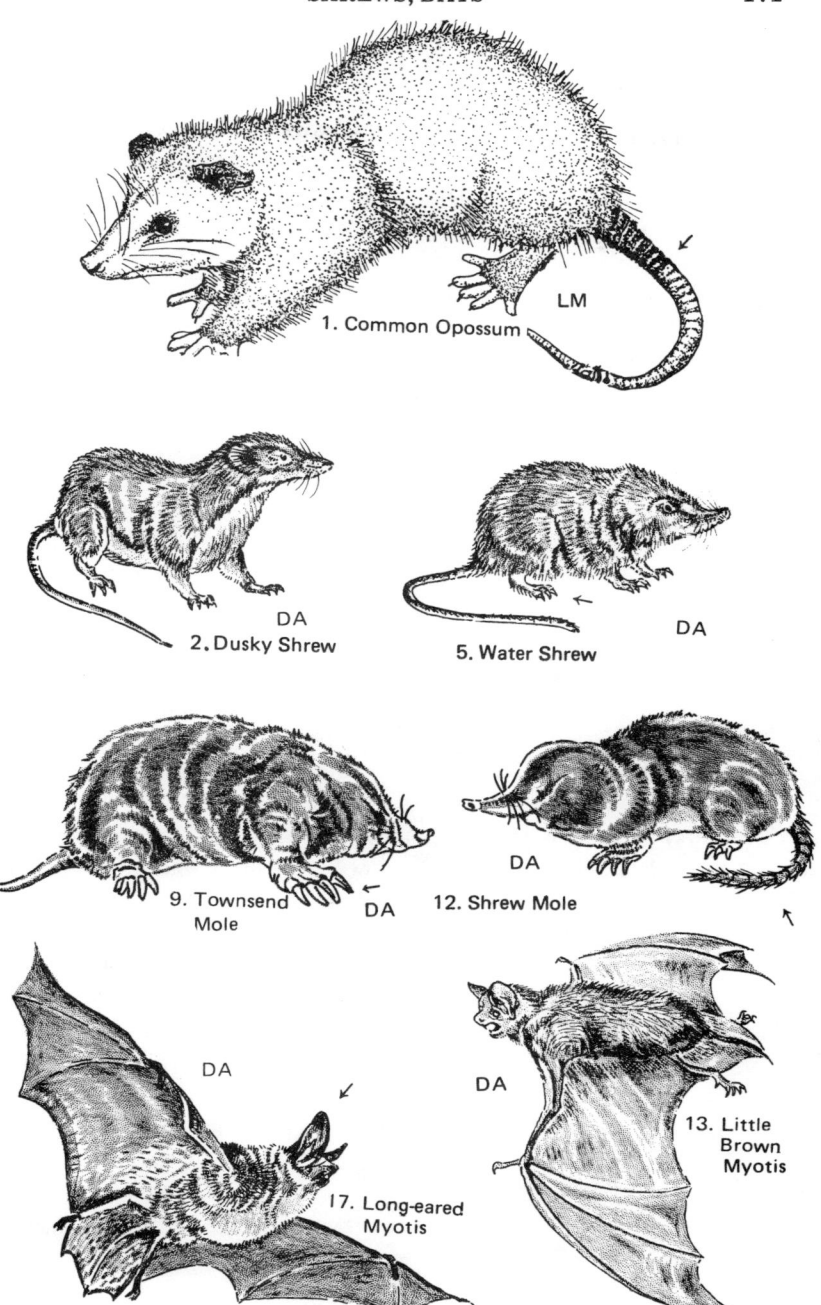

WILDLIFE AND PLANTS OF THE CASCADES

conif.
mt.mead.
str.wd.

†8. TROWBRIDGE SHREW, *Sorex trowbridgii* Mouse size; 2¼-2¾ tail 1¾-2½". Dark brown, light brown or sooty above, similar below; **tail distinctly dark above and light below.** Found in most of region in dry forest areas and Transition zone.

mt.mead.
cult.
mix.ev.
mix.con.
w.hem.

9. TOWNSEND MOLE, *Scapanus townsendii*. Rat size; 6¼-7¼"; tail 1¼-2". **Very dark black-brown or purple-black fur,** often with a metallic luster, but some are found brownish in color with markings of gray; the snout and tail are naked. **Front feet, as in all moles, are strongly clawed and adapted for digging.** Feeds mainly on insects, spiders, worms and vegetable matter. Active mainly at night, and underground in tunnels as shown. Found in most of the region except northwestern California, Transition zone.

mt.mead.
conif.
str.wd.
cult.

†10. COAST MOLE, *Scapanus orarius*. Rat -4¼-5¼"; tail 1¼-1¾". **The velvety-purple-black fur looks lead-gray at base;** snout and tail mostly naked. Food is insects, spiders, worms and probably some vegetable matter. Lives mainly in Transition Life Zone of most of our region except n.e. California and s. central Oregon.

mt.mead.
conif.
mix.ev.
str.wd.
brush
cult

†11. BROAD-HANDED MOLE, *Scapanus latimanus*. Rat -; 4¼-5¾". Dark grayish-black to coppery or brassy-brown fur, appearing somewhat silvery when smooth, especially on undersides; **tail covered with silvery hair.** Feeds as do the above moles. Found in our region in s. central Oregon and northeast California, and in Sonoran to Hudsonian zones.

str.wd.
pine
mix.ev.

12. SHREW-MOLE, *Neurotrichus gibbsii*. Mouse=;2¾-3¼";tail 1¼-1¾". The grayish-black to black fur has a silvery iridescence in parts; **the scaly tail is covered with bristly hairs. Feet not so powerfully constructed for digging, so tunnels are closer to the surface, often little more than up-turnings of the leaf-mold.** Its food is similar to the above moles. Found in most of our region, in the Transition Life Zone, but somewhat rare in n.e. California.

MOLE MOUND
Low, fan-shaped mound of fine dirt deposited at surface.

GOPHER MOUND
High, volcano-like mound of lumpy dirt upheaved from tunnel at an angle.

BATS, RABBITS

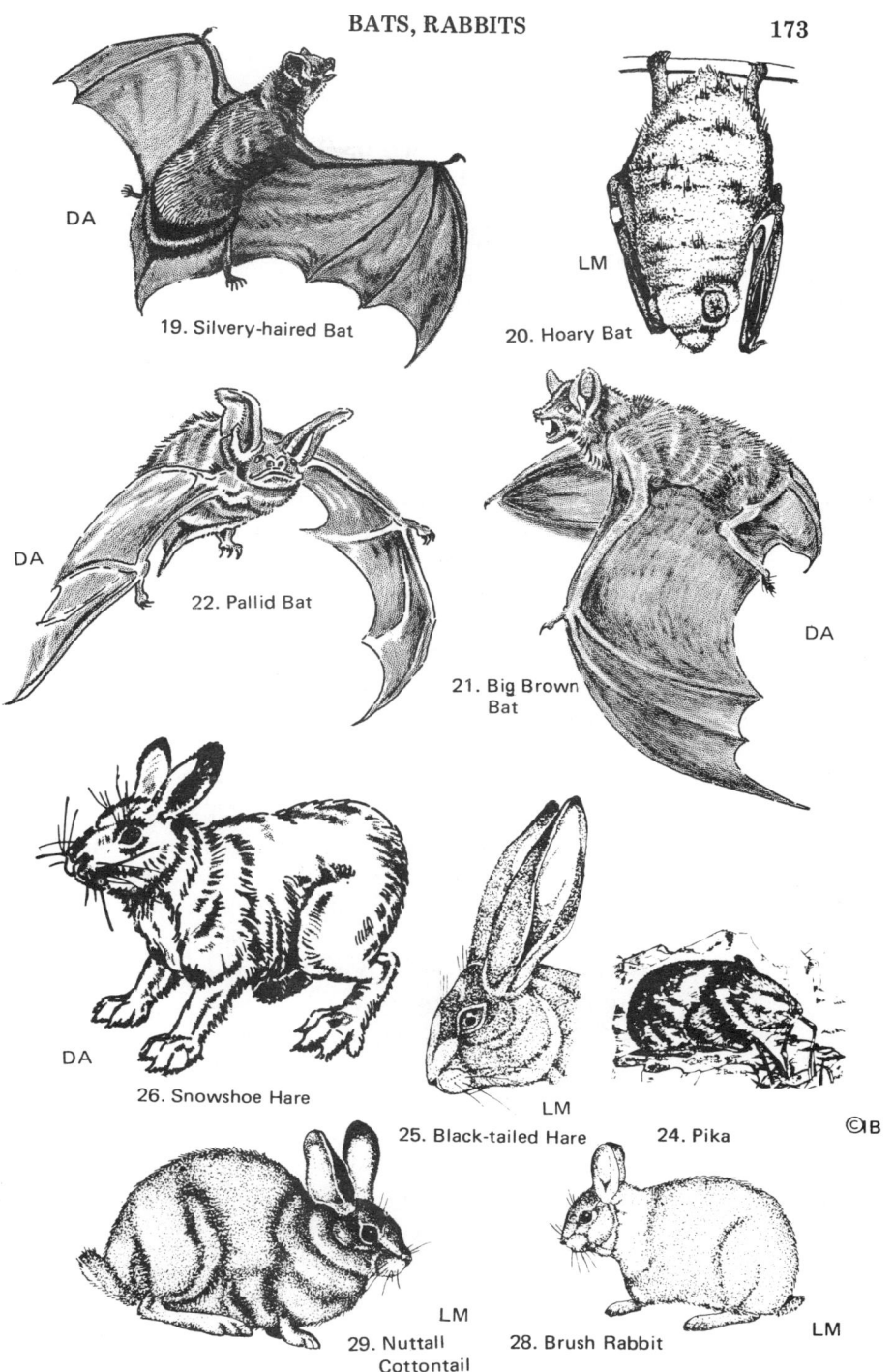

174   WILDLIFE AND PLANTS OF THE CASCADES

III. Order Chiroptera (Bats)

Our bats are all insect-eaters, catching them on the wind. Some fly south in winter, while others hibernate in caves, hollow trees or old buildings. Bats catch insects by aid of sonar, or the echoing return of their high-pitched cries (unheard by humans) from insect bodies. Bats rest and sleep by hanging upside down.

Family VESPERTILIONIDAE (evening bats)

These bats are characterized by having the tail nearly or completely enclosed in the hind wing membranes, and by the ears usually not being connected by a ridge of skin.Tail length included in body measurement.

Water
mt.mead.
conif.
str.wd.
bldg.

13. LITTLE BROWN MYOTIS, *Myotis lucifugus*. Mouse size; 3-3¾" long. Upper body a glossy yellow brown; light brown or tan below. Feet usually larger than in other Myotis; no hard keel between hind foot and tail on wing-membrane; no bony crest on top of head. Found over most of region in Canadian and Hudsonian Life Zones.

jun.
str. wd.
mix.ev.
water
brush
bldg.

†14. FRINGED MYOTIS, *Myotis thysanodes*. Mouse size. 3-3¾"; tail 1½-1¾". Color dull yellowish-brown; **wing membrane near tail noticeably fringed with stiff hairs**; wing membrane extends to the base of the toes on feet. Found in Upper Sonoran Life Zone, mainly in open woods of California and Oregon.

most
habitats

†15. CALIFORNIA MYOTIS, *Myotis californicus*. Mouse size. 3-3½". **The dark ears and wing-membranes contrast sharply with the light golden-brown or tawny fur of the back**; hairs of fur dark gray at base, a distinct keel along the edge of the wing-membrane between foot and tail; face rather blackish, but not altogether so. Found in all of region except upper two life zones.

mix.ev.
str.wd.
jun.
cult.
cliff.
bldg.

†16. HAIRY-WINGED MYOTIS, *Myotis volans*. Mouse size. 3½-4"; tail 1½-2". Color yellowish-brown to dark brown on back; **ear-membranes and wings black;** the short ears barely touch the nose when held foreward. Found in most of region in open woods of the Upper Sonoran and Transition Life Zones.

str.wd.
conif.
mix.ev.

17. LONG-EARED MYOTIS, *Myotis evotis*. Mouse size; 3-4". Fur dark to light yellow-brown; wing-membranes and ears are black; **ear unusually long**, ¾-1". Found in most of our region in Upper Sonoran, Transition and Canadian Life Zones.

BATS 175

†18. YUMA MYOTIS, *Myotis yumanensis.* Mouse size; 3-3½". Color above buffy or light brown, whitish below, with no shining or glinting; ears and wing membranes very light brown; front of head very high; no crest on top; lobe appears on wing-membrane near foot and toward tail. Found in most of region in Sonoran Transition zones, mainly in fairly open areas or open woods.
brush
water
streams
sage
conif.
mix.ev.
cult.

19. SILVERY-HAIRED BAT, *Lasionycteris noctivagans.* Mouse size; 3½-4". The dark brown to black fur is tipped with silver; **a distinct band of dark fur covers the wing-membranes around the tail end of the body.** Roosts in the branches of trees. Found mainly in Transition Life Zone in most of region.
conif.
water
str.wd.
mix.ev.
mt.mead.

20. HOARY BAT, *Lasiurus cinereus.* Mouse +; 5-5¾"? **The long soft fur is grayish-yellow or brownish-yellow and tipped with white;** white patches of fur appear on the upper surface of the elbow and wrist; the rounded ears are partly furred, but with naked black rims. Also roosts in tree branches. Migrates south in winter but found rest of the year in Sonoran to Canadian Life Zones of region.
conif.
mix.ev.
str.wd.
mt.mead.

21. BIG BROWN BAT, *Eptesicus fuscus.* Mouse +; 4-5". The **long bright glossy brown fur contrasts with the black nose,** ears, feet and wing-membranes; the short ears can barely touch the nose if held forward. Found in all of region in Upper Sonoran and Transition Life Zones.
cult.
cliffs
water
brush
mix.ev.
str.wd.
mt.mead

22. PALLID BAT, *Antrozous pallidus.* Mouse +; 4¼-5¼". Color brownish-yellow to dull gray, but ears and wing-membranes blackish-brown. **Large wide-apart ears distinctive and could reach far beyond the nose; two spiral grooves above nostrils below a c-shaped ridge.** Edge of mountains in Sonoran Life Zones.
grass
brush
sage
str.wd.

†23. LUMP-NOSED BAT, *Plecotus townsendii.* Mouse size. 3½-4¼". Color brownish-gray; **very long narrow ears are joined together above forehead; big glandular lumps appear between eyes and nose.** Found on edges of mountains in Sonoran Life Zones.
brush
grass
water
sage

Bats can do extraordinary feats of dodging objects in their way when travelling at high speed. This is because the echoing of their very rapid and shrill cries (too high to be heard by most humans) tells them exactly where each object is. The 1-4 young are usually born in the spring and cling to the fur of the mother until they can fly after a few weeks. Bats are good allies of man; they kill harmful insects; do not kill bats!

WILDLIFE AND PLANTS OF THE CASCADES

IV. Order Lagomorpha (Rabbits and Hares)

rocks
mt.mead.
s.a.mead.
alp.

24. PIKA, *Ochotona princeps.* (Family Ochotonidae.) Rat -; 6½-8½"; **no tail visible.** Color grayish-brown to dark brown, with white-tipped ends; **distinctive round short ears.** Found in lava beds, but mainly in Hudsonian and Arctic-Alpine Life Zones of mountains, where it gathers grass, dries it and stores in rock caves like hay to be used in winter. Gives a shrill, whistling cry or squeaks.

Family LEPORIDAE (Rabbits and Hares)

Rabbits are born naked and have shorter ears than hares. They depend more on dodging and hiding in thickets or holes than on straightaway running, like the hares. Hares are larger, with longer ears, and are born well-furred and immediately able to travel. The name Jackrabbit· is misleading to call our species of western hares.

conif.
grass
sage
brush
pume.
cult.
mix.ev.

25. BLACK-TAILED HARE (or Jackrabbit), *Lepus californicus.* Cat plus size; averaging a little less than 20" long; tail 2-4½ ". **Tail black above, extending up into rump, grayish-brown below;** general color above brown or brownish-gray; ear 4-5¾"; hind foot 4¼-5¾". Often leaps 15' or more to escape enemies. Found in Sonoran and Transition Life Zones in foothill country.

conif.
mt.mead.
str.wd.

26. SNOWSHOE HARE,*Lepus americanus,* Cat size - ; 13-18"; tail 1-1¾"; ear 2½-2¾"; **hind foot very broad and hairy for travel on snow, 4½-6"** long. Tail above blackish-brown, grayish-brown below. Found in most of region except Klamath Mts., in Transition and Canadian Life Zones. Turns white in winter.

sage
brush
jun.
pine
pume

†27. WHITE-TAILED HARE (or Jackrabbit),*Lepus townsendii,* Cat plus size; 20-22"; tail 2½-4½"; ear 3¾-5"; hind foot 5¾-7¼". Color grayish-brown in summer, but **tail white except for occasional grayish stripe above;** color usually white in winter. Found on e. edge of Cascades in Transition and Upper Sonoran zones.

brush

28. BRUSH RABBIT, *Sylvilagus bachmani.* Cat-; 11-13¼"; tail ¾-1½"; ear 2-2¾"; hind foot 2½-3¼". **General brown color,** but with some white hairs on tail and belly. Upper Sonoran w.

jun.
sage

29. NUTTALL COTTONTAIL, *Sylvilagus nuttallii.* Cat -; 12-13½"; tail 1¾-2"; ear 2¼-2¾"; hind foot 3½-4". **Brownish-gray above, whitish below; ears black-tipped.** Upper Sonoran and Transition Life Zones. Similar Eastern Cottontail has brown ears.

SQUIRRELS

V. Order Rodentia (Rodents)

A. Family APLODONTIIDAE (Mountain Beavers)

30. MOUNTAIN BEAVER, *Aplodontia rufa*. Cat -; 11-17"; tail not visible. The blackish-brown color all over (good camouflage in a dark forest), distinctive shape and **whitish blotch below the ear** make this strange animal easy to recognize. It is not related to the true beaver except very remotely. The teeth are very peculiar with a tiny and nearly cylindrical upper premolar, and with the other grinding teeth rootless and with little cups on their surfaces. Found from Transition to Hudsonian Life Zones. Has a whimpering cry, and is strictly nocturnal, living in numerous burrows.

str.wd.
pine
red fir
sitk.-spr.
w.hem.
streams
lodg.

B. Family SCIURIDAE (Squirrels and Marmots)

31. YELLOW-BELLIED MARMOT, *Marmota flaviventris*. Cat plus size; 14-20"; tail 5¼-8". **Distinctive yellowish-brown color with white-tipped hairs making it grizzly in appearance;** belly drab yellow; **dark bar on face; whitish around eye.** Found in most of our region except Klamath and Olympic Mts. in Canadian and Hudsonian Life Zones. Eats in meadows, hides in rocks.

rocks
mt.mead.
s.a.mead.
conif.

32. HOARY MARMOT, *Marmota caligata*. Cat plus size; 11-22"; tail 6¾-10". Back a mixture of grayish and black, underparts whitish; **distinctive dark bar across face with white below and above; dark rusty-brown tail.** Usually has burrow in rock talus, but sometimes in open meadows. Hudsonian zone in Washington.

rocks
mt.mead.
s.a.mead.

✝33. OLYMPIC MARMOT, *Marmota olympus*. Cat plus size. 10-21"; tail 7¾-10". The **generally dark brown color is distinctive;** the bar across the face is not so dark or distinctly-marked as in the Hoary or even the Yellow-bellied Marmot; some yellowish appears on back. Digs burrows under rocks of talus slopes, but sometimes in open meadows. Found only in the Olympic Mts. in the Hudsonian Life Zone.

rocks
s.a.mead.

Marmots are the largest of all the squirrels, but do not have cheek pouches inside the mouths as do the ground squirrels. Also they do not store food, as do most squirrels, but stuff themselves with herbs and grass in the high mountain meadows in the summer and fall until they build up enough fat to make about half the weight of the body. This then serves them as food to be drawn on during the long cold winter when they hibernate in deep sleep.

grass
mt.mead.
s.a.mead.
conif.

†34. COLUMBIAN GROUND SQUIRREL, *Citellus columbianus.* Cat size. 10½-11½"; tail 3-5". Gray-brown above, mottled with white specks; gray on head and neck, but **tail, legs and face reddish;** belly dark yellowish-orange to pale yellow-buff. Found in our region only in northern Washington and British Columbia in Transition to Canadian and Hudsonian Life Zones, in open forests.

grass
mt.mead.
jun.
pine
red fir
lodg.

35. BELDING GROUND SQUIRREL, *Citellus beldingi.* Rat=; 7¾ - 9"; tail 2¼-3". **A wide band of grayish, brownish or grayish-brown down the back;** under parts and sides light brownish or light brownish-white; **tail very short** and reddish or reddish-brown on underside. Often called "picket pin gopher" because of its habit of sitting up straight like a stake. Found in our region only in n.e. California and adjacent Oregon from Sonoran to Canadian Life Zones. A shrill whistle of alarm as squirrel darts into hole.

grass
mt.mead.
s.a.mead.
brush
mix.ev.
mix.con.
jun.
str.wd.

36. BEECHEY GROUND SQUIRREL, *Otospermophilus beecheyi.* Rat+size; 9¾-12"; **tail 5½-7¾" or more than ½ body and head length.** The general gray color of the body is flecked with light spots in rear, **while a dark gray to gray-brown band extends from the head down the back;** a lighter gray appears on sides of head and shoulders, with under parts light brown. Found in all life zones up to Hudsonian, but not in n. Washington or B. C.

conif.

†37. CASCADES GOLDEN-MANTLED GROUND SQUIRREL, *Callospermophilus saturatus.* Rat−; 7½- 7¾ "; tail 3¾-4½". **A broad white stripe on the side of the body is bordered by two black stripes, which usually vary in length, one sometimes disappearing;** general color tawny, but paler beneath. Found in Washington and B. C. in Transition mainly, but also Canadian zones.

conif.

38. SIERRA NEVADA GOLDEN-MANTLED GROUND SQUIRREL, *Callosphermophilus lateralis.* Rat−size; 6- 7¾"; tail 3¼-4". Tawny below and on legs; tail bordered with white hairs; **broad white stripe on side bordered by two black stripes of nearly equal length; shoulders and head bright golden-yellow.** Found in Transition and Canadian Life Zones of Oregon and California.

The ground squirrels described above usually combine the ability to store fat in their bodies, to use as emergency food during their long sleep when the weather is too hot and dry or too cold, with the instinctive wisdom to store food under ground for later use. All have shrill cries.

SQUIRRELS

30. Mountain Beaver DA

32. Hoary Marmot DA

31. Yellow-bellied Marmot DA

36. Beechey Ground Squirrel JB

38. Sierra Nevada Golden-mantled Ground Squirrel DA

40. Yellow Pine Chipmunk DA

41. Townsend Chipmunk DA

35. Belding Ground Squirrel CL

NOTE: Chipmunks are easily told from Golden-mantled Ground Squirrels, which superficially look like them, by the stripes found on the faces of the chipmunks, and by their smaller size.

jun.
sage
brush
pume.
pine

†39. LEAST CHIPMUNK, *Eutamias minimus*. Mouse+;4-4½"; tail 2¾-3½" (notice that chipmunk tails are much longer in proportion than in golden mantled ground squirrels). Generally rough grayish in color with **5 distinct black strips and 4 distinct whitish stripes on the back, all reaching the base of the tail; ear uniform grayish; the round tail is grayish-yellow to bright yellow on the under side.** A dull black stripe through eye on face, brownish stripe below medium white stripe. Found on the eastern edge of our region, mainly in Upper Sonoran.

pine
jun.
west hem.
mix.con.
dg.fir

40. YELLOW PINE CHIPMUNK, *Eutamias amoenus*. Mouse+; 4½-5¼";tail 2¾-4¼". Brightly colored, with stripes quite distinct. **The inner whitish stripes usually broader and more distinctive than outer whitish stripes, which appear yellowish-tinged;** tail with dark tip and yellowish-brown under edge; belly whitish-yellow. Found in most of region in Transition to Hudsonian Life Zones.

conif.

41. TOWNSEND CHIPMUNK, *Eutamias townsendii*. Mouse+; 5¼-6";tail 3½-5". This large chipmunk is **distinctive for reddish to yellowish-brown under tail; back side of ear with distinct white rim against black; a whitish stripe followed by brownish stripe below the ear; and brownish undersides.** Found in most of our region on floor of forests in Transition Life Zones and Canadian.

str.wd.
pine
mix.ev.

42. WESTERN GRAY SQUIRREL, *Sciurus griseus*. Cat minus; 10¼-12"; tail 9½-11" (or about 95% of head and body length). Easily identified by **large size, silvery-gray color above, large bushy tail with white edges and white belly and throat.** In most of region except n. Washington and in B. C. in Upper Sonoran and Transition Life Zones, climbing most of the time in the trees. Chatters.

conif.

43. DOUGLAS SQUIRREL, *Tamiasciurus douglasii*. Rat - ; 5¾-6"; tail 5-6". Also easily identified by **dark olive color above, yellow-white to dark orange below and whitish edge surrounding the dark tail.** Very noisy chatterer. Found in most of region from Transition to Hudsonian Life Zones.

Chipmunks screech, while tree squirrels chatter; both are daylight lovers and both store seeds, dried fruit, etc., in holes.

MICE

181

Ear tufts in winter

43. Douglas Squirrel DA DA

42. Western Gray Squirrel

44. Northern Flying Squirrel DA

45. Camas Pocket Gopher DA

53. Dusky-footed Wood Rat LM

52. Deer Mouse DA

54. Bushy-tailed Wood Rat DA

49. Western Harvest Mouse DA

conif.

44. NORTHERN FLYING SQUIRREL, *Glaucomys sabrinus.* Rat +; 5½-6½"; tail 4½-5¾". Fur a rich soft lead gray in texture and color; a **well-furred skin membrane stretches between fore and hind limbs to enable the squirrel to glide (not fly) between the branches of one tree and the base of another; membrane has white border;** belly creamy-white. Escapes most enemies by gliding, but owls can often catch it. Feeds on fungi mainly in summer, and lichens in winter, but also seeds, insects, fruits, etc. Found in most of region in Transition and Canadian Life zones.

GEOMYIDAE (Pocket Gopher Family)

Gophers are distinguished by their powerful front feet for digging (longer than the mole), their fur-lined cheek-pouches for carrying food, and their comparatively short, lightly-furred tails. The comparison of a gopher mound and tunnel to those of a mole are shown on page 172. Gophers live mainly on plant tubers, roots and leaves, living underground.

grass
cult.

45. CAMAS POCKET GOPHER, *Thomomys bulbivorus.* Rat –; male 8-8½"; hind foot 1½-1¾ inches. Female 7¼-8". **Incisor teeth protrude far out; tail almost naked;** general color blackish-brown; white spot on chin and around anus. Found along edge of Cascades in Willamette Valley, Oregon, Transition Life Zone.

grass
mt.mead
s.a.mead.
alp.
cult.

†46. **MAZAMA POCKET GOPHER,** *Thomomys mazama.* Rat-size; ♂5½-6¼";hind foot 1-1¼". Female 5¼-6": Reddish-brown or (rarely) black above, slightly paler below; **black area around ear; so similar to** *T. talpoides* (below) that the best way to tell difference is by locality. **Found mainly from crest of Cascades to the west in Oregon;** also in Olympic Mts. and Puget Sound area of Washington, in most life zones.

grass
mt.mead.
str.wd.
pine
sage
cult.

†47. **NORTHERN POCKET GOPHER,** *Thomomys talpoides.* Rat-:♂5-6¼; hind foot 1-1¼". Female 4¾-5¾". Color in summer grayish to yellowish-brown, gray on belly, often with much white under chin and on throat; **black area around ear 3 x size of ear. Found mainly east of Cascades in Upper Sonoran and Transition zones.** Gophers sometimes chatter or growl.

grass
mt.mead
cult.

†48. **BOTTA POCKET GOPHER,** *Thomomys bottae.* Rat -. Male 5¼-7"; hind foot 1-1¼"; female 5-6". Dark brown to light yellow color above; below grayish to whitish; **dark area around ear same size as ear.** S. Ore. and n. Calif., Sonoran to Canadian.

RATS

Family CRICETIDAE (Native Mice and Rats)

This family differs from the old world mice and rats (Muridae) by having the cusps or tubercles on the tops of the molar teeth in two longitudinal rows instead of three. Also they are silkier haired and brighter-eyed, altogether looking much more attractive.

49. WESTERN HARVEST MOUSE, *Reithrodontomys megalotis*. Mouse -:2¾-3": tail 2¼-3¾". A blackish-brown band runs down the back, while the sides are light brownish, and the **belly and throat are grayish touched with light brown; hind foot is distinctively a small ½-¾" long; the ear 2/5-3/5"**. Found in southern part of our region and as far north as Crater Lake from Sonoran to Hudsonian Life Zones. A distinctive feature of the harvest mouse is the **grooved incisor teeth**. Nocturnal seed & fruit eaters.
grass
mt.mead.
cult.
conif.
brush
s.a.mead.

†50. FOREST DEER MOUSE, *Peromyscus oreas*. Mouse size. 3¼-4"; tail at least 4" long, usually longer than head and body together, generally white-tipped. Color grayish-brown above, white below. Found in Transition and Canadian Life Zones.
wh.fir
dg.fir
mix.conif.
gr.fir

†51. PINYON MOUSE, *Peromyscus truei*. Rat-:3¾-4¼"; **tail 3-5", usually over 90% of body and head length, but rarely over that length, distinctly bi-colored whitish below and dark brown above.** Found mainly in Upper Sonoran Life Zone in northern California and southern Oregon.
brush
jun.

52. DEER MOUSE, *Peromyscus maniculatus* Mouse+3½-4½"; tail 2¼-3½", almost always **less than 90% of body and head length except in coastal subspecies not in our region**; tail bi-colored, but not as sharply so as in *P. truei*. Has light spot in front of ear. Found in most life zones, but rare in Cascades of Washington.
found in most habitats except water

53. DUSKY-FOOTED WOOD RAT, *Neotoma fuscipes*. Rat size; 7¼- 9"; **tail scaly and covered with short hairs, nearly as long as the body and head, 6-9½"; hind foot 1¼-1¾"**. Color grayish-brown above with black hairs, whitish underparts and feet except **dusky above on hind feet**. Found in Sonoran and Transition zones in Oregon and California, usually west of high mountains.
brush
mix.ev.
mix.con.
rocks
str.wd.

54. BUSHY-TAILED WOOD RAT, *Neotoma cinerea*. Rat size. 6¼-9¾"; **tail 4¾-8¾", with bushy hairs;** color similar to above, but white below looks ashy. Found from Upper Sonoran to Canadian Life Zones in all of region. Both wood rats make typical piled stick nests, each rat controlling a definite territory around nest.
sage
pine
ref fir
lodg.
str.wd.

The voles and meadow mice described and pictured on this and the following pages belong to the sub-family of Microtine Mice, of which the muskrat (Page 187) is also a member. They all have long hairs that cover much of the ears from the front, and all have comparatively short tails, less than half the total length, with the exception of the much larger muskrat. Most are hard to tell apart even by experts, but may usually be distinguished best by habitats and localities where found.

s.a.mead.
mt.mead.

55. NORTHERN BOG VOLE, *Synaptomys borealis*. Mouse +; 4- 4¼"; tail ¾-1", or less than 1/5 total length; ears very small. **Told best by location and habitat, in northern Washington and s.w. B. C. in cold wet meadows of Hudsonian Life Zone, making grass-covered tunnels through thick herbs.** Upper incisors differently colored.

pine
red fir
sitk.-spr.
lodg.
west.hem.
mt.mead.

56. HEATHER VOLE, *Phenacomys intermedius*. Mouse +;4-5"; tail 1¼-1½", longer than above mouse. **Body above ashy-gray, often touched with brown; tail darker above, lighter below.** Found from the Transition through Canadian, but mainly Hudsonian Life Zone in much of our region; it likes to live in patches of huckleberry and heather in open spaces in the forest, feeding mainly on huckleberry leaves and those of lousewort and bear grass.

sage
jun.
pume.

†57. SAGEBRUSH VOLE, *Lagurus curtatus*. Mouse + :3¾-4½": tail ½-1¼", or shorter than most other meadow mice. **Ashy-gray color above is distinctive, though sometimes touched with brown, belly a lighter gray, the color harmonizing with the sagebrush.** Found in Upper Sonoran and Transition Life Zones on east edge of mountains as far north as Lake Chelan in Washington.

mt.mead.
grass
rocks
brush

58. GAPPER RED-BACKED MOUSE, *Clethrionomys gapperi*. Mouse plus; 3¾-4½"; tail 1½-2", or around half as long as the head and body together. **A broad reddish band on the back is distinct from gray or silvery sides; light brownish-white below.** Found in Washington and B. C. in Transition and Canadian Life Zones.

mix.con.

59. WESTERN RED-BACKED MOUSE, *Clethrionomys occidentalis*. Mouse +; to rat-; 3¾-4¾";tail 1¾-2¼", with long hairs at the tip. Reddish-brown and black above, gray below. Found in Oregon and n.w. California in Transition and Canadian Life Zones.

60. LONG-TAILED MEADOW MOUSE, *Microtus longicaudus*. Mouse+:4¼-5"; tail 2-3¾", or about 1/3 total length, long-haired

MICE, RATS

DA
55. Northern Bog Vole

DA
56. Heather Vole

DA 58. Gapper Red-backed Mouse

DA
59. Western Red-backed Mouse

DA
60. Long-tailed Meadow Mouse

DA
64. Water Rat or Richardson Meadow Mouse

JB
65. Montane Meadow Mouse

DA
67. Pacific Jumping Mouse

str.wd.
grass
mt.mead.
s.a.mead.
conif.

at tip, and with dark color above, light below. Reddish to grayish brown band down the back, with lighter gray sides and grayish-blue belly and throat. Does not make as sharply-marked trails in the grass as other meadow mice. Found in most of our region in Transition and Canadian Life Zones. Likes wet meadows near willows.

grass
mt.mead.
marsh
conif.

†61. OREGON MEADOW MOUSE, *Microtus oregoni*. Mouse +; 3¾-4½; tail 1¼-1¾". The **dense short fur is dark brown or black to sooty gray above** with the belly brownish-gray; **the ears have little hair on them, but are almost hidden by the fur; tiny eyes.** Transition to Hudsonian zones in most of region except n.e. Calif.

grass
mt.mead.

†62. CALIFORNIA MEADOW MOUSE, *Microtus californicus*. Mouse+; 4½-5¾; tail 1¾-2¾". Color olive-brown to reddish-brown above, pale blue-gray to whitish below; **ears prominent;** very short hairs on tip of tail. Found in Upper Sonoran Life Zone at base of mountains in northern California and southern Oregon.

grass

†63. TOWNSEND MEADOW MOUSE, *Microtus townsendii*. Mouse+; 4¾-6¼"; **tail 2-2¾; tail ½ of head and body length, which is unusually long for a meadow mouse, as is also size.** Color dark-brownish above, smoky gray below. Found in western edge of region in upper Sonoran and Transition zones.

streams
marsh

64. WATER RAT or RICHARDSON MEADOW MOUSE, *Microtus richardsoni*. Mouse plus; 5-6¾"; tail 2¾-3¾. Color reddish-brown to dark brown above; brownish-gray below. **Large size and habit of burrowing along swift streams or marshes distinctive.** Canadian and Hudsonian zones in Oregon, Washington and B. C.

mt.mead.
grass
conif.
str.wd.

65. MONTANE MEADOW MOUSE, *Microtus montanus*. 4½-5¼"; tail 1¼-2¾", or less than 1/3 total length. Color is dark brown above, grayish below; **ears hidden. Digs holes in wet meadows and near springs.** Transition to Canadian Life Zones mainly in eastern parts of Cascades of Oregon and in northern California.

Family ZAPODIDAE (Jumping Mice)

mt.mead.
grass
str.wd.

†66. WESTERN JUMPING MOUSE, *Zapus princeps*. Mouse =; 8½-10"; **tail 4¾-6", or more than half total length.** Dark brown band down lower back; yellowish with black markings on upper back. Transition and Canadian Life Zones, n. Calif. and s. Oregon.

67. PACIFIC JUMPING MOUSE, *Zapus trinotatus*. Mouse =;

3¾-4"; **tail 4¾-6";** distinctly bi-colored. Blackish-brown above; orange yellow sides; **belly white.** Found in Transition Life Zone on Cascades western slopes down to Crater Lake area, and down coast to northwestern California.

mt.mead.
grass
dg.fir
sitk.-spr.
west.hem.
str.wd.

Family CRICETIDAE (Native rats and mice, con't)

68. MUSKRAT, *Ondatra zibethica.* Rat+size;10½-13"; **tail 6¾-11½", distinctively flattened from side to side; hind feet very large, 2½-3½", webbed.** Has rich reddish-brown to dark brown fur. An excellent swimmer, building house of water plants and brush in pond (smaller than beaver's) or digging underwater hole in bank of pond or stream up to air and room for nest; principal enemy is the mink. Found mainly in lakes, slow-moving streams, etc. in foothills, but some may get as high as Canadian zone.

water
marsh
str.wd.

Family CASTORIDAE (Beavers)

69. BEAVER, *Castor canadensis.*Raccoon size; 2-2½";tail 13½-17", **very large, flat and largely hairless;** hind feet very large, 7-8". **Fur rich dark to golden brown on back, lighter underneath.** Feeds mainly on bark, storing parts of small cottonwoods, etc. under water for winter supply; builds dam to make pond and builds house of sticks, mud and water plants in and above water. Found in most of our region from Upper Sonoran to Canadian zones.

water
stream
str.wd.

Family CAPROMYIDAE (Nutrias)

70. NUTRIA,*Myocastor coypu.* Raccoon size; 20-26"; **tail 12-17", or 2/3 or more of body length, scaly and round; very large, webbed hind feet.** Brownish general color, with silky underfur beneath coarse guard hairs that are colorless. It has been introduced from South America and spread to many of our streams, where it digs large holes in banks and may wander ashore to attack cultivated crops, thus becoming a dangerous pest. Sonoran and Transition.

water
marsh
stream
cult.
str. wd.

Family ERETHIZONTIDAE (American Porcupines)

71. PORCUPINE, *Erethizon dorsatum.* Raccoon =; 20-22"; tail 7-12". Color yellowish to yellowish-brown to blackish above, somewhat lighter below. **Has distinctive stiff quills and spines all over body and tail, each spine with reverse barbs so it is very hard**

conif.
jun.

188 WILDLIFE AND PLANTS OF THE CASCADES

68. Muskrat

70. Nutria

69. Beaver

71. Porcupine

to get out once it has entered the flesh. It defends itself by rolling into a ball to protect soft underbelly, and whipping about with its armed tail (rarely, however, ever throwing any barbed spines). It climbs mainly coniferous trees to eat bark, sometimes killing the tree by ringbarking. Found in dry Transition and Canadian zones of most of region, but not n.w. Washington or southwestern B. C.

VI. Order Carnivora

Family CANIDAE (dogs, foxes, wolves, etc.)

72. RED FOX, *Vulpes fulva*. Raccoon -; 22-25"; tail 12-16"; very thick and fluffy with white tip. Several color types: **an all red phase with blackish legs, whitish belly; black phase is mostly blackish, rarely with silver hairs; cross phase is like the red phase but darker and with a blackish band across the shoulders and back.** Found in most of our regions, mainly in Canadian and Hudsonian Life Zones (not in Olympic Mts.). A clever hunter of mice.

mt.mead.
conif.
s.a.mead.

73. GRAY FOX, *Urocyon cinereoargenteus*. Raccoon =; 23-29":tail 11-17½", less fluffy, but with distinctive **black crest running down the upper side to the black tip.** General gray color, except for reddish in front, black nose and whitish undersides. This fox has been known to climb trees to escape pursuit or hunt birds eggs, but it mainly hunts gophers, wood rats, mice and rabbits, so is very good at keeping these animals under control and should be considered a fine ally of man, hence should not be shot, trapped or poisoned. Both foxes prefer making dens in rock slides or caves, but sometimes dig burrows. Men, dogs, eagles and greathorned owls are their chief enemies. Found mainly in Upper Sonoran and Transition Life Zones in California and Oregon.

brush
sage
str.wd.
mix.ev.
mix.con.
jun.

74. WOLF, *Canis lupus*. 3-5'; looking like very large grayish-brown German Shepherd Dog, with **black-tipped tail, about 14-20" long, held high when running, and quite bushy in appearance;** hind foot very large, leaving track about 5" long. May hunt in packs in winter, giving long deep howls, and running down animals as large as elk and deer. Found in northern Wash. and in B.C.

conif.
mt.mead.
s.a.mead.
str.wd.

75. COYOTE, *Canis latrans*. 2-3½' long; **tail 11-16", not so bushy as the above animal;** ears more long and pointed than wolf; tail always held low when running, sometimes between legs. The mountain variety of coyote may be as much as foot longer than

most
habitats

190   WILDLIFE AND PLANTS OF THE CASCADES

73. Gray Fox LM

72. Red Fox
DA

74. Wolf
DA

75. Coyote
DA

BEARS

the desert variety. Track of coyote about 2½-3½". Since the chief food of coyotes is mice, rats, rabbits, ground squirrels, hares, gophers and large insects, all possible pests to crops, they help maintain balance in nature, and should be destroyed only when they attack sheep. At such times, unfortunately, men too often try to poison them, killing in the process many useful birds, dogs and other valuable creatures. Very widespread in all zones.

*76. BLACK BEAR, *Euarctos americanus*. Head and body 4½-5'; **tail usually under 6", often concealed in fur;** hind foot up to 9" long, placed with both heel and toes on the ground; claws of front feet up to 2¾"; the face curves outward instead of inward as in the grizzly. General color all black or cinnamon brown except for brown face. This bear feeds mainly on small mammals, insect grubs, berries and vegetable matter, going into hibernation in a den during the cold part of the year. Dangerous to feed or tease. Found in most of region in Transition and Canadian zones.

conif.

str.wd.

mt.mead.

s.a.mead

mix.ev.

brush

* 77. GRIZZLY BEAR, *Ursus chelan*. 4-7' long; tail very small. 3-5' high at the shoulders; claws of forefeet 3-4" long. Brown to brownish-yellow color has **grizzly appearance because of numerous white-tipped hairs.** The grizzly is more aggressive than the black bear and more likely to attack sheep, cattle, horses or even man, which explains why the species is now near extinction. It uses powerful muscles and claws to overturn boulders and logs to get at mice, ground squirrels, gophers, etc., that it finds underneath. It is estimated that only about 10 individuals may still be roaming the wilderness in far-northern Washington, though a greater number can be found in British Columbia. **Notice hump above shoulders.**

mt.mead.

rocks

s.a.mead.

conif.

str.wd.

brush

Family PROCYONIDAE (Raccoons and Ringtails)

Members of this family walk flat on their hind feet like bears.

78. RACCOON, *Procyon lotor*. 18-28"; tail 8-12", usually grayish-brown like rest of body, but ringed with black. **Black mask on face is very distinctive. The chunky, powerful body and aggressive personality make the raccoon a formidable fighter;** it is a good swimmer also and may drown an attacking dog in the water by holding its nose under water. Color grayish-brown above, with some black hairs, lighter gray below. It is very clever with its hands, catching fish and crayfish with them. It has a unique long

str.wd.

water

mt.mead.

conif.

mix.ev.

and rather sad "whoooo-ooo-ooo" call, heard mostly on rainy nights. It feeds on most anything, loving dried grapes, berries and figs. Found over most of our region up to the Canadian zone.

79. RINGTAIL, *Bassariscus astutus.* (Also called ring-tailed

78. Raccoon
79. Ringtail
80. Long-tailed Weasel
Weasel tail in winter
Summer
83. Fisher
84. Mink
81. Ermine
82. Marten

cat and cacomistle).   Cat size; head and body 12-18"; tail 12-
18" or same length about as head and body, not completely circled   rocks
with black rings. Wide white areas surround and are surrounded   brush
by narrower black areas on face; general color brownish shading   str.wd.
to black, lighter below. Comes out mainly in the middle of the
night, hunting small rodents. S. Oregon and n. Calif. in Upper
Sonoran and the bottom edge of the Canadian zone.

Family MUSTELIDAE (Weasels, badgers, skunks, etc.)

The short legs with 5 toes on each foot, the fine and valuable fur, and the strongly developed scent glands are distinctive.

80. LONG-TAILED WEASEL, *Mustela frenata*.   Cat -;8-15";
tail 4-6½" or usually more than 45% of head and body length,   conif.
with black tip and white on first third of lower side. Color gener-   str.wd.
ally brown above and yellowish white on throat, belly and feet; a   mix.ev.
white spot between the eyes; white all over except for tail tip in   mead.
winter, in higher mountains, but remains brown in lower warmer
areas. Hunts mice, gophers, etc. so is active ally of man. Found
in most of our region in almost all life zones.

81. ERMINE, *Mustela erminea*. Rat to rat + size,   5½-11";
tail always less than 45% of head and body length or 1¾-2½", also   red fir
tipped with black, but without white underneath in summer pel-   lodg.
age.   Generally brown above and white below, but usually pure   sub.alp.
white all over in winter except for black tip of tail. Found mainly
in higher mountains of region in Canadian and Hudsonian zones.

82. MARTEN, *Martes americana*.   Cat plus size; 14-19";
tail 7-9"; ears 1-1¾", unusually pointed and large for weasel family. General color yellowish or golden brown above, with feet and   conif.
tip of tail blackish; orange, yellowish orange or yellowish on chest
and throat; tail rather bushy. Hunts mainly squirrels in trees and
rock slides, travelling at high speed. Found in most of our region,
mainly in Canadian Life Zone, but also in Hudsonian and Transition.

83. FISHER, *Martes pennanti*. Raccoon -; 19-24"; tail 13½-
17". Dark or blackish-brown general color, but grayish shoulders,   yel.pine
grizzled fur on top of head with white hairs and whitish spots on   red fir
belly and throat. It does not really fish at all, but feeds mainly on   lodg.
large rodents and birds. They even run down and kill martens
and are probably the most successful killers of porcupines. They
are very rare and should not be killed or trapped. They are found

77. Grizzly Bear, 6-7'

76. Black Bear, 5-6'

COLOR PLATE 1 - BEARS

COLOR PLATE 2 - 96. Mountain Goat, height 3-3½′.

in most of our region mainly in Canadian, but also neighboring zones.

water str.wd.
84. MINK, *Mustela vison*. Cat plus size ; 12-21"; tail 6-7½"; ear very short, hidden in fur; toes partially webbed for swimming. **Dark brown color all over, rarely with whitish spots on chest.** Found in most of our region, except rare in northern Washington and s.w. B. C., up to Canadian Life Zone. Lives largely on fish.

sub-alp.
alpine
85. WOLVERINE, *Gulo luscus*. 26-38"; tail 7½-10½", very thick. General color smoky brown or blackish, **with 2 large light brownish or yellowish bands running along sides and meeting at the base of the tail; large powerful claws appear white against dark legs; body very thick and powerful.** This rare animal is quite a sight to see; it rarely attacks men, but is so ferocious when attacked that even bears and mountain lions leave it alone. It feeds largely on large rodents such as the marmots; it has a very strong smell. Found in wildest parts of our region from Hudsonian to Arctic-Alpine Life Zones. Because of rarity, it is protected by law.

sage
pine jun.
conif.
mead.
str.wd.
grass
86. BADGER, *Taxidea taxus*. Raccoon - ; 18-24"; tail rather short, 3½-6", and roughly-haired. The brownish-gray fur appears and feels very rough; **the white single stripe down back and head, the black and white markings on the face, and the long, powerful claws for digging are very distinctive.** It has a peculiar method of running at a steady trot that makes it look as though it is gliding. The body is whirled around swiftly when attacked and a hissing snarl given. It digs out marmots, ground squirrels and other rodents from their burrows. Found from the Upper Sonoran into the Transition Life Zone in southern part of our region, but found only on eastern edge of Cascades in n. Ore. and in Wash.

str.wd.
mix.ev
conif.
mead.
87. STRIPED SKUNK, *Mephitis mephitis*. Cat minus ; 14-17", **tail 7½-15½", very long and fluffy. Distinctive black color, but with two broad white stripes down back, one narrow white stripe down face, and some whitish hairs in tail.** Skunks have two glands in the rear that are activated by powerful muscles, but they use these almost solely when attacked, ejecting a fine spray, up to 15 feet down-wind, that temporarily, but rather painfully blinds and nauseates the attacker. Since they feed mainly on insects and mice, they are generally helpful allies of man and should not be killed. Found from Sonoran up into Canadian Life Zone.

88. SPOTTED SKUNK, *Spilogale putorius*. Cat-; 9-12"; tail

WOLVERINE, SKUNKS, OTTERS

85. Wolverine DA

86. Badger LM

87. Striped Skunk ED

88. Spotted Skunk JB

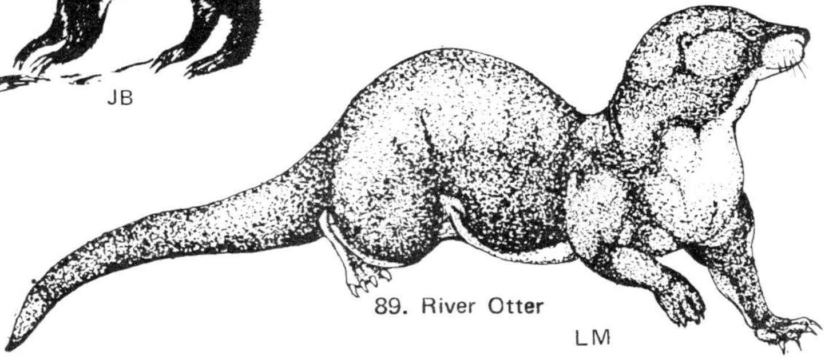

89. River Otter LM

COLOR PLATE 3 - 94. Columbia Black-tailed Deer, height 3-3½'

COLOR PLATE 4 - 93. American Elk, height 4½-5'

200 WILDLIFE AND PLANTS OF THE CASCADES

water
str.wd.
5-7". The smaller size and incomplete and scattered white stripes and spots are distinctive; also white-tipped tail. Found from Sonoran up into Transition Life Zone in much of region.

89. RIVER OTTER, *Lutra canadensis.* 2-2½'; tail 1-1½'. The slim, slick shape, overall brown color, webbed feet and long, tapering tail are distinctive. Feeds mainly on fish. Found in most regions up to Canadian Life Zone. Loves to slide down banks.

92. Mountain Lion

Family FELIDAE (Cats)   LM

rocks
conif.
str.wd.
mix.ev.
cult.
mead.
90. BOBCAT, *Lynx rufus.* 2-2¼'; tail 5-8", comparatively short, and with dark bands near tip. Color generally tawny with numerous dark bars and spots; tufted and pointed ears. It hunts mainly rodents and rabbits and is one of man's greatest allies in destruction of these crop-destroying pests. The few game birds it kills are small pay indeed for this aid, and no more harmful work has been done than the wide-scale poisoning of so-called "varmints" urged on by misguided farmers and sportsmen. Found everywhere.

sub-alp.
conif.
mead.
91. CANADA LYNX, *Lynx canadensis.* 2½-2¾'; tail 3¾-5", tipped with black instead of barred; ear also tipped with black. General color soft gray with somewhat yellowish tinge; lighter gray below with some dark spots; fur more reddish in summer;

ELK, DEER

long hairs form ear tufts. Only in n. Washington and B. C. in high zones.

92. MOUNTAIN LION, *Felis concolor.* 3-6¼' long; tail 1¾-2½', with black tip. **Distinctive long slim body, rounded ears and long tail, plus great size; a reddish brown color phase contrasts with a smoky-gray phase**, both phases are whitish below and white inside the ears. Cubs are usually spotted. The mountain lion is particularly useful in keeping deer populations normal by weeding out the weaklings. Found in most of region in Sonoran and Transition zones.

brush
rocks
sage
conif.
mt.mead.
caves

VII. Order Artiodactyla (Hoofed animals)
Family CERVIDAE (Elk and Deer)

* 93. CANADIAN ELK or WAPITI, *Cervus canadensis.* 4½-5' high; females weight 500-600 pounds, males 700-900 pounds; length 5½-8'. **Has distinctive grizzly brown color, and darker brown mane, about throat; more grayish-brown farther back and on sides; yellowish-brown rump patch; has canine teeth in upper jaw;** the very long heavy horns of the bulls are very different from those of deer. Bulls begin gathering their herds of cows in the fall when the thrilling bugling of the great herd bulls can be contrasted with the rather shriller whistling of the young bulls. Fights between mature bulls last till one is driven away or killed. Bulls often leave "sign posts" to mark the limits of their territories by scraping the bases of trees with a burr at the base of the antler. Man and the mountain lion are the main enemies. Found mainly in the Transition and Canadian Life Zones in the central and south Cascades of Washington, scattered places of the Cascades of Oregon and northern California, and in the Olympic Mountains.

mt.mead.
str.wd.
conif.

* 94. MULE DEER, *Odocoileus hemionus.* 4-6' long, 3-3½' high. **The antlers do not rise from a single main beam as in the white-tailed deer, but keep branching out in two directions, and there are no forward overhanging brow and bez tines as in the elk, the color varies from a summer reddish or yellowish-brown to a winter bluish gray;** fawns are spotted; the tail has a black tip, and there is **a white rump patch.** The Black-tailed deer of the coast has the tail almost entirely black. It is a subspecies of the mule deer, and has a much smaller and narrower white rump patch. As the tines of the antlers of the bucks grow in summer they become covered

mt. mead.
s.a.mead.
str.wd.
conif.
sage
brush
mix.ev.
pume.

with a soft velvet-like fur, which is rubbed off in fall when the buck prepares for combat over harems of does. Found in most of our region in all life zones up to Hudsonian. Bounds high on run.

Family ANTILOCAPRIDAE

sage
grass

95. PRONGHORN ANTELOPE, *Antilocapra americana.* About 3' high. The bright white markings and rump against the yellowish-brown body are unmistakable. E. side Sonoran Life Zones.

Family BOVIDAE (cattle, sheep, goats, etc.)

rocks
s.a.mead.

* 96. MOUNTAIN GOAT, *Oreamnos americanus.* Height 3-3½'; 4-6' long. **Distinctive curved, sharp black horns and white massive body.** Cascades of Washington and B. C. Tremendous rock climbers.

95. Pronghorn Antelope

COMMON BIRDS

Birds of the Cascades are very numerous, interesting and beautiful, especially in the warm months of the year, but, even in winter, there are many of interest to see. Because of the wings of birds, they can move about easily from one region to another. So we observe that some are resident all the year, some are winter visitors, others spring and fall migrants. **Unless otherwise noted in the descriptions, a bird may be assumed to be an all year resident.**

On account of limited room, the descriptions of birds that follow cover only the important points so as to give some space for habits. In watching birds, note particularly the types of bills(see illustrations below), types of feet, sizes and shapes of bodies, methods of feeding, flying and acting, and the kinds of wildlife areas or habitats a bird lives in. The most important facts about each species are emphasized by **darker type** in the text and arrows with the pictures.

Because the pictures of the birds in the pages that follow are not always in proportion to the actual sizes of the birds described, it is important to give you a proper feeling of size. To aid in this five familiar birds are taken as examples of bird sizes. Study their pictures carefully and compare the warbler (4-5"), the sparrow (5-6½"), the robin (8-10"), the dove or pigeon (11-13"), and the crow (18-24"). In descriptions sizes are given in comparison to the five birds pictured.

+ = **larger than comparative bird**
- = **smaller than comparative bird**
* = **illustrated on color plate**
† = **not illustrated anywhere**
♂ = **male**   ♀ = **female**

204 WILDLIFE AND PLANTS OF THE CASCADES

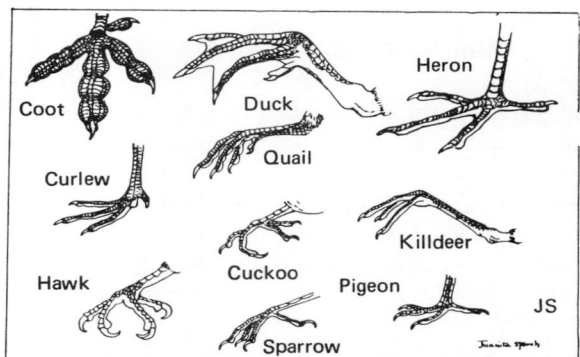

The birds are arranged in this book so as to give the maximum help in quick identification. Therefore the scientific order is sometimes bypassed so as to bring groups together that look alike, such as the swallows and the swifts. Also all the water and shore birds are grouped together.

WATER AND SHORE BIRDS

LOONS - Order GAVIIFORMES. American Loons, Family *Gaviidae*. Swimming birds, larger than ducks, **but** with shorter necks than geese; expert swimmers and divers; relatively slow wing-beats in flight, and may not be able to get out of water unless a breeze is blowing to help them.

water
1. COMMON LOON, *Gavia immer*. Size of small goose; occasional on lakes during spring and fall migration; may breed on lakes of n. Wash. and B.C. Blackish-gray general color, **with cheek, throat and underparts white; in spring, back checkered with black and white.** Long, wailing "ooo-ah-eee" call.

water
2. PACIFIC (or Arctic) LOON, *Gavia arctica*. Crow size. Resembles no. 6 at a distance, but smaller and with thinner bill. White below and grayish-black above. **In spring black bars appear on back, with black throat and gray hind neck.** Rare during migration.

1. Common Loon 28-36"

2. Pacific Loon 23-29"

GREBES AND HERONS

Order PODICIPEDIFORMES (Grebes)

Family *Podicipedidae* (Am. Grebes). Distinguished from ducks by poor flight, swift diving, narrow head and neck (always held erect), and tailless look. Usually runs across water to get started flying.

3. RED-NECKED (Holboell's) GREBE, *Podiceps grisegena*. Crow size. A large grebe with heavy, long, **yellowish bill; body grayish, with white throat and sides of head; two white patches visible on wings in flight.** Gray neck becomes reddish-brown in April; cheeks are white with black tufts on head. Migrant on lakes.   water

4. WESTERN GREBE, *Aechmophorus occidentalis*. Crow +. Blackish-gray upper parts except for single white wing patch; underparts whitish, including cheeks and front of neck; **bill yellow, long and slender. Long, slender neck and large size are distinctive.** Young of this species not striped as in other kinds, but plain gray. Found in most of the lakes of our region. Summer.   water

5. PIED-BILLED GREBE, *Podilymbus podiceps*. Pigeon size. **Distinctive thick blunt bill; also only grebe not flashing white wing patch in flight;** black ring shows near tip of bill in summer; general color brownish-black, but black throat patch only in spring and summer. Gives stuttering "kik-kik-ki" call.   water

Order CICONIIFORMES (Herons, bitterns, etc.)

These birds have long necks and long bills for using like a spear in water after fish and frogs, and long legs for wading; they often stand motionless for a long time waiting for prey to come near. In flight the head and neck are drawn back into an S-shape.

6. GREAT BLUE HERON, *Ardea herodias*. **Immense size is distinctive, standing 4' tall. Bluish-gray in color with white head and neck,** and black crest feathers. Makes low hoarse goose-like croaks as it flies with great slow wing sweeps. Found in most of our region during spring, summer and fall.   water str.wd.

7. BLACK-CROWNED NIGHT HERON, *Nycticorax nycticorax*. Crow +, **distinctively thick-bodied. Our only heron with black back and top of head;** eyes red; pale grayish-white below; wings gray; immature is grayish-brown, streaked and spotted with white. Hoarse "cwa-cwa" cry. East side Cascades in summer.   water str.wd.

206   WILDLIFE AND PLANTS OF THE CASCADES

4. Western Grebe
22-29"

3; Red-necked Grebe
18-22½"

7; Black-
Crowned
Night
Heron
23-28"

5. Pied-billed Grebe   12-15"

8. Mallard   20½-28"

6. Great Blue Heron
42-52"

9; Green-winged Teal   12½-15½"

11. Bufflehead   13-15½"

10. Pintail   25-29"

DUCKS

Order ANSERIFORMES (Ducks, geese and swans)

Sub. Fam. *ANATINAE.* Surface-Feeding Ducks. Normally obtain plant food by tipping up body in water and dabbling for it with bills. In rising from water, they usually spring straight up. Females usually plain colored.

8. COMMON MALLARD, *Anas platyrhynchos.* Crow size and +. **The only male duck with green head and neck,** a reddish-brown breast and white ring on neck; **both sexes have conspicuous white borders on both sides of metallic blue wing patch;** female mottled brown. Visits our region mainly in spring, summer and fall.   water str.wd.

9. GREEN-WINGED TEAL, *Anas carolinensis.* Pigeon size. Males have reddish-brown head with metallic-green sides; **slender white crescent appears on shoulder; a metallic green speculum (or wing patch); yellowish-white patches on each side of black area under tail;** sides of body gray. Female plain brown, but back feathers tipped with ashy color. Male has peeping cry, and sharp whistle. Found in most of our region except coldest areas in winter.   water str.wd.

10. PINTAIL, *Anas acuta.* Crow +. Male with **distinctive long slim neck, white in front, dark behind; long slim pointed tail;** wavy black lines appear on gray back. Female slender and streaked brown. Pointed tail often lost in winter. Both sexes show whitish border on hind part of wings in flight. Gives liquid "kuek-kuek" cry; soft "quack" from female. Found in most of region.   water str.wd.

Sub. Fam. *AYTHYINAE.* Diving Ducks dive deeply for plant and animal food; in rising from water, they first patter along the surface.

11. BUFFLEHEAD, *Bucephala albeola.* Pigeon size. **Male has fluffy black and white head;** light ring around neck; **large white patch in wing;** sides and undersides white. Female is dark gray above except for long white spot on side of head. **Notice rather tiny bill in both sexes,** and low zig-zag flight. Mostly spring, fall.   water str.wd.

12. BARROW'S GOLDEN-EYE, *Bucephala clangula.* Crow size. **Head of male black, with white crescent mark on cheek;** back and tail black with white markings. Head may appear glossy purple in certain lights; in spring the bill sometimes appears yellow. The wings make a whistling sound in flight; cry a harsh "quark", and, during courtship, males may make a mewing sound.   water str.wd.

Uncommon in most of region on lakes, beaver ponds, etc. in spring, summer and fall.

FISH-CATCHING DUCKS (bills with saw-toothed edges)

water
13. **COMMON MERGANSER**, *Mergus merganser*. Crow size and +. **Male has orange feet and bill, black back, greenish-black head, rest of body whitish.** Female and juvenile with white throat and streaked whitish yellow-brown breast; black wings have white patches. Found in most of region in spring, summer and fall.

GEESE AND BRANTS. Unlike ducks, these birds usually feed away from water on grain and weeds in fields. Bodies large and heavy looking.

water
str.wd.
14. **BLACK BRANT**, *Branta nigricans*. Crow size and +. **Distinctive black head and neck with white collar circling neck;** in flight, tail appears white with black edges, neck and breast black, and wings brownish. Gives low "cronk" cry. Uncommon on lakes in spring and fall.

Order GRUIFORMES (cranes and rails, etc.)

water
str.wd.
15. **AMERICAN COOT**, *Fulica americana*. Pigeon size. **Distinctive dark black neck and head; body grayish-black, whitish-blue bill;** white area under tail. Toes are lobed, not webbed; neck is pumped back and forth when swimming; bill is dabbed down at plants when feeding; paddles water with feet for some distance to start flight. Croaking, cackling calls most often heard at dawn and dusk.

Order CHARADRIIFORMES (Shore birds, gulls and terns)

Family CHARADRIIDAE (Plovers, turnstones)

str.wd.
water
grass
cult.
16. **KILLDEER**, *Charadrius vociferus*. Robin +. Brown head and back and black wings contrast with white belly and neck band; **two black chest bands very distinctive;** rump and tail base reddish-brown. Juveniles have duller colors, but more reddish above. An explosive "kee-kee-di-di!" call. During courtship mates swing and gyrate low in flight, giving loud cries. Most of region except high cold country in winter.

str.wd.
17. **SNOWY PLOVER**, *Charadrius alexandrinus*. Sparrow size. A small **whitish bird with incomplete black collar;** black bar separates white forehead from yellowish-brown top of head; back

SHOREBIRDS

pale gray; black spot appears behind eye; blackish-brown tips to central tail feathers; white stripe flashes on wings in flight. A "teet-teet" call: also a musical whistle. Found mainly on east side of Cascades in spring, summer and winter in Oregon, rare to north.

18. SPOTTED SANDPIPER, *Actitis macularia*. Robin —. Our only sandpiper with many round large spots on breast in spring and summer. Stopping between short runs, it teeters expertly; seeks insects, worms and other small creatures along stream and lake shores. Gives clear "peee-weet" call, with first note high.

rocks
water

JB
13. Common Merganser 22-27"

JB
12. Barrow's Golden-eye
16½-20'

JB
15. American Coot
13-16"

14. Black Brant
23-26"
JB

17. Snowy Plover
6-7"

16. Killdeer
9-11"
JGI

18. Spotted Sandpiper
7-8"
JB

LAND BIRDS

(Including some birds that feed in water such as kingfisher & dipper.)

Order FALCONIFORMES (vultures, hawks and eagles)

Family *CATHARTIDAE* (American vultures)

rocks
grass
sage
brush
str. wd.
mix. con
pine-jun.
sub. alp.

19. TURKEY VULTURE. *Cathartes aura.* Crow +; wingspread up to 6' or more. **Black body; black wings with ashy-gray on hind border, giving 2-toned effect; neck and head naked red.** Powerful beak for tearing flesh, but comparatively weak claws; a carrion eater. When soaring, wing tips are usually more widespread than in hawk; wings slightly tipped up; does not spread and flex tail like red-tail hawk; flaps wings heavily when rising from the ground. Found in most of our region during the warm part of the year. A useful scavenger.

Family *ACCIPITRIDAE* (hawks and eagles)

grass
brush
rocks
mix. con.
sub. alp.
pine-jun.

20. GOLDEN EAGLE, *Aquila chrysaetos.* **Wingspread 6-8'.** The large size, very long wings and powerful beak distinguish the eagles. Generally brown above, **somewhat golden-brown on head and neck; black below and usually with white at base of tail.** The juvenile has a dark-banded tail plus bright white markings under mid-wing. Occasionally whistles, more rarely yelps. Found in most of our region, but rather rare because of hunters.

water
rocks
str. wd.

21. BALD EAGLE, *Haliaeetus leucocephalus.* Wingspread 6-7½'. The brilliant white head and tail of **the adult contrast with the dark brown body and dark, two-toned wings.** Juvenile dusky brown. 20. hunts mammals on land, whereas this species hunts mainly for fish, which it also steals from other birds. Gives shrill metallic "kwee-kuck" call. Found mainly near water in region.

HARRIERS - long wings, long tail.

water
grass
mead
cult.

22. MARSH HAWK, *Circus cyaneus.* Wingspread 3½-4½'. Both male and female have a **white rump,** but the male is bluish-gray above, the female brown, and streaked with brown on breast. **Harries animals by swooping and pouncing.** Excited "kek-kek-kik" cry. Found in open areas of lower altitudes of our region.

FISH HAWKS - dive for fish from sky

HAWKS

19. Turkey Vulture 26-32" GMC
20. Golden Eagle 30-41" GMC
21. Bald Eagle 30-43" JB
21. Bald Eagle GMC
22. Marsh Hawk JB 17½-24"
23. Osprey 21-24½" ©IB
24. Red-tailed Hawk 19-25" JGi red.
26. Swainson's Hawk 19-22" CH

WILDLIFE AND PLANTS OF THE CASCADES

water
str.wd.

23. OSPREY, *Pandion haliaetus.* Wingspread 4½-6'. **Large hawk having whitish head marked with brown, white under parts; dark brown above.** Circles over water, often crying shrilly in three different tones. Occasional summer visitor to large lakes.

SOARING HAWKS - long, broad wings and short, broad tail. Fall like thunderbolts on the mammals they catch and feed on.

grass
rocks
brush
conif.
pine-jun.
sage
sub. alp.

24. RED-TAILED HAWK, *Buteo jamaicensis.* Wingspread 4-4½'. **Rounded tail in adult may show bright red in flight as the bird veers at an angle;**color varies from light brown streaked with whitish to dark brown streaked with light brown. Juvenile has light gray tail with numerous dark bars. Adult gives fierce, squealing cry, juvenile a softer "hwooo-eep" Most of our region.

grass
brush
sage

25. ROUGH-LEGGED HAWK, *Buteo lagopus.* Wingspread 4-4½'. Brownish above; **usually with blackish-brown belly and black patch on underside of wing at bend, contrasting with whitish of rest of underside;** chest streaked brownish-black; **tail white above, but with distinctive black band near end.** Some birds have lighter-colored bellies. Edge of wing shows white; less white at base of tail than in 26. This large hawk may hover with wings rapidly beating, like a sparrow hawk, watching for prey below, then dive down to seize it. Winter visitor in most of our region.

grass
pine-jun.
sage

26. SWAINSON'S HAWK, *Buteo swainsoni.* Wingspread 4-4½'. Variable in coloration, generally brownish above, but black to almost white beneath; most adults have a **dark reddish-brown breast band, also a clear yellowish-brown under-surface of the wing, and narrow dark bands under the light gray tail, which has a whitish base.** Often sits on low perches; flight sluggish; scream not so fierce as in other buteo hawks. Spring, summer and fall in most of our region, but avoids the thicker forest areas.

ACCIPITER HAWKS

Long tail and short broad wings; secretive hawks who often dive through foliage to seize birds.

conif.
sub.-alp.

27. GOSHAWK, *Accipiter gentilis.* Crow size; wingspread 3½-4'. Bluish-gray above, light gray below; **distinctive black cap is marked off by white line above eye. Fierce killer of birds to as large as grouse;** flies, as do other accipiters, with first flapping of wings, then gliding. Found in most of our region.

HAWKS

28. COOPER'S HAWK, *Accipiter cooperii*. Crow -; wingspread 2¼-3'. Similar to Goshawk, but **reddish below; tail rounded** instead of square as in Sharp-shinned. Found in most of our region.

str.wd.
mix.ev.
conif.
pine-jun.

29. SHARP-SHINNED HAWK, *Accipiter striatus*. Pigeon size and -. Very similar to 28, but has **square tail and 1¾-2' wingspread**. Has soft, wailing "whee-whee" call. Found all over.

conif.
str.wd.
mix.ev.

Family FALCONIDAE

Long tails and long, pointed wings are characteristic. They hunt and strike with high-speed dives. Most often catch birds in flight.

30. SPARROW HAWK, *Falco sparverius*. Wingspread 1½-2'. **Male with distinctive reddish-brown tail and back, also bluish crown of head,** and wings bluish. Both sexes have two **black stripes down whitish side of head;** also black band near tip of tail. Often hovers with swiftly-beating wings, then dives down to catch prey, such as insects or mice. High-pitched "kee-kee, kee-kee" or "killy-killy-killy" cry. Found in most of our region.

grass
mix.ev.
cult.
str.wd.
pine-jun.
rocks
sage
sub.alp.

31. PIGEON HAWK, *Falco columbarius*. Wingspread 1¾-2¼'. Male bluish-gray to nearly black above; **tail barred with black;** under parts white, streaked with black. Female and juveniles brownish. **When perched, folded wings reach about to tail tip.** Often dashes low over ground or in thickets, after small birds. Found in most of region, but usually in California only in winter.

grass
str.wd.

32. PRAIRIE FALCON, *Falco mexicanus*. Wingspread 3¼-3½'; crow - to crow-size. Pale brown color, **but black patches at base of wings contrast sharply with whitish wings;** faint white line over eye; brown stripe down each side of head; under parts streaked with brown. Boldly dashes among bird flocks. Has cackling and screeching cries. Found mainly in drier areas of region.

rocks
grass
sage

†33. PEREGRINE FALCON, *Falco peregrinus*. Also called Duck Hawk. Wingspread 3¼-3¾'. Mainly dark bluish-black above, but head whitish below and dark grayish above; **a dark stripe appears down each side of head; under parts whitish with narrow dark bars.** Flies with dazzling speed; has harsh "kek-kek" cry. Catches and kills fast-flying ducks and other large birds on the wing. Found in most of our region, but rather scarce due to too much shooting by hunters. A wonderful bird, worth saving.

water
grass
rocks

214 WILDLIFE AND PLANTS OF THE CASCADES

GYRFALCON, CHICKEN-LIKE BIRDS

34. **GYRFALCON,** *Falco rusticolus.* Wingspread 4-4¼'; **much larger than our other falcons. A generally uniform grayish or whitish color is also distinctive.** The gyrfalcon appears to beat its wings slower than does the peregrine, but this is deceptive as it actually can reach tremendous speeds in its pursuit of ducks, geese and other large birds. It is a rather uncommon winter visitor to the higher and more barren areas of our region. The Gyrfalcon's more common home is in the barren tundra region of the Arctic.
s.a.mead.
rocks
mt.mead.

Order GALLIFORMES (Chicken-like birds)
Family *TETRAONIDAE* - grouse

35. **WHITE-TAILED PTARMIGAN,** *Lagopus leucurus.* Pigeon size or -. Our only ptarmigan in this region. **Distinctively all white in winter except for black bill and eyes; brown above with a white belly, tail and wings in summer.** Found in the highest mountains of B. C. and Washington, coming lower in winter. Often hides in snow, from which it bursts out when disturbed.
alp.
s.a.mead

36. **SAGE GROUSE,** *Centrocercus urophasianus.* Male, crow +; female, crow size. Grayish-brown color above, whitish on breast; **large black patch on belly; both a black and white neck ring; a spike-like tail.** During courtship of female, the male puffs out his chest, shows yellow air sacs on the neck, raises and spreads his spike-like tail feathers and dances about, showing off, often making a popping noise. Alarm note is a "tuk-tuk-tuk" call.
sage

37. **SPRUCE (Franklin's) GROUSE,** *Canachites canadensis.* Pigeon +. **Distinctive row of white spots at base of black tail in the male; also white bars on dark tail and orange-red on forehead;** general color blackish brown; female a heavily barred reddish-brown. Found mainly on east side of Cascades and mostly north.
conif.

38. **BLUE GROUSE,** *Dendragapus obscurus.* Pigeon+to crow size. Has dark gray general color; **tail black with broad light-gray band at tip; orange color around eye;** the female more brownish. Male makes hollow, hooting call; both sexes give loud "kuk-kuk-kuk" cry, but female gives whining cry in spring. Found in most of our region in mountains.
conif.
brush

39. **RUFFED GROUSE,** *Bonasa umbellus.* Crow - and crow size. Mostly reddish-brown in color, **broad black band near tip of tail;** black feathers form ruff on neck; yellowish-brown below with
str.wd.
brush
mix.ev.

brown bars. When flushed from brush, bird flies off with a loud whirring noise. When courting, the male usually struts up and down a log making a loud drumming noise with its wings; the female makes a clucking sound. The male's mysterious slow thumping noise, gradually rising to a startling "whirrrrrrr", something like that made by a helicopter, is one of the most amazing sounds of the wilderness, frightening when first heard and not understood. Found in most of our region, but in more open forests.

Family *PHASIANIDAE* - quail, partridges, pheasant, etc.

brush
conif.
str.wd.

40. MOUNTAIN QUAIL, *Oreortyx pictus*. Pigeon -. Ground color bluish-gray; **reddish-brown throat; long straight plume on the head;** sides barred with white against reddish-brown. Gives loud resonant "t-woook!" or "ti-yoork" cry; females call "cut-cut-cut" to young; a "kwep-kweep" is the mating call. Also give tremulous whistles of alarm. Found in most of our region.

brush
grass
cult.
str.wd.

41. CALIFORNIA QUAIL, *Lophortyx californicus*. Robin size and +. Bluish-gray ground color above; **black plumes curve forward from crowns; male with black throat, circled with white;** under parts yellowish-brown with some reddish on belly. Males have distinctive white and black throat and face pattern; females duller. Clan rallying cry of "quer-ca-go!"; mothers call young with a sharp "pt-pt-pt", and there is a clucking "tik-tik". Found in our region in northern California and southern Oregon.

Order COLUMBIFORMES - Pigeons and doves

Family *COLUMBIDAE*

Pigeons and doves, eat seeds and grains.

str.wd.
brush
conif.
cult.
mix.ev.

42. BAND-TAILED PIGEON, *Columba fasciata*. Dark gray above, with some greenish high lights, especially on neck,but head and throat purplish-gray, and **white neck band; broad bluish band at end of fan-shaped tail;** white belly; outer wing feathers black. Gives an owl-like "hoo-hoo" or "hoo-ooo-hoo" call. Found in most of our region at lower elevations, rare in winter.

str.wd.
mix.ev.
pine-jun.
grass
cult.
brush

43. MOURNING DOVE, *Zenaidura macroura*. Robin + to pigeon -. **The long central pointed tail feathers are brown, with other tail feathers gray, tipped with white, and bordered with black; feet red;** back is brownish; pinkish-brown breast, head reddish-brown and rather small proportionately to body. Gives soft

WILD FOWL

38. Blue Grouse 15½=21"
35. White-tailed Ptarmigan 12-13"
36. Sage Grouse 26-30"
39. Ruffed Grouse 16-19"
37. Spruce Grouse 15-17"
40. Mountain Quail 10½-11½
41. California Quail 9½-11"

plaintive "ooah-coo-coo-cooo" call, the first syllable rarely heard. Flies in pairs in breeding season, otherwise in flocks. Tail flashes white when seen in swift, whistling flight. Found in most of our region, but rather rare in winter.

Order CUCULIFORMES - cuckoos

Family *CUCULIDAE*

str.wd.
44. YELLOW-BILLED CUCKOO, *Coccyzus americanus*. Pigeon -. A slender long-tailed brownish bird, with three long blackish outer tail feathers **showing large white spots; lower mandible of bill is yellow. Explosive, repeated "kowlp" cry. Summer visitor.**

Order STRIGIFORMES - Owls, large eyes face forward

Family *TYTONIDAE*

Barn owls, heart-shaped monkey face.

rocks
bldg.
grass
cult.
45. BARN OWL, *Tyto alba*. Pigeon to crow size. **General color yellowish-brown and white; distinctive white heart-shaped face; eyes quite dark.** Flies like a giant moth on silent wings, appearing ghost-like. Rather knock-kneed and long-legged in appearance. A **very distinctive snoaring hiss call, high-pitched.** A helpful scourge of small rodents, particularly mice. In most of our region.

Family *STRIGIDAE* - typical owls

conif.
†46. FLAMMULATED SCREECH OWL,*Otus flammeolus.* Sparrow +, very tiny owl. Resembles a grayish screech owl, but has **distinctive brown eye and short ear tufts.** It has conspicuous repeated musical "hoot" calls. Found in mountains of most of our region, but rather uncommon. Nests in woodpecker holes.

mix. ev.
str.wd.
pine-jun.
sitk-spr.
cult.
bldg.
47. SCREECH OWL, *Otus asio*. Robin size. **This is the only small gray owl with large ear tufts;** black streaks on body; wings barred with yellowish-brown. Sometimes this species appears in a brownish color phase, instead of gray. Young birds appear gray in summer with few dark markings and no ear tufts. Frequently nests in woodpecker holes. Call made up of repeated echo-like whistles merging into a long tremulous whistle. Found in most of our region and fairly common in wild areas.

48. SHORT-EARED OWL, *Asio flammeus*. Pigeon +. General

PIGEONS, OWLS 219

42. Band-tailed Pigeon 14-15½"
43. Mourning Dove 11-13"
47. Screech Owl 7-10"
44. Yellow-billed Cuckoo 11-13½"
45. Barn Owl 14-20"
49. Long-eared Owl 13-16"
50. Great Horned Owl 18-25"
48. Short-eared Owl 13-17"
56. Spotted Owl
54. Saw-whet Owl 7-8½"
52. Pygmy Owl 7-7½"
51. Burrowing Owl 9-11"

water
grass
cult.

color yellowish-brown; **ear tufts quite short and black; pale patches show on wing when flying.** Often flies by day, but floppy flight differs from hawk's; swoops back and forth low over ground with slow wing beats when hunting prey, suddenly dropping down to seize it. The yellow eyes against the dark face disks may appear startling. Gives loud, nasal "teee-yow!" call or bark. Found in open areas in much of our region.

str.wd.
mix.ev.
conif.
pine-jun.

49. LONG-EARED OWL, *Asio otus.* Pigeon size. Has slender grayish body and reddish-brown face; **ear tufts or horns very close together, narrow and conspicuous. Calls include a soft "coo", a whine and a "meow".** It is told from the Great Horned Owl by smaller size, close together horns and the fact that the body is streaked lengthwise instead of barred. Very hard to see in woods because it stands frozen close to tree trunk. In most of region.

conif.
mix.ev.
str.wd.
brush
rocks
s.a.mead.
jun.
sage
grass

50. GREAT HORNED OWL, *Bubo virginianus.* Crow +. Only **very large owl with large ear tufts or "horns" and these spread far apart;** body generally dark brown or blackish with light brown under parts that are barred crosswise with ligh brown. **Distinctive, white collar on throat; body very thick.** Has deep "hoo-hoo, hoo-hoo, hoo" cry of 5 or 4 notes, but may vary to 3 or 8 at times. Fierce hunter of rats, rabbits, even skunks and foxes. All over.

grass
sage
cult.

51. BURROWING OWL, *Speotyto cunicularis.* Robin size or +. Brownish general color with light markings; **white line over eye; very long legs for an owl.** Has queer way of bobbing up and down when it alights; often flies in daylight and comes to ground squirrel holes, inside of which it may nest; also likes fence posts to stand on. Gives shaky chattering "kvik-vik-vik-vik" call, or soft "coo-coo", but higher than call of dove. Found in most low open areas of our region, but goes to lower altitudes or south in winter.

conif.
mix.ev.
jun.

52. PYGMY OWL, *Glaucidium gnoma.* Robin -. A small gray brown or red-brown owl; **with narrow black breast stripes; conspicuous dark brown tail barred with white;** black neck patch; white throat; dark brown collar across upper breast. Often flies in daylight with dip-up motion at end of flight, like that of shrike. Head rather small for owl. Has soft whistled "tewk-tew-kew" call, frequently repeated rapidly. Found in most of our region.

s.a.mead
mix.con.
mix.ev.

†53. RICHARDSON'S OWL, *Aegolius funereus.* Robin size or robin +. Often called Boreal Owl. This large-headed, **earless owl**

has the face disks rimmed with black, and a yellowish bill; front of head strongly dotted with white, general color brown. Has a song that sounds like dripping water or a soft-toned bell with a high pitch. Found in northern Washington and British Columbia.

54. SAW-WHET OWL, *Aegolius acadicus*. Robin -. Small brown owl with **wide-brown markings down light-colored undersides;** no ear tufts; the brownish upper parts are somewhat whitespotted; **wings when open show rows of white spots;** tail rather short. Gives variable, slow or rapid whistle, usually repeated slowly in beginning, then faster, sounding like file on saw.   conif. s.a.mead.

55. SNOWY OWL, *Nyctea scandiaca*. Crow size and +. Generally **white all over, but flecked with black above;** yellow eye and bill. Rather rare winter visitor to most of our region.   grass marsh cult.

56. SPOTTED OWL, *Strix occidentalis*. Crow -. **A large dark brown and earless owl having many white spots on head and back;** face yellowish-brown, as are the under parts, which are barred or spotted with white. Also **has large dark eyes,** while all other large owls have yellow eyes, except the barn owl in our region. Has a high-pitched "whoo-hoo-hoo" or 4 "hoos", each group rapidly repeated, and sounding like a dog barking. Uncommon and found mainly in Olympic Mts. and lower west slopes of Cascades.   conif. str.wd.

57. HAWK OWL, *Surnia ulula*. Pigeon size to crow -. Shaped somewhat hawk-like and flies by day. Dark brown above, except for head, which is black with many white spots; yellowish-brown barred against white below. **The small head, long rounded tail and white face with black border are distinctive.** Even the chittering "kee-kee-kee-kee" call is more hawk-like than like an owl. An uncommon visitor, mainly in winter, as far south as Washington.   conif. mt.mead.

58. GREAT GRAY OWL, *Strix nebulosa*. Crow +; the largest owl in North America and with an unusually long (12") or more) tail. **The lack of ear tufts, the very large and comparatively dark facial disks with large yellow eyes, and the conspicuous black chin spot are distinctive;** general color brownish-gray. Call is a deep drumming "whooo-whoo-whoo", or single "whoo's". Found in most of our region, but uncommon, though more often in winter.   conif. mt.mead.

Order CAPRIMULGIFORMES - goatsuckers

Family *CAPRIMULGIDAE* - nightjars and nighthawks
Feeds on insects in the air.

222 WILDLIFE AND PLANTS OF THE CASCADES

sage
brush
rocks
jun.-

59. POOR WILL, *Phalaenoptilus nuttallii.* Robin -. Gray-brown in color with blackish markings; **white band on throat with black below; outer tail feathers with white tips.** Flutters up from ground like giant moth to snap up insect on wing with its wide, hair-lined mouth, doing most of catching at dusk or dawn. Soft "poo-woo" call, or a startled "phweek!". Found on east border of Cascades in late spring, summer and fall.

mix.con.
s.a.mead.
bldg.
grass
sage

60. COMMON NIGHTHAWK, *Chordeiles minor.* Robin size. Streaked brownish-gray above; plain brownish-gray below, but with **whitish band across throat, band of white near tip of tail, and white wing bar about half way out long narrow wing.** Flies high in sky, uttering nasal "pee-ent" cry or dives earthward to make loud booming sound, especially at mating time. Late spring, summer and fall visitor to more open areas of our region.

Order CORACIIFORMES - kingfishers
Family ALCEDINIDAE

water
str.wd.

60a. BELTED KINGFISHER, *Megaceryle alcyon.* Dove size. Big-headed and big-billed, blue-gray above, ragged crest.

Order PASSERIFORMES - perching birds, in part.

Family HIRUDINIDAE - swallow and martins

We put the swallows here because they and the swifts look so much alike. Both only visit us in warm months. Notice that the swifts have shorter tails. See color plate on page 236.

grass
str.wd.
water
cult.
bldg.

* 61. CLIFF SWALLOW, *Petrochelidon pyrrhonota.* Sparrow size. Top of head and back steely blue; **pale orange-brown rump; gray throat patch and whitish forehead patch; square-shaped tail.** The long ellipse of its glide, ending in a quite steep climb is characteristic. Builds a mud gourd-shaped nest on cliffs or under eaves of buildings. Has "kyeeer-kyeeeer" alarm note and low "chrrrr".

rocks
grass
brush
str.wd.
cult.
bldg.
water

* 62. BARN SWALLOW, *Hirundo rustica.* Sparrow +. Bluish-black above; **orange-brown below plus forked tail are distinctive;** also white tail spots; throat darker than belly. Does not glide nearly as much as above; flight more direct. Builds open mud nests on cliffs and buildings. Found in most of our region. Soft twitter.

water
str.wd.
mt.mead.
cult.
grass

* 63. TREE SWALLOW, *Iridoprocne bicolor.* Sparrow size. **Male bright bluish-black or green above, bright white below;** female and juvenile with brown upper parts; juvenile with dark collar partly across the neck. A "keeely-keely-tsee-keely" call. Glides in a circle, ending glide with 3-4 fast wing flaps and quick climb.

OWLS, KINGFISHER 223

55. Snowy Owl 20-27"

57. Hawk Owl 14½-17½"

58. Great Gray Owl 24-33"

59. Poor Will 7-8½"

60. Common Nighthawk 8½-10"

60a. Belted Kingfisher 11-14½

224 WILDLIFE AND PLANTS OF THE CASCADES

rocks
water
str.wd.
brush
water

* 64. ROUGH-WINGED SWALLOW, *Stelgidopteryx ruficollis.* Brownish above and with white belly; **brownish-gray breast, but without distinct collar.** Has direct flight like barn swallow's, but wings are folded back at end of their stroke. Nests in holes in banks like no. 65, but in smaller groups or alone. Constantly gives harsh, but weak "prrreet" call. In summer over most of region.

water
str.wd.
grass

*65. BANK SWALLOW, *Riparia riparia.* Sparrow size. Like above, but with distinct **dark band across white breast. Has a fluttery and irregular flight, with short hesitant glides.** Gives soft "brrrt" note. Likes to live in holes in banks in large colonies.

most
hab.

* 66. VIOLET-GREEN SWALLOW, *Tachycineta thalassina.* Sparrow size. Beautiful green and purple glossy colors above, white below and around eye. Light rapid twittering call.

conif.
mt.mead.
brush
cult.
str.wd.
bldg.

* 67. PURPLE MARTIN, *Progne subis.* Robin - to robin size. **Male distinctive blue-black all over;** female brown above, with whitish belly and grayish neck, but purplish gloss on head and back. **Both have forked tails.** Found in most of our region in summer.

Order APODIFORMES - swifts and hummingbirds

Family *APODIDAE*

Swifts; unlike swallows, wings of swifts move so fast they seem to twinkle. Very narrow, scythe-like wings. Very short tails.

rocks
conif.

68. VAUX'S SWIFT, *Chaetura vauxi.* Warbler size. Brownish-black above; brown on rump and tail, **which is distinctive by being short and inconspicuous; ashy-gray belly and throat. Very small for a swift,** but with typical stiff somewhat curved wings. Found in most of our region in late spring, summer and fall. Nest in trees.

rocks
brush
mix.ev.
cult.
grass

69. WHITE-THROATED SWIFT, *Aeronautes saxatalis.* Sparrow +. **White on throat and middle of breast and flanks, but rest of bird blackish or dark gray.** It is amazing to watch the gyrations of a group of these birds high in the sky, chasing insects, and seeming to lace the blue with dazzling speed. Unlike the almost silent Vaux's Swift, these birds send down a shrill and adjectival "jee-jee-jee-jee" twitter, in lowering scale. Summer in our mountains.

rocks
conif.

70. BLACK SWIFT, *Cypseloides niger.* Robin -. **The slightly forked tail and all black color, except for white blotch on forehead are distinctive.** In flight it gives an effect of moving slower than the other two swifts. Gives a sharp "pik-pik-pik-pik" twittering call. 69 and 70 nest on high cliffs. Summer in mountains of region.

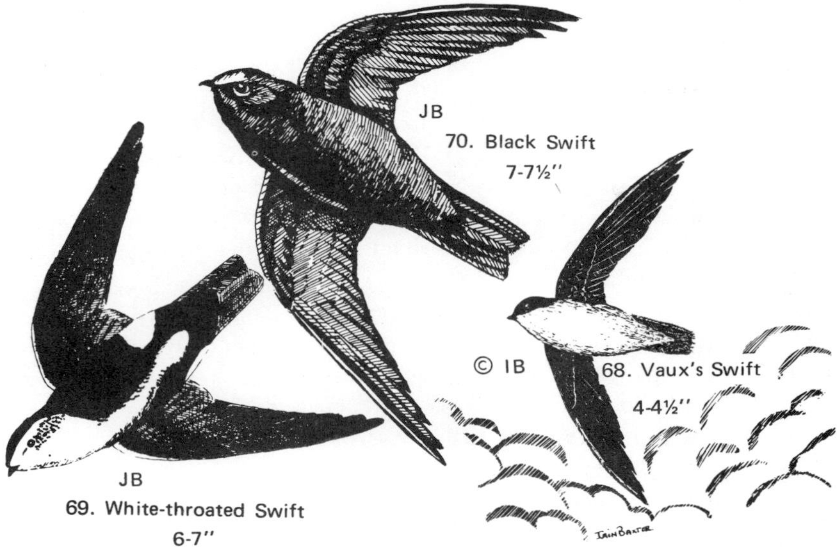
JB
JB
© IB
IAIN BAXTER

70. Black Swift
7-7½″

68. Vaux's Swift
4-4½″

69. White-throated Swift
6-7″

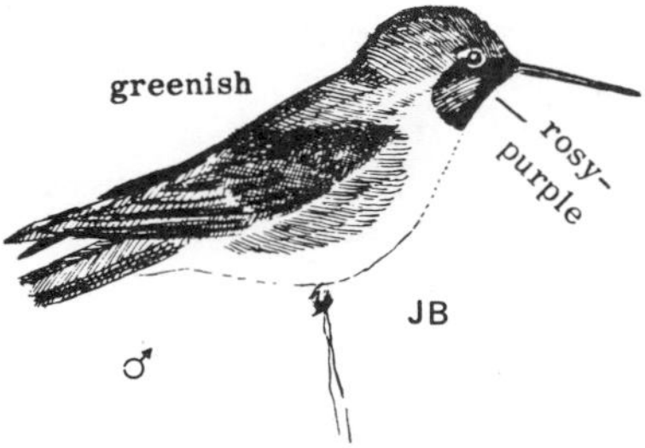
greenish
rosy-purple
JB
♂

72. Broad-tailed Hummingbird
4-4½″

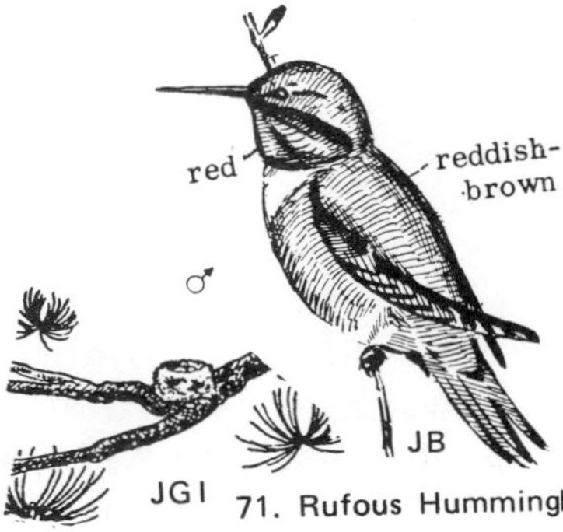
red
reddish-brown
♂
JB
JGI

71. Rufous Hummingbird
3¼-4″

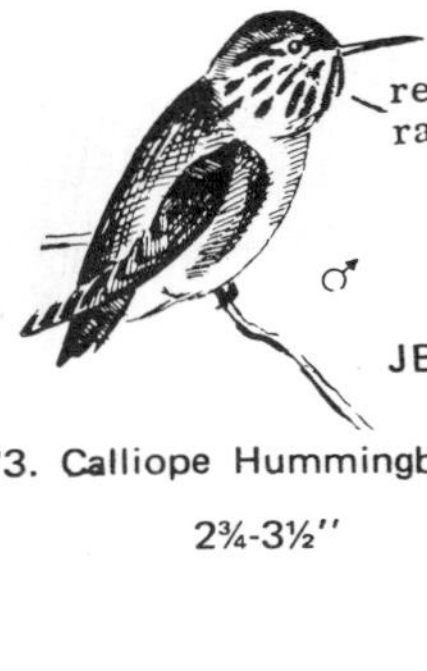
red rays
♂
JB

73. Calliope Hummingbird
2¾-3½″

71.
brush
mix.ev.
str.wd.
conif.
cult.
mt.mead.

72.
conif.
brush
jun.
cult.
mt.mead.
str.wd.

73.
s.a.mead.
conif.
brush
str.wd.

71. RUFOUS HUMMINGBIRD, *Selasphorus rufus*. Warbler -. A rich **reddish-brown above**; throat coppery-red and shining; a white band below it; duller and greenish-olive. Migrant in high meadows. ♂in courting makes ellipse⊖with diagonal axis.

72. BROAD-TAILED HUMMINGBIRD, *Selasphorus platycercus*. ♂With green upper parts, whitish under parts and **rosy purple throat**; ♀greenish above, whitish below, with buff on sides. Both noisy in flight, making constant rattling trill with wings. E. side of mountains.

73. CALLIOPE HUMMINGBIRD, *Stellula calliope*. Warbler-; the tiniest bird of the mountains; ♂with upper body golden-green, whitish below; **beautiful lilac-colored feathers radiate out from white throat**. ♀Dull olive-green. Females of these 3 hummers look much alike. ♂makes shallow ⌣ dive in courting.

Order PICIFORMES - woodpeckers

Family *PICIDAE*

Usually fly with an undulating flight and have chisel-shaped bills.

str.wd.
mix.ev.
jun.
grass
bldg.
cult.
conif.

74. RED-SHAFTED FLICKER, *Colaptes cafer*. Dove plus size. Brown above, but black bars on wings; cream to white under parts with black spots; **white rump, red under wing and tail; black crescent mark on breast**; male with red marks on cheeks. Often bobs head vigorously, and mainly feeds on ground on insects, worms. Has many calls; "wick-wick", "flick-ah-flick-ah"; "kee-er", a queer "whroooooo!". Found in most of region.

s.a.mead.
conif.
mix.ev.

75. PILEATED WOODPECKER, *Dryocopus pileatus*. Crow-to crow size. Our largest woodpecker, with black general color, **with pointed crest and top of head a flaming red; narrow white line above the eye**; white zig-zag streak down side of neck; **red stripe back from base of lower bill**; white patch on under side of wing. Makes thundering tat-too when pecking tree; common call is a loud "wi-wii-wii" or "kek-kek-kek". Wilderness areas of our region.

conif.
cult.
bldg.
mix.ev.
str.wd.

76. ACORN WOODPECKER, *Melanerpes formicivorus*. Robin size. **Only lowland and foothill woodpecker showing white wing patches in flight; yellow throat and white rump are distinctive**; red on top of head, white on forehead; black back and black around eye and back of head; tail black. Often seen hammering

WOODPECKERS 227

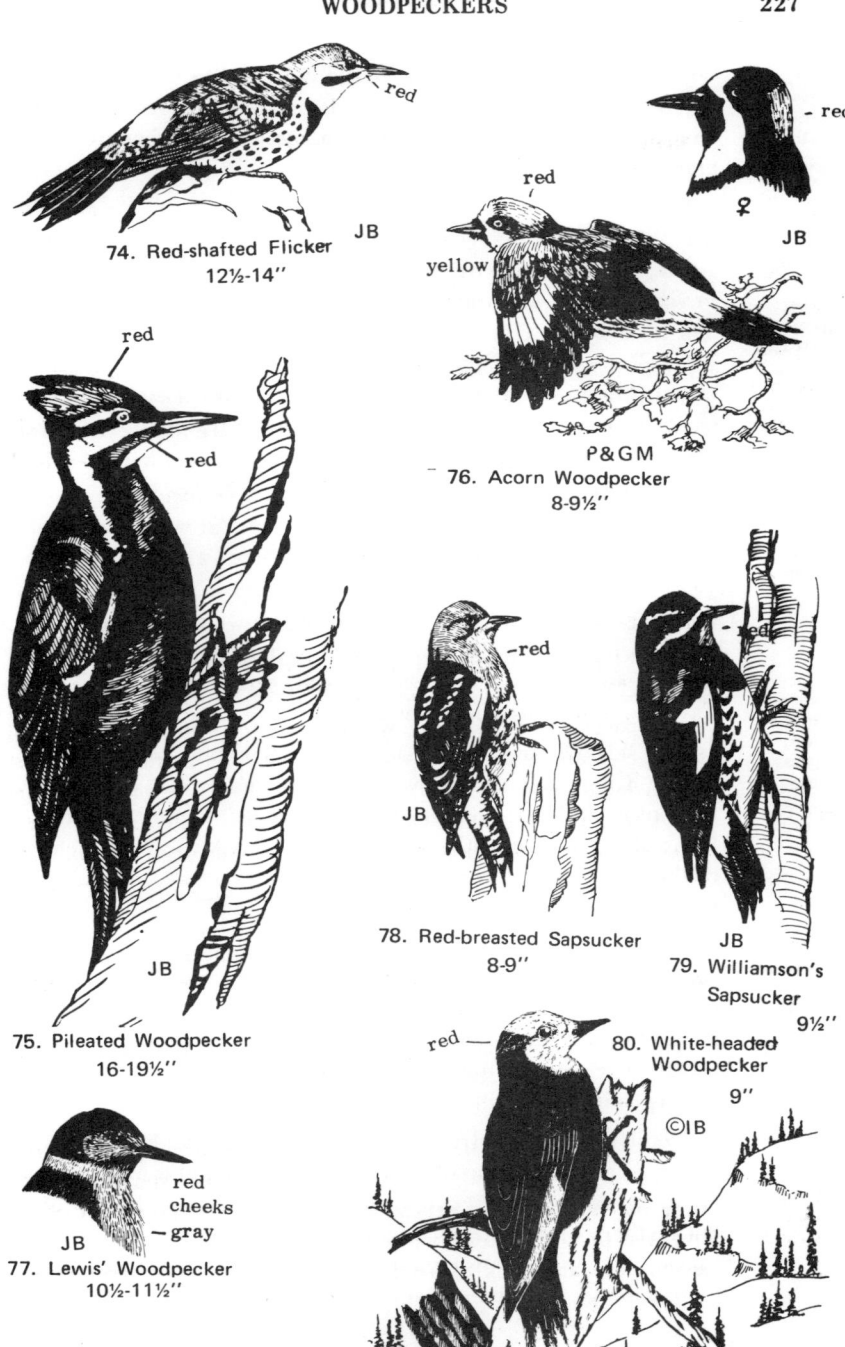

74. Red-shafted Flicker
12½-14″

75. Pileated Woodpecker
16-19½″

76. Acorn Woodpecker
8-9½″

77. Lewis' Woodpecker
10½-11½″

78. Red-breasted Sapsucker
8-9″

79. Williamson's Sapsucker
9½″

80. White-headed Woodpecker
9″

acorns into dead trees or stumps for storage. "Wick-up, wick-up" call may change to "jay-cup, jay-cup". S. Oregon and n. Calif.

conif.
mix.con.

77. LEWIS' WOODPECKER, *Asyndesmus lewis*. Robin +. Our only all-dark woodpecker with **rose red belly and cheeks; gray neck and breast collar.** Rarely gives any sound except an occasional "chrrrr" in spring. Found in most of our region, but winters from Oregon south and at lower elevations in winter.

conif.
str.wd.
s.a.mead.
mix.ev.
cult.

78. RED-BREASTED SAPSUCKER, *Sphyrapicus varius*. Robin size. Black wings and back spotted with white; **breast, neck and head bright crimson red; whitish rump;** white on middle of tail; yellow belly. Juvenile duller and with mottled gray. Digs circle of holes around tree to suck sap, also eating insects in sap. Gives nasal "chrrr" or squeal. Breeds in our region, but winters lower.

s.a.mead.
conif.
brush

79. WILLIAMSON'S SAPSUCKER, *Sphyrapicus thyroideus*. Robin size. **All of upper parts black except for white stripes behind and below eye and white patch at bend of wing;** white rump; yellow belly; red chin. Female duller with brown head and throat; the wings, flanks and back barred brownish-white on black; black band on breast. May drum with bill at high speed, then give 3-4 short beats. A nasal "weeee-er" call. Breeds on east slope of Cascades, but winters in lower areas.

s.a.mead.
conif.

80. WHITE-HEADED WOODPECKER *Dendrocopos albolarvatus*. Robin size. **Distinctive white head and throat, with red on nape of neck;** black over rest of body except for white patches on bases of outer wing feathers. Gives shrill "wick-wick" or a sharp rattling cry. In California found on both sides of the Cascades and near coast in mountains, but north it is found on the east side.

conif.
s.a.mead.
str.wd.
jun.

81. HAIRY WOODPECKER, *Dendrocopos villosus*. Robin size. The **white back and large size, along with white and black color design are distinctive;** outer tail feathers white; red patch on back of head. Has loud "kink" note; also a long rattling cry all at the same pitch. Rolling drum beats on tree grow loud during mating time. Found in most of our region.

str.wd.
mix.ev.
cult.

82. DOWNY WOODPECKER, *Dendrocopos pubescens*. Sparrow +. Looks like twin of 81, but smaller, and **bill is much smaller; white back is distinctive;** male scarlet on back of head; outer tail feathers white with inconspicuous black bars. Gives metallic "kink" cry; also sounds rapidly descending notes much like whinny of a horse. Found in most of our region.

WOODPECKERS, FLYCATCHERS 229

82. Downy Woodpecker
6-7"

81. Hairy Woodpecker
8½-10½"

83. Black-backed Three-toed Woodpecker
9-10"

84. Northern Three-toed Woodpecker
8-9½"

86. Western Kingbird
8-9½

85. Say's Phoebe
7-8"

WILDLIFE AND PLANTS OF THE CASCADES

s.a.mead.
83. BLACK-BACKED THREE-TOED WOODPECKER, *Picoides arcticus*. The yellow cap on the head of the male is lacking in the female; **rest of upper parts black except for white marks on the face**; white below; black and white barred on sides; central tail feathers black, outer white. Sharp "tik" or "tsik" cry. Peculiar method of tearing off chunks of bark. Most of region.

conif.
s.a.mead.
84. NORTHERN THREE-TOED WOODPECKER, *Picoides tridactylus*. Robin size. This and 83 are the only woodpeckers in our region with 3 instead of the normal 2 front and 2 back toes. They also are the only two with **yellow caps**. Both look alike except this one has a **white back, somewhat ladder-backed in appearance, and both have barred sides**, unlike the similar-appearing Hairy Woodpecker. Voice is like that of number 83. Found as far south as southern Oregon Cascades in our region.

Order PASSERIFORMES - Perching birds - 1 toe back, 3 forward

Family *TYRANNIDAE*

Tyrant flycatchers; most often seen perching on an outer branch from which they make a circle outward to snap up an unwary fly or other insect. Most of them do their singing in the very early morning.

rocks
bldg.
sage
brush
grass
85. SAY'S PHOEBE, *Sayornis saya*. Robin -. Tail blackish-brown; **dark to grayish-brown above; reddish-brown under parts** except for grayish-brown throat and breast. Has "phee-ee" call; also stuttered and repeated "pt-see-ar". Found mainly on east side of Cascades in spring, summer and fall.

grass
jun-
cult.
86. WESTERN KINGBIRD, *Tyrannus verticalis*. Robin size. Yellowish below; **black tail bordered with white**; pale gray head, chest and back; wings brownish. Has shrill, peevish cries and often attacks other birds. Most of our region in spring, sum., fall.

conif.
str.wd.
brush
mix.ev.
87. OLIVE-SIDED FLYCATCHER, *Nuttallornis borealis*. Robin -. Very similar to 88, but slightly larger and darker; **two dark chest patches are separated by white stripe down the center of breast and belly**; two white patches on sides of rump often show in flight. Has "pee-pwee" or "pee-pee-pa" cry. Two cotton-like tufts may sometimes poke out from behind the wings. Found in most of our region in late spring, summer and fall.

conif.
mix.ev.
str.wd.
88. WESTERN WOOD PEWEE, *Contopus sordidulus*. Sparrow size. **Plain dark olive-gray-brown in color with no white eye**

FLYCATCHERS

ring; the two white wing bars are inconspicuous; breast has two dark sides separated by light line down middle. Likes to sit partly hid and still for long times. Common nasal "pee-weeee!". Found in most of our region in late spring, summer and fall.

Empidonax flycatchers; the three following species are almost identical in appearance, but told by calls and habitats.

89. HAMMOND'S FLYCATCHER, *Empidonax hammondii.* Sparrow -. Olive-brown body, yellowish underside, white eye-ring and two white wing-bars are common to all three. This one lives in upper branches of deep forest. Sum. Low "see-werl" note.
conif.
mix.ev.

†90. TRAILL'S FLYCATCHER, *Empidonax traillii.* Sparrow -. Calls "seepeh-dee-rr" or sneezing "sitz-bee-oh". Summer.
str.wd.

†91. WESTERN FLYCATCHER, *Empidonax difficilis.* Sparrow size. More yellowish below. Wheezy "tss-eet" note. Summer.
mix.ev.
conif.
str.wd.

88. Western Wood Pewee and nest
JB
6-6½"

87. Olive-sided Flycatcher
7-8"

89. Hammond's Flycatcher,
5-5½"

Family CORVIDAE - jays, magpies, crows

conif.
mix.ev.
str.wd.

* 92. PINON JAY, *Gymnorhinus cyanocephala*. Robin +. Generally **dull blue in color; throat white or white-streaked; brighter blue on head.** Usually flies in loose flocks, often foraging on the ground, the ones at the rear of the flock flying over those ahead to get in front of them, this process repeating itself. These flocks are very noisy, with much shrill nasal "kaah, karnh", going down in scale; sometimes mews and chatters "jh-jeh-jeh-jeh". Individuals walk about with stiff-legged way of crows. Found along lower east slopes of Cascades in dry areas.

conif.
s.a.mead.

* 93. GRAY JAY, *Perisoreus canadensis*. Dove to pigeon -. Most of upper parts grayish-brown; blackish on upper neck; lower neck has grayish-white collar; conspicuous white forehead; belly and breast grayish white. Juvenile is dark gray above, blackish on head; breast dark gray; belly pale gray. Very soft and fluffy plumage. Has harsh, screaming calls of "ker-weep!", also softly whistled "wheeeyooo" or soft "shuck".

conif.
mix.ev.
s.a.mead.
str.wd.

* 94. STELLER'S JAY, *Cyanocitta stelleri*. Dove - to pigeon size. **Upper back, chest and head dark brown-black; rest of body deep blue. The only jay in our area with a crest.** Has many harsh notes, especially very rapid "chey-chey-chey!" call; may copy shrill scream of red-tailed hawk; also loud "kweechkweech"; squeaking rusty-wheel-like note; more rarely a soft warble. Like most jays, it is a camp robber, and may sometimes rob bird's nests, acting sneaky, like it has a guilty conscience, when doing so. Found in most of our region, mainly in forests.

brush
str.wd.
jun.
cult.
mix.ev.

*95. SCRUB (California) JAY, *Aphelocoma coerulescens*. Dove-. Back brown; rest of upper parts blue; **under parts light gray, except for dark band across breast;** crest absent; tail often hangs straight down when bird is perched. Flies with pitching motion in long shallow curves; bobs head energetically when it alights. Common cry is harsh "chey-chey-chey", higher and usually slower than that of Steller Jay; also has harsh "krr-hweek" and low warble. Found in more open and lower country than 94, from southwest Washington south in our region.

Jays are noted warners about anything unusual that moves in their territory. The increasing excitement of their cries will indicate that something big is coming, and a combative note will often indicate they are attacking or teasing an owl, wildcat, and so forth.

COLOR PLATE 5 - JAYS

92. Pinon Jay, 10-11½"
93a. Gray Jay, Juvenal Form
93b. Gray Jay, 10-13"
94. Steller's Jay, 11-13"
95. Scrub Jay, 11-13"
99. Clark's Nutcracker, 12-13"

96. BLACK-BILLED MAGPIE, *Pica pica.* Crow - to crow size.
Easily recognized because of black and white color design, large size, black bill and very long tail with wedge-shape. In flight the greenish-black tail gleams with iridescent lights, and large white wing patches flash. Call a harsh "kek-kek-kek!" often machine-gun-like, also a nasal and solitary "maagh" and several soft whistling or chuckling notes. Largely a scavenger, but sometimes attacks and kills small animals or birds, and flocks have been known to worry and wound a sheep to death by pecking at its eyes. In our region mainly east side of Cascades in open country.

str.wd.
sage
cult.
pine,jun.
brush

97. COMMON RAVEN, *Corvus corax.* Crow size and +.
Black all over like crow, **but has very rough-looking feathers on throat. Has distinctive manner of flying with wings held horizontal (unlike crow), half the time soaring, half heavily flapping;** also generally appears larger and tail is wedge-shaped. Gives a deep and croaking "krrruack" cry. It is largely a scavenger of dead creatures, and is noted for its wisdom and cunning. Found in most of region.

rocks
sage
sub.alp.
conif.

98. COMMON CROW, *Corvus brachyrhynchos.* **Black color all over. Soars with wings bent up at an angle, not horizontal.** Calls with a loud "caw-caw-caw-caw!". Outside the breeding season, crows generally fly in flocks, under the direction of a wise leader or leaders. They show extraordinary ability to outwit enemies, including man. Note that a crow flock comes quickly together into a tight mass when threatened by a large hawk or eagle so that the attacker finds it hard to strike a single bird alone. Found in most of our region, but at lower altitudes, and winters mainly south of the Canadian border.

cult.
str.wd.
mix.ev.

99. CLARK'S NUTCRACKER, *Nucifraga columbiana.* Dove -. Looks like a small, light-colored crow; most of body, neck and head pale gray except for white forehead; **white tail has contrasting black central feathers, while large white wing patch contrasts with black wing.** Juvenals generally brown in color. Gives a harsh, rasping "caw-caw" or "kraaw-kraaw" cry. The light color harmonizes with the snow in the high mountains where this bird likes to live, coming lower only in the middle of the coldest winters. It feeds largely on pine nuts, but also acts as a scavenger. It is found in most of our region at high altitudes.

sub.alp.
mead.

BIRDS

96. Black-billed Magpie
17½-22"

97. Common Raven
21½-27"

98. Common Crow
17-21"

102. Chestnut-backed Chickadee
4½-5"

100b. Boreal Chickadee
5-5½"

101. Mountain Chickadee
5-5¾"

100. Black-capped Chickadee
4¾-5¾"

COLOR PLATE 6 - SWALLOWS

61. Cliff Swallow, 5-6"
62. Barn Swallow, 6-7 ½"
63. Tree Swallow, 5-6"
64. Rough-winged Swallow, 5-5 ¾"
65. Bank Swallow, 5-5 ½"
66. Violet-green Swallow, 5 ½-5 ¾"
67. Purple Martin, ♂ & ♀, 7 ½-8 ½"

COLOR PLATE 7 - THRUSHES

119. Robin, ♀ & ♂, 9-11"
120. Varied Thrush, ♂ & ♀, 9-10"
121. Hermit Thrush, 6½-7¾"
122. Swainson's Thrush, 6½-7½"
123. Western Bluebird, ♂ & ♀, 6½-7"
124. Mountain Bluebird, ♂ & ♀, 6½-7½"
125. Townsend's Solitaire, 8-9½"

Family *PARIDAE*

All tiny birds that glean insects among twigs of trees and bushes, often, especially the chickadees, holding body upside down while eating.

sub.alp.
conif.
pine,jun.
mix.ev.
str.wd.

100. BLACK-CAPPED CHICKADEE, *Parus atricapillus*. Warbler size and +. Dark to pale gray back; **white sides of head contrast sharply with black top of head;** dark gray wings usually edged with whitish; under parts whitish except for black throat; sides tinged with yellowish-brown in fall, lighter colored in spring. Gives "tee-dee-deed-dee" and "dee-dee-dee" notes. Most regions.

conif.

100b. BOREAL CHICKADEE, *Parus hudsonicus*. Sparrow size. 5-5½". Same as 100 but with brown cap and sides.

conif.
str.wd.
mix.ev.

101. MOUNTAIN CHICKADEE, *Parus gambeli*. Warbler size and +. White cheeks contrast with black throat, **but black head cap broken by white bar over eye and bill;** rest of upper parts gray; lower parts grayish-white in middle, brownish-gray on sides. Has lisping "see-dee-dee" call (most often 3, but sometimes 4 notes); also has several other soft, gurgling or lisping cries, or a shrill "tseek-ah!". Three clear high and whistled notes, like "thee-bee-dee" start the song, with other notes going down the scale. Found in most of our region in mountain forests.

str.wd.
cult.
sitk.-spr.
w.hem.
mix.ev.

102. CHESTNUT-BACKED CHICKADEE, *Parus rufescens*. Warbler size. The black cap and throat and white cheeks are as in other chickadees, but **the reddish-brown back is distinctive;** also chestnut-colored on sides. Call, a rasping "sick-sick-a-dee-dee!" that is harsher than the other chickadees; also a harsh "see-see." Found in much of our region, but in moister, lower forests.

mix.ev.
pine,jun.
cult.

103. PLAIN TITMOUSE, *Parus inornatus*. Warbler +. Our only small gray-brown bird with a pointed crest. Has "sick-a-dee-dee" call, but springtime song is a soft, melodious "sweety-sweety-sweety". These birds hide themselves among the leaves of a tree, but, when singing or curious about the watcher, may show themselves in a more open part of the foliage. Found in southern Oregon and northern California in our region at lower elevations.

oak
pine,jun.
brush.
str.wd.
sitk.-spr.

104. COMMON BUSHTIT, *Psaltriparus minimus*. Warbler size. **Our only tiny gray-backed and brown-capped bird with a comparatively long tail;** grayish-white below. Flies in small, twittering flocks that dart from bush to bush, but in spring the pairs build elaborate hanging nests. In our region at lower elevations.

BIRDS

104. Common Bushtit
3¾-4¼"

103. Plain Titmouse
5-5½"

107. Pygmy Nuthatch
3¾-4½"

106. Red-breasted Nuthatch
4½-4¾"

105. White-breasted Nuthatch
5-6"

108. Brown Creeper
5-5¾"

109. House Wren
4½-5¼"

110. Winter Wren
4-4½"

COLOR PLATE 8 - RED FINCHES

161. Red Crossbill, ♂ & ♀, 5-6½"
162. Purple Finch, ♂ & ♀, 5½-6¼"
163. Cassin's Finch, ♂ & ♀, 6-6½"
164. Pine Grosbeak, ♂ & ♀, 8-10"
165a. House Finch, ♂ & ♀, 5-5¾"
165b. House Finch, paler form of ♂
165c. House Finch, ♀ with yellow
166. Gray-crowned Rosy Finch, ♀ & ♂, 6-7"

NUTHATCHES, CREEPER

Family *SITTIDAE* - nuthatches

These lively, but stout-bodied tree trunk climbers are **the only birds that go both up and down the trunks head-first.** They have powerful feet to aid in such climbing, but their stubby tails are not used to brace their bodies while climbing as with the woodpeckers. Their strong bills are useful for not only prying aside bark to get at insects and grubs underneath, but to crack seeds and nuts.

105. WHITE-BREASTED NUTHATCH, *Sitta carolinensis*. Sparrow size. **White under parts and face contrast sharply with black cap and back of neck, and bluish-gray back;** reddish-brown area is under tail; white spots appear on outer tail feathers. Has a nasal "kyeer-kyeer" call; also a low but nasal whistled song in series of "whee-whee-whee-whee or hoo-hoo-hoo", and so forth. Found in most of our region, but lower or a little south in winter.   conif. mix.ev. jun. cult.

106. RED-BREASTED NUTHATCH, *Sitta canadensis*. Warbler - to sparrow size. **Distinctive black stripe through eye and black cap on head are separated by white bar above eye;** back and most of tail bluish-gray; under parts whitish brown or reddish-brown; white spots appear on outer tail feathers. Has nasal "yhank-yhank" calls; also a high-pitched "ket-ket-ket-ket!". Found in most of our region, but may winter at lower levels.   s.a.mead. conif. mix.ev.

107. PYGMY NUTHATCH, *Sitta pygmaea*. Warbler size. Back and wings bluish-gray; **the gray-brown cap comes down over eye;** the throat is white, the belly gray. Gives a shrill and chattering rapidly-repeated "tee-dee, tee-dee" call; also a weaker, but more flute-like "teet-teet-teet" piping. Very selective in its habitats, as shown. Found only among these trees with rare exceptions.   conif.

Family *CERTHIIDAE* - creepers

108. BROWN CREEPER, *Certhia familiaris*. Sparrow-. Whitish-streaked on brown back and head; whitish below. This slender-bodied, **slender down-curved billed bird, is best told by watching its actions, for it invariably starts at the bottom of a tree trunk and slowly spirals upward, stopping now and then to probe into cracks in the bark for tiny insects. When it reaches where the trunk gets small, it flies to the bottom of another tree and starts spiralling up again.** It has a soft but high-pitched, lisping "tsee-tsee-tsee" song, and a single "seee" note. Found in most of our region, but usually at lower elevations in winter.   conif. mix.ev.

Family TROGLODYTIDAE - wrens

Energetic, small, often scolding, brown-backed birds with barred and often cocked-up tails.

brush
mix.ev.
cult.
bldg.

109. HOUSE WREN, *Troglodytes aedon.* Warbler size. **Dark markings on gray-brown above; uniform brown below and no white marks anywhere.** Likes to nest in buildings or wren houses. Has gurgling and stuttering song, loud in beginning, then softer; several scolding call notes. Notice sharp and slender bill, typical of wrens. Spring, summer, fall in most of region, south in winter.

conif.
mix.ev.
brush
rocks

110. WINTER WREN, *Troglodytes troglodytes* Warbler size, but a little smaller than 109. Dark brown above and with light line over eye; brownish belly with dark bars; **a very stubby tail is characteristic.** The rapid song has a peculiar high-pitched and long drawn quavering trill to it; call note a harsh hard "kt-kt". Found in most of our region, but at lower altitudes in winter.

str.wd.
brush
jun.
cult.

111. BEWICK'S WREN, *Thryomanes bewickii.* Sparrow size. Brownish above, white below; barred tail with white tips on the outer tail feathers; **long tail has narrow beginning; distinctive white streak over the eye.** Calls include gurgling "kut-kt-kt", harsh "chpee!" and high-pitched "tick-tick" or softer "whit-whit-whit"; song begins with 2-3 thin notes, then becomes buzzing and ends with soft and delicate trills. Tail may be waggled from side to side. Found from northern Washington south at lower altitudes.

water

112. LONG-BILLED MARSH WREN, *Telmatodytes palustris.* Warbler size to warbler +. **Distinctive white and black striped on back, black head and white stripe over eye;** dark brown bars on brown tail; sides of head and back brown; white under parts. Sibilant, gurgling song of many notes finishing in a throaty rattle; a low "tuck" call note, or a "ct-ct-rrrrrrrrr-er" sound at night. Found in late spring, summer and fall in lower areas.

rocks
str.wd.
bldg.

113. CAÑON WREN, *Catherpes mexicanus.* Sparrow size. **Brown color above and reddish-brown belly markedly contrast with white throat and breast;** some speckling of black and white on tail and wings. Sneaks in and out of rock crevices or piles of logs or goards with constant "tsee" note. Sweet liquid spraying song, starting rapidly, then drawing out into double notes and ending in deep "twee-twee-twee". Found in most of region.

grass
rocks
bldg.

114. ROCK WREN, *Salpinctes obsoletus.* Sparrow size. **Grayish general color with white breast lightly streaked with brown;**

113. Canon Wren 5½-5¾"
111. Bewick's Wren 5-5½"
112. Long-billed Marsh Wren 4¼-5½"
114. Rock Wren 5-6¼"
115. Dipper 7-8½"

yellowish-brown tail tips; white streak over eye, whitish below. Characteristically bobs body up and down as it sits on rock. Has harsh and chanting song, a rattling trill, and a "tak-keer" call note. Found in most of our region from late spring to mid-fall.

Family *CINCLIDAE* - dippers. Stout body; stubby tail.

water str.wd.

115. DIPPER (water ouzel), *Cinclus mexicanus*. Robin - to robin size. Looks like a large, thick-bodied, short-tailed wren, but always found in or near water, and color slate-gray. Swims through water with wings, walks on bottom, feeding on various small water life, including tiny fish; often bobs body up and down. Found in most of our region.

Family *ALAUDIDAE* - larks

sage grass s.a.mead. mt.mead. cult.

116. HORNED LARK, *Eremophila alpestris*. Robin -. Streaked brownish in color, but **black collar below yellow throat; black stripe above yellow forehead; small black horns on head;** tail black. Moves by walking instead of hopping like most similar birds. Song like "tsp-tsp-se-dee-dee"; shrill "tzeeee!" note; male may fly high in a circle and sing. Most of region, but lower in winter.

Family *MIMIDAE* - thrashers and mockingbirds

sage brush

117. SAGE THRASHER, *Oreoscoptes montanus*. Robin - to robin size. General brownish color, **but whitish breast and belly distinctively streaked with brown; white corners on tail; 2 narrow white bars on wings; white throat.** Male in spring may fly zig-zag over sage, then lights with upraised and fluttering wings. Very long, warbling, even-pitched song; also "kuk-kuk" alarm call, and weak, whistled "whurrr". Found east of Cascades, spring to fall.

brush cult.

118. CATBIRD, *Dumetella carolinensis*. Robin size. Slimmer than robin. **Distinctive slate-gray general color, but black cap and reddish-brown rump.** Mewing note very cat-like; song a disorganized succession of musical and non-musical notes. Hides in brush, often flipping tail jerkily. Spring-summer-fall mainly east of Cascades.

Family *TURDIDAE* - thrushes, bluebirds, solitaires. Fine singers.

* 119. ROBIN, *Turdus migratorius*. **Male always recognized in**

CATBIRD, WAXWINGS

118. Catbird 8-9¼"

116. Horned Lark 7-8"

130. Water Pipit 6-7"

117. Sage Thrasher 8-9"

128. Northern Shrike 9-10¾"

129. Loggerhead Shrike 8-10"

6½-8"

126. Bohemian Waxwing 7½-8 ¾"

127. Cedar Waxwing

cult.
mix.ev.
str.wd.

spring and summer by rusty-red breast and gray back; yellow bill; blackish head and tail. Female with grayish head and tail; breast pale reddish-brown; both sexes in winter become browner above and outer edge of breast is obscured by white markings. Tail is often pumped up and down. Juvenile is black spotted on breast and white-spotted on back. Low "pip-pip" sound, followed by "tet-tet", then more shrieking "pip-pip-pip"; a shrill "tzeee" call given in flight; song very cheerful, four rising and falling notes. Found in most of region in spring, summer, and fall. Winters to the south.

conif.
str.wd.
mix.ev.

* 120. VARIED THRUSH, *Ixoreus naevius*. Robin size or -. Looks like robin, but **has distinctive black band between reddish-brown throat and breast; orange-brown stripe over eye and bars on wings.** Female has gray breast band. Gives soft "tchoooook!" note; song a clear, quavering, long whistled note, with a following breezy similar note at different pitch. Most of region.

conif.
mix.ev.
cult.

* 121. HERMIT THRUSH, *Hylocichla guttata*. Sparrow +. All gray-brown or olive-brown above; the light-whitish to rose-tinted breast is dark-brown spotted; **reddish-brown tail and rump. Has curious habit of raising tail slowly.** Sounds nasal "pseee" and clear "kee" notes; also "chuk" alarm note; gives exquisitely lovely flute-like song at different pitches after **long beginning note**. Most of region in late spring, summer and fall; winters to the south.

str.wd.
brush
conif.

* 122. SWAINSON'S THRUSH, *Hylocichla ustulata*. Sparrow +. Olive-brown or gray-brown on upper parts; **eye-ring yellowish-brown; dark brown spots on buffy breast.** Very soft and beautiful song, spiralling slowly upward in pitch; "wheet" or "whee" call; also file-like "chrrrr". Lower elevations of our region.

conif.
brush
mix.ev.
cult.

* 123. WESTERN BLUEBIRD, *Sialia mexicana*. Sparrow +. Male distinctively **blue or dark blue on head, tail, throat and wings, but back and breast reddish.** Female more brown in color, though reddish-brown on sides. Gives rapidly-sounded "puw-puw-puw" call, and weak "chew-chew-chew". Found in most of region in late spring, summer and fall; winters to the south.

mix.ev.
grass
mt.mead.

* 124. MOUNTAIN BLUEBIRD, *Sialia currucoides*. Sparrow +. **Male distinctively pale azure blue except for white belly.** Female brown except for blue on tail and wings in part. May hover

in the air. Infrequent "turr", or simple "cu-cu-cu" song. Found mainly east of Cascades in late spring, summer and fall; winters to the south.

* 125. TOWNSEND'S SOLITAIRE, *Myadestes townsendi.* Robin - or robin size. Much slimmer than robin, gray above and pale gray below; tail edged and tipped with white; wing feathers also edged with white; white ring around eye; yellowish-brown bar or patch shows on spread wing. Juvenile spotted yellowish-brown. Male flies in high spiral in late spring, fluttering about and singing loudly, then dives earthward in steep zig-zags to nest. Calls creaking "eeesk". Most of region in spring, summer, fall; winters to the south.

conif.
str.wd.
brush
jun.

Family *BOMBYCILLIDAE* - waxwings. Sleek-looking.

126. BOHEMIAN WAXWING, *Bombycilla garrula.* Robin -. Reddish-brown on head grades gradually into grayish-brown on back to ashy-gray on rump and tail; wings blackish; crest on head may be high or low; black streak through eye; black chin; white spots on wing; some wing feathers tipped with red wax; belly gray; tail tipped with yellow. A rough or harsh "zzrreee" note. Found rather uncommonly in B.C. and northern Washington in spring, summer and fall; rare winter visitor to south and lower.

conif.
mix.ev.
cult.

127. CEDAR WAXWING, *Bombycilla cedrorum.* Robin -, but somewhat smaller than 126. Very similar in appearance, but more brownish above and yellowish and white below, and without white spots on wings; white under tail instead of reddish; ashy-gray on sides of head and tail. Sometimes catches insects like a flycatcher; travels in berry-hunting flocks, stripping trees and bushes. Gives high-pitched whistling note in flight or perched. Found in most of our region, wintering at lower altitudes.

mix.ev.
cult.
brush

Family *LANIIDAE* - shrikes

Upper bill strongly hooked; feed on large insects, lizards, mice, small birds, killing with bill, but using thorn or barb wire, etc. to tear apart before eating.

128. NORTHERN SHRIKE, *Lanius excubitor.* Robin size. The white, black and gray color design is distinctive of shrikes, particularly the black mask, but this species differs from 129 by having the whitish-gray under parts barred with faint but dark

grass
cult.

248 WILDLIFE AND PLANTS OF THE CASCADES

wavy lines. Juvenile brownish-gray above; lines on breast and belly more distinct than in adults. Like most shrikes it often sits alone on a wire or branch. Has "sek-sek" note or rasping "jhaeeg" call. Winters irregularly in our region.

grass
jun.
sage
cult.

129. LOGGERHEAD SHRIKE, *Lanius ludovicianus*. Robin - or robin size. Exactly like above, but smaller and breast unmarked. Sings rather haltingly; note like "jack-jack". Found in drier parts of our region in late spring, summer and fall; winters to the south.

Family *MOTACILLIDAE* - pipits. Walks instead of hops.

grass
water
cult.

130. WATER PIPIT, *Anthus spinoletta*. Sparrow +. Looks like grayish-brown sparrow with streaky-brownish-yellow belly and breast, but has **slender bill and frequently bobs tail up and down**; outside tail feathers are white. "Seep" or "seep-seep" call. Found in mts. of our region in spring, summer, fall; lower down in winter.

Family *SYLVIIDAE* - kinglets. Tiny, nervous and quick-moving.

conif.
s.a.mead.
cult.
mix.ev.

131. GOLDEN-CROWNED KINGLET, *Regulus satrapa*. Warbler -. **Bright orange or yellow crown bordered by black and yellow; gray-green to gray above; dull whitish below;** white wing bars; white line over eye. Like 132, feeds on tiny insects among small branchlets of tree. "see-see-see" notes like weak hisses. Found mainly in high mountains; winters lower down.

s.a. mead.
conif.
str.wd.
mix.ev.
cult.

132. RUBY-CROWNED KINGLET, *Regulus calendula*. Warbler size. Generally olive-gray in color above; gray to gray-green below; **bright but broken white eye-ring; bright red head patch seen only when bird is excited;** generally shorter-looking tail than warbler and often flits wings. "Cheep-chep" alarm note; harsh "kaar" note; rapidly repeated "eel-eel-eel". Song first shrill, then soft, repeating "ti-dee-dee" notes 2-3 times. Found in our region in high mts. in spring, summer, fall; lower down in winter.

Family *VIREONIDAE* - Vireos.

Rather slow-moving plain-looking gray or olive-backed birds; carefully hunting insects under leaves.

mix.ev.
brush
str.wd.
cult.

133. HUTTON'S VIREO, *Vireo huttoni*. Warbler size. This and 134 have white wing bars; Hutton's has **incomplete eye-ring**

KINGLET, WARBLER 249

131. Golden-crowned Kinglet
3¼-4″

132. Ruby-crowned Kinglet
3¾-4½″

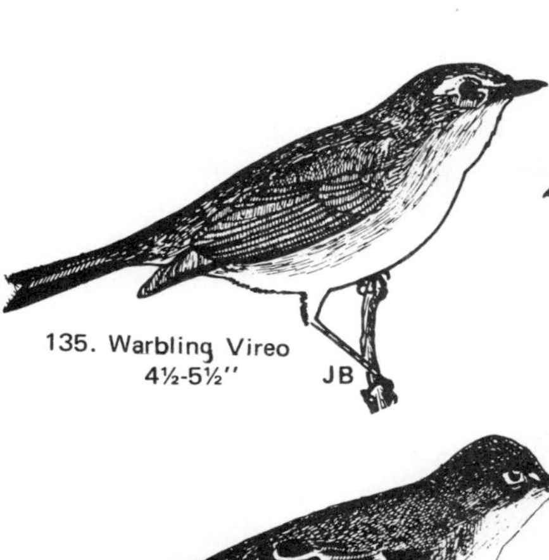

135. Warbling Vireo
4½-5½″

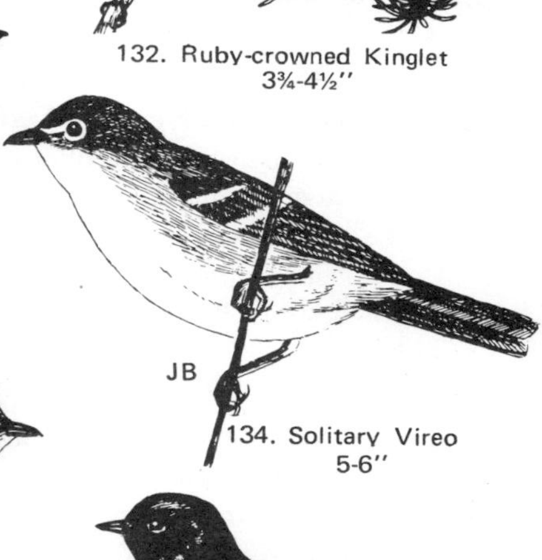

134. Solitary Vireo
5-6″

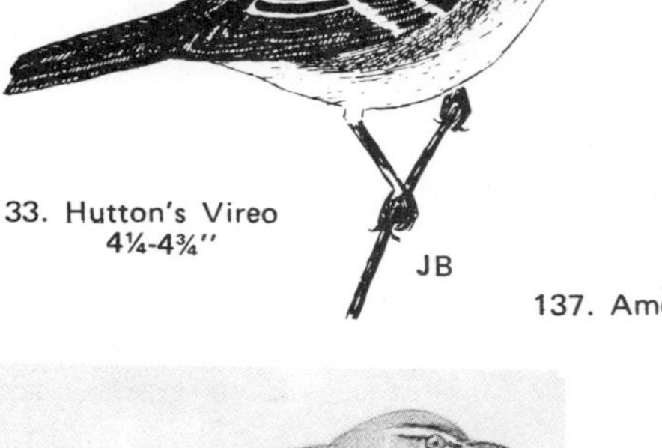

133. Hutton's Vireo
4¼-4¾″

137. American Redstart
4½-5¾″

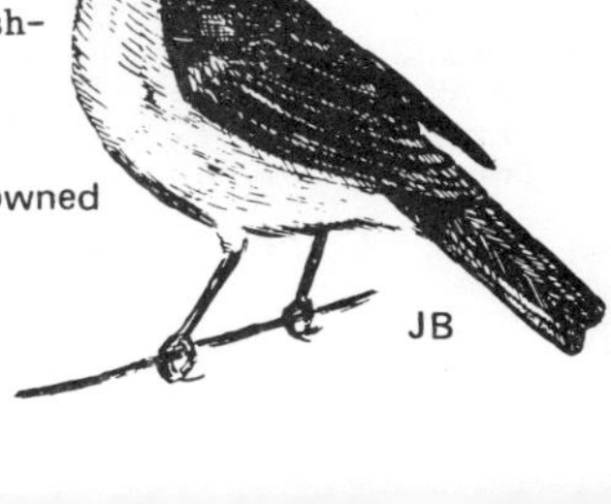

yellowish-green

138. Orange-crowned Warbler
4½-5½″

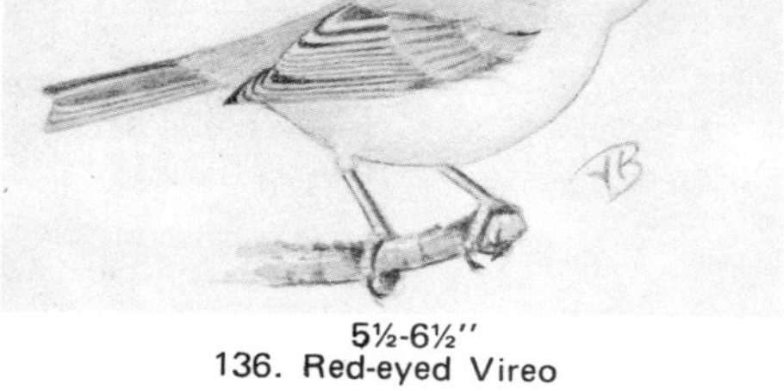

5½-6½″
136. Red-eyed Vireo

with black spot breaking ring above eye. Has peevish or hoarse "tsu-weep" note, often repeated; and a "that-thee-thee-thee" call. Found in most of region, but goes south or lower in winter.

mix.ev.
conif.
str.wd.

134. SOLITARY VIREO, *Vireo solitarius*. Sparrow size. Similar to 133, but **bright white spectacle eye-ring complete, and throat bright white.** Variable song with "chee-whee" and "whee-wee" notes. Most of region in spring, summer, fall; winters farther south.

str.wd.
mix.ev.
cult.
s.a.mead.

135. WARBLING VIREO, *Vireo gilvus*. Warbler size. Dull grayish-brown color; **no eye ring. Song an even-toned, endlessly repeated slow warble;** soft, scolding and querulous notes. Found in most of region in spring, summer, fall; winter south or low elevations.

mix.ev.
str.wd.
cult.

136. RED-EYED VIREO, *Vireo olivaceus*. Sparrow size. **Gray cap and white eye-brow stripe with black borders are distinctive.** Song has swift clear phrases, separated by pauses, 30-40 a minute; call note a nasal whinny "thway". Summer visitor, north Oregon and up.

Family *PARULIDAE* - wood warblers.

Small active flitters, hunting insects among twigs; thin needle-pointed bills; colorful.

The following are warblers with mostly unstreaked fronts.

str.wd.
cult.

137. AMERICAN REDSTART, *Setophaga ruticilla*. **Male has lustrous black head, back and throat; reddish-orange flanks and sides of breasts; and salmon-orange bars on black wings and tail;** belly white. Female has grayish-white throat, gray head, and yellow instead of orange markings. Two songs, one starting with "see-see-see", the other "seetsa-seeta-seetsa--". Found on east side of Cascades, migrating south of our area in winter.

brush
mix.ev.
cult.
str.wd.

138. ORANGE-CROWNED WARBLER, *Vermivora celata*. A plain-looking warbler, olive-green above and yellowish-green below with very faint markings on breast. Song, a weak repeated trill, soft at end; faint "chip" call. Most of region; winters to south.

brush
str.wd.
conif.
s.a.mead.
mix.ev.

139. MACGILLIVRAY'S WARBLER, *Oporornis tolmiei*. Male **with dark gray hood, white ring about eye; back olive; belly yellow.** Female has paler hood. Secretive in thick brush, much jerking of tail. Changeable song may start as rocking chant of "siddle-siddle" or "sweeter-sweeter" repeated. Most of region, but winters to the south.

WARBLERS

140. YELLOWTHROAT, *Geothlypis trichas*. Distinctive black back and yellow throat in male. Female and juvenile also have yellow throats, but are mainly dull olive-brown above. "Tchek", scolding note; distinctive "wit-chee-chee" song. Found in most of region, but winters from northern California south.
  marsh
  str.wd.

141. YELLOW-BREASTED CHAT, *Icteria virens*. Sparrow + . This very large yellow-breasted warbler has bright white spectacle-like eye-rings; dull olive-brownish above; white belly. Has loud harsh song of odd whistled notes. Most of region in lower levels.
  str.wd.
  brush

142. WILSON'S WARBLER, *Wilsonia pusilla*. (Pileolated Warbler). Yellow below, olive-greenish-yellow above; male with distinctive black cap. Females usually without the cap; juveniles always. Song a rapid chattering "chit-chit-chit-chit", lowering in pitch; hoarse "chup" call. Most of our region, wintering to south.
  str.wd.
  brush

The following Warblers have strongly streaked or marked breasts.

143. NASHVILLE (Calaveras) WARBLER, *Vermivora ruficapilla*. The male has a bright yellow belly and sharply marked white eye-ring; back plain olive-green; top and sides of head ashy-gray. The female and juvenile are duller in color. Has shrill "tspp" call; song a high "see-lit, see-lit, see-lit", continuing into rapid and varied notes. Found in most of region, but winters far to the south.
  conif.
  mix.ev.
  brush

144. YELLOW WARBLER, *Dendroica petechia*. Only all yellow warbler in our region, though with light reddish-brown streaks below and some greenish-gray on wings and tail; some yellow spots appear on tail. Has soft and light "see-see-weetse-see" song and "tsick!" note. Found in most of region, but winters far to south.
  str.wd.
  cult.

145. AUDUBON'S WARBLER, *Dendroica auduboni*. Both sexes all through year have bright yellow patches on sides of breast and bright yellow rumps; the male shows yellow crown in summer and spring; also black breast patch. In winter both sexes have streaky white breasts, are brownish above with yellow throats and white edges on 4-5 outer tail feathers. Has monotonous trilling song of "tseet-tseet-tseet", followed by lower pitched trill; soft "tseep" note. All region, winters low elevation.
  s.a.mead.
  conif.
  grass
  str.wd.
  cult.
  mix.ev.
  brush

str.wd.
conif.
mix.ev.
cult.

146. MYRTLE WARBLER, *Dendroica coronata*. Looks like a twin to 145, but **throat white and white spots appear on both sides of 2 or 3 outer tail feathers**. The harsh but soft "tsip" call is also distinctively different, but the junco-like trill of the song is much like Audubon's, either rising or falling in pitch at the last. Winter visitor in Oregon and northern California at low levels.

mix.ev.
conif.
jun.

147. BLACK-THROATED GRAY WARBLER, *Dendroica nigrescens*. **Male distinctively gray with black and white-striped face and black throat**; female with white throat. The wheezy and variable song starts with "tzeedle-tzeedle" or "zee-zee, zee-zee" in a lazy swinging cadence; a buzzing note. All region, winters south.

mix.e v.
conif.
cult.

148. TOWNSEND'S WARBLER, *Dendroica townsendi*. **Adult male in spring and summer has black crown and throat patch; greenish-gray patch back of eye is surrounded by wide yellow area; gray wings with white bars and feathers tipped with black; back is grayish-yellow-green; yellowish-white breast streaked with black**; song like that of above. Breeds B. C. and Washington; winters in southern Oregon.

conif.
s.a.mead.
str.wd.
mix.ev.

149. HERMIT WARBLER, *Dendroica occidentalis*. **Bright yellow head and black throat combination of male is distinctive; the gray back streaked with black**; white bars on wings; outer tail feathers mostly white; under parts unstreaked white except on upper sides. Head of female more dullish yellow and mottled black. Variable lisping "sweety-sweety" song spaced with abrupt notes "tsskk" call note. Found from Wash. south; winters in tropics.

Family *ICTERIDAE* - meadowlarks, blackbirds, orioles.

grass
marsh
cult.

150. WESTERN MEADOWLARK, *Sturnella neglecta*. **Male streaked brown in color, with bright yellow breast marked with black V; white-sided tail**. Female duller. Bubbling, cheerful song of 7-10 notes; "tchuk" call. Most of region at lower elevations.

marsh
cult.
grass

151. YELLOW-HEADED BLACKBIRD, *Xanthocephalus xanthocephalus*. Robin size. **Male black except for bright yellow head, neck and chest, and white wing patch**. Female has yellow throat and streaky breast, but otherwise brown. Has raspy and creaky "ka-ka-kow" or "kik-klook-kah" song; a rough "kick" or "kack" call. Most of region at low elevations; winters to south.

WARBLERS 253

139. MacGillivray's Warbler 4¾-5½"
140. Yellowthroat 4½-5¾"
143. Nashville Warbler 4-5"
141. Yellow-breasted Chat 6½-7½"
142. Wilson's Warbler 4¼-5"
145. Audubon's Warbler 5-5½" ♂ Spring
147. Black-throated Gray Warbler 4½-5"
146. Myrtle Warbler 5-6" ♂ Spring
144. Yellow Warbler 4½-5¼"

marsh
grass
cult.
str.wd.

152. RED-WINGED BLACKBIRD, *Agelaius phoeniceus*. Robin -. Male entirely black except for red and yellow patch on wing. Female streaky brown, but with striking dark brown markings on brown breast. Has gurgling metallic "onk-ka-la-reee" song; note a loud "keck"! Most of region at lower elevations.

grass
conif.
str.wd.
marsh
sage
jun.

153. BREWER'S BLACKBIRD, *Euphagus cyanocephalus*. Robin -. Male with purplish-green reflections on black feathers; eye white. Female brownish-gray with dark eyes. Flies in big flocks except when nesting; often rests on wires. The non-musical song wheezes and creaks; metallic "teck" call. Most of region.

str.wd.
grass
sage
jun.
cult.

154. BROWN-HEADED COWBIRD, *Molothrus ater*. Sparrow +. Male black with brown upper neck and head; stout short bill. Female uniform brownish-gray. Often holds tail very high. Song gurgles and whistles and also sounds like a rusty-spring; a "kuk" note, and sharp whistled "wee-tee-tee" flight call. Found in most of our region, but winters to south. Lays eggs in other bird nests.

str.wd.
mix.ev.
grass
cult.

155. BULLOCK'S ORIOLE, *Icterus bullockii*. Robin -. Male black on top of head and upper back, black streak through eye; black throat; breast, belly and side of head orange; white wing patch and white markings on dark wings; yellow at base and sides of dark tail. Female yellowish with gray wings and back. Juvenile looks like female, but shows black throat. Song a variable "kit-kit-ick, kit-ick, shee-wheet", plus 2-3 piping notes; a sharp "skit!" call. Found in most of our region, but winters in tropics.

Family *THRAUPIDAE* - tanagers. Bright colors, seed-eaters.

conif.
s.a.mead.
jun.
cult.
mix.ev.

156. WESTERN TANAGER, *Piranga ludoviciana*. Male has bright yellow body, black tail and wings, bright red face; yellow wing-bars. Female grayish-green above; yellowish below; yellow or white wing bars. Song falls and rises like robin's, with short "peer-re, peer-ree, pee-wee, peer-ree" phrases. Found in most of our region, but winters south into tropics.

157
brush
grass
str.wd.
mix.ev.
cult.
sage

Family *FRINGILLIDAE* - sparrows, finches, grosbeaks, etc. Have short stout bills, useful for eating or breaking open seeds.

157. LAZULI BUNTING, *Passerina amoena*. Sparrow size. Male bright blue on upper parts; tail and wings dusky-blue; white wing bars; white belly; cinnamon-brown sides and breast. Female

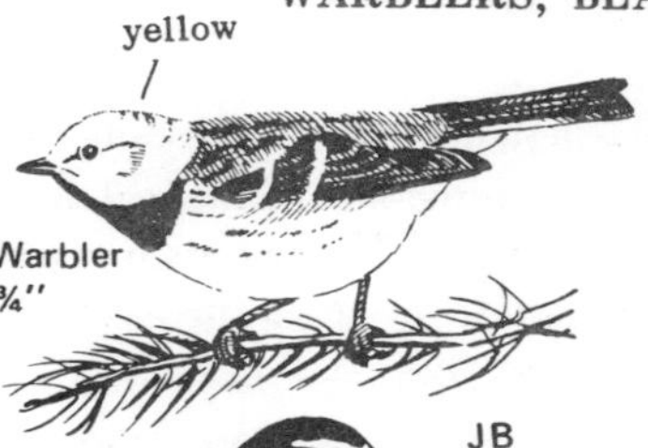

WARBLERS, BLACKBIRDS 255

149. Hermit Warbler
4½-4¾"

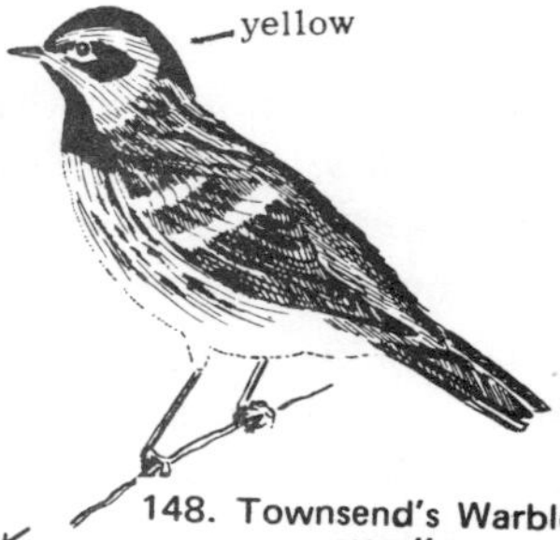

yellow

JB

148. Townsend's Warbler
4¼-5"

yellow

JB

155. Bullock's Oriole
7-8½"

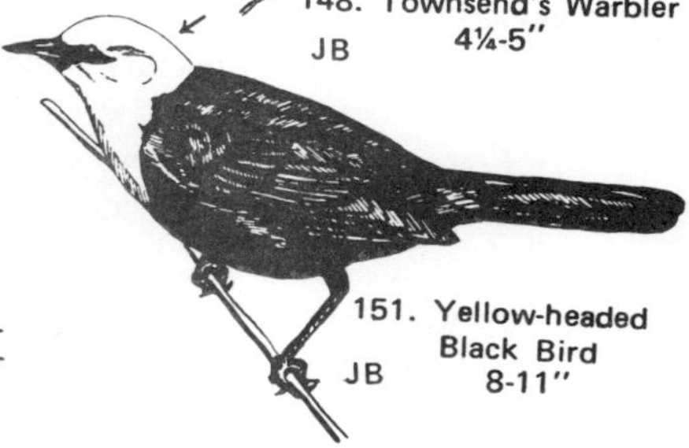

JB

151. Yellow-headed Black Bird
8-11"

JB

150. Western Meadowlark
8½-11"

JGl

154. Brown-headed Cowbird
6-8"

♂

JB

152. Red-winged Blackbird
JB
7-9½"

153. Brewer's Blackbird
8-10"

JB

dusty-brown with whitish wing bars. The high shrill song starts with a "weet-weet" or "hew-hew"; has "tskik" alarm note. Male may fly high when singing; tail often jerked nervously. Found in most of our region, but winters to the south.

158. EVENING GROSBEAK, *Hesperiphona vespertina.* Rob-

s.a.mead.
conif.
str.wd.
mix.ev.

in -. **Male black on wings, tail and top of head; yellow forehead with line over eye; tail well-forked; large white patch on wing;** breast is smoky brown; as are neck and back of head; belly and lower back yellow; black wing and tail feathers edged with black. Female is brownish-gray, washed with yellow; black tail and wing feathers edged with white. Both sexes possess large greenish-yellow bills. A rough "tseer-eep, grrreeea" song. All of region; winters lower.

159. BLACK-HEADED GROSBEAK, *Pheucticus melanoceph-*

str.wd.
mix.ev.
conif.
jun.
cult.

alus. Sparrow +. **Male with reddish-brown neck and breast, black head; yellow on belly; black and white wings and tail.** Female with striped head and duller general color. The mellow and liquid song rises and falls, sometimes with great strength; a sharp "eek" note; sweet "wee-wee-yoo" call. All of region; winters south.

160. WHITE-WINGED CROSS-BILL, *Loxia leucoptera.* Spar-

s.a.mead.

row size to sparrow +. **Two distinctive broad white wing-bars plus cross-bills in both sexes. Male a faded rose-pink,** except for dark brownish wings and tail. Female with yellow on rump and olive-gray general color. Song a series of loud trills at different levels. Found mainly from Washington north. Bill used to crack pine nuts.

* 161. RED CROSSBILL, *Loxia curvirostra.* Sparrow size.

sa. mead
conif.
str.wd.

Male dull red all over, but brighter on head and rump; blackish on wings and tail; sometimes yellow-green to orange. Female dull grayish-green, more yellowish-tinged on head and rump, brownish on wings and tail. Juvenile streaked brownish-black on gray. Song a warbled "tu-tee-tu-tee, tay-tay, gip-gip-gup" with the "gips" harder; loud "pip-pip" call.

* 162. PURPLE FINCH, *Carpodacus purpureus.* Sparrow size.

conif.
mix.ev.
str.wd.
cult.

Male rose-red on head, rump, and breast, whitish below and brown elsewhere, but no dark streaks below like similar house finch; tip of tail notched instead of square as in house finch. Female has streaked grayish-brown body, yellowish-green tinged above; streaked on whitish below; pale stripe over eye and dark blotch back of

GROSBEAK, GOLDFINCHES

7-8½"
158. Evening Grosbeak

156. Western Tanager
6¼-7½"

159. Black-headed Grosbeak
6½-7-¾"

— reddish-brown orange

157. Lazuli Bunting
5-5½"

5-5½"
167. Common Redpoll

6-6¾"
160. White-winged Cross-bill

4½-5¼"
168. Pine Siskin

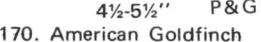

4½-5½"   P&GM
170. American Goldfinch

3¾-4¼"
169. Lesser Goldfinch

eye. Male often flies high to warble swift rippling and rolling song; a metallic "pt" or pick note. Found in most of region.

s.a.mead.
conif.
str.wd.
mix.ev.

* 163. CASSIN'S FINCH, *Carpodacus cassinii*. Sparrow size. Male is paler red on breast than 162; square red patch on crown sharply contrasts with brown neck and back; tail notched deeply; no sharply-marked belly streaks. Female like 162, but has 5 brownish belly streaks. The vibrant warble rolls to a "chrrrrr" ending; startling "tay-dee-yeep" alarm note. Found in most of region in mountains, but winters at lower elevations.

s.a.mead.
conif.

164. PINE GROSBEAK, *Pinicola enucleator*. Robin - to robin in size. Much larger than above finches; male with red on breast, back and head; black wings show white wing bars; belly brown and tail dark brown. Female has white wing bars, but elsewhere brown. Rich and melodious song, whistles and twitters. In our mountains.

grass
mix.ev.
rocks
bldg.
cult.
str.wd.
jun.
sage
brush

* 165. HOUSE FINCH, *Carpodacus mexicanus*. Sparrow size. Very similar to 162, but male has bright red rump, forehead, breast and eye-stripe; narrow dark streaks on belly and sides; tip of tail more squarish; sometimes yellow or orange enters coloring. Female has no black blotch on cheek as in 162. Has loose and sunny musical song, ending in nasal "chee-wheer". All of region.

rocks
mt.mead.
s.a.mead.
sub.alp.

* 166. GRAY-CROWNED ROSY FINCH,*Leucosticte tephrocotis*. Sparrow size. The head cap of the male, black in front and gray in the rear; rosy-brown head, throat and sides of breast; rosy-red wings with black and white markings; rump pink with brown bars; tail and upper back brown. Females duller in color. Gives rough "cheep-cheep" or "chee-chee" calls. Alpine peaks; winters to east.

brush
grass
sage

167. COMMON REDPOLL, *Acanthis flammea*. Sparrow size. Black chin and bright red cap are distinctive; otherwise streaked grayish-brown except for whitish rump. Male has pink breast. Acts more like goldfinch than purple finch, with quick nodding motions. Trilling song ends in rattling "chet-t-t t-t-tet-tet", which is also a call given in flight. Winters in our region in open country.

s.a.mead.
conif.
grass
brush
cult.

168. PINE SISKIN, *Spinus pinus*. Warbler +. Both sexes look strongly-streaked with yellowish-brown to dusky all over; some yellow seen in center of tail, and also in patch on wing when outstretched. The bill is finely pointed. Song a wheezy "kee-see-ee",

punctuated at times by a queer "who-ee"; also has distinctive "shzz-rrrrrreee" call; a loud "shee-ip" or "chilee-eep", and soft talkative twittering "tee-di-di". Most of our region, but winters in lowlands.

169. LESSER GOLDFINCH (Green-backed), *Spinus psaltria*. Warbler size. **Male has black cap, greenish-black back, black and white wings and is yellowish below.** Female more dull-looking. Gives plaintive sweet "teee-yeeer" call; song made of paired musical notes. Found from western Oregon south.

mix.ev.
str.wd.
brush
cult.
jun.
sage

170. AMERICAN GOLDFINCH, *Spinus tristis*. Sparrow -. **The bright yellow male has black wings with white bars; also black forehead and tail in spring and summer;** more like female in winter except for black and white wings. Female brownish-green on head and back; gray bars appear on blackish wings and tail; throat bright yellow; belly and breast duller yellow. Juveniles are similar to the female but browner. Most of region; lower altitudes in winter.

str.wd.
brush
grass
cult.

171. SLATE-COLORED JUNCO, *Junco hyemalis*. Sparrow size. **Male is uniform slate-gray on breast and upper parts, contrasting sharply with white belly;** white edges to tail. The insect-like song is short but musical trill; hard "tek" call. Rare winter visitor.

conif.
sage
cult.

172. OREGON JUNCO, *Junco oreganus*. Sparrow size. **Male has distinctive black head and breast, reddish-brown back, yellowish-brown sides and white belly.** Female is grayer on head. May appear in large flocks. Has trilling, insect-like and quivering tone at same level; also clicks and twitters. Found in most of region.

s.a.mead.
conif.
mt.mead.
mix.ev.
cult.

171. Slate-colored Junco
5½-6¼"

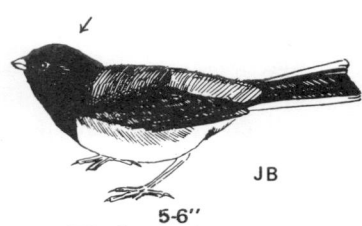

5-6"
172. Oregon Junco

260   WILDLIFE AND PLANTS OF THE CASCADES

brush
sage
pine

173. GREEN-TAILED TOWHEE, *Chlorura chlorura*. Common summer visitor in brushy areas. Sparrow +. Plain olive-green above; gray below; under surfaces and edges of wings yellow; sparrow-like bird with **bright white throat and reddish-brown crown**, bordered with black streaks. Has churring, burring song and a soft "mew" call. Song often opens with soft sweet notes.

brush
mix.ev.
str.wd.
cult.
jun.

174. BROWN TOWHEE, *Pipilo fuscus*. **The only robin-size plain brown bird with rufous-brown under tail**; throat streaked against light color. Has metallic "tink" note, which is repeated rapidly in the song, ending in a trill; also has quarrelsome, buzzy noises. Found from S.W. Oregon south at lower altitudes.

brush
str.wd.
sage
sitk.-spr.
jun.
cult.

175. RUFOUS-SIDED TOWHEE, *Pipilo erythrophthalmus*. Robin -. **Distinctive white spots on black wings and back plus reddish-brown sides**; male with black neck and head; breast and belly white; long, black tail with white at tips of outer feathers; eyes red. Female with brown head. Call an insect-like "to-whee" while song is a loud and buzzing trill. From B.C. south, low alt.

SPARROWS WITH MAINLY PLAIN BREASTS AND BELLIES

brush
sage
cult.

176. BREWER'S SPARROW, *Spizella breweri*. **Finely streaked with black on brownish head and back**; cheeks grayish-brown and not streaked. The slender blackish-brown tail is notched; underparts gray and unstreaked. Weak "tskip" call; song in series of buzzing trills and runs in different pitched notes. Generally found on E. side of Cascades in brushy areas.

conif.
sub.alp.
jun.
str.wd.
cult.
mt. mead.

177. CHIPPING SPARROW, *Spizella passerina*. **A small sparrow with reddish-brown crown**; dark line through eye with white line above; plain grayish-white underparts. Call note a "sip"; song a dry "insect-like trill." Breeds from British Columbia south generally at lower altitudes.

grass
cult.

178. GRASSHOPPER SPARROW, *Ammodramus savannarum*. **Small sparrow with apparently large flat head and very short tail**; pale stripe through crown; grayish-buff, unstreaked breast; reddish-brown stripes down dark back. Flight rather feeble and fluttering. A "tlilick" note; a "zit-tick-zzeee" buzzing song; also a dry insect-like buzz or trill; the first song often jumbled. From British Columbia south generally in dry areas.

179. GOLDEN-CROWNED SPARROW, *Zonotrichia atricapilla*. **Yellow band through crown of black-sided head**; rest of

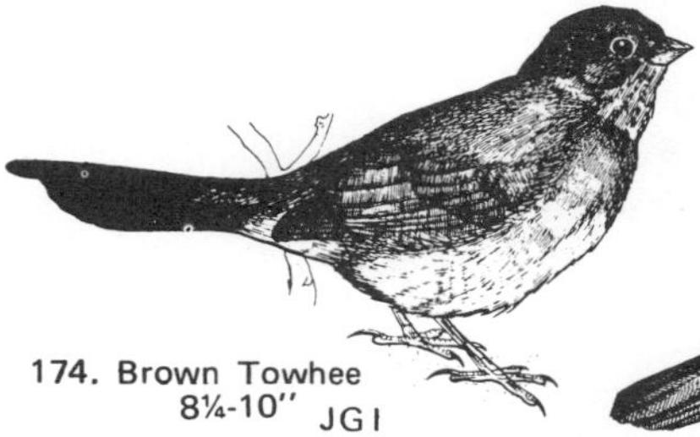

TOWHEE, SPARROWS 261

174. Brown Towhee
8¼-10" JGI

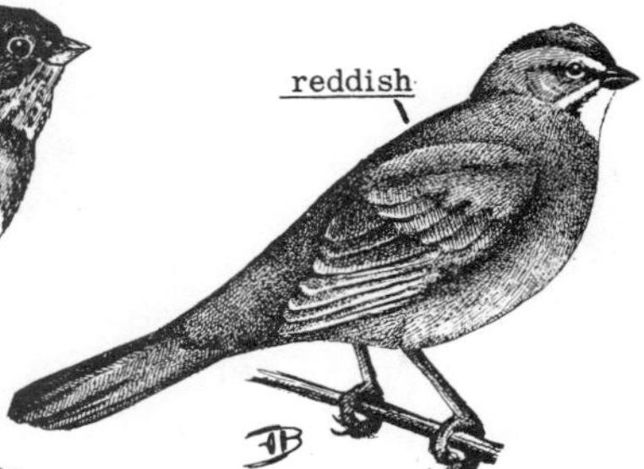

reddish

173. Green-tailed towhee
6¼-7"

175. Rufous-sided Towhee 
7-8½"
JB

176. Brewer's Sparrow
5-5¼"
JB

177. Chipping Sparrow
5-5¾"
JB

yellow

179. Golden-crowned Sparrow
6-7"
JB

178. Grasshopper Sparrow
4½-5¼"
JB 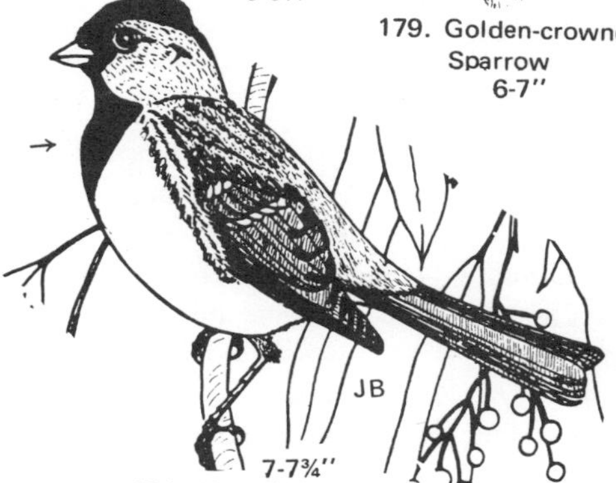

180. White-crowned Sparrow
5½-7"
JB

181. Harris' Sparrow
7-7¾"
JB

brush
str.wd.
sitk.-spr.
cult.
grass

upperparts brownish-gray except for dark brown streaks on wings and brown outer tail feathers; belly whitish; breast brownish-gray. Juveniles have no light stripes over eyes as in white-crowned. Has a plaintive 3-noted song, coming down scale like "3 blind mice." Winters in brushy areas of lower mountains.

brush
grass
cult.
mt.mead.

180. WHITE-CROWNED SPARROW, *Zonotrichia leucophrys*. Adult with black and white stripes on head; throat and breast grayish; upper back streaked with brownish-black. Juveniles with dark and light brown stripes on head. Song starts with "saay-see-say", which may be repeated, often followed by dry trill or series of trills or "lillipip" sounds. Breeds in high alt., winters lower.

str.wd.
cult.
s.a.mead.
mix.ev.

181. HARRIS' SPARROW, *Zonotrichia querula*. Large, black-throated, black-crowned sparrow with general dark gray color; blackish streaks on back and wings; white belly and breast; juveniles with brown heads. Has low-keyed song of minor whistles generally at same pitch or very close. Winters in lower altitudes, generally on east side of Cascades.

SPARROWS WITH DARK SPOT ON BREAST OR SIDE OF BREAST

grass
brush
mix.ev.
sage

182. LARK SPARROW, *Chondestes grammacus*. Sharp white and dark markings on face; reddish-brown cheek patch; round tail with white corners; crown reddish-brown with white stripe; black spot on white breast. Young have no central spot and are lightly-streaked on breast. Very variable song, with churrs, buzzes and clear notes and trills; weak and soft "tsip" call note. Usually seen flying up into bushes when frightened. -Breeds in most of our region at lower altitudes.

sage
brush

183. SAGE SPARROW, *Amphispiza belli*. General gray color has distinctive black marks on sides of throat and single black spot on breast; a few dark streaks on sides of breast. Often jerks tail, which is fairly long and square. Soft "kik-kik" call; thin high jerky song like "seet-sooo-seeeee-tzay". Breeds in dry brushy areas.

alp.
str.wd.
brush
cult.

184. WESTERN TREE SPARROW, *Spizella arborea*. Reddish-brown cap and round spot on plain-colored breast are distinctive; back brownish with light streaks; reddish-brown mark on shoulder. Sweet notes of song very variable, starting with clear high notes, gives musical "teelweet" note. Winters generally east side of the Cascades.

SPARROWS

P&GM

5½-6¾"
182. Lark Sparrow

5-6"
183. Sage Sparrow

5½-6½"
184. Western Tree Sparrow

6-7¼"
185. Snow Bunting

6¼-7¼"
186. Fox Sparrow

187. Lincoln's Sparrow
5-6"

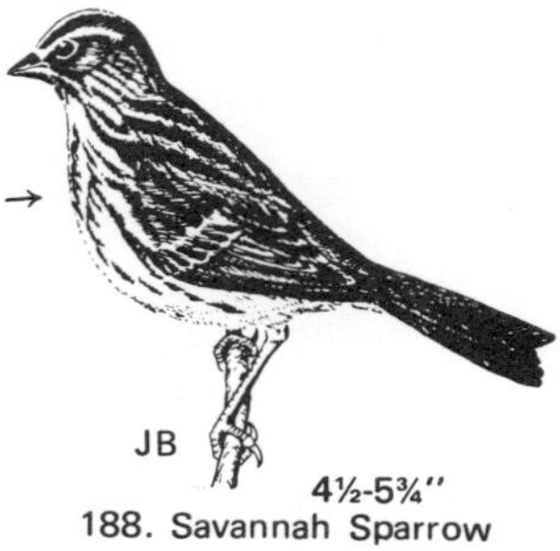

4½-5¾"
188. Savannah Sparrow

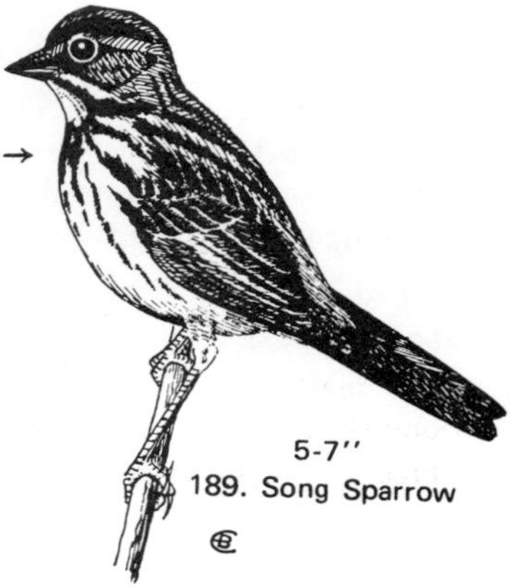

5-7"
189. Song Sparrow

185. SNOW BUNTING, *Plectrophenax nivalis*. Much white in color, especially below; **dark mark on side of breast;** some appear brown, but large white patches appear in flight. Call note a "seer" or "teew"; song like lark's "tee-tee-chuw-reee" repeated. Winters in middle areas of mountains.

grass
cult.
mt.mead.

SPARROWS WITH STREAKED BREASTS

186. FOX SPARROW, *Passerella iliaca*. Very large, dark brownish-gray sparrow, **heavily streaked and spotted on breast,** especially on upperpart; **reddish-brown tail;** much variations in appearance, especially in browns and grays, some with brown heads and others with gray. **Does much vigorous scratching under bushes, bird jumping forward, then scratching back with both feet.** Song, 2 soft sweet notes "swee-chu", followed by loud trills. A metallic "sisp" note. Breeds up to tree limit; winters lower elevation.

brush
str.wd.
cult.

187. LINCOLN'S SPARROW, *Melospiza lincolnii*. Similar to Song Sparrow, but no large spot on chest; instead **underparts are finely streaked with blackish-brown and a buff-colored band crosses the breast;** also tail shorter. Soft to loud "tsee" call; song of gurgling low notes, rising and lowering rapidly, often with pauses between phrases, dropping at end. Breeds in Canadian zone, migrates at lower elevations and winters from S.W. Oregon south, often seen skulking in bushes.

grass
marsh
cult.
mt.mead.

188. SAVANNAH SPARROW, *Passerculus sandwichensis*. Has many varieties, but generally **with whitish breast and sides streaked geometrically with dark brown; tail slightly forked.** Song, a sibilant, soft "tsee-tsee-tsee, zee-tzee", with last note low; a soft "tseep" or loud "tsup" note. Breeds along coast and E. side of mountains; winters in lower, drier areas.

grass
marsh

189. SONG SPARROW, *Melospiza melodia*. Whitish underparts are **dark streaked, combining to form distinctive central large breast spot.** "Tchik" call; beautiful song starts with soft "seet-seet-sweet", followed by some buzzy notes. Bird often seen pumping its tail when flying. Most of region.

str.wd.
marsh
brush
cult.

190. VESPER SPARROW, *Pooecetes gramineus*. Brown above, streaked with dusky; **chestnut patch at bend of wing; best field mark is flash of white outer feathers in tail when flying.** Song starts with 2, long, clear, whistled notes, flute-like and like "taps". Breeds in foothills of mountains; winters to the south.

sage
grass
brush

SPARROWS

191. **LAPLAND LONGSPUR,** *Calcarius lapponicus.* Walks or creeps, rarely hops. Shows many narrow brownish-black streakings on back and sides; reddish-brown at nape of neck; some white on sides of tail. Dry rattling call. Rather rare winter visitor in open areas of mountains.

grass
cult.

191. Lapland Longspur
6-7"

190. Vesper Sparrow
5-6½"

REPTILES

Reptiles have a covering of hard scales to protect them against enemies and against drying out, whereas amphibians, such as frogs and salamanders, have a smooth and moist skin. Reptiles appear mainly during the warm months of the year, going into winter dormancy in various hiding places when cold weather comes. This is because their blood remains the same temperature as the air. Most of the reptiles in our region are most active in daylight, particularly the lizards, but the rubber boa and ring-neck snake are also active at night.

Remember that no native reptile in our region is dangerous except the Western Rattlesnake, which has poisonous fangs and should be carefully avoided. It is told from other snakes by its very wide head, much wider than the neck, and its rattles. If you are struck by a rattlesnake, do not run, as this pumps the poison into your heart. If you are struck in the hand or arm, you can keep the poison away from the heart by swinging the arm in a circle as you walk to get help. Carry a snake-bite kit at all times on hikes.

The reptiles described below are divided into three sections, A. turtles, B. lizards, and C. snakes. When you are trying to identify a reptile, turn to the proper section and study the pictures and descriptions until you find the one you have in your hand or see. Remember to carefully observe what kind of habitat or wildlife area (meadow, yellow-pine forest, brush, etc.) that you find it living in, and compare this with the description, as this may help you be more sure of your identification.

A. Turtles

water
str.wd.

1. WESTERN POND TURTLE, *Clemmys marmorata*. 3½-7½"; tail about ¼ body length. The yellowish shell is usually blotched with black or brown, though sometimes unmarked, and often has a network of lines-and spots on each of the shields that radiate out from the center; plastron, 6 pairs of plates. The head has blackish spots or a network of lines. It lives most of the time in the water of ponds or slow streams, and spends much time basking on logs or rocks in the sun. If disturbed, it dives quickly into the water where it hides among the water plants. Feeds on insects, water plants and dead animals or birds or other carrion. Found in lower streams of the Cascades and ponds west of the divide, rare in Washington and absent in British Columbia. The

female may go inland a ways to lay eggs, but otherwise this turtle is quite aquatic.

2. PAINTED TURTLE, *Chrysemys picta.* 3½-10"; tail about 1/5 length of body. Shell or carapace low and unkeeled; **shields with front edges yellow** or, more rarely, the shell will have a central stripe of yellow down the upperside and be covered with an open network of lines. **Yellow lines appear on legs and head, while there is a red bar or spot behind the eye.** The generally black or olive upper shell is smooth; the under-shell (plastron) is usually with a large dark blotch in the center, with dark lines extending out along the furrows or grooves, but in the young turtles the plastron is orange or red outside the dark center. The male is much smaller than the female and has very long fingernails, which are used to carress the female while swimming beneath her at mating time. This is a completely aquatic turtle in ponds, marshes and small lakes or sluggish streams. It often basks on logs or banks in the sun, sometimes in large groups; it feeds mainly on insects, worms, water plants, crayfish, frogs, etc. Found in foothills of Cascades, eastern side in Washington and B. C., but in branches of Willamette River in Oregon.

water str.wd.

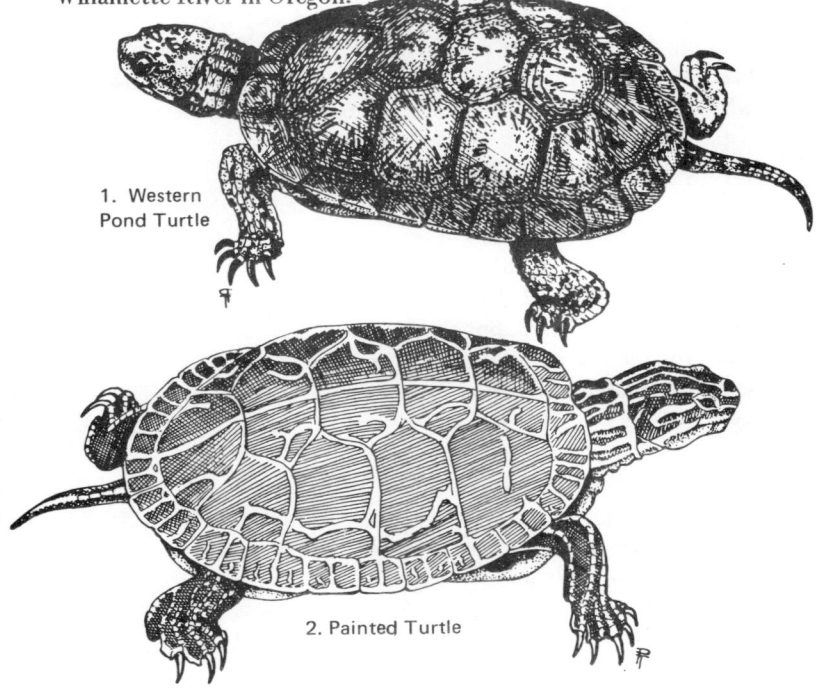

1. Western Pond Turtle

2. Painted Turtle

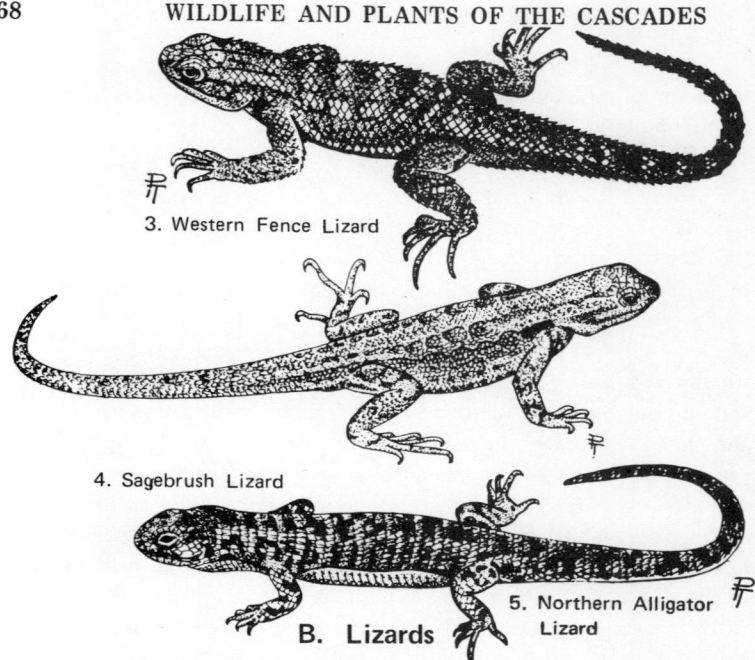

B. Lizards

3. Western Fence Lizard
4. Sagebrush Lizard
5. Northern Alligator Lizard

rocks
brush
conif.
mix.ev.
str.wd.
cult.
mt.mead.
grass

3. WESTERN FENCE LIZARD, *Sceloporus occidentalis*. 2-3¾"; tail up to 2¼" or longer than head and body combined. Grayish, blackish or brownish in color, with darker blotches on back in regular rows; tail appears dark-banded; **belly whitish but with blue patches on sides; male has base of tail swollen and blue patch appears on throat, while the blue belly patches are bordered with black;** female has less bright blue coloring and never any green or blue coloring on back; young have blue color faintest of all. Found in most of region, except B. C. and Olympic Mts., up to the lower limits of the Canadian Life Zone.

sage
brush
str.wd.
conif.

4. SAGEBRUSH LIZARD, *Sceloporus graciosus*. 2-2½". Similar to above lizard, **but has definite black bar on shoulder and more rusty color on sides of neck and body;** has relatively smaller scales than above lizard. Like above lizard, feeds mainly on insects, spiders, etc. Found up to Canadian Life Zone in southern Cascades.

mix.ev.
conif.
str.wd.
grass
sage

5. NORTHERN ALLIGATOR LIZARD, *Gerrhonotus coeruleus*. 3-5¼"; tail about 1½ x length of body and head. **A distinctive dark longitudinal stripe down belly between the scale rows.** Greenish, bluish or olive above with dark bars and blotches. **Fold of skin along side is distinctive.** Feeds on insects, worms, spiders, etc. Found in all our region up to Hudsonian Life Zone.

C. Order Serpentes (Snakes)

6. RUBBER BOA, *Charina bottae.* 14-30". A heavy-bodied snake **with tail end so thick it looks like head-end, and with large symmetrically-placed plates on top of head.** Color brown or chocolate brown above, yellowish below, the skin feeling smooth and looking shiny; young snakes more pinkish or light brown in color. It can climb, swim and burrow, though ground movements are not very fast. It eats small mammals and birds, which it kills by constriction, hunting often at night. It is most likely to be found under rocks, rotting logs, and the bark of dead or fallen trees by day. Found in most of our region up to Canadian Life Zone.

grass
brush
conif.
str.wd.
mix.ev.
water

†7. RINGNECK SNAKE, *Diadophis punctatus.* 13-31". Body slender, blackish, bluish or olive in color **with a bright orange or yellowish neck ring; belly yellowish-orange becoming bright red under tail.** When fearing attack, the snake may coil its tail like a spring, exposing the bright red under-color, evidently as a method to frighten the attacker. Usually found in daylight under boards, logs, rocks, debris, etc. Feeds on insects, frogs, lizards, worms, salamanders, etc. Found up to Transition zone in Ore. and Calif.

mix.ev.
grass
brush
cult.

8. WESTERN YELLOW-BELLIED RACER, *Coluber constrictor mormon.* 21-78". Plain olive or brown color above and plain yellow on belly, the young, however, look almost leopard-like with brown saddle blotches on back and spots on sides. These slim snakes travel at comparatively high speed, including rapid climbing through bushes and up trees, and may often lift the front part of body and head high to see about them, even weaving it from side to side. Chases lizards, frogs, small mammals and insects; fights aggressively when caught or cornered. Widespread in Oregon and Calif. up to Canadian zone, east of Cascades in Wash.

mt.mead.
brush
grass
mix.ev.

9. GOPHER SNAKE, *Pituophis melanoleucus.* 3-8' long, our largest snake. Generally cream or yellowish-colored, with reddish-brown, blackish or brownish blotched on back, wider-spaced on tail; dark line often appears from side to side in front of the eyes; yellowish to whitish on belly, often with black spots. **Each back scale has a keel down middle. A very good ally of man, hunting mainly rodents and rabbits, but unfortunately often killed because its diamond-shaped blotches and the aggressive vibrating of the tail in dry grass or leaves make people think it is a rattlesnake.** Found in most of region up to Canadian Life Zone.

grass
brush
mix.ev.
conif.
cult.

270 WILDLIFE AND PLANTS OF THE CASCADES

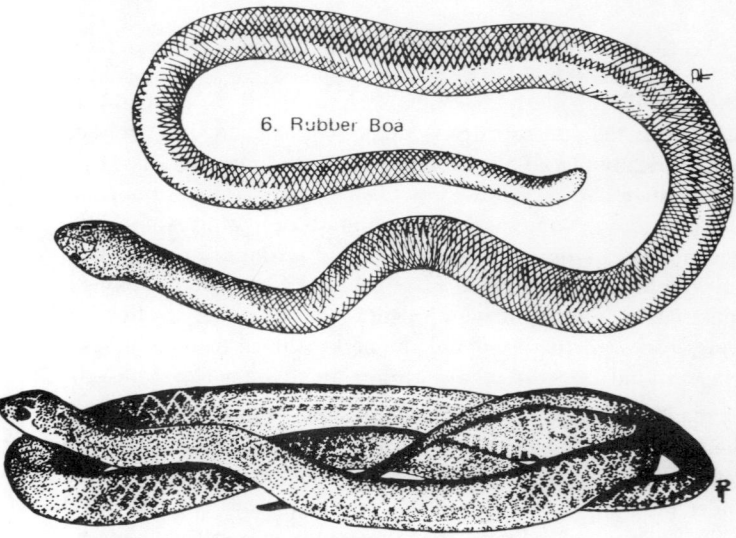
6. Rubber Boa

8. Western Yellow-bellied Racer

9. Gopher Snake

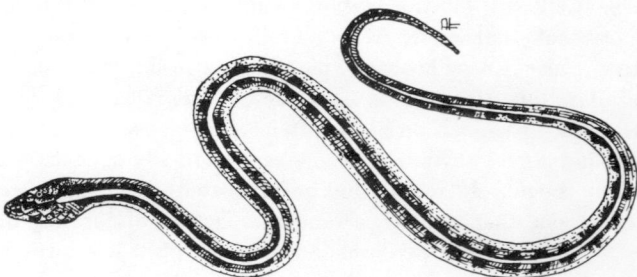
10. Common Garter Snake

GARTER, RATTLE SNAKES

10. COMMON GARTER SNAKE, *Thamnophis sirtalis*. 18-50". Like the gopher snake, garter snakes have keels on their scales, but they are entirely different in other ways, being more slender, having more yellow in the color and giving off a bad smell when handled. The count of scales that form a row along the neck, mid-body and above the vent (or beginning of tail) are important in telling differences between species, and are read as 17-19-17, which is the scale count of this species. Since color is very variable, from brown through, red, grey and black, and sometimes striped yellow on sides and sometimes whitish, it is more important to notice the **red blotches on the side and the usually 7 upper and 10 lower scales along the lips. This snake often fights savagely when picked up;** feeds mainly on tadpoles, frogs, salamanders, birds, fish, mice, slugs, etc. Common everywhere up to Canadian zone.

water
grass
mt.mead.
mix.ev.
brush
str.wd.
cult.

11. WESTERN TERRESTRIAL GARTER-SNAKE, *Thamnophis elegans*. 18-43". Scale count 19-19-17. Has a sharply-marked—**yellow stripe down back**, but varies greatly in other color patterns, so it is more important to notice that there are **8 scales along upper lips, of which the 6th and 7th are specially large and usually taller than wide, while the two main scales between the nostrils are usually broader than long and not pointed at the front. Found mainly on land** in most of our region up to Canadian Life Zone.

grass
brush
mix.ev.
str.wd.
cult.

12. WESTERN AQUATIC GARTER SNAKE, *Thamnophis couchi*. 18-58". The representatives of this garter snake in our region are easily told from the above snake by the **irregular dark blotches against the olive general color, and the weak or absent yellowish back stripe;** 8 scales along upper lip; **the two main scales between the nostrils are usually narrower than long and are pointed at the front.** Found in northern Calif. and s.w. Oregon, up **to** the Canadian Life Zone.

water
str.wd.

†13. NORTHWESTERN GARTER SNAKE, *Thamnophis ordinoides*. 14-27"; variously brown, green, blue or black, but usually with **red blotches on yellow belly; 7 upper lip scales. W. side of Cascades.**

mt.mead.
mix.ev.
conif.

14. WESTERN RATTLESNAKE, *Crotalus viridis*. 14-63"; general color varies greatly through brown, green, gray, yellow, pink, black, etc., to camouflage with surroundings, but is much

most
habitats

blotched and has light stripe behind the eye and the corner of the mouth. This is the only species of rattlesnake in our region, and is found on east side of Cascades in Washington and B.C.

Class Amphibia (Frogs, Toads and Salamanders)

All these animals have moist, smooth skins, and usually hatch from eggs into gill-using tadpole forms, which metamorphose into lung-breathing adults with four legs. Most hibernate secretly in winter or drought.

Salamanders

Family AMBYSTOMIDAE (Mole and Tiger Salamanders)

Our only salamanders with a band or broken band of teeth across the roof of the mouth. Length given is from snout to vent (tail base).

conif.
str.wd.
water

1. PACIFIC GIANT SALAMANDER, *Dicamptodon ensatus*. 4-6", size; massive-appearing body and head are marbled black spotted against gray, purplish or brown general color; 3 segments in 4th toe of hind foot. Gives low or hoarse rattling cry when attacked! Larvae like cold mountain streams or lakes. Found in most of our region, mainly west of Cascade Divide.

water
str.wd.
rocks

2. OLYMPIC SALAMANDER, *Rhyacotriton olympicus*. 1½-2½". **Distinctive large eyes combined with small size;** also noted for its long body and legs, contrasting with short tail and small head. The northern subspecies (from central Oregon north) is brown above, but with white specks on sides; belly yellowish-orange with a few specks of black. The southern subspecies is mottled brownish on olive; belly greenish-yellow, heavily dotted with black. Likes cold mountain streams, springs, etc, or hiding among wet rocks nearby. Found mainly west of Cascade crest as far north as Olympic Mountains, but not in B. C.

grass
mix.ev.
conif.
str.wd.
water

3. NORTHWESTERN SALAMANDER, *Ambystoma gracile*. 3-4½". General color brownish or blackish; **has particularly large paratoid glands back of eyes, and a glandular ridge down top edge of tail;** openings of glands give out poison when animal is attacked. In British Columbia light spots appear on the back. Found hiding under rocks, logs, etc. near water in most of our region, but west of Cascade crest and up to Canadian Life Zone.

4. LONG-TOED SALAMANDER, *Ambystoma macrodactylum*. 2-3¼'. Dark brown or black general color, with mottled

SNAKES, SALAMANDERS

11. Western Terrestrial Garter Snake

12. Western Aquatic Garter Snake

14. Western Rattlesnake

Proportions different

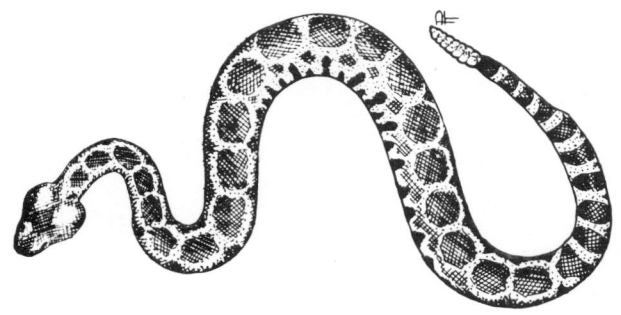

1. Pacific Giant Salamander

2. Olympic Salamander

water
sage
grass
mt.mead.
rocks
str.wd.
conif.

markings or nearly solid band of yellow, light brown or olive green down the back. Found in most of our region up to Arctic-alpine Life Zone, usually hiding in rotten wood, under bark, logs, rocks, etc. near to fairly quiet water.

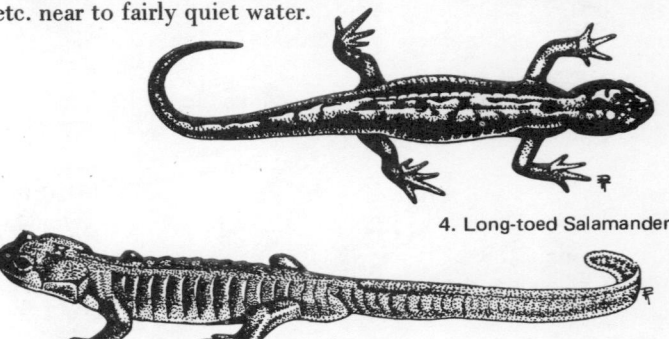

4. Long-toed Salamander

3. Northwestern Salamander

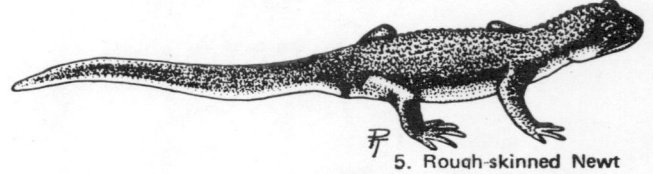

5. Rough-skinned Newt

Family SALAMANDRIDAE (Newts)

grass
mix.ev.
conif.
water
str.wd.

5. ROUGH-SKINNED NEWT, *Taricha granulosa.* 2-3½". Color dark brownish to blackish, rarely light brown; reddish-orange to yellow below; **rough skin except in breeding males; which also develop a flattened tail and are found in water.** When attacked, it suddenly develops a threatening posture with curled and uplifted tail. Found in most of region west of Cascade crest.

Family PLETHODONTIDAE (lungless salamanders)

mix.ev.
str.wd.
conif.
mt.mead.

6. ENSATINA or OREGON SALAMANDER, *Ensatina eschscholtzi.* 1½-3". Color of the subspecies in our region is plain brown to black above; pale yellowish to white on belly with fine dark specks; **tail appears swollen but is constricted at base.** Found in most of region up to Canadian zone, mainly w. of high mts.

7. WESTERN RED-BACKED SALAMANDER, *Plethodon*

SALAMANDERS

vehiculum. 1¾-3". The dark brownish body is sprinkled with white flecks on sides; **broad, even-edged, yellowish to reddish-brown, to orange or yellow stripe down back to tail;** sometimes all body becomes suffused with same color as back stripe. Found from central Oregon north, west of Cascade summit.

str.wd.
rocks
sitk.-spr.
west.hem.
water

8. VAN DYKE'S SALAMANDER, *Plethodon vandykei.* 2-3". Looks like number 7, but thicker body, and broad back stripe of reddish, yellowish-brown or yellowish, usually has wavy edges. The light yellowish throat often contrasts with a black or dark brown belly, dotted with white, though sometimes belly lighter. Some adults of large size may be plain yellowish or yellowish-brown or pinkish-red all over. **Usually vertical grooves on side of body 14, rarely 15.** Found in western Washington up to Canadian zone.

rocks
str.wd.
grass
conif.
mix.ev.

9. OREGON SLENDER SALAMANDER, *Batrachoseps wrightī.* 1½-2¼". Generally dark brownish, but has large white blotched dark belly, and some have brick red tails and reddish or yellowish-brown stripes on back. **Quickly identified by tiny feet and legs.** Found in northern Oregon on lower w. slope of Cascades.

mix.ev.
str.wd.

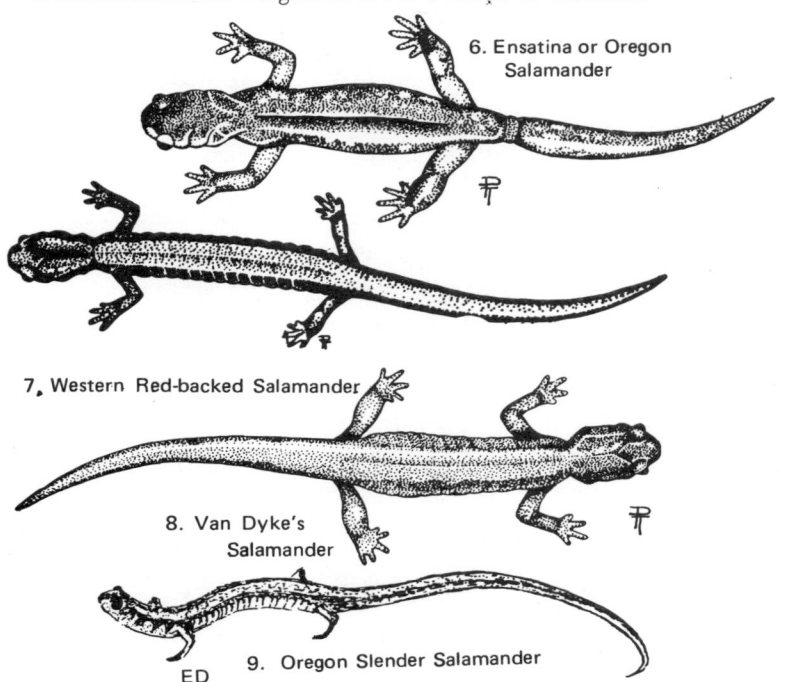

6. Ensatina or Oregon Salamander
7. Western Red-backed Salamander
8. Van Dyke's Salamander
9. Oregon Slender Salamander

TOADS AND FROGS

Family BUFONIDAE (True Toads, walk more than hop)

cult.
water
grass
mix.ev.
mt.mead.
str.wd.

10. WESTERN TOAD, *Bufo boreas*. 2-5". The only toad in our region, easily identified by thick body, short legs and **the light-colored stripe down the dark-colored warty-looking back**. All over.

Family ASCAPHIDAE (Tailed Frogs)

water
str.wd.

11. TAILED FROG, *Ascaphus truei*. 1-2". Variously reddish, brown, grayish or olive colors above, often with a pale greenish or yellowish triangle on nose and dark stripe through eye; a very large outer toe on hind foot; tail-like organ on male. Found in most of our region in Transition Life Zone, rarely Canadian.

Family HYLIDAE (Tree Frogs, having suction disk toes)

mt.mead.
water
str.wd.
grass

12. PACIFIC TREEFROG, *Hyla regilla*. ¾-2". **Varies in color from green through gray to tan, brown and black, changing its color to fit its environment; black stripe through eye is distinctive.** Cream-colored to yellowish below. Found from most of our region up to Hudsonian Life Zone, usually found near water.

Family RANIDAE (True Frogs, no suction disks)

water
str.wd.
grass

13. RED-LEGGED FROG, *Rana aurora*. 2-5". Red **on underside of hind legs is distinctive,** also some reddish on belly; **a dark mask on face is bordered below on upper jaw by whitish streak;** often is coarsely mottled black, gray, reddish or yellowish on inside of upper leg; dark bands on outer legs. Likes permanent or slow water in lowlands and foothills up to Transition zone.

water
str.wd.

14. CASCADES FROG, *Rana cascadae*. 1¾-2½". General color brownish above; **very black spots on back stand out sharply;** legs also dark spotted; yellowish below, but mottled on groin. Found from border of B. C. south in main part of Cascades, up to Hudsonian Life Zone. Call a rough, low-pitched chuckle, as above.

water
str.wd.

15. SPOTTED FROG, *Rana pretiosa*. 2-4". General light to dark brown color with rather vaguely-defined spots with light centers. Mask not so distinct as in 13, **but light jaw stripe very evident;** colors not as strong or permanent-looking as in 13. Found more on eastern side of Cascades, but some in western foothills.

TOADS AND FROGS

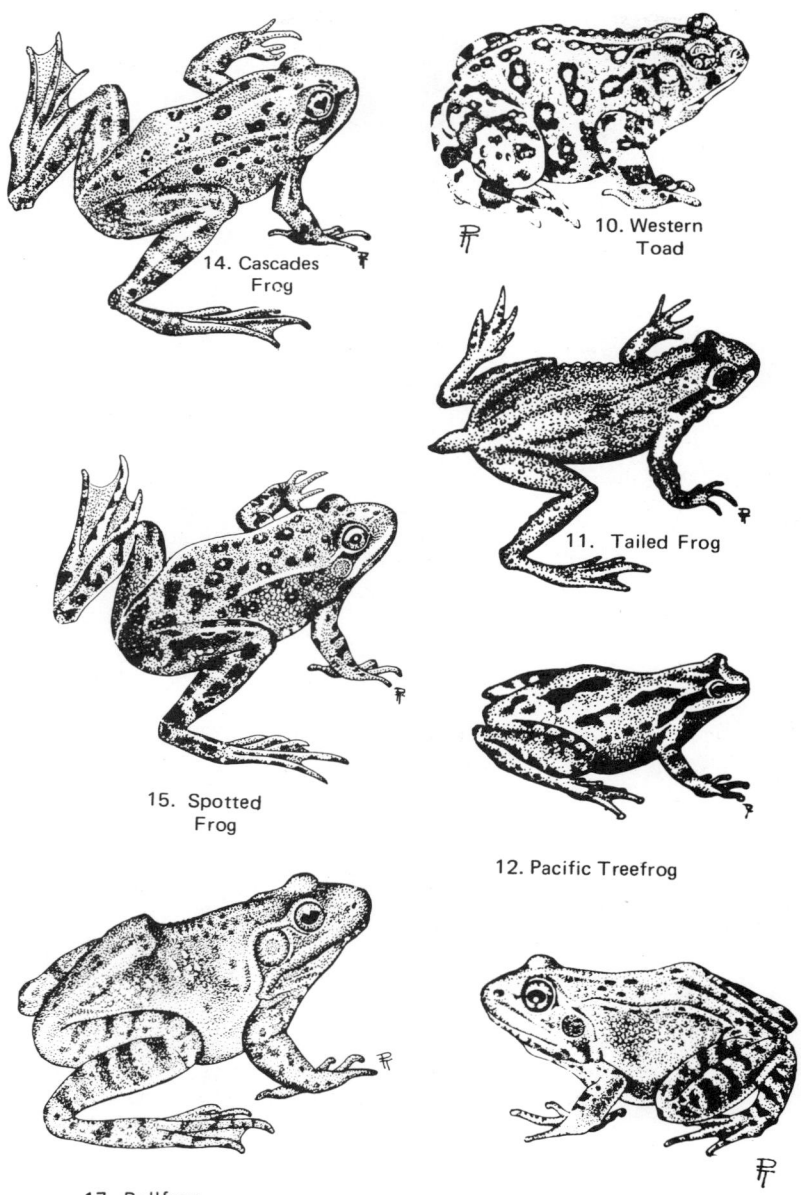

WILDLIFE AND PLANTS OF THE CASCADES

water

†16. FOOTHILL YELLOW-LEGGED FROG, *Rana boylei.* 1½-2¾". Best distinguished by yellow under **legs and on belly, and by a triangular-shaped light brown patch on nose.** Found on west side of Cascades in Oregon and in much of n. Calif., to Canadian zone. Cry; a rasping, gutteral sound in one pitch but some rising.

water

17. BULLFROG, *Rana catesbeiana.* 3¾-8". This very large greenish-yellowish-brown frog, with blackish bands on legs, has **distinctively large ear-drums;** grayish-white mottled below with touch of yellow on chin and on hindquarters; the male has a yellow throat. Lives most of life in water. Introduced from the east, but widespread in ponds, lakes and foothill areas.

FISHES

The fishes described in this book are those that are usually most common in our region, but there may be many you will see that are not described here. Before looking at the descriptions of the different fish, study carefully the drawing of a generalized fish at the top of page 279, so you will understand the names of the different parts of the body. The enlarged picture of a dorsal fin shows how to count fin rays. In identifying a fish, make sure it is very close to the description and picture shown in this book.

Family SALMONIDAE (trouts and salmons)

Pacific salmon travel from the sea up streams to spawn, after which they die, but steelhead and trout do not. Pacific Salmon spawn between March and December, while steelhead spawn usually between October and March. The other trout spawn at times given under their descriptions. We picture the two most common salmon, but describe others.

1. KING SALMON, *Oncorhynchus tschawytscha* (also called Chinook Salmon and several other names). Up to 70 lbs. and to 4' long; silvery-bluish color; anal fin rays usually 15-17; scales usually 25-31 above the lateral line, and 23-24 below. Found in ocean and fresh water.

2. SILVER SALMON, *Oncorhynchus kisutch.* Up to 15 lbs. and to 20". Silvery color; anal fin rays usually 12-15; scales numbered as in King Salmon. Found in ocean and fresh water. (Also called Coho.)

†3. SOCKEYE SALMON, *Oncorhynchus nerka* (also called Blueback and Red Salmon). At time of fall spawning they generally become

SALMON 279

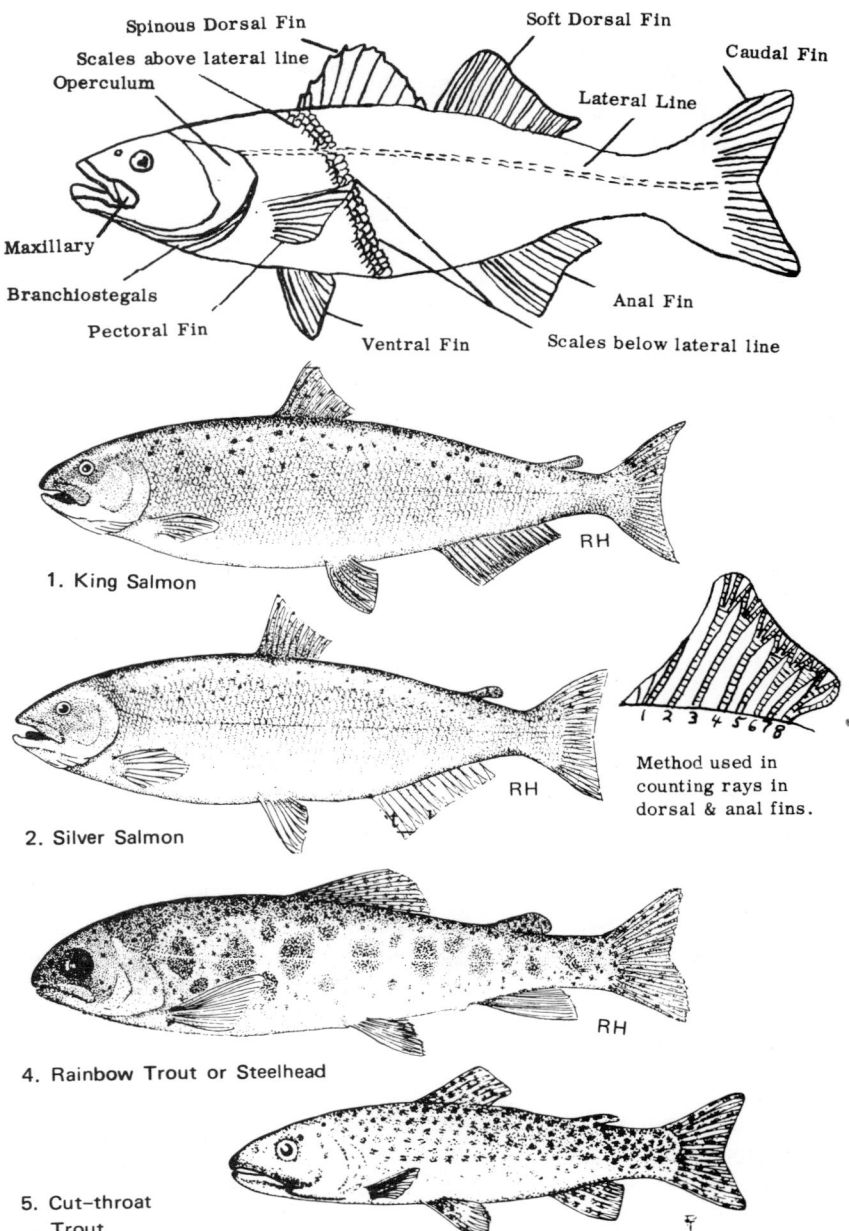

1. King Salmon

2. Silver Salmon

Method used in counting rays in dorsal & anal fins.

4. Rainbow Trout or Steelhead

5. Cut-throat Trout

bright reddish with a greenish head, otherwise steel blue to grayish on back and upper sides. 5-12 pounds in weight; up to 18". A variant of this salmon is the little kokanee salmon, 10-14", and usually little more than 1 pound, which becomes red at spawning, and spends its life in fresh water in the mountains.

4. RAINBOW TROUT or STEELHEAD, *Salmo gairdnerii*. Up to 40 pounds, but averages 2-8; up to 34", but usually under 18"; 9-13 rays in anal fin. Breeding males become bright red, but most of the time the fish are silvery with a greenish or bluish black near salt water (the steelhead type), or dark spotted on the silvery sides and with a rosy lateral band (fainter up the streams in the rainbow type).

5. CUT-THROAT TROUT, *Salmo clarkii*. Up to 41 pounds; usually less than 6 pounds; length usually less than 16". Generally bluish on back, and silvery below, often covered with many small spots; dorsal rays 9-11, mostly 10; lateral line scales greater than 150; a red or pink bar appears on each side of lower jaw; caudal and dorsal fins heavily spotted. Mountain lakes and streams.

6. GOLDEN TROUT, *Salmo aquabonita*. Usually 8-12", some up to 20"; 8 to 11 pounds. Sides often brilliantly colored with yellow or orange; around 8 vertical dark blotches appear on sides. Introduced from California into Oregon and Washington high mountain streams.

7. BROWN TROUT, *Salmo trutta*. Length up to 24"; averages 7-10 pounds, but up to 39. General color yellowish or yellowish-brown, but **heavily brown-spotted on back; caudal fin with no spots or only a few restricted to upper portion;** red spots on sides may be surrounded with light rings. Often lives in warmer water than the Brook Trout. An import from Europe that has become common in many of our streams.

8. EASTERN BROOK TROUT, *Salvelinus fontinalis*. Usual size 7-12"; up to 9 pounds, with record of 14. Back mottled with olive and black, often appearing as "wormy streaked"; **front edges of lower fins are white; scales of body very tiny;** has square tail. Likes cold clear water and has been introduced from the east to many of our mountain streams.

9. DOLLY VARDEN, *Salvelinus malma*. Length to 20"; up to about 12 pounds. Back **light-spotted on dark background; no mottling on dorsal and caudal fins;** general olive-brown to dark silver color, with red **spots of eye-size on sides. Caudal fin somewhat forked.** This is a native char rather than trout, but usually called a trout.

TROUT AND BASS

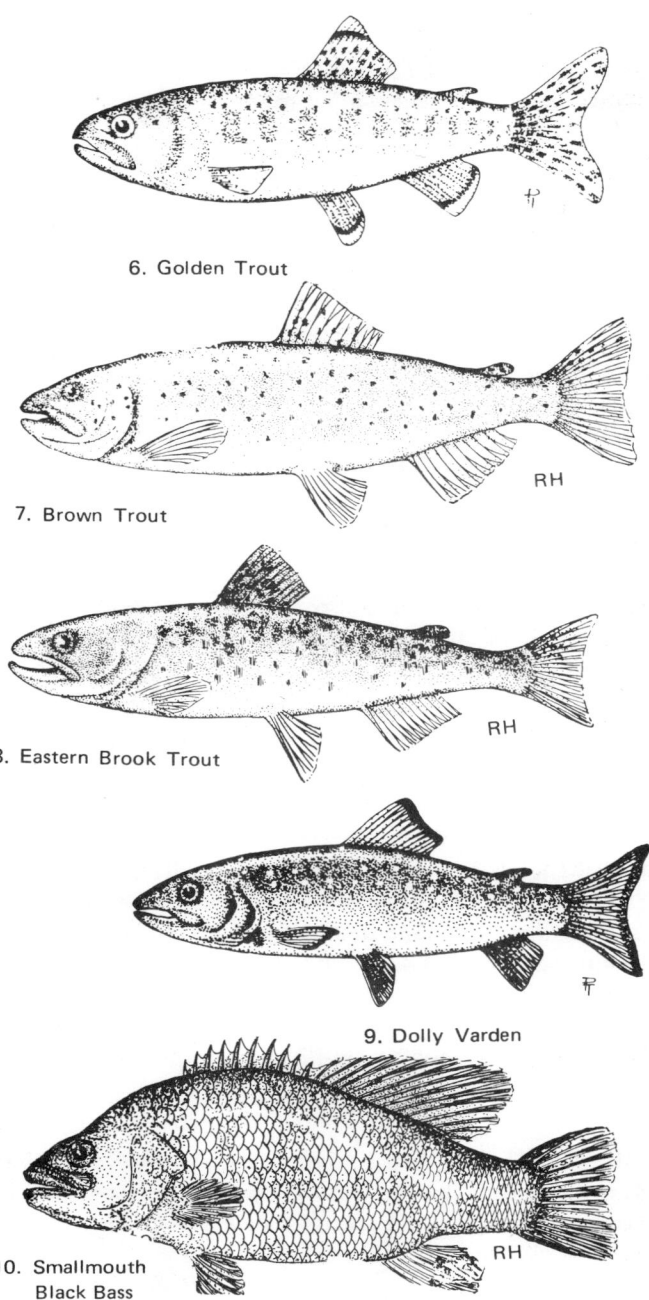

6. Golden Trout

7. Brown Trout

8. Eastern Brook Trout

9. Dolly Varden

10. Smallmouth Black Bass

Family CENTRARCHIDAE (Black Basses, Sunfish, Crappies)

Body bass-shaped or sunfish shaped, with depth about 1/3 of length in bass type and upto 3/4 of length in sunfish type. The ventral fins are placed just below the pectoral.

10. SMALLMOUTH BLACK BASS, *Micropterus dolomieu*. Usually under 16"; soft dorsal rays (those in the second or larger back fin) 13-15; **greenish to greenish-yellow above, barred with dark gray, dark silvery below**. The spinous, or front, dorsal fin is not separated from the soft, or rear dorsal fin by a deep notch as in the Largemouth Black Bass. A fish of the lower streams of our mountains.

11. LARGEMOUTH BLACK BASS, *Micropterus salmoides*. Usually under 20". Brownish-green above, only slightly lighter below, thus dark all over and with no narrow stripes; **dorsal fins united by a membrane; the anal and soft dorsal fins with no membrane or scales near the base.**

12. GREEN SUNFISH, *Lepomis cyanellus*. Up to 12", body often up to ¾ as broad as long; anal fin spines 3; dorsal fin spines 9-12; **maxillary reaching just beyond middle of eye.** Back greenish-brown mottled; belly yellowish; pectoral fins short and round. In lower altitudes.

13. BLACK CRAPPIE, *Pomoxis nigro-maculatus*. Usually under 1'. **Dark greenish-brown mottled above, yellowish with dark markings below; dorsal fin spines 7-8** (rarely 6 or 9), anal fin spines 6-7. May reach 4 pounds. Vertical spines are spotted. Males of both *Pomoxis* species build interesting nests in which the females lay the eggs. This fish has been introduced from the east into our lower streams.

14. WHITE CRAPPIE, *Pomoxis annularis*. Usually under 1'; unlike the Black Crappie, the front base of the dorsal fin is farther back, usually at about the top of the hump. **Has light greenish-brown mottlings on back and white sides; yellowish on belly.** Usually 6 (rarely 5 or 7) dorsal fin spines; anal fin spines 6 or 7. Both crappies spawn in deep water over gravel in early summer; both feed on aquatic insects and both crappies and sunfish are good to eat. Found mainly at lower levels.

Family GADIDAE (Cods)

15. FRESH WATER BURBOT, *Lota lota*. Up to 30"; 6-12 pounds. **The peculiar shape of the fins (see picture), and the very tiny scales and strangely and profusely mottled grayish-olive color are distinctive.** A single barbel is carried under the chin. This fish spawns in the middle of winter, and likes living in deep cold lakes, though found elsewhere too.

SUNFIRE, BURBOT 283

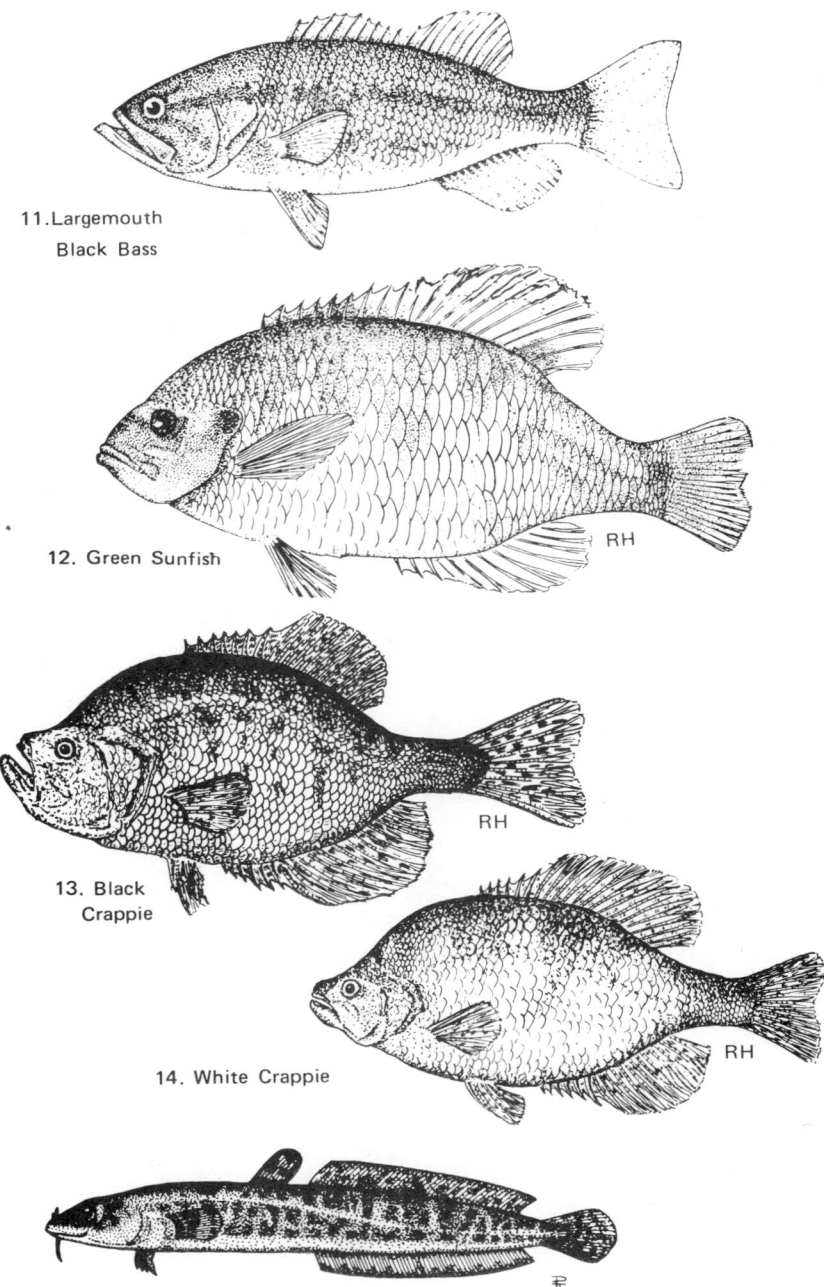

11. Largemouth Black Bass

12. Green Sunfish

13. Black Crappie

14. White Crappie

15. Fresh Water Burbot

Family PERCIDAE (Perches)

16. YELLOW PERCH, *Perca flavescens.* Usually under 14". Yellowish general color with dark greenish vertical bands; pelvic fins quite close together, the space between being less than the width of the base of one of the fins. Anal fin with only 1 or 2 spines; the dorsal fins well separated; notice concave shape of head just above eyes. Feeds on all forms of small water creatures, likes quiet water in streams, rivers and ponds, not very high up in the mountains.

Family CYPRINIDAE (Minnows, etc.)

17. NORTHERN SQUAWFISH, *Ptychocheilus oregonensis.* Up to 2'. Lateral line scales are 67-75; 46-56 of the scales are before the dorsal fin; the dorsal rays are 9-10; rays in the anal fin, 8. General color is dark greenish above and silvery or yellowish below. Found in streams.

Family ACIPENSERIDAE (Sturgeons)

18. WHITE STURGEON, *Acipenser transmontanus.* May grow over 8' and past 200 pounds. Bony plates appear between pelvic and anal fins in 2 rows of 4-8 each; dorsal fin rays about 45. General color grayish-brown. Found in rivers at lower altitudes.

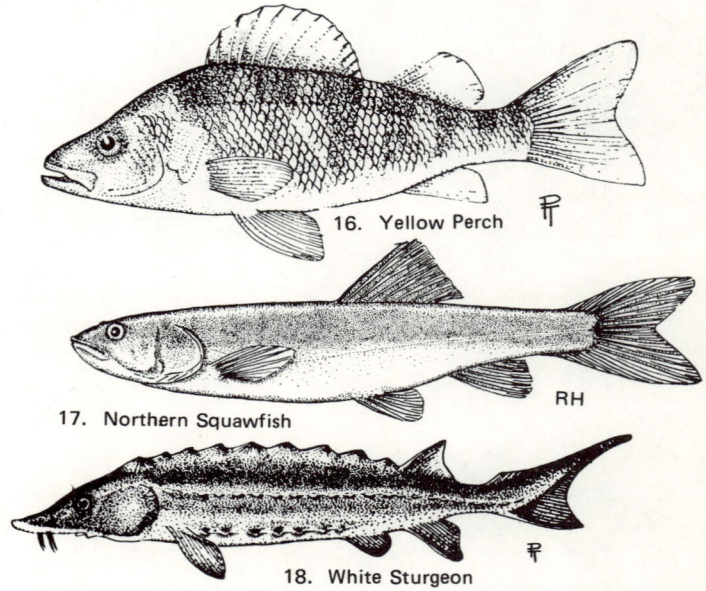

16. Yellow Perch

17. Northern Squawfish

18. White Sturgeon

REFERENCES

Abrams, LeRoy. ILLUSTRATED FLORA OF THE PACIFIC STATES 4 vols. 1923-1963. Stanford University Press.

Baerg, Harry. HOW TO KNOW THE WESTERN TREES. W. C. Brown Publishing Co. 1955

Brown, Vinson, Weston, Jr., Henry M. and Buzzell, Jerry. HANDBOOK OF CALIFORNIA BIRDS. 2nd Rev. Edit. Naturegraph 1971

Burk, William H. and Grossenheider, L.P. FIELD GUIDE TO THE MAMMALS, 1964. Houghton-Mifflin.

Eddy, Samuel. HOW TO KNOW THE FRESH WATER FISHES. 2nd. Edit., 1970. W. C. Brown Publishing Co.

Franklin, Jerry F. and C.T. Dyrness. VEGETATION OF OREGON AND WASHINGTON. U.S. Dept. of Agriculture, 1969.

Ingles, Lloyd G. MAMMALS OF THE PACIFIC STATES. Stanford University Press. 1965

Kirk, Donald. WILD EDIBLE PLANTS OF THE WESTERN U.S. 1970. Naturegraph Publishers.

Peterson, Roger T. FIELD GUIDE TO WESTERN BIRDS, Rev. Edit. 1969. Houghton-Mifflin.

Schultz, Leonard P. KEYS TO THE FISHES OF WASHINGTON, OREGON AND CLOSELY ADJOINING REGIONS, 1936, University of Washington Press.

Stebbins, Robert. FIELD GUIDE TO THE WESTERN REPTILES AND AMPHIBIANS. Houghton-Mifflin, 1966.

ACKNOWLEDGMENTS

We owe grateful thanks for their contributions or other help with this book to the following persons: Robert W. Morris, Assistant Director of Watershed, Recreation, Range and Wildlife Habitat Research at the Pacific Northwest Forest and Range Experiment Station in Portland, Oregon, for the fine photographs of northwest plant communities he sent us from the files of his office; to Jerry F. Franklin and C. T. Dyrness for the valuable information about northwest plant communities in their book on "Vegetation of Oregon and Washington", published by the U.S. Department of Agriculture in 1969, parts of which we paraphrased in our book; to the artists who contributed so many useful pictures to this book and whose names and initials (as marked on their art) follow:

Douglas Andrews, DA, mammals
Iain Baxter © IB (whose pictures are copyrighted in his name), birds;
Jerry Buzzell JB, birds
Gene M. Christman, GMC, birds,
  (whose drawings were originally in the book by Dr. A. Starker Leopold on "Game Birds and Mammals of California", with permission to use kindly granted by the author.)
Ben Cummings,   birds
Elizabeth Dasmann, ED, mammals and slender salamander
Corrine Hansen, CH, birds
Rune Hapness, RH, fish
James Gordon Irving, JGI, birds
Janice Kirk, JEK, No. 284, Rosy Everlasting Flower
Carol Lyness, CL, mammals
Peggy and George Matson, P&GM, birds
Lynn Maxwell, LM, mammals
Juanita Storch, JS, birds
Phyllis Thompson, reptiles, amphibians, fish, PT,
Dr. Charles Yocom, plants, ℂ

* INDEX TO COMMON NAMES

Alder, oregon, 75,76
Anemone,
   wood,132,133
Antelope,
   pronghorn,202
Antelope Bush,91,92
Arnica,
   cordilleran,162,164
   heart-leaved,165,166
   seep-spring,162,164
   sierra, 164,166
   streambank, 166
   subalpine, 165,166
Arrowhead,
   common, 54,55
Ash,
   sitka mountain, 96,97
Aspen, quaking, 75,76
Aster,
   cascade, 160,163
   common, 160,161
   shasta, 160,163
Azalea,
   mock, 104,106
   western, 102,105

Badger, 196,197
Balsam Root,
   arrow-leaved,158,159
Bass,
   largemouth black,
     282,283

   smallmouth black,
     281, 282
Bat,
   big brown, 173, 175
   hoary, 173,175
   lump-nosed, 175
   pallid, 173,175
   silvery-haired,173,175
Bear,
   black,169,191,194
   grizzly,191,194
Beaver,187,188
   see mountain beaver
Bedstraw,
   northern, 156,159
Bistort, western,128,129
Blackberry,
   cut-leaf, 94,95
   pacific, 94,95
Blackbird,
   brewer's, 254,255
   red-winged, 254,255
   yellow-headed, 252,255
Blazing Star, 142,143
Bluebell, scotch, 158,159
Blueberry,
   western bog, 109,111
Bluebird,
   mountain, 237,246
   western, 237,246

Blue flag,
   western,122,124
Bobcat,200,200
Boxwood,
   oregon,98,99
Brant,black,208,209
Brodiaea,
   common,117 119
   harvest,116,117
Buck Brush,100,103
Buckthorn,
   cascara,98,99
Buckwheat brush,127,128
Bullfrog,277,278
Bunchberry,142,143
Bunting,
   lazuli ,254,257
   snow',263, 264
Burbot,
   freshwater,282,283
Bur-reed,
   narrow-leaved,52,53

   small,52,53
Bushtit,common,
   238,239
Buttercup,
   sagebrush,132,135
Butterweed,165,166
Calypso,125,126
Catbird,244,245
Cattail,
   common,52,53
Cedar,
   giant red , 72,73
   incense,72,73
   port orford,72,73
Chaenactis,
   hoary, 160,161
Chat,
   yellow-breasted,251,253
Cherry,
   bitter,96,97
   western choke,80,83
Chickadee,
   black-capped,235,238
   boreal,235,238
   chestnut-backed,
     235 238
   mountain235,238
Chinquapin,
   bush,giant,76,77
Chipmunk,
   least,180
   townsend, 179,180
   yellow pine,179,180
Cinquefoil,
   mount rainier,136,138
   sticky, 136,139
Clintonia,
   single-flowered,
     120,121
Coffeeberry,98,99

Columbine,
   northwest crimson,
     132,133
Comparative sizes, 169,203
Cone-flower, 160,161
Coot, american, 208,209
Cottontail,
   nuttall, 173,176
Cottonwood, black, 76,77
Cowbird,
   brown-headed, 254,255
Coyote, 189,190,191
Crappie,
   black, 282,283
   white,282,283
Cream Bush,91,92
Creeper, brown,239,241
Cross-bill,
   red,256,240
   white-winged,256,257
Crow,common,203 234,235
Cuckoo,
   yellow-billed,218,219
Curlew,204
Currant,
   crater lake,87,88
   red flowering,87,88
   squaw,87,88
   sticky,87,88
   swamp,87,88
Cycladenia,146,147

Daisy,
   hairy,162,164
   showy,162,163
   wandering,162,163
Dandelion,
   common,167,168
   false,167,168
Deer,
   columbia,black-tailed,198
   mule,201,202
Deer Brush,100,101
Desert sweet ,91,92
Devil's club,102,103
Dipper,243,244
Dock,veiny,128,129
Dogbane,spreading,146,147
Dogwood,
   california,102,103
   pacific,82,83
   red osier,102,103
Dove,mourning,216,219
Duckweed,greater,54,56
Duck,
   bufflehead, 206,207
   common mallard, 206,207
   merganser, 208,209
   pintail, 206,207
   teai, green-winged,206,207

Eagle,
   bald, 210,211
   golden, 210,211

*Numbers underlined indicate picture pages.

Elderberry,
  blue,110,113
  pacific red, 110,113
Elephant heads,155,156
Elk,
  american, 199,201
  (canadian)
Eriogonum,
  naked-stem,127,128
  wicker,127,128
Ermine,192,193
Eupatorium, western,
  167,168
Everlasting flower,
  pearly,167,168
  rosy,165,167
Fairy Bells,
  hooker's,120,123
  large-flowered,122,123
Falcon,
  peregrine,213
  prairie, 213,214
Fescue,
  blue bunch,59,60
Figwort,
  coast,154,155
Filaree,
  red-stem,140,141
Finch, .203
  cassin's,240,258
  gray-crowned rosy,
  240,258
  house, 240,258
  purple,240, 256
Fir,
  douglas,68,69
  grand, 70,71
  noble, 72,73
  pacific silver, 68,69
  red, 70,71
  shasta red,70,71
  subalpine, 70,71
  white, 70,72
Firecracker flower,117,119
Fisher, 192,193
Flax,
  western blue, 141,142
Fleabane,162
Flicker,
  red-shafted,226,227
Flycatcher,
  hammond's,231
  olive-sided,230,231
  traill's,231
  western,231
Fox,
  gray,189,190
  red, 189,190
Foxglove,
  purple, 150,152
Fritillary,
  yellow, 118,119

Frog,
  cascades,276,277
  foothill yellow-legged,
  278
  red-legged,276,277
  spotted,276,277
  tailed,276,277
Gilia,
  scarlet,146,147
Ginger,
  wild, 125, 126
Goat,mountain,195,202
Golden-eye,
  barrow's, 207,209
Goldfinch,
  american,257 259
  lesser,257, 259
Gooseberry,
  gummy, 89,90
  plateau, 88,90
  sierra,89,90
  siskiyou, 87,88
  white-stem,87,88
Gopher,
  botta pocket,182
  camas pocket,181, 182
  mazama pocket,182
  northern pocket, 182
Goshawk,212,214
Grape,
  california wild,100,102
  oregon, 85,86
Grass,
  bear,115,116
  downy brome,59,60
  downy oat,59 60
  gray rye,60,61
  squirrel-tail,61,62
  western wild oat,59,60
Grebe,
  pied-billed,205,206
  red-necked (holboell's)
  205,206
  western,205,206
Grosbeak,
  black-headed,256,257
  evening,256,257
  pine,240,258
Grouse,
  blue,215, 217
  ruffed, 215,217
  sage, 215,217
  spruce (franklin's)
  215,217
Gyrfalcon,214, 215
Hairgrass,tufted,59, 60
Hare,
  black-tailed, 173,176
  snowshoe, 173, 176
  white-tailed, 176
Harebell, california, 158

Hawk,   203,204
  cooper's,213,214
  marsh,210,211
  pigeon,213,214
  red-tailed,211,212
  rough-legged,212,214
  sharp-shinned, 213,214
  sparrow, 213, 214
  swainson's, 211,212
Hazelnut. California, 85,86
Heather,
  cream mountain, 104,106
  red mountain, 104,106
  white, 106,108
Hellebore,false,115,116
Hemlock,
  mountain,68,69
  western, 68,69
Heron, 203,204
  black-crowned night,
  205,206
  great blue,205,206
Honeysuckle,
  orange,112,114
  purple flower,112,113
  rocky mountain,112,113
Horehound,common,
  148,149
Hornwort,54,56
Horsebrush,
  spineless,115,116
Horse-mint,
  nettle-leaved, 148,149
Huckleberry,
  dwarf,109,111
  evergreen,109, 111
  littleleaf,109,111
  red,109,111
  thinleaf,109,111
Hulsea,dwarf,160,161
Hummingbird,
  broad-tailed,225,226
  calliope,225,226
  rufous,225,226
Indian Pink,130,131
Indian Warrior.154,155
Inside-out-flower, 134,135
Iris, douglas, 122,124
Jay,western blue flag,122,124
  gray,232,233
  juvenal form,gray,233
  pinon,232,233
  scrub,(california),232,233
  stellers,232,233
Junco,
  oregon,259
  slate-colored,259
Juneberry,96,98
Juniper,
  dwarf,74
  western,74

Kalmia,
    alpine bog, 104,105
Killdeer,204,208,209
Kingbird,western 229,230
Kingfisher,belted,222,223
Kinglet,
    golden-crowned,248,249
    ruby-crowned,248,249
Kinnikinnick,107,108
Knotweed,
    alpine,128,129
    newberry's, 128,129
    swamp,128,129

Larch, western,66,67
Lark,horned,244,245
Larkspur,red,132,133
Lily,
    desert,120,121
    leopard,118,119
    washington,118,119
    yellow fawn,119,121
Lily-of-the-valley,
    false,120,123
Lizard,
    northern alligator, 268
    sagebrush, 268
    western fence, 268
Longspur, lapland, 265
Loon,
    common, 204
    pacific, 204
Lupine,
    low, 139, 140
    small flowered, 139,140
Lynx, canada, 200

Madrone, 82,84
Magpie,
    black-billed, 234,235
Mahonia, piper's, 85,86
Manzanita,
    greenleaf, 107,108
    pinemat, 107,108
Maple,
    big-leaf,82,84
    mountain,82,84
    vine,82,84
Mare's-tail,57,58
Marmot,
    hoary,177,179
    olympic,177
    yellow-bellied,177,179
Marten, 192,193
Martin, purple, 224,236
Meadowlark,
    western, 252,255
Meadow Sweet, 89,90
Milfoil,
    american, 57,58
    whorl-leaved, 57,58
Mink, 192,196

Mission Bells,118,119
Mock Orange,85,86
Mole,
    coast,172
    broad-handed,172
    shrew,171,172
    townsend,171,172
Monardella,
    mountain,148,151
Monkey-flower,
    common large,150,152
    dwarf purple,150,152
    lewis, 148,151
    primrose,150,151
Montia.heart-leaved,130,131
Mountain Beaver, 177,179
Mountain Lion, 200,201
Mountain Mahogany,
    desert, 80,83
    mountain, 80,83
Mouse,
    california meadow, 186
    deer, 181,183
    forest deer, 183
    gapper red-backed,
        184,185
    long-tailed meadow,
        184,185,186
    montane meadow,185,186
    oregon meadow,186
    pacific jumping,185,186,
        187
    pinyon,183
    richardson meadow,185,
        186
    western harvest,181,183
    western jumping,186
    western red-backed,184,
        185
Mouse-tail,132,133
Muskrat,187,188
Mustard,tumble,134,137
Myotis,
    california,174
    fringed,174
    hairy-winged,174
    little brown,171,174
    long-eared,171,174
    yuma,175
Myrtle,oregon,80,81

Najas,slender,52,55
Nettle,hoary,125,126
Newt,
    rough-skinned,274
Nighthawk,
    common,222,223
Ninebark,90,91
Nutcracker,clark's,233,234
Nuthatch, 203
    pygmy,239,241

Nuthatch(continued),
    red-breasted,239,241
    white-breasted,239,241
Nutria,187,188
Oak
    california black,78,79
    canyon,78,81
    huckleberry,80,81
    oregon white,78,79
    sadler's,78,81
    tanbark,77,78
Ocean spray,
    desert,91,92
Onion,
    watson's, 116,117
Opossum,
    american.170.171
Oriole, bullock's, 254,255
Osprey,211,212
Otter,river,197,200
Oval-leaved alum root,
    136,138
Owl,
    barn,218,219
    burrowing,219,220
    flammulated,screech,218
    great gray,221,223
    great horned,219, 220
    hawk,221,223
    long-eared,219,220
    pygmy,219, 220
    richardson's,220
    saw-whet,219,221
    screech,218,219
    short-eared,218,219
    snowy,221,223
    spotted,219,221
Paintbrush,
    desert,156,157
    great red indian,156,157
    pine,156,157
    pumice indian,156,157
    scarlet,156,157
Parrot's feather,57,58
Partridgefoot,136,138
Pasque flower,132,133
Penstemon,
    ashy,150,152
    cliff,153,154
    creeping,154
    davidson,154
    gay,153,154
    rock,150,153
    showy,150,153
    woodland,154,155
Pewee,
    western wood,230,231
Perch,yellow,284
Phacelia,
    silverleaf,148,149

Phacelia,(continued),
    virgate,148
Phlox,spreading,110,111
Phoebe,says,229 230
Pigeon, 204
    band-tailed,216,219
Pigweed,130,131
Pika,173,176
Pine,
    digger,64 ,67
    foxtail,64,65
    jeffrey,64,65
    lodgepole,66,67
    oregon, 68, 69
    sugar,62,63
    western white,62,63
    western yellow,64 65
    whitebark,63,65
Pinedrops,145,146
Pintail,206,207
Pipit,water,245, 248
Plantain,
    common water, 54,55
    rattlesnake,125,126
Plover, snowy,208,209
Pond-lily,yellow,54,56
Pondweed,small,52,53
Poor Will, 222,223
Poppy,california,134,135
Porcupine,187,188,189
Ptarmigan,
    white-tailed,215,217
Purple fringe,146,149
Pyrola,
    leafless,144
    one-sided,144,145
Quail,
    california,216,217
    mountain, 216,217
Rabbit,brush,173 176
Rabbit Brush,
    bloomer's 112, 114
    gray,112,114
Raccoon,169,191,192
Racer,
    western yellow-bellied,
    269,270
Raspberry,
    creeping,92,93
    white-stem,93, 94
Rat, 169
    bushy-tailed wood,
    181,183
    dusky-footed wood,
    181,183
    water,185,186
Raven,common,234,235
Red-bud,western,96,98
Redpoll,common,257,258
Redstart,american,249, 250
Rhododendron,
    white-flowered,102,105

Ringtail,192
Robin,203,237,244
Rose,
    nootka,94,95
    spalding's wild,94,95
    wood,94,97
Rose-bay,
    california,104,105
Rush,drummond's 61,62
Sage,
    giant, 112,115
    gray ball, 110,111
Salal, 107,108
Salamander,
    ensatina,274,275
    long-toed,272,274
    northwestern,272,274
    olympic,272,273
    oregon,274,275
    oregon slender,275
    pacific giant,272,273
    vandyke's, 275
    Western red backed,
    274, 275
Salmon,
    king,278,279
    kokanee,280
    pacific,278
    silver,278,279
    sockeye,278
Salmon berry,92,93
Sandpiper,spotted,209
Sandwort,130
    pumice,130,131
Sapsucker,
    red-breasted,227,228
    williamson's,227,228
Saxifrage,alpine,134,137
Service-berry,
    pacific,96,97
    pale-leaved,96,97
Shorebird,203
Shrew,
    dusky, 170, 171
    marsh, 170
    masked, 170
    pacific, 170
    trowbridge, 172
    vagrant, 170
    water, 170,171
Shrike,
    loggerhead, 245,248
    northern, 245,247
Silk-tassel,
    fremont's,102,105
Silver flower,165,166
Siskin,pine,257,258
Skunk,
    spotted,196,197
    striped,196,197
Skunk brush,98,99

Snake,
    boa,rubber,269,270
    common garter,270.271
    gopher,269,270
    northwestern garter,271
    ringneck, 269
    western aquatic garter,
    271,273
    western rattlesnake, 271
    273
    western terrestrial garter,
    271,273
Snowberry, common, 110,113
Snow Plant, 146,147
Solitaire, townsend's, 237,247
Solomon's-seal,
    false, 120,123
    nuttall's false, 120,123
Sorrel,redwood,140,141
Sparrow,
    brewer's,260,261
    chipping,260,261
    fox,263,264
    golden-crowned,260,261
    grasshopper,260,261
    harris',261,262
    lark,262,263
    lincoln's,263,264
    sage, 262,263
    savannah,263,264
    song,263,264
    vesper,264,265,
    western tree,262,263
    white-crowned,261,262
Spiraea,
    douglas,89,90
    shiny,89,90
Spruce,
    engelmann,66,67
    sitka,66,69
Squaw carpet, 100,103
Squawfish,northern,284
Squirrel,
    beechey ground,178,179
    belding ground,178,179
    cascades golden-mantled
    ground, 178
    columbian ground, 178
    douglas, 180,181
    northern flying, 181,182
    sierra nevada golden-
    mantled ground 178,179
    western gray, 180,181
Steelhead, 278,279,280
Strawberry, wild, 139,140
Sturgeon, white, 284
Sugar-scoop, 136,137
Sugarstick,144,145
Sulphur Flower,126,127
Sun-cup,
    pinnatified,142,143
Sunfish,green,282,283

Swallow, 203
  bank,224,236
  barn,222,236
  cliff,222,236
  rough-winged,224,236
  tree,222,236
  violet-green,224,236
Swift,
  black,224,225
  vaux's, 224,225
  white-throated,224,225
Syringa,gordon's,85 86

Tanager,western,254,257
Tea,labrador,104,106
Tea tree,oregon,99,101
Thimbleberry,92,93
Thistle,russian,130,131
Thrasher,sage,244,245
Thrush,
  hermit,237,246
  swainson's,237, 246
  varied,237,246
Titmouse,plain,238,239
Toad,western,276,277
Tobacco,coyote,148,151
Tobacco brush,100,101
Towhee,
  brown, 260,261
  green-tailed 260,261
  rufous-sided,260,261
Treefrog,pacific,276,277
Trillium,120,121
Trout,
  brown,280,281
  cut-throat,279,280
  eastern brook,280,281
  golden,280,281
  rainbow,279,280
Turtle,
  painted,267
  western pond,266,267

Twayblade,122,125
  heart-leaved,122,125
Twinberry,black,110,113
Twin flower,156,159
Twisted stalk, 122,124

Valerian,158,159
Vanilla leaf,134,135
Varden,dolly,280,281
Vetch,140,141
Violet,
  yellow wood,142,143
Vireo,
  hutton's,248,249
  red-eyed, 249 250
  solitary,249,250
  warbling,249,250
Vole,
  heather,184,185
  northern bog,184,185
  sagebrush,184
Vulture,turkey,210,211

Wake robin, 120,121
Wapiti,201
Warbler, 203
  audubon's, 251,253
  black-throated gray,
    252,253
  hermit,252,,255
  macgillivray's,250,253
  myrtle,252.253
  nashville(calaveras),
    251,253
  orange-crowned,249 .250
  townsend's,252,255
  wilson's 251,253
  yellow,251,253
Water-shield,54,56
Waxwing,
  bohemian,245,247
  cedar,245 247

Weasel,long-tailed,192,193
Wheat grass,blue bunch,59,60
Whitethorn,mountain,100,101
Willow,red,75, 76
Windflower,
  columbia,132,133
Wintergreen,
  alpine,107,108
  bog,144
  oregon,107,108
  white-veined,144,145
Wolf,189,190
Wolverine,196,197
Woodpecker,
  acorn, 226,227
  black-backed three-toed
    229,230
  downy,228,229
  hairy,228,229
  lewis,227,228
  northern three-toed,
    229,230
  pileated,226,227
  white-headed,227,228
Wood-rush,smooth,61,62
Wren,
  bewick's, 242, 243
  canon, 242,243
  house, 239,242
  long-billed marsh, 242,243
  rock, 242,243
  winter, 239,242

Yarrow,162,164
Yellowthroat,251,253
Yerba de selva,136,138
Yew,62,63
Youth-on-age,136,137

INDEX TO GENERIC NAMES OF VERTEBRATES

Acanthis, p. 258
Accipiter,212, 213
Acipenser,284
Actitis, 209
Aechmophorus,205
Aegolius,220,221
Aeronautes, 224
Agelaius, 254
Ambystoma, 272
Ammodramus, 260
Amphispiza, 262
Anas,207
Antilocapra,202
Anthus, 248
Antrozous, 175
Aphelocoma, 232
Aplodontia, 177
Aquila, 210

Ardea, 205
Ascaphus, 276
Asio, 218, 220
Asyndesmus, 228

Bassariscus. 192
Batrachoseps,275
Bombycilla, 247
Bonasa, 215
Branta, 208
Bubo, 220
Bucephala, 207,208
Bufo, 276
Buteo, 212

Calcarius, 265
Callospermophilus, 178
Canachites, 215
Canis, 189

Carpodacus ,256,258
Castor.187
Cathartes, 210
Catherpes, 242
Centrocercus, 215
Certhia, 241
Cervus, 201
Chaetura, 224
Charadrius, 208
Charina, 269
Chlorura, 260
Chondestes,262
Chordeiles, 222
Chrysemys, 267
Cinclus, 244
Circus, 210
Citellus, 178
Clemmys, 266

INDEX TO GENERIC NAMES OF VERTEBRATES

Clethrionomys, 184
Coccyzus, 218
Colaptes, 226
Coluber, 269
Columba, 216
Contopus, 230
Corvus, 234
Crotalus, 271
Cyanocitta, 232
Cypseloides, 224

Dendragapus, 215
Dendrocopos, 228
Dendroica, 251, 252
Diadophis, 269
Dicamptodon, 272
Didelphis, 170
Dryocopus, 226
Dumetella, 244

Empidonax, 231
Ensatina, 274
Eptesicus, 175
Eremophila, 244
Erethizon, 187
Euarctos, 191
Euphagus, 254
Eutamias, 180

Falco, 213, 215
Felis, 201
Fulica, 208

Gavia, 204
Geothlypis, 251
Gerrhonotus, 268
Glaucidium, 220
Glaucomys, 182
Gulo, 196
Gymnorhinus, 232

Haliaeetus, 210
Hesperiphona, 256
Hirundo, 222
Hyla, 276
Hylocichla, 246

Icteria, 251
Icterus, 254
Iridoprocne, 222
Ixoreus, 246

Junco, 259

Lagopus, 215
Lagurus, 184
Lanius, 247, 248
Lasionycteris, 175
Lasiurus, 175
Lepomis, 282
Lepus, 176
Leucosticte, 258
Lophortyx, 216

Lota, 282
Loxia, 256
Lutra, 200
Lynx, 200

Marmota, 177
Martes, 193
Megaceryle, 222
Melanerpes, 226
Melospiza, 264
Mephitis, 196
Mergus, 208
Micropterus, 282
Microtus, 184, 186
Molothrus, 254
Mustela, 193, 196
Myadestes, 247
Myocastor, 187
Myotis, 174, 175

Neotoma, 183
Neurotrichus, 172
Nucifraga, 234
Nuttallornis, 230
Nyctea, 221
Nycticorax, 205

Ochotona, 176
Odocoileus, 201
Oncorhynchus, 278
Ondatra, 187
Oporornis, 250
Oreamnos, 202
Oreortyx, 216
Oreoscoptes, 244
Otospermophilus, 178
Otus, 218

Pandion, 212
Parus, 238
Passerculus, 264
Passerella, 264
Passerina, 254
Perca, 284
Perisoreus, 232
Peromyscus, 183
Petrochelidon, 222
Phalaenoptilus, 222
Phenacomys, 184
Pheucticus, 256
Pica, 234
Picoides, 230
Pinicola, 258
Pipilo, 260
Piranga, 254
Pituophis, 269
Plecotus, 175
Plectrophenax, 264
Plethodon, 274, 275
Podiceps, 205
Podilymbus, 205

Pomoxis, 282
Pooecetes, 264
Procyon, 191
Progne, 224
Psaltriparus, 238
Ptychocheilus, 284

Rana, 276, 278
Regulus, 248
Reithrodontomys, 183
Rhyacotriton, 272
Riparia, 224

Salmo, 280
Salpinctes, 242
Salvelinus, 280
Sayornis, 230
Scapanus, 172
Sceloporus, 268
Sciurus, 180
Selasphorus, 226
Setophaga, 250
Sialia, 246
Sitta, 241
Sorex, 170, 172
Speotyto, 220
Sphyrapicus, 228
Spilogale, 196
Spinus, 258, 259
Spizella, 260, 262
Stelgidopteryx, 224
Stellula, 226
Strix, 221
Sturnella, 252
Surnia, 221
Sylvilagus, 176
Synaptomys, 184

Tachycineta, 224
Tamiasciurus, 180
Taricha, 274
Taxidea, 196
Telmatodytes, 242
Thamnophis, 271
Thomomys, 182
Thryomanes, 242
Troglodytes, 242
Turdus, 244
Tyrannus 230
Tyto, 218

Urocyon, 189
Ursus, 191

Vermivora, 250, 251
Vireo, 248, 250
Vulpes, 189
Wilsonia, 251
Xanthocephalus, 252
Zapus, 186
Zenaidura, 216
Zonotrichia, 260, 262

INDEX TO GENERIC NAMES OF PLANTS

Abies,69,71,72
Acer,82
Achillea,162
Achlys,134
Agastache,148
Agoseris,167
Agropyron,60
Alisma,54
Allium,116
Allotropa,144
Alnus,76
Amelanchier,96
Anaphalis,167
Anemone,132
Antennaria,167
Apocynum,146
Aquilegia,132
Arbutus,82
Arctostaphylos,108
Arenaria,130
Arnica,162,166
Artemisia,112
Asarum,126
Aster,160

Balsamorhiza,158
Berberis,86
Brasenia,54
Brodiaea,116,119
Bromus,60

Calochortus,120
Calypso,126
Campanula.158
Cassiope,108
Castanopsis,76
Castilleja,156
Ceanothus,99,100
Ceratophyllum,54
Cercis,96
Cercocarpus,80
Chaenactis,160
Chamaebatiaria.92
Chamaecyparis,72
Chenopodium,130
Chrysothamnus,112
Clintonia,120
Cornus,82,102,142
Corylus,86
Cycladenia,146

Danthonia,60
Delphinium,132
Deschampsia,60
Digitalis,150
Disporum,120,122

Elymus,60
Erigeron,162
Eriogonum,126,128
Erodium,140
Erythronium,119
Eschscholzia,134
Eupatorium,167

Festuca,60
Fragaria,140
Fritillaria,119
Galium,156
Garrya,102
Gaultheria,108
Gilia,146
Goodyera,126

Haplopappus, 112
Heuchera, 136
Hippuris,58
Holodiscus,92
Hulsea,160

Iris,122

Juncus,62
Juniperus,74

Kalmia,104

Larix,67
Ledum,104
Libocedrus,72
Lilium,119
Linnaea,156
Linum,142
Listera,122
Lithocarpus,78
Lonicera,110,112
Luetkea,136
Lupinus,140
Luzula,62

Machaeranthera,160
Maianthemum,120
Marrubium,148
Mentzelia,142
Menziesia,104
Mimulus,148,150
Monardella.148
Montia,130
Myosurus,132
Myriophyllum,58

Najas,52
Nicotiana,148
Nuphar,54

Oenothera,142
Oplopanax,102
Oxalis,140

Paxistima.99
Pedicularis,154,156
Penstemon, 150,154
Phacelia,148
Philadelphus,86
Phlox,110
Phyllodoce,104
Physocarpus,90
Picea,67,69
Pinus,62,65,67
Polygonum,128
Populus,76

Potamogeton,52
Potentilla,136
Prunus,80,96
Pseudotsuga,69
Pterospora,146
Purshia,92
Pyrola,144

Quercus, 78,80

Raillardella, 166
Ranunculus, 132
Rhamnus, 99
Rhododendron, 102,104
Rhus, 99
Ribes, 87,90
Rosa, 94
Rubus, 92,94
Rudbeckia, 160
Rumex, 128

Sagittaria,54
Salix,76
Salsola.130
Salvia,110
Sambucus,110
Sarcodes,146
Saxifraga,134
Scrophularia,154
Senecio,166
Silene,130
Sisymbrium,134
Sitanion,62
Smilacina,120
Sorbus,96
Sparganium,52
Spiraea,90
Spirodela,54
Streptopus,122
Symphoricarpos,110

Taraxacum,167
Taxus,62
Tetradymia,116
Thuja,72
Tiarella,136
Tolmiea,136
Trillium,120
Trisetum,60
Tsuga,69
Typha,52

Umbellularia,80
Urtica,126

Vaccinium,109
Valeriana,158
Vancouveria,134
Veratrum,116
Vicia,140
Viola,142
Vitis,100

Whipplea,136

Xerophyllum,116

NOTES

NOTES

SOME OTHER BOOKS BY NATUREGRAPH

THE SWALLOWTAIL BUTTERFLIES OF NORTH AMERICA, by Hamilton A. Tyler, illustrated by Don Phillips. This manual has everything the amateur or professional will wish to know about this fascinating group. All known recognized species, subspecies and forms are described. Illustrated with maps, line drawings, and 16 color plates. 192 pages.

THE PACIFIC COASTAL WILDLIFE REGION—Revised Edition, by Charles Yocom and Raymond Dasmann. This finely illustrated handbook identifies common plants, mammals, birds, reptiles, amphibians and fish of the humid coastal forest belt from Monterey County, California, north to the southern part of British Columbia. 117 pages.

WILD EDIBLE PLANTS OF THE WESTERN UNITED STATES—Color Edition, by Donald Kirk, illustrated by Janice Kirk. 16 color plates by Donald Kirk. This popular handbook covers nearly 2000 species of useful plants found in the western United States, southwestern Canada and northwestern Mexico. Over 400 drawings included in 343 pages.

COMMON MOSSES OF THE PACIFIC COAST, by Marion Harthill, illustrated by Irene O'Connor. This pocket-sized book describes 68 common mosses, beautifully illustrated with delicate line drawings. A key is included for identification. Mosses are a fascinating small world to explore. For both the hiker and the beginning student. 108 pages.

REPTILES AND AMPHIBIANS OF THE WEST, by Vinson Brown. 80 pages, 16 color plates, 12 black and white plates, an illustrated key, and illustrations to show how to catch these animals alive and how to take care of them in captivity. This handy guide will be welcomed by all who are interested in the array of reptiles and amphibians found throughout the West.

WILD EDIBLE FRUITS AND BERRIES, by Marjorie Furlong and Virginia Pill. For each of the 42 wild edible fruits and berries covered, there is a full-color photograph and description. Locations are given and conservation principles encouraged. A recipe section also adds to the readers enjoyment. This book is useful throughout the U. S. and Canada.

Ask for these books at your local bookstore, or order from Naturegraph Books, Happy Camp, CA 96039. Catalogs are free upon request.